When Pitt
Ruled the Gridiron

When Pitt Ruled the Gridiron

Jock Sutherland's Five-Time National Champions, 1929–1937

DAVID FINOLI

McFarland & Company, Inc., Publishers
Jefferson, North Carolina

ALSO BY DAVID FINOLI

*For the Good of the Country:
World War II Baseball in the Major
and Minor Leagues* (2002)
BY DAVID FINOLI AND BILL RANIER

*When the Bucs Won It All: The 1979
World Champion Pittsburgh Pirates* (2005)

*When Cobb Met Wagner:
The Seven-Game World Series of 1909* (2011)

ALL FROM MCFARLAND

Photographs are courtesy of the University of Pittsburgh Athletics unless otherwise noted.

ISBN 978-0-7864-9426-2 (softcover : acid free paper) ∞
ISBN 978-1-4766-1750-3 (ebook)

LIBRARY OF CONGRESS CATALOGUING DATA ARE AVAILABLE

British Library cataloguing data are available

© 2015 David Finoli. All rights reserved

*No part of this book may be reproduced or transmitted in any form
or by any means, electronic or mechanical, including photocopying
or recording, or by any information storage and retrieval system,
without permission in writing from the publisher.*

On the cover: Marshall Goldberg (left) celebrates a victory
with his teammates in 1936 (courtesy of the University of Pittsburgh
Department of Athletics)

Printed in the United States of America

*McFarland & Company, Inc., Publishers
Box 611, Jefferson, North Carolina 28640*
www.mcfarlandpub.com

To my inner circle that I hold so dear.
Living my dreams through the pages of my books pales
in comparison to the experiences I treasure with them.

Also to the memory of my mother Eleanor, the kindest
woman I've ever known. I treasure everything
she did to help me live the life I enjoy today.

Table of Contents

Acknowledgments — viii
Introduction — 1

1. The Building Blocks — 3
2. 1929: Uansa's Boys — 12
3. 1930 Rose Bowl: A California Nightmare — 43
4. 1931: A Quick Rebuilding Process — 51
5. 1932: The Program Up and Running — 88
6. 1933 Rose Bowl: A Rematch Gone Bad — 112
7. 1933: Close but No Championship — 121
8. 1934: A Forgotten Title — 147
9. 1936: Everything for Football — 176
10. 1937 Rose Bowl: Pitt's Greatest Day — 209
11. 1937: The Troubled Championship — 219
12. The End of the Glory Days — 253

Appendix — 261
Notes — 264
Bibliography — 268
Index — 270

Acknowledgments

There are many people who were instrumental in the completion of this book that deserve my gratitude. First off there is my supportive family: my wife Viv and my three children Tony, Matt, and Cara. Then there is my incredible extended family that includes my father Domenic, the memory of my mother Eleanor, brother Jamie, his wife Cindy, my nieces Marissa and Brianna, my sister Mary, her husband Matthew, and all my loving aunts, uncles and cousins as well as my in-laws Vivian and Salvatore Pansino.

A thank-you also has to go to E.J. Borghetti and Celeste Welch of the University of Pittsburgh Sports Information Department who as always were very generous with the photos that appear in this book as well as any information I needed. Phil Marwill of the National Football Foundation and nationally renowned journalist Dan Jenkins, who helped point me in the right direction when I was at a standstill with my research, were both certainly a valuable resource for the project.

Finally, I offer a huge thank-you to my partners in crime—my good friends Bill Ranier, Tom Aikens, Chris Fletcher, Sam Christian, Ray Stefanacci, Pat Didiano, Bob O'Brien, Dan Russell, Rich Boyer and Matt O'Brotka—who not only help out when needed with these projects, but with whom I've had the pleasure of talking about our favorite college football team over the years. We all share the hope that they will return to the championship levels the Pitt fans during the 1920s and 1930s had the satisfaction of witnessing so many years ago.

Introduction

Former president of the NCAA Walter Byers once made the statement that "I've never seen a school that appears to be as embarrassed by winning as Pitt."[1] It was a common theme throughout the history of the program: a successful run by the program, followed by tighter-than-normal academic restrictions that led to the downfall of what was a national power. It happened in the 1980s when the school arguably had the best program in the country; the administration instituted restrictions that rendered the team inconsequential until the late 1990s. It happened in the 1960s after John Michelosen appeared to have the team about to compete at a championship level on an annual basis. As bad as those times were, perhaps the most confusing battle between football and the administration happened in the late 1930s when one of the greatest coaches in college football history, John Bain "Jock" Sutherland, who led the University of Pittsburgh football squad to five national championships in a nine-year period, lost a tussle with the school's chancellor John Bowman, first over whether to subsidize his players as he had during his national championship run, then over what level the team should play at after he lost the first argument.

John Gabbert Bowman was president at the University of Iowa before becoming the University of Pittsburgh's tenth chancellor in 1921. As successful as Sutherland was in making the football program a national power, Bowman was just as successful in raising money to construct some of the school's, as well as the city's, iconic landmarks such as the Cathedral of Learning, the Heinz Chapel and the Stephen Foster Memorial.

In 1924, he made his first major contribution to the school by hiring Sutherland to replace another football coaching icon, Glenn "Pop" Warner, who accepted the same position at Stanford. As it turned out, Sutherland did what was a very difficult task as he took a championship program and improved on it. In his 15 seasons patrolling the Panther sidelines he amassed an incredible 111–20–12 mark producing no less than 24 first-team All-Americans. His defenses were the hallmark of his squad, shutting out opponents on 79 occasions.

To reach such levels, the team generously subsidized their athletes which not only allowed them to recruit the best players in the fertile football areas of Western Pennsylvania but to become perhaps the most dominant team in the history of sports in the city of Pittsburgh. Unfortunately the aggressive subsidies also led to massive criticism from schools throughout the land, which became an embarrassment for Bowman. He first instituted a more restrictive subsidy program, then ended them altogether after the team turned down a bid to the 1938 Rose Bowl, reportedly over the lack of expenses the school had been willing to give them to make the trip. Sutherland would support the new policy only if the administration took the program to a minor football status so it could at least have a chance to win; Bowman naively felt the team could still compete at the major level even with the restrictions. The conflict not only led to the resignation of Sutherland but to the destruction of the championship program; the school appeared indeed to be embarrassed by winning.

This book tells the story of how the program was built to a championship level, concentrating on the period between 1929 and 1937, when it lost only nine contests while winning five of the nine national championships that the school recognizes. It also takes a thorough look at how the team was quickly brought down.

As controversial as the program eventually turned out to be, in its prime the team not only thrilled countless college football fans, but produced a feat that no major team in the city has ever done and may never do again. It was a time when the University of Pittsburgh truly had the kings of the college football gridiron, and whether or not the administration was embarrassed of that fact, it is remembered as one of the greatest dynasties college football has ever produced.

1

The Building Blocks

It is very difficult for a new coach to replace a legend. In 1924, a former Pitt All-American by the name of John "Jock" Sutherland would get a chance to learn that lesson as he was tabbed by University of Pittsburgh chancellor John Bowman to replace an icon, Glenn "Pop" Warner—one of the greatest college football coaches to ever grace the sideline.

Warner was hired by the university in 1915 to replace Joseph Duff. Duff had graduated from law school that year and would become an American hero as he was killed in action during World War I three years later.

Pop was an innovator who preached discipline with his teams at Iowa State, Georgia, Cornell and Carlisle before being lured to Pitt with the promise of more money and better facilities. Some of the innovations the hall-of-fame coach brought to the game were the reverse, which he developed as a player at Cornell, lightweight uniforms to enhance his players speed, and tackling dummies.

According to a biography of Warner written for the Buffalo Sports Hall of Fame website, the coach "was a trailblazer who led football out of the wilderness of masses, closed-order, push-pull and huddle into the open game of speed, deception and brains."[1]

He brought his innovations and discipline to the Oakland section of Pittsburgh and immediately turned the University of Pittsburgh into a national power. Warner won his first 30 games at the helm of the Panthers, capturing Pitt's first three national championships in 1915, 1916 and 1918. While those would be the only titles he would win at the school, his teams never suffered from a losing record.

As his tenure with the Panthers was coming to an end in 1923, the championship contending teams had turned into mediocre ones with the squad losing nine contests in his final three seasons (Warner only lost 12 times in his tenure at Pitt). Warner had announced before the year that this would be his last at the school, accepting a job at Stanford for the 1924 campaign. The team struggled as they hadn't in the Warner era, sporting a 4–4–0 mark going into his final contest as coach of the Panthers, where the team would face their state rivals from Penn State in the coach's swan song.

Pitt fans celebrated the end of what was at the time their most successful era with a loud ovation before the game started as Warner came to midfield. They presented him with a diamond scarf pin as the students spelled out the name Pop with the crowd cheering wildly for their soon-to-be-departed coach.

Warner showed his appreciation the best way he could, leading his club to a 20–3 victory over the Nittany Lions. It was a fitting way to end his tenure. *Pittsburgh Press* columnist Ralph Davis said it best following the contest. "He is a real gridiron wizard," Davis commented. "One of the few men who give their entire thought to football. Pitt will miss him beyond question, for his equal is hard to find."[2]

It was certainly what Pitt fans everywhere must have felt; his equal would be hard to find. As tough as that feat would prove, Bowman hoped he had found Warner's equal

Pictured is a uniform worn by the Panthers in the 1920s when coach Jock Sutherland first took over the program. Worn by such All-Americans as Gibby Welch and Bill Kern, the uniform is part of a rich football tradition at the university that included being the first football team in the history of the sport to wear numbers on their uniform as they first used them in 1908 (photograph by the author).

at Lafayette College in Easton, Pennsylvania, hiring their head coach, John "Jock" Sutherland, to try and continue Pitt's championship ways.

A graduate of the Pitt school of dentistry, Sutherland quickly found that success would come easier as a football coach than a dentist. Taking over a mediocre 3–4 Lafayette team in 1919, he quickly turned them into winners. By 1921 the school finished 9–0–0, outscoring their opponents 274 to 26 that included a 6–0 win against Warner's Panthers. For their efforts, Sutherland and his team captured the national championship.

After a 33–8–2 record in five seasons at Lafayette, Sutherland came home to take on the challenge of maintaining the dominant program that Warner had built by signing a three-year contract with the school. Following his first season in 1924, he had to wonder if he made the right choice coming back.

The team was very inexperienced in 1924, only five starters returning from 1923, and not much was expected from Pitt on the gridiron. They shut out Grove City to begin the season before facing Sutherland's last employer, Lafayette, in the second contest.

Lafayette chose another former Panther, Herb McCracken, to replace Sutherland, and on this afternoon in Forbes Field, they dominated play in a 10–0 victory. The *Pittsburgh Press* said it best when it declared, "McCracken had better individual players to his plans than was Sutherland's lot."[3]

While it may have been one of the lower points of the Pitt coach's regime, two things were very apparent from the loss: Sutherland did a wonderful job building the Lafayette program and left McCracken a team loaded with quality players, and the second was a belief that he could do the same for the Panther program.

The team continued its inconsistency in his inaugural season, being shut out at the hands of both of the school's local rivals in Carnegie Tech and Washington and Jefferson, before Sutherland secured a winning campaign by soundly beating yet another Pennsylvania foe, Penn State. It was Thanksgiving Day, and while it may be remembered by most as the day they had the first Macy's Thanksgiving parade, for Pitt football historians, the 24–3 thrashing may be known as the moment Sutherland's dynasty was born. The Pitt coach felt that three losses in a season were unacceptable, and the dominance over Penn State showed fans what possibility the future held for Pittsburgh.

With the newfound confidence from their victory over the Nittany Lions, Panther fans hoped that 1925 would see them return as one of the elite programs in the country. The pressure for success had to be felt by the coaching staff as 1925 would also mark the opening of the school's new magnificent $2.1 million stadium. The stadium had an original capacity of 56,150 and was built with the option of adding a 30,000-seat upper deck, which was never utilized.

Despite the fact that it cost $2.1 million to construct—well over the budgeted $1.1 million—Pitt Stadium opened on September 26, 1925, as the Panthers defeated Washington and Lee 26–0. The Stadium's original capacity was 69,400, but it was also built to allow the addition of an upper deck which would have increased the capacity by 30,000.

    The problem with the facility was that the original budget called for the stadium to be constructed for almost half that amount, $1.1 million. Chancellor Bowman was incensed at the increased debt that had occurred, and he named an athletic director post to oversee the department, with the hope the AD would rein in what he felt was an out-of-control football program. The problem was that to make the money to pay for the stadium, it became the job of new AD Don Harrison, who was selected after Bowman's first two choices died suddenly, to schedule big-money games to fill it.

    To garner the interest in filling the stadium with high-level opponents, they had to have a team that could win often, so they needed the incredible talent that was found around the steel mills in Pittsburgh. They would entice the players to come to Pitt by offering them an average of $55 a month plus tuition and books, a generous amount at the time. In essence they were paying players to play college football, a situation that as the years went on would cause the university major issues. The strategy worked incredibly, better than probably Sutherland and Harrison could have hoped.

With the talent starting to come to the school, the team faced Washington and Lee to christen Pitt Stadium and thoroughly destroyed the club coached by Jimmy DeHart, who was a teammate of Sutherland's at Pitt on the national championship squad in 1916, 26–0.

Pitt was a very deep team in 1925 and looked for revenge against Lafayette in the Panthers' second contest of the season. A win would show the country that they were national championship contenders while a loss could make another mediocre season a possibility.

As much as Pitt wanted this to be a measuring stick to show how they'd improved, what happened was just the opposite. After spotting the Panthers an early 9–0 lead, Lafayette thoroughly controlled the contest, scoring 20 unanswered points and handing Pitt their worst loss in six years, 20–9.

It was a devastating moment for the program, but one where Sutherland showed that his style and tenacity would be able to lead Pitt to overcome such adversity. They began the next week by beating the West Virginia Mountaineers 15–7 and never looked back. Six consecutive victories followed, including revenge wins against Carnegie Tech and Washington and Jefferson, to finish the year 8–1 while capturing the eastern football championship. While given no consideration for the national championship at the time, years later when Denmark's Soren Sorensen, a physics professor at the University of Tennessee, decided to develop his college football computer rankings, he calculated that the Panthers were the best team in the nation. It's an honor that, while not recognized by the university as an official championship, showed the power of the 1925 squad.

The next campaign saw the squad not ready to compete for the national championship as they had ties against Georgetown and Washington and Jefferson as well as losses to Carnegie Tech and Lafayette; it was only a momentary lapse as Sutherland would lead Pitt to his first undefeated regular season a year later.

The Panthers had an experienced team in 1927 and began the campaign against Thiel. Led by unanimous All-American Gibby Welch's two touchdowns and Dick Booth's three, Pitt crushed Thiel 48–0 and never looked back. Surrendering only seven points in their first seven contests, a streak that included a scoreless tie against Washington and Jefferson, Pitt ended the regular season with two tough foes if they hoped to complete their undefeated campaign in Nebraska and Penn State.

Nebraska came into this game as a big, tough physical opponent led by running back Glenn Presnell. Presnell showed his talent by rumbling over the Panther defense for 148 yards. Unfortunately for the Cornhuskers, Welch was on the other side of the line. The Pitt All-American took the opening kickoff

With the ball is Gibby Welch, an All-American at the University of Pittsburgh in 1927, pictured above returning a kickoff 105 yards for a touchdown against West Virginia University, a school record which still stands today. Welch had 4,108 all-purpose yards in his career, a school record until Tony Dorsett broke it almost 50 years later.

96 yards for a touchdown and then snagged a toss from future athletic director Jimmy Hagan, who would have a large hand in the dismantling of this powerful program, and rambled 52 yards with it. All told, Welch had 208 total yards in leading the Panthers to a 21–13 victory.

With Army upsetting Notre Dame and Yale topping Princeton, there was serious talk of Pitt as strong national championship contenders. A one-sided 30–0 win over the Nittany Lions not only kept them in the championship picture but garnered the school its first bowl invitation, a Rose Bowl matchup against Pop Warner and his Stanford Cardinals.

The game was a fierce defensive battle as Pitt broke out in front 6–0 on a touchdown by Hagen in the third quarter. It was at that point a rule, which in 45 years Pittsburgh fans would see again in the Steelers' famous Immaculate Reception play, backfired against the Panthers on a controversial touchdown. On a fourth-and-two from the Panther two-yard line, the Cardinals' Frankie Wilton tossed a pass in the end zone to Bob Sims. Sims tipped the ball which was picked up by Wilton, who was rushing toward him. He secured the ball and then took it over the goal line for the score. The problem was that at the time, the rule read that after securing a forward pass, an opposing player had to touch the ball before a member of the same team could pick it up and regain possession. The referee claimed that a Pitt player had in fact touched the ball first; many others who were there were certain no Pitt player had.

According to the *Pittsburgh Press*'s Max Hannum, who was covering the game, "No Pitt man touched the ball at all.... Ten thousand eyes will attest that fact."[4] He further went on to explain that while Pitt lost on a questionable call, Sutherland showed nothing but sportsmanship, not making any excuses. "Sutherland undoubtedly has an opinion on the play but he won't express it," Hannum went on to say. "His evident care that he say nothing, even hinting at an alibi, is admirable."[5]

Unfortunately for the Panther faithful, the score stood, and the successful extra-point attempt gave Stanford a 7–6 lead which held up for the victory. To make matters worse, while they captured their second eastern championship in three years, they were recognized as national champions only by two very minor polls, the Esso Gas ratings and the Veterans Athletes Body ratings, neither of which are recognized by the University of Pittsburgh as official championships. Illinois was given the nod as the official national champions by every major source.

A year later, losses to West Virginia and Carnegie Tech were the low points in a 6–2–1 campaign that saw the staunch Panther defense allow only 15 points. Despite the setbacks, the table was now set for the championship run that the school was about to embark on. Sutherland truly did have a difficult challenge in replacing the legendary Pop Warner. His first five seasons may have shown that he was up for the challenge, but with the impressive local talent that he was bringing to the university, the next nine campaigns would show that he was able to do the impossible and take the Panthers to the next level.

National Champions selections made by modern-day analysts are noted "(retrospective)." Players rated as ***First Team All-Americans*** by a plurality of NCAA-recognized selectors are noted as "(consensus)." Players rated by all NCAA-recognized selectors are noted as "(unanimous)."

1924 Scores

Date	Opponent	Score	Record
9/27	Grove City	14–0	1–0–0
10/4	Lafayette	0–10	1–1–0
10/11	West Virginia	14–7	2–1–0
10/18	@Johns Hopkins	26–0	3–1–0
10/25	Carnegie Tech	0–6	3–2–0
11/1	@Syracuse	7–7	3–2–1

Date	Opponent	Score	Record
11/8	Geneva	13–0	4-2-1
11/15	Washington and Jefferson	0–10	4-3-1
11/27	Penn State	24–3	5-3-1
		98–43	

1925 Scores

Date	Opponent	Score	Record
9/25	Washington and Lee	26–0	1-0-0
10/3	Lafayette	9–20	1-1-0
10/10	West Virginia	15–7	2-1-0
10/17	Gettysburg	13–0	3-1-0
10/24	Carnegie Tech	12–0	4-1-0
10/31	Johns Hopkins	31–0	5-1-0
11/7	Washington and Jefferson	6–0	6-1-0
11/14	@Pennsylvania	14–0	7-1-0
11/26	Penn State	23–7	8-1-0
		151–34	

Selected as National Champions by:
Soren Sorensen Ratings (retrospective)*

*Not Recognized as Official National Championship Selector by University of Pittsburgh.

Selected as First-Team All-American
Ralph Chase (consensus)

1926 Scores

Date	Opponent	Score	Record
9/25	Allegheny	9–7	1-0-0
10/2	Georgetown	6–6	1-0-1
10/9	Lafayette	7–17	1-1-1
10/16	Colgate	19–16	2-1-1
10/23	Carnegie Tech	0–4	2-2-1
10/30	Westminster	88–0	3-2-1
11/6	West Virginia	17–7	4-2-1
11/13	Washington and Jefferson	0–0	4-2-2
11/25	Penn State	24–6	5-2-2
		170–73	

1927 Scores

Date	Opponent	Score	Record
9/24	Thiel	42–0	1–0–0
10/1	Grove City	33–0	2–0–0
10/8	West Virginia	40–0	3–0–0
10/15	@Drake	32–0	4–0–0
10/22	Carnegie Tech	23–7	5–0–0
10/29	Allegheny	62–0	6–0–0
11/5	Washington and Jefferson	0–0	6–0–1
11/12	Nebraska	21–13	7–0–1
11/24	Penn State	30–0	8–0–1
1/2	Stanford–Rose Bowl	6–7	8–1–1
		289–27	

Selected as National Champions by:
  Esso Gas Ratings*
  Veterans Athletes Body Ratings*

*Not Recognized as Official National Championship Selector by University of Pittsburgh.

Selected as First-Team All-Americans
  Bill Kern
  Gilbert Welch (unanimous)

1928 Scores

Date	Opponent	Score	Record
9/29	Thiel	20–0	1–0–0
10/6	Bethany	53–0	2–0–0
10/13	West Virginia	6–9	2–1–0
10/20	Allegheny	29–0	3–1–0
10/27	Carnegie Tech	0–6	3–2–0
11/3	Syracuse	18–0	4–2–0
11/10	Washington and Jefferson	25–0	5–2–0
11/16	@Nebraska	0–0	5–2–1
11/29	Penn State	26–0	6–2–1
		177–15	

Selected as First-Team All-American
  Mike Getto (consensus)

2

1929: Uansa's Boys

In 1928 he led the Pittsburgh Panthers in passing; a year later Toby Uansa was the ultimate triple threat for Pitt leading the team in rushing, interceptions and scoring. A superstar back out of McKees Rocks who was a multi-sport star that won 16 letters in his high school career, Uansa became the most important cog what would be the first national championship squad in the Jock Sutherland era.

Born in Germany, of parents who were of Romanian descent, Uansa was known much more for his prowess on the diamond than he was on the gridiron, as he was a very effective power hitter for a local amateur team called the Stowe Civics. While professional scouts might have been salivating at his baseball talent, it was on the football field at Pitt Stadium where Uansa earned his superstar status. An elusive runner, who was as dangerous returning kicks as he was behind center, Uansa was the leader of a very talented and deep team that Sutherland would command in 1929.

Dr. Sutherland was in sixth year at Pitt after a less-than-stellar start in 1924 when the "downtown coaches and over-enthusiastic alumni were hot after his scalp."[1] He lost to local rivals Washington and Jefferson and Carnegie Tech that season, but since then he had led the team to two eastern championships, an undefeated regular season and their first bowl bid. There were now very few fans, alumni or newspapermen who were calling for his job by the beginning of 1929 as he had continued the toughness and discipline that his predecessor Pop Warner began 14 years earlier.

Its not surprising that Sutherland was able to follow in his footsteps; after all it was Warner that helped form his football philosophy. Born in Scotland and raised in nearby Sewickley after his family sent him to America to live with relatives that had settled here with the hope that he could escape a life of poverty in his native land, the future hall-of-fame coach started his athletic career playing the favorite game of his native country, soccer.

He entered the University of Pittsburgh in 1913 as a student in the school of dentistry and a year later witnessed his first collegiate football game as the Panthers faced off against the Naval Academy. He was a lineman on Joe Duff's club at Pitt in 1914, and the Scotsman entered the game as a reserve one afternoon. So impressive was Sutherland that he became a fixture in the starting lineup the next week and remained there for the next four seasons, the final three under the tutelage of Warner.

In 1917, the kid who never saw a college football game until the day he actually played his first game ended his career at Pitt losing only one game under Duff and Warner. For his excellence at guard, Sutherland was named as a first-team All-American by the International News Service.

He finished his education the following spring, earning his degree before spending a year in the army overseas. He returned in 1919 to begin his legendary coaching career, starting as the head man at Lafayette, that in its tenth season in 1929 would take the 40-year-old coach from great to icon.

As a coach, he was most likely comparable to Vince Lombardi, inasmuch as his teams relied on attention to detail and discipline rather than a complex innovative offensive or defensive system. Like Lombardi's power sweep, it was said of Sutherland's squads that you knew what was coming, but you still couldn't stop it. All-American Ave Daniell claimed that "Winning the game was the way to do it, the only way to do it. We were sort of machine like. We did our job as we were trained to do our job and that was it. In 1934, we lost one game. In 1935 we had a bad year; we lost one game and tied four of them [there were actually two ties in 1935]. In 1936 we lost to Duquesne and tied Fordham. 1937 we didn't lose a game. You know you can't get too excited about wining if you never lose."[2] One of the greatest running backs ever to wear the Panther uniform, Marshall Goldberg remembered, "We were highly trained; we were in great physical condition. We were like a symphony orchestra. You didn't think, all you were concerned about was playing your part. I knew that if I got my man every time I was supposed to get him and everyone else did the same, we were going to win that ball game."[3]

The coach, who was elected to the College Football Hall of Fame in 1951, was able to acquire some of the best talent in the area by offering them a stipend of $500 a year plus tuition and books. In 1929, they raised it to $650, an amount that was more aggressive than almost any other school in the country, which allowed Sutherland to recruit enough quality players that he had superb depth at every position.

On the spot at the University of Pittsburgh where Pitt Stadium used to reside is not only the Petersen Event Center, which is home to, among others, the championship Pitt Panther basketball team as well as the Panther statue pictured above. Below the Panther are plaques celebrating the retired numbers of the greatest players ever to take the gridiron for the school (photograph by the author).

He worked his team hard as they began practice for the campaign. Sutherland had an impressive club that caught the attention of one of the sport's leading authorities, Tad Jones, who was a former successful head coach at Yale University and leader of the prestigious national football rules committee along with such luminaries as Knute Rockne, Warner and Georgia Tech's Bill Alexander.

Jones, who was the only retired coach of the group, decided to take an extensive trip through the northeast in the pre-season, visiting some of the better programs in order to get a thorough view of as many teams as he could. Pitt and Carnegie Tech were two of the 12 schools he visited on his journey, and the University of Pittsburgh was his first stop.

While not ready to scrimmage with his players yet, Sutherland put his club through an intense workout for Jones showing his various formations he learned from Warner. What impressed the former Yale coach was not only the impressive physical shape that Sutherland had his Panthers in, but their speed and discipline in the formations and plays, all very indicative of Sutherland teams. While disappointed he didn't get a chance to see Joe Donchess, the great left end who was not at practice due to the classes he was attending at the university's medical school, Jones nonetheless marveled at what he saw, which was a deep team that by season's end would be considered one of the country's best.

The depth was particularly impressive to Jones as the Panthers had 22 players capable of filling the 11 starting spots. The *Pittsburgh Press* said it well when it stated that "there are just two evenly matched elevens with not much to choose between them."[4]

As the opener against Waynesburg was creeping closer, there was heavy concern on the face of the coach as his first team was looking sluggish in one of the finals scrimmages of the pre-season against their backups. Such heavyweights as Uansa, Donchess, Thomas Parkinson and Ray Montgomery were being pushed around by a second-team crew led by quarterback Eddie Baker, Bucky Wagner, Franklin Hood and Hart Morris. Time and time again the second team would rip through the frontline defense causing Sutherland to blow the play dead before the backup runners reached the end zone, with the coach directing his ire toward his stars.

Sutherland teams were successful not having to depend on such undisciplined moments and the quiet coach, who despite his less-than-animated personality expected perfection from his players. Defensively he formed a philosophy he learned from Warner that was simplistic yet effective. His guards were fast and his tackles were described as a "tall, rangy type, tall and weighing from 185 to 200 pounds."[5] Sutherland wanted his center of the defensive line to be "the mobile defenseman who played the roving game."[6] He didn't believe in interchangeable positions as he wanted his players to master their position, which is why his practices were always intense. He truly believed in the famous quote that his mentor Pop Warner muttered so many times: "You play the way you practice."[7] As the pre-season was ending, he had his team practicing passionately as Sutherland had his team prepared for perfection, much to the dismay of his opening-day opponents.

Game 1—September 28, 1929, at Pitt Stadium
WAYNESBURG COLLEGE YELLOW JACKETS 0
UNIVERSITY OF PITTSBURGH PANTHERS 53

The Yellow Jackets of Waynesburg College would have their hands full as they would be the first opponent for the University of Pittsburgh in what was predicted to be a rainy, warm late summer afternoon in the Steel City.

In an effort to give the Panthers a perfect field to play for its fifth season in Pitt Stadium, the groundskeepers laid a brand new turf two days before the game was to be played, hoping it would be a lightning-fast track for what was a small, yet young Pitt backfield.

The Yellow Jackets had been beaten thoroughly the week before against St. Vincent and were led by two Pittsburgh local players, quarterback Frank Demoise and tackle Sammy Smith. Pitt of course was completely healthy and from all accounts was expecting a relatively easy time in the opener as they were hoping to stay healthy for their second contest against a much tougher Duke team.

It was an experienced Panther club with only two new starters on the offensive line, center Ralph Daugherty and tackle Jim MacMurdo, who had the unenviable task of replacing unanimous first-team All-American Mike Getto from Jeannette, who had been the Panthers' MVP in 1928. The tackle, who eventually had head-coaching stints at Kansas and in the NFL replacing Sutherland in 1942 with the Brooklyn Dodgers while also noted for prompting his hometown high school to adopt the Jayhawk nickname after his Kansas squad, was certainly difficult to replace, but on this day MacMurdo was more than up to the challenge.

With his experienced offensive line intact, the Panther coach had a difficult choice in naming his starting quarterback. While Baker was impressive in the Panthers' final intra-squad scrimmage, Sutherland decided to go with the incumbent starter, Charley Edwards, to start the season.

Luckily for the 9,000 fans that turned out to watch Pitt open the 1929 campaign as well as the players on the field, the rain held off as it was a very warm sunny day in Oakland. The small possibility that Waynesburg could make this a close game ended very early when the Yellow Jackets chose to send out their defense first after winning the toss.

Uansa, Parkinson and Josh Williams started in the backfield alongside Edwards, and each looked masterful running behind an offensive line that manhandled Waynesburg on almost every play. After the initial kick went out of bounds, Parkinson took the second at the 20 and returned it 14 yards to get the day started for the Panthers. Williams took the opening play 8 yards around the right side, before Parkinson went for 12 more in two plays up the middle. Uansa rambled with runs of 8 and 14 yards behind left tackle to put the ball on the Yellow Jacket 21. Parkinson shot up the middle twice to the 15 before Uansa showed his talent once again with a nine-yard stroll to the six. Three plays later Parkinson gave Pitt its first score of the year. Daugherty sent a low snap back on the conversion leading to a blocked extra point to leave the Panthers up by six.

Waynesburg had its only highlight of the day with a first down on its first series before fumbling the ball at their own 33, which was recovered by Parkinson. Williams then got a reverse for 13 yards, and after Uansa and Parkinson combined to bring it to the five, Williams sprinted to his right and danced in untouched to double the lead to twelve. In what would probably be the only negative for Pitt on that day, another bad snap led to a Uansa fumble on the point-after and another block by Waynesburg.

After the Yellow Jackets finally stopped the Pitt attack on downs late in the first quarter, their defensive prowess proved temporary as the Panthers continued the onslaught with Uansa sprinting around left end 20 yards to the Waynesburg 23. Parkinson took over with consecutive runs of 5, 12 and 7 through the hole to the right of center for his second touchdown of the day. With Edwards now holding, Parkinson put the kick through the uprights for a 19–0 lead.

On their next possession, the Pitt offensive line continued to punish the Waynesburg defense. Williams and Parkinson took the ball to their own 42 before a 19-yard dash on a reverse by Uansa put the Panthers back into Yellow Jacket territory where they spent the majority of the first half.

So dominant was Pitt that Sutherland started to give his first team a rest at this point, replacing Edwards with Baker. A Waynesburg defensive holding call, coupled with a Parkinson 12-yard run in which his helmet was ripped off, put the Panthers once again inside the 20. Williams and Parkinson ran it to the 7 where Uansa took it in the rest of the way to make it 26–0.

The Pitt coach continued to substitute liberally, replacing his entire backfield. Williams, Parkinson and Uansa gave way to Franklin Hood, Whitey

Walinchus and Jimmy Rooney without missing a beat. In the next offensive possession, Sutherland replaced his entire front line as the backups crushed the Yellow Jacket defensive wall. After methodically moving to the opposing 25, Hood ran 12 to the 13. Three plays later, Walinchus ripped through the middle of the Yellow Jacket defense for the score, ending the first half with a 33–0 advantage.

Sutherland sent his first team in to begin the second half, which started with Uansa taking the opening kickoff from his ten to the 39 where the Panthers were stopped for only the second time in the contest. Pitt's defense quickly held, then blocked the Yellow Jacket punt, taking over at the 39. It turned out to be a power drive with Hood ripping through for two five-yard runs after Williams rambled for nine. Uansa and Hood took it down to within inches of a touchdown, when the McKees Rocks native powered it into the end zone for his second touchdown of the day and a 40-point lead.

With the game thoroughly out of reach, Walinchus torched the exhausted Waynesburg defense for a 49-yard touchdown jaunt before the Panthers finished the one-sided affair scoring on a five-yard run after jumping on a Yellow Jacket fumble following a punt to put the final touches on a 53–0 shutout as the team finished what was almost a perfect game.

Game 2—October 5, 1929, at Duke Stadium in Durham, North Carolina

UNIVERSITY OF PITTSBURGH PANTHERS 52
DUKE UNIVERSITY BLUE DEVILS 7

Following a very one-sided contest against Waynesburg College in the opener, the Panthers traveled to Durham, North Carolina, to meet a team that figured to be a much tougher opponent, the Duke Blue Devils.

The Blue Devils were led by former Panther Jimmy DeHart, a teammate of Dr. Sutherland, and like the Panther coach a disciple of Pop Warner. While Sutherland had added some wrinkles to the attack he learned from his mentor, DeHart had stuck true to the system. His team was led by Harry Kistler and four sophomore linemen in Bill Bryan, Leon Matthews, Sam Lemons and Don Hyatt, which gave Duke fans optimism for the 1929 campaign.

On their way to Durham, the Panthers stopped off for a couple of days in Washington, D.C. They were guests of Georgetown University and Hoya coach Lou Little where the team spent time practicing. Concerned about the Blue Devils' passing attack, the coach spent more time preparing at Georgetown against the pass, as he knew DeHart would be aggressive through the air trying to take advantage of what was perceived to be Pitt's biggest weakness defensively. The preparation against Duke's effective pass game certainly would pay off by week's end.

While in the nation's capital, the team got the chance to meet President Herbert Hoover and have their picture taken with him as they visited the White House. They would have the honor of being the first college football team to visit the White House in Hoover's tenure.

As Pitt left from Washington for the game, the Panther coach had to feel lucky that his injuries were very minimal after their opening game. Only backup Leo Murphy, who injured his shoulder against the Yellow Jackets, was questionable. Third-string quarterback Bucky Wanger, who was spiked above his right eye, and Donchess, who hurt his arm, were the only other reported injuries, although both were thought to be minor.

Knowing he was facing a healthy national power, despite the confidence he had with home-field advantage, DeHart expressed his apprehensions clearly when asked how he thought the game would turn out. "We cannot expect to win," the former Panther stated. "I just only hope Jock won't run it up too high on me."[8]

Even though the Panther injuries were not severe and DeHart was "sure" Pitt would crush him, the hall-of-fame coach wasn't as convinced he would exit Durham victorious. Concerned with his opponent, Sutherland replaced Edwards at quarterback with Baker. He considered Edwards a safe quarterback that wouldn't make mistakes, but Baker was a gambler, a high-risk, high-reward type of player. By choosing Baker it was clear he wanted to open up the game in a contest he felt would be high scoring. Besides quarterback, the coach made one more change in his starting lineup, inserting Rip Collins at right end for Bill Loehr.

While he had reason to be concerned, DeHart had a group of young exciting players and another hopeful advantage for the contest. The Pitt game represented a milestone for the Duke program, the opening of their brand new state-of-the-art facility, Duke Stadium. Renamed Wallace Wade Stadium in 1967 and still in use by the Blue Devils currently, Duke Stadium was the facility that DeHart hoped would help vault Duke into the upper echelon of collegiate football programs in the nation.

While smaller than Pitt Stadium, with a capacity of 35,000 fans, Duke Stadium would have the unique distinction of hosting the only Rose Bowl outside of California when it was moved to Durham in 1942 for safety reasons shortly after the Pearl Harbor attack.

The teams would be christening the new facility in what were very colorful uniform combinations. According to the *Pittsburgh Press*, "Duke will wear a striking uniform of blue and white with white jerseys, blue helmets, white stockings and blue silk trousers. Pitt will wear a special hot weather uniform of blue silk with gold trim across the shoulders and blue helmets with gold cross pieces."[9]

It was a celebratory atmosphere with many local dignitaries in attendance for the festivities. Twenty thousand thrilled Duke fans showed up, excited to see if the Blue Devils could go 2–0 after their 19–6 victory over Mercer in the opener; it didn't take long until they would find out that wasn't going to happen.

Within the game's first two minutes, Pitt ripped through the Duke defensive line for the first touchdown of the day. Toby Uansa ran 48 yards with the opening kickoff, giving the Panthers an excellent field position inside Duke territory. Later on Uansa ran the ball 15 yards then took a pass and rambled for 17 more. After Tom Parkinson ran the ball to the 6, Josh Williams ended the drive on a 6-yard sprint around right end for the early lead.

Their next possession was just as destructive to the spirit of the Blue Devils. Parkinson and Williams combined for 17 yards rushing before a wrinkle in the wide-open offense just about ended Duke's hopes before the game was ten minutes old. Williams caught a pass, faked a pitch to Uansa, then turned and ran through the right side of the Duke defense for 40 yards and a quick two-touchdown lead.

As it turned out, Sutherland was correct in preparing for a wide-open Duke aerial attack as their quarterback Sam Buie would pass 47 times and took his team to the Pitt 20 before being stopped by the Panther defense. Pitt's quickly took advantage as Uansa took the ball 78 yards for a score to end the first period with the Panthers up 19–0.

Buie once again found success through the air as he sent two long completions, one of 25 yards and the other for 27 yards, which gave DeHart his second scoring threat of the afternoon. While looking as if they would finally cut into the Panther lead, the Pitt defense stiffened and stopped Duke at the 24.

On the next play, Uansa showed what a superstar he was as he sprinted around the right end and didn't stop for 76 yards, crossing the goal line and putting the game out of reach as the first quarter was coming to an end. Sutherland was very satisfied at what he had seen to this point and pulled his entire starting lineup out for the rest of the game as they opened up a 26–0 lead. Unfortunately for DeHart and his squad, he was about to experience Pitt's incredible depth.

In the second quarter after the starters were removed, the Blue Devils did see more success against the Panther backups as a completion of 40 yards took them down to Pitt's 12 yard line, and the next drive saw them get inside the ten to the seven. Each time, Sutherland's defensive crew showed they would not break, keeping them scoreless as the half ended.

The success of the second quarter would not extend to the third as the Panthers' second-team offense showed their big-play ability. Rooney had touchdown runs of 58 and 45 yards, while Walinchus rambled 47. Added to the embarrassment was a Pitt safety as the game entered its final quarter with a 46–0 Pitt thrashing.

Ed Schultz made it 52–0 before the Panther defense was finally penetrated for the first time in 1929. Buie, who completed 17 passes, took them to the five-yard line before Robert Beaver crossed the goal line for the final score of this rout, ending the game 52–7.

As it turned out, both Panther teammates from the national championship 1916 club were correct. DeHart was right for understanding he had no chance to beat his former teammate, while Sutherland seemed to better grasp what the mentor to both understood: you play like you practice, and the intense Pitt practices surely showed in this one-sided affair.

Game 3—October 12, 1929, at Pitt Stadium

WEST VIRGINIA UNIVERSITY MOUNTAINEERS 7
UNIVERSITY OF PITTSBURGH PANTHERS 27

The Backyard Brawl—that's how the intense rivalry between West Virginia University and the University of Pittsburgh came to be known. By the end of the 1920s the two schools, separated by only 75 miles, were playing contests that were anything but a brawl, as there was a huge diference in the quality of their football programs.

It wasn't that the games weren't competitive; after all, WVU had defeated the Panthers in Pop Warner's final two seasons as well as a 9–6 upset over Sutherland's club the year before. They even had some recent successful campaigns including an undefeated 10–0–1 mark in 1922. The difference between the two schools was after Warner came aboard in 1915: Pitt played a schedule against some of the best programs in America and was always seemingly competing for a national championship, while the Mountaineers usually played a less-than-stellar slate against several non-descript schools.

Regardless of the disparity, the two universities would face off in the twenty-fifth version of what has become one of the most celebrated rivalries in college football.

Pitt was certainly looking for revenge after the 1928 contest. They had crushed their first two opponents in 1928, very similar to what Pittsburgh had done so far in 1929. The Panthers had taken a slim 6–0 lead against

WVU but had dominated the game so thoroughly that a victory was a foregone conclusion; or so they thought. A long pass to the two-yard line to Mountaineer Eddie Bartrugg, a short TD pass, then a safety when Rooney picked up a fumble in his own end zone gave West Virginia the stunning 9–6 victory.

Unfortunately the Mountaineers did not have a great start to their campaign this season, losing to Davis and Elkins and tying Duquesne in the first three encounters. Despite that fact they were 1–1–1, they still had a dangerous backfield that would face the Panthers at Pitt Stadium. Led by "Little Sleepy" Glenn, "Bus" Larue, a lightning-fast back by the name of "Speed" Waggoner, who ran the 100-yard dash in ten seconds, and quarterback Eddie Stumpp, the WVU backfield was one of the most dangerous Sutherland's defensive squad would face in 1929.

Stumpp was considered, alongside Carnegie Tech's Howard Harpster, as being one of the most dangerous passers in the nation. He had been injured early in September and there was a fear he would miss a portion of the campaign, but Stumpp was a tough player and found his way back on the field, which would cause the Pitt coach some anxious moments during the week as they prepared for him.

While he didn't expect them to be as aggressive in the air as Duke was the week before, Sutherland considered Stump a much more accomplished and accurate passer than the Blue Devils' Sam Buie, so he had his defensive troops concentrating on stopping the pass once again in practice during the week. A difficult week of practice ended with a spirited scrimmage against the freshman squad, who mirrored the Mountaineer offense; Sutherland not only wanted his defense well schooled, but his offense too as they went against the then-tough West Virginia defensive line.

To try and perplex the WVU defense, he chose Eddie Baker and his aggressive, gambling style over Charley Edwards for the second consecutive week at quarterback. It was apparent that Baker was now the coach's choice for the season and would be expected to make his offense explosive.

Even though Sutherland was taking no chances and was giving the Mountaineers extreme respect, the newspapers and experts alike were claiming the Panthers as big favorites to crush their opponents. The *Pittsburgh Press*'s Max Hannum stated, "The Panther players are determined; despite the fact they believe they have an edge on the visitors." He further went on to explain that the main factor in his opinion was retribution for the previous season's loss. "Their defeat last year rankled as few beatings have. They frankly want revenge and a team in that frame of mind is dangerous."[10] What was also apparent was that in big games, superstar talent comes to the forefront. For the University of Pittsburgh, that meant that two of their biggest stars, Toby Uansa and Tom Parkinson, would shine.

After taking the opening kickoff, the Panther defense quickly thwarted the Mountaineers' first offensive efforts, turning them back on three straight plays. Pitt took over at their own 25 after the WVU punt, and while they turned over the ball on a fumble, they showed the Mountaineers they were the more physical team.

Nicknamed "Pug," Parkinson was a powerful, physical runner, who was also adept at catching passes. A native of California, Pennsylvania, with parents who were born in England, Parkinson began to wear down the WVU defense on this possession. He ripped through the center of their line for 12 yards on two consecutive plays before fumbling on his third carry at the 43.

Sutherland certainly had his defense prepared as they once again forced a punt on a three-and-out. The West Virginia defense was their equal early as the offenses struggled for most of the first period. Finally as the quarter was winding down, Pitt showed it was a more physical team with Parkinson leading the way.

The All-American ran the ball four consecutive times for 18 yards, giving Pitt its first real threat of the day at the Mountaineer 41. A couple of more powerful Parkinson rambles put the ball on the 30. Uansa slid through for nine yards before a crushing four-yard Parkinson run gave the Panthers a first down at the 17. Josh Williams ended the drive with a magnificent touchdown, going through several WVU defensive players for a 7–0 advantage.

Early in the second quarter, Stumpp struck with a 25-yard completion to the Pitt 25, but West Virginia's first scoring threat was stopped right there. While the Panthers lost Williams to injury the next drive on a 24-yard reception, they still were opening up huge holes, taking it to the WVU four. At that time the Mountaineers' defense came through with a tough stance holding the Panthers at that point while taking over on downs.

With Pitt dominating, yet only up by a touchdown, the game was looking eerily like the loss the year before. Just as it looked like WVU might have a chance, the Panthers' "Rip" Collins intercepted Stumpp at their own 49. Walinchus, who replaced Williams, began the drive with a 6-yard run around the right end before a 24-yard sprint gave them the ball at the 17. James Clark came in for Parkinson and ran the ball four straight times before Uansa pulled in a Baker pass at the two and fell into the end zone for a 14–0 lead which Pitt held on to at the half.

Williams and Parkinson joined Uansa in the backfield for the start of the third quarter and proceeded to power down the field against what was a tiring WVU defense. After Parkinson went up the middle, this time for ten yards to the opposing 14, Uansa showed his skill with a tough 13-yard touchdown jaunt to put the Panthers up by what seemed like an insurmountable 20 points.

Just when it seemed like the rout was on, Stumpp found William Behnke, who pulled it in at the Pitt 40. Uansa looked like he would stop him there when he slipped and Behnke bolted past him to cut the lead to 20–7.

With momentum now on their side, WVU forced a Uansa fumble at their own 45, where they picked it up in an effort to cut the once dominant lead to a mere touchdown. Looking to capitalize, Stumpp once again took to the air. Instead of being the hero, Uansa made up for his mistakes, stepping in front of the errant Stumpp pass at the Mountaineer 40 and then deftly going through the West Virginia offense for the 60-yard touchdown, giving the Panthers the 27–7 victory.

In the end, the Mountaineers did prove to be much tougher opposition than Pitt had had all season. Despite that, the outcome was never really in doubt as Pitt was now 3–0–0 before a game that would show the nation whether or not they were true national championship contenders: a contest at Nebraska against the Cornhuskers.

Game 4—October 19, 1929, at Memorial Stadium in Lincoln, Nebraska

UNIVERSITY OF PITTSBURGH PANTHERS   12
UNIVERSITY OF NEBRASKA CORNHUSKERS   7

The year before, when the Panthers visited Lincoln, Nebraska, to play the University of Nebraska Cornhuskers, Pitt hoped to somehow make up for a disappointing two-loss season by beating the favored Cornhuskers in their own field. Unfortunately for Pitt, while they dominated the contest, neither offense crossed the goal line in a scoreless tie. It would be the second consecutive weekend where Coach Jock Sutherland's boys tried to garner retribution for their less-than-stellar 1928 campaign, the difference being that the massive Nebraska defensive line became the first team that year to frustrate the explosive Panther offense.

The Cornhuskers were the defending Big Six champions after a 7–1–1 campaign and sported one of the fastest backs in the nation, Clair Sloan, who ran behind a massive Nebraska offensive line. They were not enjoying one of their best starts in 1929 as they opened the season with a 0–0 tie against SMU in a contest where, despite the fact they were without Sloan and "Dutch" White, they clearly dominated the game. They made up for the costly tie with a 13–6 defeat of Syracuse, but coach Dana X. Bible, who previously led Texas

A&M to five Southeastern Conference championships in nine seasons, knew he would be an underdog against the Panthers.

On their second road trip of the season, 29 Pitt players boarded the train, four less than their first excursion to Duke two weeks earlier. The Panthers stopped first in Chicago, where they spent some time preparing at the University of Chicago's Stagg Field, before finishing their long train trip scrimmaging at the Ak-Sar-Ben fairgrounds in Omaha on Friday where Sutherland would be trying some new formations that he designed especially for the Cornhuskers. Sutherland used the practice time to decide whether Baker or Edwards would start at quarterback as well as at right end, where Loehr and Collins had battled for the starting position all season.

With the home-field advantage and the fact that they had revenge on their minds themselves as they had not beaten Pitt in the past two campaigns, Nebraska certainly had all the intangibles on their side. Despite this fact, the experts still felt that the Panthers were one of the best teams in the nation and would emerge victorious. Hall-of-fame coach Knute Rockne said in his weekly column, "Pittsburgh has possibly one of the best teams in the east this year if not the country and they will carry too many guns for Coach Bible's men." Rockne further went on to say, "Nebraska showed nice improvement last week at Syracuse, but they are not ready for a team the caliber that "Jock" Sutherland will send on to the field this Saturday afternoon."[11]

The *Pittsburgh Press*'s beat writer Max Hannum said it best when he described the Panthers' effort against the Cornhuskers as "great, mediocre and poor."[12] For Sutherland's crew, the poor existed for the better part of the first quarter. Thirty-five thousand Nebraska fans were thrilled, as the Cornhuskers had been the dominant team in the opening frame. While Nebraska did have the better of play, the Pitt defense continually made clutch plays to keep them off the board, while Tom Parkinson was a magnificent punter, giving Nebraska poor field position to start their drives. The Panthers needed both to excel, as the offense, for the first time in the 1929 campaign, was completely inept.

Things were certainly looking difficult for Sutherland and his club with the way Nebraska was moving the ball; it seemed like only a matter of time before the Panthers were behind for the first time that season. It seemed even worse when Josh Williams left the contest with an injured leg; enter Bill Walinchus.

The reserve back finally broke through the big Husker defense early in the second period. Walinchus pulled in a short pass from Baker, whom the hall-of-fame coach decided to start for the third consecutive game. The speedster caught the ball at his own 45 and sprinted 53 yards to the Nebraska two.

Two plays later Parkinson ripped through the Nebraska line for his first touchdown of the day and a 6–0 Pitt advantage.

Invigorated by the touchdown, the Pitt offense methodically dissected Nebraska on a powerful drive led by Parkinson, who was showing the experts why he should be an All-American. The drive finally culminated with another short rush by Parkinson, and what looked like it would be a difficult afternoon for Pitt now showed much more promise with a 12–0 lead at the half.

When it seemed like the Panthers could garner a comfortable lead despite their inept play, even backing up the Cornhuskers to their own goal on two occasions, the bad came out again for Pitt as Sloan showed what a dynamic player he was, completing a 25-yard scoring toss to Cliff Morgan early in the final quarter bringing Nebraska to within five points at 12–7.

With disaster looming, the Pitt defense held firm after the Nebraska touchdown, preserving Pittsburgh's slim advantage. While Uansa was held in check by the Nebraska defense with his worst game of the season, Tom Parkinson had arguably his best. Parkinson's punting and running led the way for the Panthers, playing almost the entire game. The California, Pennsylvania, native was finally given a rest in favor of Jimmy Rooney as the game was coming to an end.

The final whistle blew as the game ended with their fourth victory of the season. As happy as Pitt should have been with the important victory, the team knew they did not perform as consistent and as well as they could have. They were also beaten physically. Williams had a bruised leg and had to be helped onto the train home, and lineman Ralph Daugherty went straight to his bunk in the train to rest after the physical beating he took by the huge Husker linemen. Making matters worse for the team was the fact that many players on the team were suffering from bad burns due to the lime that the Nebraska groundskeepers used to line the field. Every time the lime came into contact with a Panther player it burned painfully.

Regardless of the physical beating and questionable groundskeeping, Pitt was still undefeated and was now being mentioned as serious national championship contenders. The Associated Press mentioned many programs, but specifically Southern California and the Panthers as the top two, giving Pitt the nod due to their win over the Huskers, claiming that the "Panthers gave Nebraska a more decisive beating than the score of 12 to 7 indicates."[13] Even though it was close, Pitt found a way to win against arguably the best team it would play in the regular season.

Game 5—October 26, 1929, at Municipal Stadium in Erie, Pennsylvania

UNIVERSITY OF PITTSBURGH PANTHERS   40
ALLEGHENY COLLEGE GATORS   0

They were the one of the kings of college football at this point and time of the season, not only in the very competitive college football scene in Western Pennsylvania, but in the nation as well. Despite this fact, during the week following their huge win over Nebraska, the University of Pittsburgh football squad took a backseat not only to the Carnegie Foundation report that was released during the week detailing some of the problems in collegiate sports, but to the Carnegie Tech–Notre Dame tilt that was taking place in Pittsburgh the same day as Pitt would travel to Erie to face Allegheny College.

While Pitt Stadium was technically built on Pitt turf, fans and newspapermen alike were referring to it simply as the Stadium, since Tech and Pitt both shared the facility. The Tartans were considered a national power in the 1920s and beat the Panthers four times in the previous six seasons, but they definitely took a backseat to Pitt in the yearly national championship race, although the matchup against the Fighting Irish was about to set an attendance record at the five-year-old facility.

The other major news of the week in college football was the announcement of the results in the Carnegie Foundation report on college athletics. The unique thing about the report was the lack of specifics or the fact that at several universities like Pitt, there were no investigators reported on campus. Regardless of the inadequacies, it brought to light the issues of paying athletes in college football and began a national debate on the ethics of the policy, a policy that would be uncovered at the University of Pittsburgh toward the end of the next decade and would eventually lead to the downfall of their powerful national championship program.

For the time being, the pay-for-play issue was on the back burner, as was the fact that a record 65,000 fans would be jammed into Pitt's own field to see two teams that were not representing the university. The week was about the Panthers trying to increase their record to 5–0 against what was perceived as an undermanned Allegheny squad.

Eight thousand fans showed up at Erie's Municipal Stadium, a far cry from the record crowd that entered Pitt Stadium on this day, to see what they had in fact expected when they entered the gates. One of the most powerful teams in the nation facing off against one that had no business being on the same field with them.

Allegheny entered the game winless with an 0–2–1 mark, being manhandled by one of Pitt's main competitors for the 1929 national championship, Dartmouth, the week before. They were led by a formidable backfield that included two Harrys, Dennison and Smith, as well as their star Nick Varano.

For his part, Dr. Sutherland decided to hold out his starters for most of the contest, giving them a rest after the physical toll that the Nebraska contest took on them. They instead went with Edwards at quarterback as well as Rooney; Walinchus, the star of the Cornhusker clash; and Clark in the backfield to join him. It made no difference as the Panthers scored early and often against their undermanned foes.

After stopping Allegheny on their first series, Clark showed just how long a day it was going to be for the small Meadville school. Pitt started at their opponents' 42, and on the second play Clark rambled 33 yards to the six. Three plays later Walinchus took it in for the day's first touchdown and an early 7–0 Panther advantage.

The Pittsburgh defense frustrated the Allegheny attack once again and Pitt began their second possession at midfield. After an 11-yard run, Rooney skirted around the end on a 17-yard sprint, being tossed out of bounds at the 22 for the first down. Clark and Walinchus advanced the ball 17 yards on the next two plays before the Gators sacked Clark for a one-yard loss giving the Panthers a second-and-goal from the six. Rooney ended the drive on the next play with a touchdown that gave Pitt the 14-point lead.

Following almost a full quarter of domination, Allegheny began their first major threat of the game when Varano rolled through the right side of his line for a 21-yard gain. As the first quarter was coming to an end, the Panthers' opponents from northwestern Pennsylvania were at the Pitt five with a second-and-goal. The Pitt defense stiffened as Allegheny was threatening to cut the lead in half. With a fourth down at the nine, Walter Milligan picked off a pass for Pitt, returning it to the ten.

What only moments ago looked like a close game turned into a three-touchdown lead for Pitt. It was a methodical 90-yard drive, at least for the first 44 yards highlighted by a 20-yard Rooney run. At that point a lateral from Edwards to Clark made it 21–0 when Clark took the pitch 46 yards around the right end and down the sideline for the score.

Backed up at their own eight after a fine punt by Rooney pinned them back, Allegheny could not advance the ball, as a short punt to the Panthers' 30 gave Pitt wonderful position when Rooney grabbed it and took it 11 yards to the 19. Walinchus sprinted ten yards in the first play followed by a nine-yard touchdown by Rooney to end the half with the Panthers holding an impressive 27–0 lead.

The third quarter was every bit as dominant as the first half when Rip

Collins secured the opening kickoff, sprinting 34 yards to the Allegheny 46. Rooney ended the short seven-play drive with a 25-yard jaunt and an insurmountable 33-point lead. As fun as the afternoon had been for the Panther backups at this point, Walinchus had been hurt on the touchdown drive and left the game. It made no difference; the next time Pitt had the ball, Rooney continued his phenomenal afternoon, tossing a scoring pass to Walinchus's replacement Murphy for 52 yards, ending the scoring 40–0 late in the third quarter.

Sutherland put in his first team late in the contest just to get them warmed up for their anticipated matchup against a much tougher foe the following week—Ohio State at Pitt Stadium—as the undefeated streak reached five games with Pitt heading into November with a perfect 5–0–0 mark.

Game 6—November 2, 1929, at Pitt Stadium

OHIO STATE UNIVERSITY BUCKEYES   2
UNIVERSITY OF PITTSBURGH PANTHERS   18

Following their impressive shutout win against Allegheny in their last road contest of the season, the undefeated Panthers returned home to face a difficult test: a matchup against the equally undefeated Ohio State Buckeyes. While Ohio State had challenges offensively, only scoring 33 points in their three victories over Wittenberg, Iowa and Michigan, the defense had been impenetrable, allowing only six points, that being in the 7-6 win over the Hawkeyes. In their previous game before the Pitt contest, the Buckeyes suffered their lone blemish of the campaign to date in 1929, a scoreless tie against the Hoosiers of Indiana. Regardless of the tie, they were undefeated in the tough Big Ten Conference and were expected to give Pitt yet another formidable challenge in their quest for the national title.

Ohio State coach Sam Willamans' squad was led by three-time All-American end/fullback Wesley Fesler, who not only earned nine letters at the university in football, basketball and baseball, but was elected to the College Football Hall of Fame in 1954. Outside of his magnificent playing career he spent one season as head coach at Pitt in 1946. Willaman also had a solid backfield that included quarterback Alan Holman, halfbacks Arden McConnell, Bill Nesser and Bob Horn, as well as fullback Stuart Holcomb. As good as their backfield was, it was their magnificent defensive line, though, that could be the difference for the Buckeyes in this contest.

The biggest matchup on the front line was thought to be between Pitt's center Ralph Daugherty and Ohio State's big lineman Fred Barratt. Daugherty was athletic, quick and nimble, but the Buckeye senior was 6'2", 239 pounds, a full 60 pounds heavier than his Panther opponent. Should Barratt be able to dominate his lighter foe, it would create a huge obstacle for Tom Parkinson, who had yet to be stopped at fullback for Pitt during the season.

With the two coaches spending time preparing for battle, the main emphasis in the newspapers in Pittsburgh was the expected record college football crowds that would reportedly descend on Pittsburgh during the weekend. Aside from the Ohio State–Pitt clash, Duquesne and Geneva were competing just down the street from Pitt Stadium at Forbes Field the evening before. It was a significant contest as it was the first night football contest in the city's history. Over 20,000 fans were at Forbes Field for the historic game that saw Duquesne win 27–7. As impressive as it was, it would pale in comparison to Pitt Stadium on Saturday afternoon.

By Tuesday, only 400 reserved seats remained, and the demand seemed to be growing for the general admission seats by the day. While the vast majority of fans would certainly be rooting for the University of Pittsburgh in this home tilt, many Ohio State aficionados would make the trek from Columbus to the Steel City. A huge armada of Buckeye faithful traveled to Pittsburgh by train and automobile. On the train were 47 players and coaches as well as the 110-piece Ohio State band and 1,100 undergraduates. This would be in addition to over 8,000 Buckeye fans who were on hand at the stadium.

With his undefeated record on the line, Pitt Coach Jock Sutherland had potential issues in his star-studded backfield. Josh Williams was still suffering from the injuries acquired in the Nebraska game two weeks earlier and was limited in practice earlier in the week. His main backup, Bill Walinchus, was doubtful himself after injuring his leg against Allegheny. Sutherland moved Jimmy Rooney into their spot in the early practices as an insurance policy in case both couldn't play against Ohio State. The Buckeyes were not without issues themselves as they would be missing an important part of their backfield with Al Hess out with a bad knee.

It had rained in Pittsburgh several times during the week, and there was fear by the Pitt coach that a wet, muddy field could affect Pitt more than their opponents, taking away one of the main advantages the heavily favored Panthers had—their incredible speed. As it turned out, the rain came just as feared and kept the contest from topping the stadium record set the week before by Carnegie Tech and Notre Dame, but 51,000 rabid fans still filled Pitt Stadium. The rain muddied the field which gave the defenses a huge advantage.

Two weeks before, Parkinson was the hero against Nebraska while Toby Uansa was almost nonexistent; on this day it would be a different story from the outset. The Pitt defense held Ohio State in the first series and took over at the opposing 30-yard line. After Williams, who was deemed healthy enough to play, recovered his own fumble on the first offensive play of the game for the Panthers, Uansa showed very quickly that he would be a star as he took the ball around left end, dashing through the vaunted Buckeye defense for 68 yards and a 6–0 Pitt advantage. On the play, Daugherty, who many wondered before the contest whether or not he could handle the bigger opponents, administered a crushing block that allowed Uansa to travel the final 30 yards with no Ohio State defenseman in sight.

Late in the first quarter Pitt once again drove deep into Buckeye territory thanks to the long runs around the end from Williams and Uansa which took the ball to the Ohio State four. The highlight of the drive was the battle between the two All-American ends Joe Donchess and Fesler. While Fesler ended his career in Columbus as the three-time All-American, in this game he was vastly inferior to Donchess.

Growing up in nearby Youngstown, Ohio, Donchess was a child of German immigrants as he left school in seventh grade to work and help his family financially. A true Horatio Alger story, Donchess was a very hard worker who impressed one of his bosses where he worked. The boss made sure that the future All-American had all the requirements to enter the University of Pittsburgh where he not only became one of the school's greatest players, but an orthopedic surgeon, impressively being able to enter medical school after two years at Pitt.

On this rainy day his blocks had Pitt on the verge of an early blowout; that is until Baker tossed an interception to McConnell to end the threat. After making the game's biggest play for the Buckeyes, McConnell gave points to the Panthers, fumbling the ball in the end zone where he was downed for a safety.

As the second quarter began, the shower turned into a downpour. Pitt was stuck deep in their own territory and Parkinson's uncharacteristically bad punts in the wet conditions kept Ohio State on Pitt's side of the field. As the Pitt defense was very strong, keeping the Buckeyes off the scoreboard, the Panther offense was not so lucky. After a poor pass, Uansa had to run into his own end zone following a fumble, which he secured, unfortunately giving Ohio State what would turn out to be its only points of the game with a safety of their own to cut the Panther lead to six.

Now only ahead 8–2, the Pitt began to win the field-advantage war now, thanks to a poor punt by McConnell that gave the Panthers the ball at the Buckeye 16. After a couple of less-than-stellar runs, Pitt did something that it hadn't all season; they were successful on a field-goal attempt as Rooney hit from 32-yards, making it 11–2.

In the second half, the offenses were bogged down by poor field conditions and staunch defenses as they went through the third quarter scoreless with Pitt threatening deep in Ohio State territory as the final quarter began. The Buckeyes stopped Pitt at the 25 as Rooney went back to punt. Instead of trying to pin Ohio State down, he threw a pass toward the 13-yard line that was snatched by Uansa. The Panther star took the ball and then slashed through the Buckeye defense for the final 13 yards to give the home team an 18–2 lead.

The Pitt defense was able to keep the Buckeyes from threatening the rest of the contest as Pitt held on for the tough win, sending the huge Ohio State throng home unhappy which began a tailspin that saw them lose three of their final four games.

For the Panthers it was the end of a perfect college football weekend in the Steel City as Uansa, who had not been heard from the previous two weeks, once because of ineptitude and once because Sutherland sat his regulars, came to the forefront once again as a great player to lead Pitt to its sixth consecutive victory.

Game 7—November 9, 1929, at Pitt Stadium
WASHINGTON AND JEFFERSON COLLEGE PRESIDENTS   0
UNIVERSITY OF PITTSBURGH PANTHERS   21

In the 1920s and 1930s, the collegiate football rivalries in Western Pennsylvania were of a very intense variety. With what was turning out to be a very successful 1929 campaign for the University of Pittsburgh coming to an end, three very difficult local schools would be the final three hurdles for the Panthers in their quest for an undefeated regular season and a shot at their fourth national championship. First up would be the Washington and Jefferson College Presidents.

While only defeating a Jock Sutherland Pitt squad once, a 10–0 shutout in his first season in 1924, W & J nonetheless usually gave the Scotsman fits with two scoreless ties and a close 6–0 loss in 1925. Finally in 1928, the Panthers showed they were superior to their rivals with a 25–0 thrashing of the Presidents and were hoping they could make the same statement once again.

As tough as they had been against the Pitt hall-of-fame coach, they had been equally difficult against the school itself over their 29-game series to this point with the Panthers holding a slim 14–13–2 advantage. With the confidence they gained holding Pitt's next opponent, the tough Carnegie Tech Tartans, to a scoreless tie earlier in the season, the Presidents had hopes they could figure out a way to similarly shut down the Panthers' vaunted attack.

Both teams were preparing for this important contest amid the backdrop of the beginnings of the great stock market crash of 1929. While the headlines over the previous week were dominated by the impending doom, the sports sections were full of stories of what a formidable opponent Washington and Jefferson would be.

Led by fullback Stew Wilson, the Presidents came into this contest undefeated with a stellar 4–0–2 mark despite the fact they were a young sophomore-laden team. Their only blemish was the aforementioned scoreless tie versus Carnegie Tech as well as one against Temple. W & J was coming off an impressive 20–0 victory over Lafayette and had outscored their opponents 124–6, yielding a single touchdown to Bucknell. The top player on the stalwart Washington and Jefferson defense was future Steeler coach Jap Douds.

Offensively, Wilson was joined in the Presidents backfield by three players that included Maury Rush, Lewis and Butler, who was the W & J quarterback. The four were having a great season to this point, but most of the experts felt they paled in comparison to the Pitt foursome of Uansa, Parkinson, Baker and Josh Williams, who seemed to be 100 percent healthy for the first time in three weeks after his injury against Nebraska.

An impressive victory against the formerly undefeated Ohio State Buckeyes coupled with the fact that Dartmouth, who was one of the few schools mentioned in the same breath as the Panthers for the national championship, lost to Yale 16–12, left the Panthers, along with Cornell and Notre Dame, as the only schools who had not been beaten or tied in 1929.

The Irish had been considered the favorites to capture the national crown with impressive victories against Indiana, Navy, Wisconsin and Georgia Tech to go with their 7–0 squeaker against Carnegie Tech, but if Pitt could win their final three contests and defeat the Tartans in a much more decisive manner than Notre Dame did, they would certainly would make a serious claim for the championship themselves.

Surprisingly as the sectional ratings were announced by mid-week, Yale had forged ahead of the Panthers in the eastern ratings. It was said by United Press writer George Kirksey, "Despite an early season loss at the hands of Georgia 15–0, Yale's eastern record is far more impressive than any other team in this section. Pittsburgh is unbeaten, but Pitt's victories over West Virginia, Nebraska and Ohio State can't match Yale's triumph over Brown, Army and Dartmouth."[14]

Despite the disappointing news on the ratings front, the potent Pitt attack was ready for W & J. Over the first ten years of Sutherland's impressive coaching career, his teams had scored more points than any other team in the country other than Knute Rockne's Notre Dame Fighting Irish and would add to that impressive number against their nearby rivals.[15]

A huge favorite despite their struggling record against the Presidents, Sutherland worked against his team being overconfident against W & J. Wanting to show that they in fact were taking the game seriously, Pitt won the toss and began a grinding opening drive that took the ball to their opponents' 13. Unfortunately the President defense did stiffen as Douds stopped Williams and then Parkinson only inches from a first down taking over on downs.

The W & J momentum was short-lived when Lewis dropped a reverse in which Charles Tully recovered at the 24. Parkinson then made up for his last carry with a 19-yard ramble up the middle to the one where he fumbled, but fortunately picked up at the four. Two plays later he finally made it over the goal line, then kicked the extra point for the 7–0 advantage. The rest of the first half was played mostly between the 30s as the two teams ended the second quarter with Pitt hanging on to its precarious seven-point lead.

The beginning of the third quarter looked much like the last, with no serious scoring threats before the Panthers took over midway in the stanza. On this drive, Sutherland made sure his offensive line continually double-teamed Douds. Pittsburgh took a time out for their All-American candidate Joe Donchess, who had his pants ripped off, and then started to churn downfield. After Uansa and Parkinson were stopped by the tough Washington and Jefferson defense, Jimmy Rooney hit Baker with a pass at the President's 35. Baker then rambled to the 23 to set up Pitt's second score. W & J appeared to have the Panthers stopped as Pitt had the ball with a fourth-and-three from the 12 and Uansa apparently injured. Uansa stayed in the game and took the fourth down carry through the staunch defense for the touchdown, putting Pittsburgh up 14–0.

As the contest turned to the final quarter, the Panther opponents finally broke when Uansa took a punt at his own 24, returning it 14 yards where he was

JOSEPH DONCHESS
PITTSBURGH   END
1927-29

Joe Donchess was one of four first-team All-Americans for the 1929 national champion University of Pittsburgh Panthers. The end, who was elected to the College Football Hall of Fame in 1979, had a successful career as an orthopedic surgeon following his graduation from Pitt's renowned school of medicine.

thought to be tackled. The rules at the time stated that when a runner was tackled, he had to be in the grasp on the ground or he could get up and keep advancing the ball. In this case Uansa was not in the grasp and got up to continue his return for 56 yards to the W & J 20.

While the Washington and Jefferson coaches and fans were screaming at the officials for not blowing the whistle, Uansa was injured once again and did leave the game this time. Seven plays later Walinchus, who like Williams was finally healthy after a previous leg injury, took it in the last two yards for the final score of the game and an impressive 21–0 win.

Now standing at 7–0–0, Pitt continued to make a strong case for themselves as the greatest team in the nation, an argument they would continue a week later against their Forbes Avenue neighbors.

Game 8—November 16, 1929, at Pitt Stadium

CARNEGIE TECH TARTANS	13
UNIVERSITY OF PITTSBURGH PANTHERS	34

As the economy worsened in the country and the stock market continued to be dangerously volatile, football fans in the city of Pittsburgh tried for forget their financial worries as they focused on a battle of two of the country's strongest college football teams, who just happened to be separated by less than a mile. While in the mid–1930s the more intense Steel City rivalry was between Pitt and the Dukes of Duquesne, in the 1920s it was these two close neighbors that would have the more historic battles.

By the end of the decade Carnegie Tech had become one of the stronger programs in the country. They had beaten Knute Rockne and his Fighting Irish of Notre Dame twice, 19–0 in 1926 and 27–7 two years later, and just missed a third victory earlier in the season with a close hard-fought 7–0 loss in front of a record 65,000 at Pitt Stadium. Against Pitt they had been equally if not more successful than they had against the Irish. After dropping the first nine games to the Panthers, the Tartans had taken control of the series in the previous six seasons. Carnegie Tech had defeated Pitt four times, including a very muddy 6–0 shutout of Pittsburgh in 1928.

Losing to the Irish aside, 1929 was shaping up to be another strong season for the Tartans. Along with a scoreless tie against Washington and Jefferson, those two contests were the only blemishes on what was an otherwise fine campaign that included one-sided wins against Bethany, Thiel, Case Reserve and Washington (MO).

Coaches Walter Steffen and Bob Waddell were preparing their team against arguably their toughest opponent of the season to date. Led by All–

American candidate John Dreshar and his huge punishing fullback Johnny Karcis, who was compared to Pitt's own physical fullback Tom Parkinson, the Tartans were expected to be formidable foes despite the fact they were underdogs. According to *Pittsburgh Press* writer Max Hannum, "It is hard to find any soul who will claim that the Panthers will walk away with an easy victory. The greatest effort is always made against Pitt." He further went on to claim that "those who saw the Plaid defensive fight against Notre Dame will realize that Sutherland's club can hardly hope to ride rough-shod over the Steffen-Waddell clan."[16] While there would be no problem for the Tech coaches to get their team inspired for the contest, Coach Sutherland seemed concerned once again that his club would take its opponents lightly.

The Panthers were a confident bunch, and the hall-of-fame coach at times mistook that for overconfidence. They may not have been at their peak against Washington and Jefferson, but he shouldn't have had to worry about his players' incentive for this contest. After all, it was a game against a college that was only a stone's throw from their university. The Tartans helped turn 1928 into a disappointing season for Pitt with the upset, so they were looking for revenge. There was a bigger reason for the Panthers to be focused on defeating their rivals in this game: a more realistic chance at the national championship.

With the one-sided shutout against W & J in their corner and a 7–0–0 perfect record, their title hopes took an upward turn the previous week when Yale, who had previously been the top-rated team in the east, was tied by Maryland, leaving Pitt as the unquestioned top collegiate squad in the region.

It was a team that was being compared in the local media to the Panthers' 1916 national championship squad, considered at the time to be the finest the university had ever produced. The main comparison between the two powerful teams was the fact that despite the fact the opposition knew exactly what was coming, Pitt was so strong that there was no way they could stop it. Hannum stated in his article a few days before the game that Waddell "has been building to stop the reverse, the triple pass and the fake reverse, almost neglecting his own attack. If something new is rung in on Saturday, the plaid bosses fear the worst."[17]

To make matters worse for the Tartans, their star fullback Karcis, while expected to play, was not at 100 percent, suffering with several injuries during the season and been held out for most of the game the previous week against Washington (MO) hoping to rest him for the city championship tilt.

Despite the fact Karcis was hurt and Carnegie Tech came into the game as an underdog, they were the defending "city champions," and with the championship, they were the holders of a $6,000 silver bowl that the Pittsburgh city council purchased for the winner of the contest.

The two schools would battle for the bowl in front of 54,000 rabid fans in a sun-drenched Pitt Stadium. The student leaders of both institutions gathered together for a meeting earlier in the week in an effort to try and agree to keep their fellow alumni under control during the contest. The excitement in the past had led to unseemly graffiti, property damage and throwing rolled-up papers from the stands, which when wet caused potential injuries. Many of these issues were similar to ones that had occurred by fans at rivalries over the years, and while they were serious about curbing it, the attempt didn't stop the emotion in the crowd during the game, although the domination by the Panthers on this sunny fall afternoon did quiet the Tartan faithful.

The revenge that the Panthers were seeking was quick and decisive as the Tartans were stunned before the game was 15 minutes old. Uansa showed his All-American form early, returning the opening kickoff 38 yards to their own 42. On the next play he rambled through the middle of the line looking like he was about to be tackled. He then reversed his field and shot 58 yards to give Pitt the early lead two plays into the contest, 7–0. A few plays later the Panthers extended their advantage as a poor snap on a punt flew over McCurdy's head into the end zone. While he picked it up and tried to punt, it was blocked, and Tech fell on it for a safety and a quick nine-point lead.

With the Tartans reeling, Uansa continued his spectacular first quarter intercepting a pass at the Pitt 25. After Baker picked up a Whitey Walinchus fumble, who was in the Pitt backfield replacing the injured Josh Williams, he took it 27 yards to the Tech 41 setting up Uansa, who scored his second touchdown of the day with a 41-yard sprint, making the score 15–0.

On the final play of the opening period, Walinchus grabbed a fumble by Karcis that popped up into the air, and returned it 14 yards giving Pitt a 21-point lead as the opening quarter came to an end. In the second quarter, Pitt all but ended the contest when Walinchus barreled over the goal line from a couple yards out to conclude the one-sided first half with a 27-point lead.

The second half was anti-climactic as reserve back Jimmy Clark scored a meaningless touchdown in the final quarter to give the Panthers a dominant 34–13 thrashing of their neighbors, wrestling away the silver bowl, emblematic of the city championship, from the Tartans.

Even though Notre Dame remained undefeated with Pitt, defeating USC 13–12 in front of 120,000 fans at Soldier Field in Chicago, Pitt made a strong claim for the national title as their victory over Carnegie Tech was much more impressive than the victory the Irish had against them earlier in the season.

The other important thing that came from this game was that with a perfect 8–0–0 record and only a contest against the undermanned Penn State Nittany Lions left on the schedule, the eastern championship was almost assured for the Panthers, and with that a bid to the Rose Bowl to play against the best the west had to offer. It was a banner day for Sutherland and his squad, a day that showed not just how powerful the Panthers were, but that the dream of an undefeated and untied campaign was now so tantalizingly close.

Game 9—November 28, 1929, at Pitt Stadium
PENN STATE UNIVERSITY NITTANY LIONS 7
UNIVERSITY OF PITTSBURGH PANTHERS 20

In the 1920s it was a Thanksgiving tradition as celebrated in Western Pennsylvania as the Detroit Lions or the Dallas Cowboys playing on the holiday currently is. Penn State University and the University of Pittsburgh would take the field annually for their battle on Thanksgiving Day, but it was a game that the Nittany Lion faithful did not seem to enjoy as much as their rivals at Pitt did.

Penn State had not been a formidable opponent for Pitt as they had not defeated the Panthers since a 20–0 shutout in 1919, but that was not the reason Penn State was upset. They were concerned about not only securing more home dates for the school, as the game had been played in Pittsburgh every season since 1903, but according to *Pittsburgh Press* columnist Ralph Davis, it was the weather and field conditions that prompted them to want a change too.

"Often the field is a quagmire of mud, or resembles an inland sea," Davis stated. "Penn State encounters cold weather in its own domain, but claims the wetness here is unusual and that its teams are not as much accustomed to such conditions as the Panthers."[18]

Whether or not there was a significant difference in the climate in Pittsburgh versus State College was debatable; the bottom line is that not only would the 1930 contest be the last Thanksgiving game scheduled in the foreseeable future, but the 1929 game was also the last step in a potential national championship run by the University of Pittsburgh.

There were not many experts giving Penn State any semblance of a chance against the Panthers. They felt that the Lions had the same chance that every other Pitt opponent had of beating them: hope the Panthers became overconfident and made enough mistakes to lose. Led by coach Hugo Bezdek, the All-American from the University of Chicago who had the unique distinction of being the only man to coach a college team, an NFL team and manage a major league baseball squad. Coming to the Steel City was a homecoming of sorts for Bezdek as he led the Pittsburgh Pirates between 1917 and 1919 to a measure of success before taking over as athletic director, football coach and baseball coach at Penn State.

Bezdek was in his 12th season as the head man at State College and came into this game with a fine 6–2–1 mark against a less-than-stellar schedule. The two notable victories came against Syracuse, 6–4 and a 6–3 defeat at the hands of Lafayette. Their offense was far from stellar, amassing only 94 points after eight contests, but they had an exciting player who led them at quarterback by the name of Cooper French. French was the catalyst of one of the most exciting plays of 1929. With time winding down and Lafayette leading 3–0, French took the kickoff by the Leopards and ran down the sideline as the clock hit 0:00. As he was about to be stopped he launched a lateral to a teammate who ran the final 60 yards for a touchdown in a thrilling victory.

While the Nittany Lions certainly would be at their best for their rivals, they would have to be aware that the Panthers wanted to send their impressive group of seniors, which included Albert DiMeolo; quarterback Charley Edwards, who lost his starting spot to Eddie Baker in the Duke game; Joe Donchess; Ray Montgomery; Toby Uansa; and Tom Parkinson, out with an impressive win.

For Donchess, Montgomery and Uansa, they were named to the United Press All-Eastern first team the week before the rivalry game, while DiMeolo was chosen for a more unique honor. He was chosen to the first-team All-Italian squad by University of Arkansas professor Luigi A. Passarelli. As far as Parkinson was concerned, the disappointment of being left off the first-team eastern squad would inspire the bruising back to have the game of his life against the Nittany Lions, which would bring him much bigger honors later on.

Amid the backdrop of this Thanksgiving Day classic was the fate of Pittsburgh's post-season plans. They were offered an opportunity to play in New York City against either Fordham or Colgate in December to benefit the Christmas Fund. The university administration declined the invitation claiming they didn't want the team to play a game that would interfere with the player's school session after a long season. Perhaps the real reason was it gave Pitt an opportunity to accept a Rose Bowl bid that hopefully would come its way with a win. Before the hopes of a Rose Bowl became a possibility, they had to take care of business at Pitt Stadium as 30,000 fans braved the cold to see what would turn out to be perhaps Pitt's biggest scare of the season.

The game started out well enough for the Panthers. Bezdek had developed a defensive game plan to stop Uansa, which turned out to be successful, limiting the Pitt superstar back as no one had in the season. What he didn't do was fully account for Parkinson, which would haunt him on this afternoon.

Almost midway in the opening quarter, Pitt took the ball at its own 40 as Sutherland decided to mix things up offensively, preparing his team with a series of triple passes and fake reverses. Even though it was wide-open attack for the time period, it was also a methodical drive which saw no play longer than the 15-yard run by Whitey Walinchus. The leader of the drive, though, was Parkinson who ripped through the Nittany Lions line for an early 6–0 lead.

While controlling the game for most of the first half, the Panthers were unable to add to their lead, a fact that hurt them as the second quarter was coming to an end. Penn State took possession of the ball at their own 43 and had taken it down to the Pitt 24 with a pass and an effective rushing attack. It was at that point that Sutherland's worst fears would become reality when French sent a perfect pass to Skip Stahley in the end zone to tie the contest. Yutz Diedrich put the conversion through the uprights successfully as it hit off the crossbar and snuck through for a surprising 7–6 Lions advantage, the first time Pitt had been behind all season. Penn State was able to hold on through the remainder of the half and went into halftime still up by one.

Bezdek and his squad continued to stymie that Panther offense through a majority of the third quarter until Pitt finally embarked on what would be the drive of the season to save their national championship hopes. Taking the ball at their 26, the Panthers slowly and powerfully wore down what had been a stout Penn State defensive wall. The Pitt backfield, once again led by the California (PA) native, continually went downfield three to five yards at a clip. Finally, almost completely worn down by the Panthers' power, Parkinson took the ball over the goal line from three yards out, then made the conversion to make the score 13–7 as the third quarter was coming to an end.

Early in the final quarter, with the Pitt defense becoming tougher, the Panthers took over at their own 47 following a 15-yard punt return by Uansa. After being frustrated for most of the day by the Lions, Uansa finally broke loose for a 32-yard run to the opposing 21. A few plays later Parkinson gave his team a commanding lead when he bolted in from the two-yard line and once again converted with a successful extra point, finishing the scoring in the 20–7 victory.

When the team needed him most, Parkinson had the game of his life with 182 yards rushing while scoring all 20 points for Pitt. His phenomenal performance coupled with the poor one by Uansa temporarily changed the minds of the experts that would choose the various All-American teams. Parkinson and Donchess found themselves on the New York Sun first team, which was announced two days after the Penn State contest, while Montgomery was placed on the second squad and Uansa was left off altogether despite his school record 964 yards rushing, a record that stood 44 years until Tony Dorsett became the school's first 1,000-yard rusher in 1973, and team high of 61 points.

Eventually Uansa would receive his just due as he was named to the first-team All-American squads by the Associated Press and the Central Press Association while expert Lawrence Perry also put Parkinson on his first team. For

Montgomery and Donchess, they were honored with a first-team designation by several organizations as they both were included on the consensus first-team All-American list.

For the Nittany Lions and their coach, it was not a celebratory time. Bezdek, who had done so much to make football successful at Penn State, unfortunately had coached his last game there. He had been embroiled in a controversy over the past few years as the Pittsburgh region of the Penn State Alumni Club had been furious at his lack of success against Pitt since 1925. The loss again this season added fuel to the fire, and while they had a difficult time getting the powers that be at the university to fire him, they found a loophole and used that to have him removed.

There was a committee called the Beaver White Committee that was making recommendations for the school's future. One of the recommendations was to have the head of the physical education department not be directly involved in intercollegiate athletics. Bezdek was the athletic director, and the Pittsburgh chapter pushed aggressively for this recommendation. According to an article on the Penn State Libraries website, "if Bezdek could not be fired outright, at least he could be rendered powerless over the football team."[19] The administration did relieve him of his job, and there was hope among the alumni that the move would hopefully end what had been a series of humiliating losses to the Panthers, which it unfortunately did not.

As the season concluded with the perfect regular season mark, there were many experts giving their opinion on who would win a mythical championship between Pitt and the Fighting Irish including an article in the *Pittsburgh Press* by legendary Carnegie Tech coach Walter Steffen where he claimed the Irish superior to the Panthers to the cries of the Pitt faithful claiming him to be nothing more than a sore loser. While most couldn't say for certainty who was better, unfortunately for the University of Pittsburgh, Notre Dame was recognized as national champions by most of the respected organizations as Sutherland and his 1929 squad would have to wait four years for the recognition they felt they deserved.

In 1933 Parke H. Davis decided to name his list of national champions retroactive from 1869 through 1932 in one of the nation's premiere periodicals at the time, the *1933 Spalding Football Guide*. A player for Princeton in the late 1800s as well as a coach for Wisconsin Amherst and Lafayette, Davis became recognized as one of the nation's most important college football historians, if not its most important. As Dan Jenkins said in an article for *Sports Illustrated* in 1967, "Perhaps a bit irritated by the flood of experts on the scene, the most noted historian football has ever known, Parke H. Davis, decided to set all the records straight in the 1933 edition of *Spalding's Football Guide*."[20]

Regardless of the reason, Davis put together his list, looking at the schedules and scores of each team meticulously before naming his choices, and named the University of Pittsburgh as his champions for the 1929 campaign. Years later, in 1967, *Sports Illustrated* did research following the disputed national championship argument between Notre Dame and Michigan State in 1966 and developed what they felt was the official list of all national champions over the years, a list that included Davis's selections, which is also now officially listed in the NCAA records guide. Because of this research, the University of Pittsburgh officially recognizes the 1929 squad as national champions. While they weren't able to celebrate the championship in a timely manner during the 1929 campaign, it is distinguished through the years as one of the best squads the university ever produced.

***National Champions** selections made by modern-day analysts are noted "(retrospective)." Players rated as **First Team All-Americans** by a plurality of NCAA-recognized selectors are noted as "(consensus)." Players rated by all NCAA-recognized selectors are noted as "(unanimous)."*

1929 Scores

Date	Opponent	Score	Record
9/28	Waynesburg	53–0	1–0–0
10/5	@Duke	52–7	2–0–0
10/12	West Virginia	27–7	3–0–0
10/19	@Nebraska	12–7	4–0–0
10/26	@Allegheny	40–0	5–0–0
11/2	Ohio State	18–2	6–0–0
11/9	Washington and Jefferson	21–0	7–0–0
11/16	Carnegie Tech	34–13	8–0–0
11/28	Penn State	20–7	9–0–0
1/1	USC—Rose Bowl	14–47	9–1–0
		291–90	

Selected as National Champions by:
The Spalding Guide (Parke H. Davis Ratings)

Selected as First-Team All-Americans
Toby Uansa
Joe Donchess (unanimous)
Ray Montgomery (consensus)
Thomas Parkinson

3

1930 Rose Bowl: A California Nightmare

Despite the fact the University of Pittsburgh had a remarkable undefeated campaign that would eventually see them as being named national champions by respected historian Parke H. Davis, there was starting to be a real concern by the powers that be at the school that Coach Jock Sutherland's squad would not be offered a bid to the Rose Bowl in Pasadena that the team so desired. The bowl committee would first have to pick the representative from the west, who then had the opportunity to request the opponent from the east that they wanted to play. There were four possible schools that had the pedigree to represent the west.

The first, Stanford, coached by former Panther coach Pop Warner, was not a possibility as they decided to play Army at home on December 28. St. Mary's of California was undefeated with an 8-0-1 mark, but despite their impressive scoreless tie against California, their schedule was considered weak and they were expected to be an underdog to receive the bid.

That left Southern California and California as the favorites. USC won the Pacific Coast Conference with a stellar 9-2 record, losing only to Notre Dame by a single point and California 15-7. As good a season as they had, it was rumored they did not have the best relationship with the Rose Bowl committee, and because of that it was thought they did not have a chance to be chosen for the bid.

That left the University of California at Berkeley as the favorites for the bid. The Bears, led by Coach Clarence Price, had fashioned a fine 7-1-1 season, losing only to Stanford in the final contest of the season. While Cal would have made a worthy choice, the problem for the Panthers was that if the Bears were chosen, they did not want to play Pittsburgh.

Before Pitt took on Penn State in the season's final contest, there was another rumor that disturbed Sutherland and his club, that if Notre Dame was extended a bid to play in Pasadena on New Year's Day, they would accept it. Coach Knute Rockne seemed to put an end to that possibility according to *Pittsburgh Press* columnist Ralph Davis who claimed that "Coach Rockne, who insists that his boys are tired, and he himself is not in condition to supervise further training."[1]

Whatever happened, the Panthers had no choice but to be patient and wait to see how this unfolded. Regardless of whether they got the bid or not, they had the knowledge that they had a magnificent campaign. Since bowl games at this point in time were considered nothing more than exhibitions, they had already staked their claim for the national championship. A bid to the Rose Bowl or not wouldn't change that.

Still the Panthers looked forward to a reward for their fine campaign and finally early in the afternoon on December 6 they received that reward. The Rose Bowl committee had made their decision on the western representative, choosing the University of Southern California. With Notre Dame taking them out of consideration the previous week, the committee chose Pitt to receive the bid as the eastern representative not long after USC was selected.

One member of the Pitt athletic family who might not have been thrilled at the prospect of the football team extending their season another month was their basketball coach H.C. Carlson. Carlson himself was about to embark on a national championship campaign as his Pitt hoops squad was named champions in the 1929–30 season by the Helms Foundation. Because of the Rose Bowl bid, Carlson lost two of his players to the football team as Eddie Baker and Ray Montgomery both had to stay with the football squad rather than join Carlson's team as planned.

The basketball team's disappointment aside, Sutherland and his players accepted the challenge to return to California and try to erase the memory of the disappointing loss to Stanford in the New Year's Day classic two years before. While playing Southern California on what was in essence their home turf would be a difficult task, most experts did not feel Howard Jones and his USC Trojans were of national championship caliber. Despite the fact that they only lost to the Fighting Irish by a single point, they did so without Knute Rockne on the sidelines for Notre Dame.

Local college football fans would get a preview of what they could expect from the Trojans a couple of weeks before they faced the Panthers as USC still had one game left on their schedule, a contest in Los Angeles against Pitt's

3. 1930 Rose Bowl: A California Nightmare

Another view of the Panther statue that sits where Pitt Stadium used to. In 1909, only a year after the school changed its name from the Western University of Pennsylvania to its current name, alumnus George Baird suggested to the administration that the panther be the official mascot of the school's athletic teams. Once regularly found in the hills of Western Pennsylvania the panther has been the proud symbol of Pitt teams since then (photograph by the author).

fiercest city rival Carnegie Tech. After playing both Notre Dame and Pitt, the game against USC would be a good barometer to see just how the Panthers would fare against the Trojans.

While a close game was expected, the Tartans stood tough only for a time in the first half. USC flexed their muscles and showed the nation just what a superior football team they could be. Crushing Carnegie Tech 45–13 was a much more impressive performance than either Pitt or Notre Dame could muster up against them.

With the Trojans showing that they might be an incredibly difficult challenge for the Panthers, the interest in the game both in Pittsburgh and California was at an extreme high. The game sold out over two weeks in advance of the contest, an impressive feat for the time, and as far as the 2,000-ticket allotment that was sent to the University of Pittsburgh, "for every one there was at least 100 applicants."[2]

Jones had many fears as he prepared to face the Panthers; perhaps his main one was the incredible depth both in the backfield as well as their tough line. In fact it was the line that gave the Trojan coach his biggest fear. There was good reason for Jones to be concerned; Sutherland's squad had been successful all season ripping through opposing defenses whether it was his first team or reserves, as there was little difference between the two. Despite the fact that Pitt seemingly had an advantage with their depth, the Pitt hall-of-fame coach certainly had his own worries with the USC lineup.

The Trojans had some good depth in their own right, especially in their very productive backfield. USC was a wide-open offense for the time that depended on many shifts compared to the Pitt attack, which was more basic yet powerful. Sophomore Emy Pinckert and senior Harry Edelson were very tough blocking halfbacks which complemented their quick fullbacks in Jesse Hill, who was thought to be one of, if not the fastest runner on the West Coast by the experts; Don Moses; sophomore James Musick; Russell Saunders, who was the key back in the destruction of Carnegie Tech; and fellow sophomore Gus Shaver, the latter two sharing the final spot on the starting squad. Hill had been a very dangerous weapon for Jones, but he had been injured most of the campaign. There were various reports that Hill would be healthy for the Rose Bowl, which would not only be a huge plus for Southern California, but another difficult player for Sutherland to prepare for.

Defensively Jones was gearing his stout defensive front wall to stop the most impressive group of backs that the Trojans had faced all season in Toby Uansa, Tom Parkinson and the speedy Josh Williams. He would employ the team's captain, Francis Tappaan, as well as Nathan Barragar, Garrett Arbelbide, George Dye and Clark Galloway on the line. Tappaan had the biggest challenge, as Jones felt that Uansa would spend most of his time running his way. The USC coach was confident that he had one of the most formidable front lines in college football as Tappaan and Barragar would be named first-team All-Americans in 1929, and he thought they would be successful at limiting the powerful Panther attack.

As Sutherland prepared his squad before the long trip to Pasadena, he was forced to practice indoors at the Hunt Armory. Unlike the dry, warm weather he would have in Southern California, the wet, cold Pittsburgh December weather had left the turf at Pitt Stadium unusable.

The team was scheduled to leave for the coast on Christmas Day and hoped for a little cooler weather than Carnegie Tech experienced in their game against USC earlier in the month. The Tartans were not as deep as Pitt, and it was thought that the warm, uncomfortable weather was probably the biggest catalyst for the close contest being turned into a rout in the second half. As worried as Sutherland rightfully was about his opponents, the weather also came into play in his fears. "You know how good Notre Dame is supposed to be and the Irish beat the Trojans by an eyelash. Carnegie Tech isn't so weak and you know what the Southern Californians did to them," the Panther coach thought. "And you know what Southern California climate has done to other eastern football teams who were not accustomed to it."[3]

As the club was about to board the train for California at Union Station, it was announced that the powers that be at the University had rewarded their Scottish coach for his impressive work in 1929 giving him a five-year contract to remain coach of the Panthers. Head of the athletic council, C.L. Woolridge, stated that they had given him the contract because it not only "considers him one of the foremost coaches in the country but also because it has a deep appreciation of his widespread influences in teaching good sportsmanship and clean living."[4]

It was a joyous way to start the long trip, a trip where Sutherland also announced that Williams, who had an injury-plagued campaign, had been practicing and expected him to play in the game. The 85-man contingent that included the players, coaches as well as notable dignitaries from the university set out on the trek and would make a few stops before reaching California. They began with a stop in St. Louis for a practice at Washington University before heading to Dallas and another workout scheduled at Southern Methodist University. At SMU, the team had a fun workout that included soccer, rugby and basketball before going through their formations. To this point the workouts had been crisp with their coach, who usually had a worrisome attitude before each game, confident his team was well prepared to play.

Even though the Panthers were a ten-to-nine favorite among gamblers, Jones had been equally impressed with the attitude and preparedness of his team. While Sutherland knew his depth would be an advantage in the Southern California climate, the Trojan coach felt his team was ready for the challenge as his front line would thoroughly outweigh his opponents from Pitt and would be able to wear them down in the heat. It was an opinion that was also held by successful Minnesota coach Clarence "Fats" Spears who thought that the bigger Trojans would simply wear Pitt down by the second half.

Luckily for the Panthers, as they finally arrived in Pasadena after the five-day trip, the weather was much more to their liking than their neighbors from Carnegie Tech experienced earlier in the month. It was 60 degrees for the first time in a while there, as well as cloudy. The excitement of the turn in weather was tempered a bit as the forecasters predicted that by game time, the warm weather would return and the clouds would dissipate.

Regardless of the weather, game time had approached and the Pitt depth versus the size of the Trojan line would finally be played out. The game would give either team the chance to prove to the nation that it was the best team college football had to offer over Notre Dame who claimed just about every major national championship selection.

Seventy thousand fans jammed the Rose Bowl as it was host to the famed bowl game, which was in its fourteenth season. Early on it appeared as if the Panthers were in for another one-sided affair as Uansa quickly quieted the heavily pro–USC crowd. After Donchess took the opening kickoff, he fumbled, recovering it at the 18-yard line. The Pitt All-American halfback Uansa then darted on the first play of the game, 68 yards with a reverse that saw the Panthers move the ball to the Trojan 14. This was where Pitt was so dangerous, powerfully pushing the ball toward the goal line when inside their opponents' red zone. Unfortunately, rather than their backfield of Parkinson, Williams and Uansa pounding the ball into the end zone as they had done so many times earlier in the season, the large Southern California defense held and took over at the 20.

The Panthers still looked like the dominant team. Not long after taking over, Saunders sent a 68-yard punt that caught Pitt, sending them to their five-yard line. Pittsburgh could do nothing and punted back to Saunders who fumbled the ball at the Panther 36 with Tully jumping on it. Whatever advantage Pitt had at that point ended quickly as the game began to get away from them. The weight advantage USC had on Pittsburgh was taking its toll at this point as the Panther offense was completely shut down. The Trojans quickly took over after their turnover, and Saunders sent a perfect pass to Harry Edelson who ran it the remaining 30 yards for the first score of the game and a 7–0 advantage.

Pitt had only been behind once during the season and that was by a single point to Penn State, but they would go into unchartered waters before the first period ended. Whitey Walinchus, who had been so successful in reserve to the oft-injured Williams, gave USC the ball back when he fumbled at his own 31. Not long after, Saunders hit Pinckert with another touchdown toss as they now led the favored Panthers by 13 points. The one advantage USC thought they had coming into this contest, the huge weight differential, coupled with the weak link in Pitt's defense, their pass coverage, had combined to put Pitt in a hole they had not come close to being in all season.

If Sutherland thought somehow his team would recover in the second quarter, he quickly would learn otherwise. Once again Pitt dominated the beginning of the quarter, twice getting inside the Trojan 20, before the tough USC defense stopped Pitt from scoring. At that point, once again turnovers plagued Pittsburgh as the Panthers gave Southern California the ball at their

18-yard line. A few plays later junior quarterback Marshall Duffield went around right end to extend the USC advantage to 19 points. Even though Jones had sent in his reserves, there was no change in the domination over Pitt as Duffield connected with Jesse Mortensen for 48 yards to the two, before taking it in himself from the one on a spin play to give the Trojans a very surprising 26–0 lead at the half.

Unlike the first two quarters, Pitt did not come out aggressively in the third. Turnovers had been the Panthers' downfall in the opening half and would lead to the Trojans' fifth touchdown very early in the second. Parkinson threw an interception to Pinckert on the opening drive which seemed to completely deflate the Pittsburgh defense. The Trojan running attack ripped huge holes in the Panther line as they methodically went downfield with Saunders ending the back-breaking drive with a 15-yard jaunt, extending their lead to 33 points.

With the contest now certainly out of hand, Parkinson made up for the interception returning the following kickoff 41 yards. Pitt once again moved downfield and looked like they would be stopped again when Uansa dropped a pass with no defender in front of him on third down. The next play, he then completed a touchdown pass to Walinchus for the Panthers first points of the game.

While a victory was out of the question, any chance that they could at least make the contest a more acceptable outcome ended immediately after their first touchdown. Not letting up, Saunders hit Edelson with a 40-yard touchdown toss as the game continued to be a humiliation with a 40–7 shellacking as the third quarter ended.

Each team scored a meaningless touchdown in the final frame, Pitt making it 47–14 on what was described as a magnificent one-handed catch off a pass by Rip Collins from Williams before Duffield completed the rout with a scoring toss to junior Ralph Wilcox to end the route.[5]

It was a deflating experience for Sutherland and his squad, one that would not be easily forgotten. Unlike Carnegie Tech, who fell apart in the second half against USC, the Trojans dominated the Panthers from the onset; blaming the weather and lack of depth as the experts had for the Tartans was not an option for Pitt.

Any argument that Pittsburgh was a better team than Notre Dame much less Southern Cal became a moot point after this annihilation, the worst defeat by any school in Rose Bowl history to that point. Luckily in the historical context, the experts of the day did not consider bowl games anything more than an exhibition, so Parke E. Davis did not consider the embarrassing effort when naming the Panthers the 1929 national champions. Regardless of the fact that this team will forever be revered in Pitt history, the coaching staff and players alike knew they were anything but the best team in the nation, and those who returned in 1930 would realize there was plenty of work to be done if they were to reach those lofty heights once again.

Box Score 1930 Rose Bowl

Team	1	2	3	4	F
Pittsburgh	0	0	7	7	14
Southern California	13	13	14	7	47

Category	Pitt	USC
Total Yards	285	454
Rushing	199	167
Passing	86	287
First Downs	10	14
Comp/Att/Int	4/19/2	8/16/4
Penalty Yards	55	65
Average Per Punt	37	40

Lineup

Pitt	Pos	USC
Donchess	LE	Tappaan
Tully	LT	Hall
Montgomery	LG	Barragar
Daugherty	C	Dye
Dimeolo	RG	Galloway
MacMurdo	RT	Anthony
Collins	RE	Arbelbide
Baker	QB	Saunders
Uansa	LH	Edelson
Walinchus	RH	Pinckert
Parkinson	FB	Shaver

4

1931: A Quick Rebuilding Process

The 1930 Rose Bowl was a truly troubling experience for Jock Sutherland and the Pitt Panthers. After a stellar 1929 campaign, Pitt went to Pasadena to show the college football world they truly were the greatest team in the land. Instead they came back to the Steel City with the embarrassment of a humiliating 47–14 thrashing at the hands the University of Southern California Trojans. It wouldn't be an easy job to overcome the thrashing. On top of trying to resurrect the confidence of his beaten staff, he had to replace an impressive senior class of 1929 that included Albert DiMeolo, quarterback Charley Edwards, Joe Donchess, Ray Montgomery, Toby Uansa and Tom Parkinson.

With all the obstacles facing Sutherland, he also had some talented lettermen coming back and began 1930 in an impressive manner, thrashing Waynesburg 52–0, and shutting out their rivals from Morgantown, West Virginia, 16–0 before rolling over Case Reserve and Syracuse 52–0 and 14–0 respectively. Four games, four victories by a 134–0 margin—everything seemed on the upswing as they hosted Notre Dame at Pitt Stadium with a chance to restore their reputation and make them a favorite to win the national championship.

A city record 75,000 fans were on hand to see if Pitt's date with destiny would be met; it didn't take long to find the answer. Rockne's squad ripped through the Panther defense to the tune of 35 first-half points as the Irish made the 1930 Rose Bowl look like a tense matchup. Following a scoreless third quarter, Pitt did make the game respectable, but the 35–19 loss clearly showed that this team was not a national championship contender.

While Sutherland tried to shrug off the one-sided loss to the Fighting Irish, saying "I am satisfied, Pitt has nothing to be ashamed of. My boys did their best and made it a battle in the second half. They met a superior team and were beaten,"[1] it nonetheless was the beginning of the end for the University of Pittsburgh in 1930. The following week, Nebraska got a measure of revenge with a scoreless tie before barely defeating Carnegie Tech 7–6. What hope was left for a successful season would be difficult as Pitt traveled to Columbus to meet Ohio State. Unfortunately the Buckeyes broke out to a 16–0 third-quarter lead and hung on for an impressive 16–7 victory in a contest where the Panthers ineffective passing game gave up three interceptions. It was a tough loss in a listless 6–2–1 campaign, and the hall-of-fame coach had is work cut out for him if he was able to mold his 1931 edition of the University of Pittsburgh Panthers into a championship contender.

Sutherland began preparation for the 1931 opener against Miami University in Oxford, Ohio, by scrimmaging his varsity with his freshman squad. After failing last season with his aerial attack, the Pitt coach was focusing on the pass in the scrimmage as well as trying to put together his line that was the key to his championship team two seasons before. Jim MacMurdo firmly held down the one tackle post while Jesse Quatse, who would eventually have a magnificent All-American campaign, was battling sophomore Johnny Merideth at the opposite tackle spot while Ralph Daugherty and

Pictured is the plaque underneath the Panther statue beside the Peterson Events Center that celebrates the retired number 42, which was worn by two-time All-American halfback Marshall Goldberg. Retired at halftime of the 1997 Pitt–Miami game, Goldberg is one of nine Panther football players to be given the ultimate honor that is bestowed on its football players by the university (photograph by the author).

4. 1931: A Quick Rebuilding Process

Tackle Jesse Quatse was one of the greatest linemen in the history of the University of Pittsburgh as he was a consensus All-American in 1931. The Rillton, Pennsylvania, native was an important part of the school's fifth national championship squad in 1931.

Joe Tormey were facing off for the starting center position. The ends would be manned by Rip Collins and Ed Hirshberg, who was the captain of the Panthers in 1931. Rounding out the offensive line at guard would be Hart Morris and Mike Milligan.

In the backfield, Pittsburgh was small yet very speedy as sophomore Bob Hogan led the charge at quarterback with Jimmy Luch and Johnny Clark battling for the fullback slot. At halfback, Sutherland had no issues as Warren Heller and Paul Reider manned the spots.

Game 1—September 26, 1931, at Pitt Stadium
MIAMI (OHIO) UNIVERSITY REDSKINS   0
UNIVERSITY OF PITTSBURGH PANTHERS   61

During the 1930s, Miami University in Oxford, Ohio, was a tiny school of approximately 1,000 students who while having a formidable football squad, was not deep and was not expecting to prove much of a challenge over the course of 60 minutes against Pitt in the 1931 opener.

Miami coach Chester Pitser learned the game from the hall-of-fame coach Bob Zuppke, who led the University of Illinois to four national championships. Zuppke was an innovator who not only invented the huddle, but the screen pass as well as the linebacker position. The fan base at Miami hoped he would have similar success in Oxford that his mentor did in Champaign. Pitser had a fine arsenal of offensive talent led by the speedy Wilbur Cartwright, who was considered the best back in Ohio the previous season, and an outstanding freshman class from 1930 that was now ready to contribute. Miami hoped to keep the game close if not actually upset them.

For the Panthers, Quatse and Merideth had been battling for the other tackle spot opposite MacMurdo. As the week was ending, the sophomore Merideth had a surprising advantage over Quatse and looked like he would get the starting nod. The senior from Greensburg began to change his hall-of-fame coach's mind as practice was coming to an end for the week and nosed out Merideth by week's end.

Born in Rillton, Pennsylvania, Jesse Quatse was a superstar at Greensburg High School (now Greensburg-Salem) who was a three-year letterman at the University of Pittsburgh. While he was embroiled in a battle for a starting spot with Merideth at this point, by the time it was over he would not only be named at a consensus All-American but embark on a three-year NFL career that saw him not only play with the New York Giants, New York Yankees and Green Bay Packers, as well as becoming a member of the inaugural Pittsburgh Steeler squad in 1933 (nicknamed the Pirates at that time until 1940).

Quatse was a stocky 5'10" tackle who was a dominant defensive player. He played very low, which made him difficult to block by opposing offensive lines. It also made him very effective halting rushing attacks too. When his NFL career ended in 1936, he spent one season as coach of the Pittsburgh Americans, a franchise that played in the second version of the American Football League. He led the Amerks, as they were known, to a 1–3 mark until they folded following a 27–7 loss to the Boston Shamrocks. Even though the future would be bright for the All-American, for now the future was uncertain. Luckily Sutherland gave him the nod, and with Quatse in the lineup, it gave the Pitt coach eight seniors in his starting 11 against the wide-open Redskin attack.

The other thing that would hinder the underdogs in the season opener was the fact that it had rained several times during the week including a hard shower that hit the day before making the turf at Pitt Stadium softer, which would slow down Cartwright and his speedy teammates.

As it turned out, whether it was a Southern California perfect day or a winter afternoon in Alaska, it made no difference as this turned out to be a mismatch of epic proportions from the first play. Miami won the toss and mistakenly decided to kickoff and play defense first. Twelve thousand fans were thrilled when Reider took the ball at his five-yard line. His forward wall blocked perfectly as Reider sprinted down the right end to give Pitt an early lead, 6–0. Amazingly, only three plays later it was 12–0 when Heller bolted through three Redskin defenders into the open for a 67-yard touchdown run that gave the Panthers a two-touchdown lead before the contest was only two minutes old.

On a day where St. Mary's defeated Pitt's antagonists from their 1929 Rose Bowl, the University of Southern California Trojans, the Panthers were in the middle of as impressive a first quarter as they have had in the history of the program. The big play offense continued in the first period when Reider made it 18–0 with a 33-yard gallop before Pitt extended their advantage to 24 points with what was described as one of the most exciting runs that was witnessed in Pitt Stadium at the time.

The play started at the Pitt 13-yard line with Heller taking the handoff. The *Pittsburgh Press*'s Lester Biederman described it as follows: "Heller began the trip around his own right end from the 12-yard line and streaked for the opposite side. He was almost brought down in the middle of the field near the sidelines, but by an effective piece of side stepping, got away from a Miami tackler and then broke loose from four more foes before he got out in front and went on from the 25-yard line without a Redskin even close to him."[2]

The sparkling 87-yard romp all but ended the contest with 45 minutes left to play, but for the experienced Panther squad, the blowout had only begun despite the fact that Sutherland pulled his entire starting lineup out, eventually inserting the fourth and fifth squads. By the end of the half, Pitt had increased the lead to 36–0 and scored four more touchdowns from reserve backs Mike Sebastian, Richard Matesic, Eric, Heller's brother, and Mel Brown to go along with the four from Heller and the two from Bulldog Reider.

The 61–0 score remarkably was not indicative of the beating the Redskins experienced on this afternoon. As effective as the offense was, the Panther defense was even more so. The best back in Ohio, Cartwright was rendered useless, losing 16 yards rushing in four attempts. Miami mustered up only a single yard rushing as a team on 22 carries while gaining only 49 through the air, amassing a paltry three first downs.

Offensively the Pitt stats were the polar opposite of their opponents. Led by Heller's school record 250 yards on 15 carries, a record that stood for 42 seasons until a freshman by the name of Tony Dorsett rambled for 265 against Northwestern in 1973, and Reider's 95, the Panthers embarrassed the Miami defense to the tune of 499 yards while gaining 113 more through the air on five completions.

It was an amazing start to the season, even though the game was against a team that was considered a less than worthy opponent. Pitt would not have it as easy the following contest as they would travel to Iowa City to face a much tougher University of Iowa opponent in the Hawkeyes season opener although Sutherland hoped that the confidence gained from the Panthers' dominant win would carry over to their first road game.

Game 2—October 3, 1931, at Iowa Stadium in Iowa City, Iowa

UNIVERSITY OF PITTSBURGH PANTHERS 20
UNIVERSITY OF IOWA HAWKEYES 0

Had the administration at the University of Iowa been more persuasive early in 1924, the course of Hawkeye football might have dramatically been altered and this contest against the University of Pittsburgh would have been an important one on a national level. Unfortunately for the powers that be at Iowa, they were unable to convince the great Knute Rockne to leave Notre Dame early that year after originally thinking they were close to signing him. Rockne sent a note in March to school president Walter Jessup that simply said, "My Duty now lies here [Notre Dame]. Further discussion is useless. I voluntarily signed a new ten year agreement on same terms as past and whole matter is now closed. Good luck."[3]

With the unfortunate telegram the administration at the university received, they turned toward Illinois graduate and Bryant, Iowa, native Burt Ingwersen and signed him to a three-year to coach the team. It was a move that further frustrated an already irritated school alumni base. They had already lost one of the best coaches in the country when Howard Jones resigned in February of 1924 because of a dispute with the school leaders over an issue where the administration wanted to combine their intercollegiate athletic teams with the physical education department to increase the academic standards of the various sports. Jones was strongly opposed to such a move and moved on to Duke then to USC in 1925 where he had the greatest success in his hall-of-fame career.

Without Jones or Rockne, the school was left with an inexperienced head coach, who while having only two losing campaigns in his eight-year career at Iowa he only finished once above fourth place in the Big Ten conference, his first season, where the Hawkeyes ended up second with a squad comprised of Jones's players.

Despite the fact Ingwersen did not have horrible teams for most of his time at Iowa, his tenure had been sullied with an episode that occurred in 1929, which caused Iowa to be dismissed from the conference for one year. Some of the frustrated Iowa alumni created a slush fund to entice recruits to come to Iowa. A representative from the University of Minnesota found out about it and lobbied the Big Ten successfully to remove them. They were readmitted in 1930 but were only allowed to play one conference game.

The Hawkeyes were coming off a mediocre 4–4–1 season in 1930 but had ended the year with optimism after defeating Penn State 19–0 and Nebraska 12–7 in its final two games. As enthusiastic as they may have been with the two victories, it was tempered by the fact that only 12 lettermen dotted the 65-man Hawkeye roster. Marcus Magnussen, Edward Dolly and Nelson Tompkins were quality linemen, that according to United Press writer George Kirksey "compares favorably with any in the Big Ten,"[4] but had little depth behind them. Alex Rodgers, James Dee and James Merten would try to capably fill the other spots on the line.

They had a decent group of backs led by fullback and team captain Oliver Sansen and Randall Hickman, but at quarterback, Ingwersen had a small group of six players no heavier than 168 pounds trying to fill in as the starter. Track star James Willer seemed to have the inside track along with Jim Graham, but regardless, unless they found some depth and quality linemen to fill out the open spots, it was threatening to be a long season for Iowa.

The problem with a lack of depth is the fact that injuries to the starting 11 can crush the prospects of a winning campaign; unfortunately for the Hawkeyes, injuries began to mount, with Dolly going down in practice a few days before the game with an injured knee, and tackle Loe Samuelson, who was determined to play, had been hobbled by injuries during the short preseason.

For the Panthers, they were coming off one of the most dominant performances in school history, crushing Miami (OH) in a dominant fashion. They had a decisive advantage over Iowa in just about every category except for one; the Hawkeyes would enjoy home-field advantage as Pitt would have to make the long trek via train to Iowa City for the contest.

The club had one last practice at Pitt Stadium and then proceeded to travel to Chicago where they were able to garner practice time at Stagg Field where the University of Chicago played. The Pitt hall-of-fame coach put his team through an intense two-hour workout in Chicago and wanted to make sure he worked them hard enough to make sure they did not get overconfident after their huge opening-game victory. After Chicago, the team was to travel to Davenport, where they would stay and practice at the city's Municipal Stadium before traveling to Iowa City an hour before the game.

There were three things Jock Sutherland wanted to concentrate on in practice before the game. The first was something he seemingly was never comfortable with: his pass defense. The second was to drill his offense to become more effective in the forward pass to make their offense more well rounded. Finally he wanted to concentrate on what was perhaps the only deficiency his squad showed in the Miami contest: their extra-point attempts. Against the Redskins the Panthers only converted on 1 of 11 attempts. Sutherland used Paul Reider and Jim MacMurdo in practice to try and convert more successfully, with MacMurdo winning the job by the end of the week. The other end of their kicking game, punting, was a competition between starting quarterback Bob Hogan and Iowa native Mel Brown, with Hogan eventually being given the nod to take over the chore.

Pitt was completely healthy for the game and thoroughly wore down their injured opponents. Ingwersen had to shuffle his line with Dolly at center and Rodgers and Dee at tackle as the three were not only unable to handle the Panther offense but were constantly beaten by the Panther defenders.

Pitt started off ripping through the crippled Iowa defense, as the Panthers' powerful running attack dazzled the 20,000 Iowa fans. Reider began the festivities with a 25-yard run around right end to midfield early in the first quarter before catching a 22-yard strike from Warren Heller. Fullback Jimmy Clark followed with a 16-yard burst up the middle that set up a touchdown run by Reider from the one. MacMurdo failed on the conversion that left Pitt with an early 6–0 lead.

Pitt challenged to make the game an early blowout, but unfortunately Heller tossed an interception by the Hawkeyes' star halfback Hickman. The Panthers then threatened to score once again, spurred by a fine Clark run, but the Hawkeye defense had a tough goal-line stance and stopped Pitt at the one-yard line. It was a momentary lapse as Pittsburgh would soon increase their lead to two touchdowns as they had been threatening to do for the better part of the first half.

Reider once again put the Panthers in good position with a 40-yard punt return to the Iowa 35-yard line. Unlike the first touchdown drive, this one was done without the big play. Constant runs put Pitt at the 12-yard line with a first down. Reider finished the drive with two consecutive six-yard jaunts for his second touchdown of the day and a 13-point advantage as the half ended.

While the Panthers wouldn't score the points they had the week before, when Clark sprinted in from 35 yards out in the third quarter and MacMurdo tacked on his second consecutive point, it became every bit as impressive a victory as they had in their opener. The only thing that kept Pitt from making this an embarrassment was their own inability to finish drives. Three times they turned the ball over on downs deep in Hawkeye territory and once with the Hickman interception while again threatening to score.

Neither team crossed the goal line in the final quarter, but the 20–0 victory by Pitt was extremely dominant. Their rushing attack was led by Clark, who had breakout performance with 151 yards on 17 attempts. Reider tacked on 102 yards with Heller adding 32 of his own.

As impressive as the offense was, the defense was even more so. They completely frustrated Iowa's leading ball carrier from the previous season, Hickman, and held the Hawkeyes to three first downs. They outgained their opponents on the ground 364 to 37 and by a 403-to-53 count in total yards while amassing 18 first downs to Iowa's aforementioned 3.

The contest was the beginning of the end for Ingwersen and his club as they only defeated George Washington 7–0 and battled Indiana to a scoreless tie, while they lost their remaining seven games. The touchdown they scored against the Colonials proved to be the only points their maligned team would produce during the campaign, being outscored 131–7. Perhaps the only positive thing that happened for Iowa during the campaign was that the alumni finally got their way as Ingwersen was relieved of his job, being replaced by Ossie Salem in 1932.

For Pitt, they would host their rivals from Morgantown in the renewal of the Backyard Brawl at Pitt Stadium the following week, a chance to show the nation they were once again contenders for the national title.

Game 3—October 10, 1931, at Pitt Stadium

WEST VIRGINIA UNIVERSITY MOUNTAINEERS	0
UNIVERSITY OF PITTSBURGH PANTHERS	34

The Backyard Brawl in 1931 brought a different dynamic to the rivalry. Following a couple of mediocre seasons by coach Ira "Rat" Rodgers, the administration at West Virginia University made a big splash by hiring Earle "Greasy" Neale to lead its program, and in a unique move Rodgers accepted a post as Neale's assistant.

Neale was one of the most interesting figures in American sports during the early part of the 20th century. He was a starting outfielder with the Cincinnati Reds, hitting .357 in the eight-game tainted 1919 World Series upset of the infamous Chicago "Black Sox." He stayed in the majors until 1924, but it was his off-season jobs that made Neale unique. He was a great player between 1917 and 1919 in the early days of professional football for the Canton Bulldogs; the Dayton Triangles, where he was a player-coach; and the Massillon Tigers, but it's what he did after that, as a coach, that would see him elected to both the college and professional football halls of fame.

Neale spent the first part of his college coaching career leading the programs at Muskingum and West Virginia Wesleyan before taking over at Washington and Jefferson College where he first made his mark. He took the tiny Western Pennsylvania school to the 1922 Rose Bowl, where as heavy underdogs they held the more powerful California Golden Bears to a memorable scoreless tie. Following a two-year stint with the Presidents, Neale took over the University of Virginia before the Parkersburg native came home to West Virginia, where the Mountaineer faithful were hoping he'd take their program to the lofty heights where their rivals from the University of Pittsburgh already were at the time.

Unfortunately for the Panthers' own legendary coach Jock Sutherland, Neale had a history of beating a Sutherland-led team. In 1922 when the Pitt coach was at Lafayette, the Leopards came into the game against W & J with a sparkling 5–0–0 mark that included a victory against Pop Warner and his current employer. The Presidents surprised Lafayette 14–13 ending the undefeated season; it was a loss that Sutherland certainly would not forget.

The Mountaineers did not have momentum on their side at this point. After their impressive 14–6 victory against the Duquesne Dukes in the season opener, they went into New York to face one of the nation's most sucessful programs, the Fordham Rams. West Virginia could not challenge the Rams as they lost 20–7. Neale knew he would have to make some changes in order to compete with the powerful Panthers, especially since his leading rusher John Doyle was injured, so he was contemplating moving sophomore Doug Stone to quarterback, replacing the incumbent Bill Parriot, while placing fullback Leo Dotson at halfback and Homer White into his former slot at fullback. Eventually he decided on Ligonier's Harry Marker to start the contest at fullback instead.

As far as Pitt's Scottish head coach went, he was considering two moves himself, replacing Bobby Hogan as punter with Rip Collins and moving in the bigger Johnny Luch at fullback, replacing Jimmy Clark who was coming off an impressive 151-yard performance against Iowa. With the week of practice coming to a close, Sutherland did in fact make both changes, feeling that the 190-pound Luch with his battering style of running gave the Panthers a better chance to continue their undefeated season against their rivals.

It was a perfect fall day for football at Pitt Stadium as 20,000 fans entered the facility to watch the 27th edition of what would become one of the nation's bitterest rivalries. Early on it was a tough back-and-forth struggle with Pitt having the only opportunity to score as they marched down to the WVU one late in the period. One of the reasons Sutherland inserted Luch into the lineup was the fact that he was bigger than Clark and could get the tough yards. On a fourth and inches, the move failed as Luch could not push the ball over the goal line with the Panthers turning it over on downs.

While unable to score, Pitt did have the field position advantage as their defense kept the WVU offense pinned deep in their territory. After a few punt exchanges they eventually took over at the Panther 47 to begin their first scoring drive of the contest. It was a very short drive that began and ended when Heller tossed a 23-yard pass to Reider at the WVU 30. The Pittsburgh back took the ball and darted the final 30 yards to make the score 6–0. It was the score that the Panthers would hold on to as they ended the half.

After a tough first half, once Pitt scored the first touchdown of the second half the game would be all but over as they would turn this closely fought contest into a rout. Taking over at their own 20, Heller ripped off a 27-yard dash. Pitt then methodically went downfield, the longest run being a 14-yard scamper by Reider, before finally reaching the end zone as Heller walked through a gaping hole from the two for the 13-point lead.

Worn down, the injured Mountaineer defense was no match for the Panthers in the fourth quarter. After failing to score from inches out in the first quarter, Luch's power was dominating the WVU front wall. He scored Pitt's third touchdown in the fourth quarter to increase the Panther advantage to 20–0 and continued to rip runs in the middle of the Mountaineer defensive line. Jack Sell of the *Pittsburgh Post-Gazette* described his running style: "he never runs around a pile-up, but takes the shortest path between the scrimmage and the goal and either blasts his way straight through or sinks his cleats on top of the struggling mass."[5]

At this point Sutherland began to pull his starting 11 and was liberally substituting. It made no difference as reserve back Mike Sebastian became the star of the fourth quarter running the ball in for the fourth score; then ending the contest was a scoring strike to Ted Daily to make it 34–0.

It was the school's third consecutive one-sided shutout and vaulted the squad firmly into the national championship talk with Notre Dame, Michigan and Stanford among several other schools. While Sutherland hoped to keep his team focused in their next game against Western Reserve, no one would have blamed the Panthers if their focus was two weeks later in South Bend where they would face the Irish in a contest that could possibly answer the question of who the best team in the nation was.

Game 4—October 17, 1931, at Pitt Stadium
Western Reserve University Redcats 0
University of Pittsburgh Panthers 32

It had been a season so far just like most in the Jock Sutherland era—a powerful running game coupled with a stifling defense that lifted the University of Pittsburgh right in the middle of the national championship chase. As similar as things were, the one difference was that this appeared to be one of the strongest defenses he had ever had, as they had been almost impenetrable, allowing not only no points but hardly even a legitimate scoring threat.

After outscoring their opponents by an impressive 115–0 margin, Pitt would get a break this week by playing the Western Reserve University Redcats. Located in Cleveland and the first college in Northern Ohio, Western Reserve would eventually merge with the Case Institute of Technology in 1967 to form what is today known as Case Western Reserve University, but in the 1930s they were two separate universities that played football mostly against smaller Ohio-based schools, occasionally branching out against bigger squads like Pitt and Carnegie Tech.

While trying to focus his team on not taking Western for granted and looking ahead to their more important outing against the Fighting Irish the following week, Sutherland seemed to have a tough time taking them seriously himself as he was preparing to start his reserves and rest his first team for their encounter in South Bend. He also was considering traveling to Indiana to scout Notre Dame in their contest against Drake. He eventually decided to stick around to make sure his Panthers were ready.

Following their impressive victory against West Virginia University, the players were very satisfied with their performance to date and thought they might be in for an easy week in practice before they pounced on their undermanned opponents. When they hit the practice field on Monday, they found out that Sutherland and his staff were not as impressed and were on a mission to work the Panthers as tough as, if not tougher than, they always had in the past.

They were facing a squad led by Coach Tom Keady, who had previous stints at Lehigh and Vermont as well as a tenure as head basketball coach at the same two universities. He had a sophomore-laden team led by quarterback

4. 1931: A Quick Rebuilding Process

Lyron Ulrich and center Joe DiDonato. Keady realized he didn't have the team to compete with Pitt, even if Sutherland started his backups. His main goal was to work with the defense in order to hold the Panthers to a much lower offensive output than the 52–0 beating they took the year before.

While not leading to victories, his philosophy led to a 28–0 loss against Purdue, who was one of the most powerful teams in the nation, and a scoreless tie against Bowling Green. Even though they didn't lose to the Falcons, it wasn't necessarily their finest moment as Bowling Green was a very small school at the time and considered an underdog against Western Reserve. Part of the blame for the tie, though, had to lie with the injuries the Redcats suffered in the contest against the Boilermakers.

As the game came closer, Keady learned that he would face the Panthers' second team. Sutherland wanted to rest his main squad for their tough battle in South Bend and felt comfortable that the reserves, who had outscored the West Virginia Mountaineers the week before 21–0 in the fourth quarter, would certainly be good enough to defeat the Redcats. Jimmy Simms, Mike Sebastian and Johnny Luch, who started in place of Jimmy Clark against WVU, were in the backfield with quarterback Rocco Cutri, while future Pitt legend, sophomore Joe "Muggsy" Skladany, would get his first opportunity to start in place of Rip Collins at the end opposite of Ted Dally, who snatched his first touchdown of the year the week before. On the line John Merideth; John Love; Bob Morris, brother of starting guard Hart Morris; Tarciscio Onder; and Francis Seigel got the nod to start. Joe Tormey had been the second-team guard but gave way to Bob Morris as he had been battling a severe cold for most of the week.

As tough as the practices were to make sure Pitt was not going to enter this contest overconfident, Sutherland also drilled his first team intensely against the

JOSEPH SKLADANY

PITTSBURGH END
1931–33

A two-time All-American for Pitt in 1932 and 1933, Joe Skladany was one of the greatest ends ever to grace the gridiron for the school. After a one-year career in the NFL with Pittsburgh, Skladany received the ultimate honor for his collegiate career when he was inducted into the College Football Hall of Fame in 1975.

freshman squad to prepare them for the contest in two weeks that would firmly put the Panthers as the favorite to win the national title with a victory over Notre Dame. With the second squad well schooled for battle, and coach Keady hell-bent on keeping the score down, everyone seemed to get what they wanted in this contest. The Pitt hall-of-fame coach was able to rest his first team, sending them into South Bend extremely healthy as his reserves put on a very solid performance.

As the only one in the backfield who had experience starting, Luch enjoyed the most success against Western Reserve as the powerful fullback crushed through the outmatched Redcoat defensive line for three touchdowns. While Luch was powering through the middle, Sebastian and Simms showed what potential at halfback they had, sprinting for long touchdowns. Sebastian, who had an outstanding fourth quarter against WVU, rambled for a 35-yard jaunt while Simms had an incredible 64-yard run to account for the five Pitt touchdowns. The only weakness for the favorites was the fact they only converted on two of five extra-point attempts. While many would have been satisfied with the performance by the backups, one person who was not was Sutherland, who spent the first practice following the game lecturing them on their effort against the Redcats.

Keady could claim a minor victory as he kept the vaunted Panther offensive attack to 32 points, 20 less than they gave up the previous campaign, although it was still a thoroughly dominant victory for the Panthers. They claimed their fourth consecutive shutout and increased their point advantage over their opponents to 147–0. After the victory, Pitt was still considered as one of the top teams in the east along with Cornell, Columbia, Harvard and Colgate. Notre Dame was almost unanimously touted as the best team in the midwest. With the Panthers' comfortable 32–0 win over Western Reserve and the Fighting Irish dominating Drake 64–0, it set up one of the most anticipated matchups of the season.

Game 5—October 24, 1931, at Notre Dame Stadium in South Bend, Indiana

UNIVERSITY OF PITTSBURGH PANTHERS   12
UNIVERSITY OF NOTRE DAME FIGHTING IRISH   25

He was considered one of if not the greatest coach ever to grace the sidelines in the history of college football. For the better part of 13 seasons, Knute Rockne patrolled the sidelines at Notre Dame and guided his teams to intimidate all who faced the Fighting Irish during the time period. Four national championships, a 105–12–5 career record, five undefeated seasons, including

1929 and 1930 when he captured his last two titles, and a victory in his only matchup against the University of Pittsburgh, a 35–19 thrashing in 1930 that destroyed the Panthers' championship hopes, Rockne had a resume that few if any coaches could ever match.

The Pitt–Notre Dame matchup in 1931 was once again one of the most important contests of the season with national championship implications on the line, the kind of game Rockne lived for. Unfortunately it was sadly a game that the legendary coach would not live to see, as he tragically died in an airplane accident earlier in 1931, on March 31, while traveling to Los Angeles to consult on a film about Notre Dame football that would pay him a handsome fee of $50,000.

Rockne had been a champion of air travel, wanting to cut the time to get to California significantly from the more acceptable train travel, claiming that "with a good pilot and a good plane, [flying is] as safe as any other method."[6] He had a great pilot in Robert Fry, a 32 year old who had vast experience in the air. Unfortunately the weather was not on the side of the TWA Flight 5 heading from Kansas City to Wichita. While in Wichita the weather was reported as clear, in Kansas City there was a cold drizzle mixed with snow. It was TWA's premiere airplane, a Fokker F-10A NC999E. Reportedly the co-pilot radioed that the weather was poor and they were going to turn around. Regrettably they never made it back and crashed on the property of a ranch in Bazaar, Kansas; there were no survivors.

The nation was devastated; 1,600 of the country's 1,700 papers ran it as their headline, coverage worthy of any heads of state. The fans of Notre Dame as well as the school itself were particularly overwhelmed with grief. The president of the school, Father Hugh O'Donnell, said, "Nothing that has ever happened at Notre Dame has so shocked the faculty and student body as the tragic news that came at noon yesterday of the accident which took Mr. Rockne's life."[7]

It was a sorrowful event that made fans wonder how the program could go on. The administration at Notre Dame decided on Heartly "Hunk" Anderson to pick up the pieces and try and lead the Irish forward. A hall-of-fame guard at the school, who played under Rockne for the first two years of the great coach's tenure, Anderson had little experience as a head coach, fashioning a 7–8–1 mark at St. Louis before being called upon for this difficult assignment. He had mixed reviews in his first three games for Notre Dame, winning two contests combined with a scoreless tie against the Wildcats of Northwestern. A victory over a national power such as the University of Pittsburgh would help convince any detractors he may have had that Anderson was worthy of the job, and also be a big stepping stone toward a third consecutive title for the Irish.

They were led by an impressive squad that included four All-Americans, unanimous choice halfback Marchy Schwartz, tackle Joe Kurth, center Tommy Yarr and guard Nordy Hoffman. Joining Kurth, Yarr and Hoffman on the line that averaged over 200 pounds per man was Ed Krause and Norm Greeney.

The backfield of Schwartz, Joe Sheeketski, George Melinkovich and quarterback Emmett Murphy was experienced and explosive behind the massive line. As good as the first team was, this Notre Dame team was as deep if not deeper than Pittsburgh with names such as quarterback Chuck Jaskwhich, halfback Ray Brancheau and Mike Koken, who were almost as dangerous as the players that stood in front of them on the depth chart.

Ask Jock Sutherland, and he would tell you that the Notre Dame depth was superior. He was very unhappy with how his backups performed the week before versus Western Reserve. He gave them an intense lecture as preparations began for the Fighting Irish, making it crystal clear that the effort they gave against the Redcats would not be acceptable in any way against Notre Dame.

The only two reserves he had playing with the first team was Cutri at quarterback, replacing Hogan who was attending a late class during the week, and Luch, who had been starting at fullback the previous two weeks. The reserves were not the only squad that caught Sutherland's ire early in the week; his place-kicking game, which had been a constant issue all season, was also being drilled intently as he didn't want to leave any points on the field against the home team.

As the week went on, the team was not fluid in practice which was frustrating their Scottish coach. While sluggish, Sutherland had hoped his troops would get off to a better start than they did the year before when Notre Dame scored on the first play which helped them race to an early insurmountable 35-point lead. For their part, the Irish seemed to understand that this game would most likely not be as easy as 1930. They knew the Panthers had basically used only one formation against inferior opposition and were doing their best to try and prepare for other formations that they believed Pitt might use, that would include the double wingback, men in motion and the spinner play that they had used effectively in the past.

Unlike Sutherland, Coach Anderson felt comfortable that his team could stop the Panthers on the ground as his defense had been successful doing so against the scout team in practice. Anderson had concerns that the Irish would have trouble containing Pittsburgh through the air, but he knew if they halted their rushing attack there was a great chance they would win.

Thirty-three players left for South Bend two days before the game as Sutherland pushed his team hard until the last moments before they left. The starting lineup at that point was set, except for fullback where he practiced

Luch and Clark equally. Eventually Luch once again got the nod just before the team took off.

On the trip, the team first stopped off in Niles, Michigan, where they continued to practice in anticipation of their final journey to South Bend Friday afternoon. When they finally finished their trip to Indiana, they found out that they were three-to-one underdogs against a team that it had never beaten in four previous tries, the only somewhat successful outcome being a scoreless tie in 1911. Early on it looked as if the streak of ineptitude by Pitt against the Irish would continue.

Notre Dame didn't get off to the quick start it did a year earlier, but it came pretty darn close. The first few series were full of turnovers with Pitt recovering a Sheeketski fumble at the Irish 32 for the first scoring threat of the afternoon. Unfortunately Luch gave it back to them on the very next play. The Panthers held Notre Dame to force a punt, but Heller fumbled the ball which was recovered by their opponents at the Pitt 33. Two offensive plays and two lost fumbles for the Panthers was most likely a worst case scenario for Sutherland. The Irish pounded the ball down to the 18 where Schwartz hit Melinkovich with a scoring toss to give the home team an early 7–0 lead.

The game was a stalemate through the rest of the first quarter as the Irish held on to the seven-point lead, but early in the second Heller and Luch finally found their rhythm, methodically taking it down to their opponents one-yard line. Heller got the honors of taking it in as he ran around right end to bring Pitt to within a point. All the practice Sutherland did on his kicking game was for naught as MacMurdo missed the conversion as the Panthers still trailed by a point.

Driving down the field to increase their advantage on the following series, Melinkovich gave the ball back to Pitt. The Irish defense was tough and stopped the Panthers as the game once again reverted to a defensive struggle. Finally as the half was coming to an end, Notre Dame took the ball over at their own 45. Paul Host took a lateral and rambled to the Pittsburgh 23. A few plays later the Irish had the ball at the four where Mike Koken found Host for a touchdown pass. Pitt blocked the extra point but was behind 13–6 as the half came to an end.

In the third quarter, the Panther attack continued to be thwarted and was stuck deep in their own territory when they punted to Notre Dame who took over at the 35. Melinkovich ran the ball 16 yards on the first play. Pitt's defense stiffened as Notre Dame remained at the 19 with a fourth-and-ten play. The Panthers had to make just one more stop to remain in this ball game; they could not. Schwartz hit Chuck Jaskwhich at the two who fell into the end zone after catching it, putting the Irish up by 13 late in the third. It wouldn't take long for the home team to make this a one-sided affair when an 11-yard run by Schwartz put the ball at the two-yard line before Melinkovich ended the drive on the next play to give Notre Dame a 25–6 lead.

Pitt scored on the next drive, a tally from the one-foot line by Luch that was set up by a 27-yard completion by Sebastian to Heller to bring the Panthers to within 13 again. It was unfortunately as close as the Panthers would get in a tough loss for the visitors. Notre Dame had all the look of a national champion yet again while Pitt had to be perfect the rest of the way to have a chance. They physically beat up the Panthers in this contest. Jesse Quatse, the soon to be All-American, was battered and his face was badly swollen in the battle.

It wouldn't be easy for Pitt as the schedule continued to be tough for the remainder of the schedule. Difficult contests against Penn State, Carnegie Tech, Army and Nebraska would show whether 1931 was just a continuation of a rebuilding era at Pitt or prove that the phenomenal beginning of 1931 was not a fluke.

Game 6 — October 31, 1931, at Beaver Field in State College, Pennsylvania

UNIVERSITY OF PITTSBURGH PANTHERS   41
PENN STATE UNIVERSITY NITTANY LIONS   6

Many things had been constant in the Pitt–Penn State series during the early part of the 20th century. The game had been played in Pittsburgh since 1902, it had generally been a Thanksgiving Day contest, and since two consecutive scoreless ties in 1920 and 1921 it had been primarily a one-sided affair with the University of Pittsburgh coming up on the winning end. As the 1931 version of the Pennsylvania classic was about to be played, two of the three constants would change. The officials at Penn State did not like playing the game on Thanksgiving in Pittsburgh, claiming that the weather patterns in the Steel City that time of the year often made for less-than-stellar playing conditions; plus they wanted to play the game occasionally on their turf.

After their previous contract was up in the series following the 1930 contest, Penn State got exactly what they wanted. This game would be played at the end of October instead of Thanksgiving, and it was contested at Beaver Field in State College, the first time the Nittany Lions would host their state rivals in 29 years. Unfortunately the third constant, the way the game had turned out the previous ten years, would not change as Jock Sutherland and his club were bitter over the way they had been treated in South Bend the week before and wanted to take it out on their hosts.

Sutherland was quite concerned with his pass defense the week before as it was the difference between winning and losing, with three of their four touchdowns coming via the pass. While the hall-of-fame coach was considering using his second squad to start against his rivals, he also knew he would be without two of his stars. Lineman Hart Morris broke his hand, while his speedy back Bulldog Reider had a bruised leg that was not considered serious, although Sutherland wanted to rest him against the Lions. This necessitated the coach starting Mike Sebastian instead, who had shown Sutherland he had a tremendous future with his play as a reserve.

With the challenges that Sutherland and his squad faced, they would at least seemingly have an undermanned opponent to fix their problems against. Led by quarterback Donald Conn and their backfield of Bob Snyder, George Collins, Phil Moonves and their captain, fullback George Lasich, who was a Western Pennsylvania native where he was a star at Clairton High School, the Nittany Lions were not having a stellar campaign to this point.

New Coach Bob Higgins, the former three-time All-American at Penn State, had the unenviable task of replacing the forced-out Hugo Bezdek in 1930 and at this point had been far from returning the Nittany Lions to their former greatness. He finished his first season 3–4–2, although he had given the Panthers a tough battle for the first time in years, losing 19–12. The Lions came into this contest 1–4, beating only an undermanned Lebanon Valley squad 19–6.

Higgins, who had previous stints at West Virginia Wesleyan and Washington University (MO) before returning to his alma mater, brought his team into this contest with some momentum, holding the powerful Syracuse Orangemen to only seven points in a 7–0 defeat, but he had a couple of major injuries of his own to deal with. While expected to play, Lasich was not at 100 percent, and it was also rumored that guard Tom Curry would definitely not be able to start with an injured neck. If that wasn't bad enough, Collins had been called home to deal with a family situation, and former Schenley High School player Tom Slusser, who had taken over the starting spot at right end earlier in the week, hurt his ankle in practice and was questionable for the game. Luckily Collins made it back in time, but even with him in the lineup, it was questionable whether they had enough talent to hold back an angry Panther squad who was looking for redemption following their loss to Notre Dame.

Sutherland was livid at his squad for the loss against the Irish and worked them hard to make sure they wouldn't take their opponents lightly. He had three consecutive difficult contests to end the 1931 campaign and knew he had to be perfect to have a chance at the national title. The *Pittsburgh Press* had reported earlier in the week the Scottish coach would go with his backups in this contest to give his starters a rest for the stretch run.⁸ Their competitors, the *Pittsburgh Post-Gazette*, had a different take and reported mid-week that the frustrated Sutherland would send out his starting squad, except for Sebastian and Onder who were replacing the aforementioned injured Panthers.⁹ Regardless of who Sutherland decided to start, it was imperative that Pitt come out and beat the Nittany Lions by a significant margin to show the country that it should once again be taken seriously for championship honors.

A season-high 10,000 fans filled the 30,000-seat Beaver Field, the precursor to the more famous Beaver Stadium. Strangely enough Beaver Field actually became part of Beaver Stadium as it was disassembled and moved to the present site, becoming part of the current facility which was built in 1960. In 1931, though, 100,000-plus capacities weren't even a consideration as Beaver Field hosted a Panther squad for the first time since they beat Pitt 27–0 in 1902.

Eventually Sutherland proved the reporters at the *Pittsburgh Press* to be correct as he did hold out his starters, giving his second squad a chance to show that they were an effective unit. The reserves did that and more, rendering the Lions helpless from the outset.

Moonves turned out to be the early goat for Penn State. He fumbled the opening kickoff at the 16, and halfback Jim Simms took four consecutive handoffs, finally taking it over the goal line for a 6–0 lead before the contest was even two minutes old. A minute later after taking the ball at the 20 on the following kickoff, Moonves once again fumbled after a four-yard gain to give Pitt the ball back at the 24 when Fran Seigel picked it up. On the next play Simms scored for the second time, sprinting in from 24 yards out to increase the advantage to 13 points.

Jimmy Clark, the former regular who was in the starting lineup after losing his spot the previous three weeks to Luch, ripped a run around left end 47 yards on the next Panther series for the third touchdown of the third quarter. Quarterback Rocco Cutri made his second consecutive point-after to make it 20–0. Before the first half came to a merciful end for Penn State, Panther fullback Bill Hasson ripped through the Lions' defensive wall for a 24-yard touchdown run, and Cutri showed he may be the answer to Pittsburgh kicking woes, increasing the lead to 27.

The Panthers' offense seemed to be stuck in neutral in the second half but were reinvigorated when they took over on the Nittany Lions' 25. The next play, Sebastian burst over the goal line for Pitt's apparent fifth touchdown on a 25-yard jaunt, but the play was called back on a 15-yard holding call. Pittsburgh methodically went down to the Lions' one where Hasson scored his second touchdown of the contest to give the Panthers a 34–0 lead into the half.

4. 1931: A Quick Rebuilding Process

The third quarter saw the Pitt defense get into the scoring act when Richard Matesic picked off a pass from Conn at the State 40, returning it 60 yards for the Panthers' final score of the afternoon. Cutri was perfect again as the rout was on with a 41–0 score. Later on in the third, the Nittany Lions had a moral victory when Conn hit Bill McMillen from the two-yard line to end Pitt's shutout attempt and make the final score 41–6.

It was the Panthers' first victory at State College in four attempts, and the 41 points represented the most points Pitt had ever scored against the Lions in the series at that point in time. It not only gave the regulars a rest that they would need for the tough stretch drive, but showed Sutherland and the rest of the college football world that this was truly a deep powerful team that should be feared.

Game 7—November 7, 1931, at Pitt Stadium

CARNEGIE TECH TARTANS 6
UNIVERSITY OF PITTSBURGH PANTHERS 14

Football fans who were eagerly awaiting the annual city championship clash between the Carnegie Tech Tartans and the University of Pittsburgh Panthers needed to look only toward the University of Notre Dame to try and project who would win this bitter rivalry. Each team had the unenviable task of facing the Fighting Irish over the past two weekends, with Notre Dame getting the best of the Panthers 25–12 two Saturdays before and then traveling to the Steel City the following weekend to shut out the Tartans 19–0.

Many thought that Pitt would have the perceived advantage as Carnegie Tech took a physical beating against Notre Dame with only six days to recover while the Panthers had the opportunity to rest their regulars versus Penn State and supposedly would come into the contest much healthier. *Pittsburgh Post-Gazette* sports editor Harvey J. Boyle had a different take on it, claiming that "whereas the Panthers in the second half resembled Napoleon's troops on the weary march back from Russia, the Tartans, even against Notre Dame's first-string troops, in the final quarter were sprightly, eager and apparently strong. This is difficult to explain, but it was apparent that the Carnegie boys can stand Notre Dame's gaff better than the Panthers." Boyle further surmised that "whether the Tech system of training the boys is superior to Pitt's is the natural question that arises."[10] In the end that would be the big question: would the injuries sustained against the Fighting Irish at Pitt Stadium the previous Saturday be a more important factor in the contest than the apparent advantage in conditioning that Boyle pointed out?

Whatever would be the more important factor, one thing was certain:

the Tartans needed this victory to somehow shift the momentum of what had been a grueling season to that point. Despite the fact that they had played a difficult schedule, Carnegie Tech stood at 2–3; the losses to Washington and Jefferson, Purdue and Notre Dame took the luster off an impressive 13–0 victory over Georgia Tech as well as an opening-day 25–0 shutout over Buffalo.

The Tartans were a young team, sporting impressive sophomores such as arguably the team's best defensive player Lib Lewis, Henry Dreshar, Jerry O'Toole and Carl Forsman, along with the captain of the squad, Murray Armentrout, Colen Stewart, Alex Ducanis, Hooks Sample and Buck Ewing. Unfortunately Lewis would not be able to play against the Panthers, breaking his leg against the Irish in the phenomenal game he played against Notre Dame and would be in the hospital for eight weeks.

When the Tartans began practice for the week, Coach Bob Waddell and Walter Steffen had to give them Monday off to recover from the physical beating they took. Lewis of course was out and was to be replaced by Tony Ostrosky. Clyde Heinzer and Tony Kebe were questionable for the Pitt contest, with Heinzer, who was knocked out against the Irish suffering a concussion, although back then it was referred to as a "severe bump on the head," as well as an injured knee on the same play.[11] Kebe also had more than a minor injury as he was described as "badly battered around the legs."[12] Sophomore fullback O'Toole was rushed to the infirmary ill, where it was feared he had appendicitis. Later doctors deduced that it was an aggravated sinus condition. The coaches would have Ewing or Bert Pouncey at their disposal to replace O'Toole if he couldn't make it to the game, eventually deciding on Pouncey. To add to Tech woes, Don Fletcher, Armentrout, Ducanis and the big tackle George Kavel were also nursing injuries.

Despite their best efforts, the trainers were unable to get Heinzer ready for the city championship game, although they were able to get Kebe healthy enough to play and replace Heinzer in the starting lineup. The problem was that Kebe weighed 22 pounds less than the man he was replacing, which could cause issues against the powerful Panther line.

What the Tartans did have as an advantage in this contest despite the injuries was an effective passing game for the time period, which was Sutherland's biggest concern for his tough defense. It was something he was working on very intently in practice. Wanting to make sure his team was well focused on the upcoming game at hand, Sutherland decided to take his team into seclusion on Friday evening, keeping them away from friends, family and rabid alumni.

Unlike the Tartans, the Panthers were pretty healthy, with even the possibility that Hart Morris, who had been out with a broken hand, would return to the starting lineup. As had been the case all season, the hall-of-fame coach was unsure of who to start at fullback. West Virginia native Johnny Luch had held on to the position for a few weeks but was suffering with an injured leg. After his stellar performance against Penn State in which he showed his incredible speed for a fullback with a 47-yard touchdown run, Greensburg's Jimmy Clark, called the midget fullback, was in line to start the critical contest.

As the week of practice was coming to an end, Sutherland decided that Luch could not play, so Clark and Bill Hasson, who scored twice against the Nittany Lions, would be the fullbacks in this contest. The Panthers also came to the conclusion, after consulting with doctors, that Morris would not be ready to play. That left the capable backup Tarciscio Ondor, the sophomore guard from Jeanette, to fill in once again. While Ondor wasn't as fast as Morris, he was a big, strong 197-pound lineman who was impressive defensively. A fullback in high school, Onder was showing the Pitt staff that the line would be very stellar the next two seasons with him in the lineup. It was also a big day for Panther national championship hopes. The week before, five undefeated teams from the east had lost, and this week Notre Dame would face the powerful undefeated Penn Quakers with hopes of sending another one by the wayside.

Twenty-five thousand fans piled into Pitt Stadium to see if either Pitt could continue to put themselves back in the national spotlight with a win, or if Carnegie Tech could salvage their miserable season with a big victory over their rivals. As the game developed, it turned into a contest of Pitt's brawn offensively against the more wide-open finesse attack of the Tartans. Early in the contest it seemed like the Panthers would defeat the Tartans soundly when they took the opening kickoff and quickly went downfield to the Carnegie Tech ten on the strength of a 40-yard pass play from Heller to Reider. Clark and Reider barreled through the Tech line to the one, where the latter squirmed through a small hole for the opening touchdown and a 7–0 lead after Mac-Murdo connected on the conversion. After Kavel fumbled the ensuing kickoff, recovering it at the two, the Tartans were forced to punt, giving Pitt great field position where they took it to the Tech eight. Unfortunately at the point, a Clark fumble, which was recovered by Kavel, took the momentum from the Panthers and put it square on the sideline of the Tartans.

Armentrout and Kavel took the Tartans downfield methodically to the red zone, but once they got inside the Pitt 20, the Tartans' captain fumbled the ball, giving it back to Pitt, ending the threat. Both teams failed to develop a serious scoring threat in the remainder of the half as Pitt held on to its precarious 7–0.

Coming out for the second half, Pitt once again resumed control of the game, taking the first two drives deep into the Tartans' territory only to have the Tech defense stop them, taking the ball over on downs each time, but the Carnegie Tech defense wasn't so lucky the third time. Pitt once again took the ball after a punt, and this time the line was opening gaping holes for Clark and Reider to run through. Finally the Tartans could hold no more when Heller tossed a 10-yard completion to Reider for the game's second touchdown. When MacMurdo showed that Pitt's kicking woes may have finally been fixed, Pitt held a 14–0 lead going into the final quarter.

Beaten and battered for two consecutive weeks, most teams would have faltered in the fourth quarter being down by two touchdowns, but this was a gutsy Carnegie Tech team and would not fall apart. Advisory coach and Carnegie Tech legend Walter Steffen and Waddell decided to put in substitute quarterback Angelo Bevivino, who proceeded to quickly march the Tartans downfield via the air. Ostrosky pulled in a 29-yarder while Kavel caught one for 13. Graveno then pulled in the touchdown score but Tech failed on the conversion so they were down by eight late in the contest. The Tartans could get no closer as Pitt took the ball on a long drive that ended at the Tech ten, effectively ending the game and giving that Panthers the hard-fought win.

If the game wasn't disappointing enough for Carnegie Tech, it got worse later on when Steffen announced the following week that he would be retiring from the school after 18 seasons following the 1932 campaign. While Wandell ran the team during practice from Monday through Thursday, since 1928 Steffen had traveled between Chicago, where he was a Cook County Circuit Judge, to where the Tartans were playing, leaving on Friday and developing a game plan that he would institute on game day. Even though he was called an advisory coach, Steffen was much more as he was the architect of Carnegie Tech's golden era of college football.

Despite the fact they lost, Steffen had to be proud as it was a noble effort by the injured Tartans who amassed a season-high 17 first downs against the Pitt defense piling up 187 led by Kavel's 91. Offensively Pitt's powerful running attack proved to be the difference with 243 yards rushing as Clark broke the century mark with 101 yards on 24 carries.

With Pittsburgh emerging victorious for the city championship, they had more good news as Notre Dame defeated Penn 49–0 to strike down another eastern power and give Pitt another leg up in being the best team in the east, a necessary step in their attempt to win the big prize of a national title. Up next was a contest against the Army, and an unexpected fall by the Fighting Irish that would give the Panthers the momentum they needed in their ultimate quest.

Game 8—November 14, 1931, at Pitt Stadium

UNITED STATES MILITARY ACADEMY CADETS   0
UNIVERSITY OF PITTSBURGH PANTHERS   26

As the University of Pittsburgh readied for one of its most important games of the 1931 campaign against the Cadets of the United States Military Academy, the excitement of the pomp and circumstance that a contest versus a military academy brings was only an afterthought when compared to the unthinkable tragedy that those involved with the Army program experienced in their game against Yale. Second-year cadet Richard Sheridan of Augusta, Georgia, who was an honor student at West Point, broke his neck trying to make a diving tackle at the Yale Bowl in New Haven where he was transported to the hospital. Sadly Sheridan never made it out as he passed away from his injuries, prompting the powers that be at the academy to consider whether or not they should cancel the rest of the season.

The administration decided that the financial fallout for their final three opponents, Pitt, Notre Dame and Navy, which would be over $1,000,000, including an estimated $400,000 donation to a fund that would help the nation's unemployed from the receipts of the game against the Midshipmen, would be too much for the institution to endure, so they decided to play the games.

Regardless of the financial ramifications, the institution was morning the loss of one of their own. Acting superintendant of West Point, Walter K. Wilson, said of Sheridan, "The officers and cadets of the United States Military Academy mourn the tragic passing of Cadet Richard B. Sheridan, as the result of injuries received in the Army-Yale football game, and extend to his bereaved parents their heartfelt sympathy. His death has filled the hearts of everyone on the post with grief." Wilson further went on to say, "Cadet Sheridan was an outstanding member of the corps of cadets and his popularity as a leader in academic, military and athletic activities was clearly evidenced when his classmates selected him as their president. His life exemplifies the West Pointer's code."[13]

Sheridan's death sparked a national debate over the safety of the game, especially the kickoff, which was felt by some to be the most dangerous single play in the game. It was thought that the blocking formations in the kickoff were too dangerous, formations that caused the death of the young cadet. It was eventually decided to keep the play as part of the game, but it is a debate that has gone on through the years, most recently by NFL commissioner Roger Goodell late in the 2012 campaign.

Without Sheridan, the game went on as the 6–1 Panthers prepared to take on a very difficult and dangerous Army team. When you prepared to play Army, the program not only had to prepare for the team, but the city also did, getting ready to welcome a who's who of Army personnel. Scheduled to arrive in Pittsburgh for the Cadets' first trip to play a game in the Steel City were General Douglas MacArthur along with Secretary of War P.J. Hurley and Wilson, all invited to the contest by Chancellor John Bowman. The cadets in the academy were scheduled to march in front of the City-County building Saturday morning with Hurley in attendance to review the troops. It would certainly be as impressive a sight as the city had ever seen.

The Academy was a school that boasted some impressive alumni at the time, including Robert E. Lee, Ulysses S. Grant, John Pershing, George Patton, Dwight D. Eisenhower and Omar Bradley, and they also had a very formidable football program. Led by their consensus All-American tackle Johnny Price as well a productive backfield that was headed by the phenomenal Ray Stecker, who was finally healthy after hurting his knee against Yale, were Bobby Carver, Ed Herb, Tom Kilday, Ken Fields and Paul Johnson, who would play against Pitt even though he had injured his ankle against LSU, the group helped propel Army to a 5–1–1 start that included dominant victories against Michigan State, Colorado and LSU. Their only blemishes came at the hands of the formidable Ivy League, which had one of the, if not the, toughest conferences in the nation in the early 1930s, as Harvard was able to get the best of the Cadets 14–13 and national power Yale tied them 6–6 in the contest that took Cadet Sheridan's life. They had outscored their opponents 213–33 and caused much concern for Jock Sutherland.

The legendary coach was not only struggling to find a strategy to defeat his difficult opponent but to find anything positive to say about his team after their unexpectedly difficult 14–6 win over Carnegie Tech the week before. While the team's captain Eddie Hirshberg, the journalism student who was considered one of the most popular captains in the school's football history and struggled to come back from many injuries during his first two seasons only to have a phenomenal senior campaign, was given kudos for his play against the Tartans, Sutherland felt the rest of the squad made too many unforgivable mistakes that caused their injury-riddled opponents to keep it so close.

Pitt would have no excuses against Army as the squad was completely healthy, with Hart Morris finally able to contribute on the offensive line, fully recovered from the broken hand he suffered earlier in the season. Johnny Luch, the huge fullback who split time with the speedy but smaller Jimmy Clark, also returned from his injury that kept him out of the starting lineup to play against the Cadets.

As practice began for the game, Sutherland, though irritated with his

4. 1931: A Quick Rebuilding Process

squad, nonetheless did not want to break up his first team that took the field against the Tartans, so Onder and Clark looked early in the week like they would keep their starting spots for the time being even though Morris and Luch were healthy. By week's end, though, Sutherland did choose to put Morris back in the starting spot that he excelled in before the injury.

He was preparing his squad defensively to correct the same deficiency that every opponent felt they had to exploit to defeat the Panthers—their pass defense, which was the major factor in the loss to Notre Dame. Sutherland knew how effective the Cadets' quarterback Bobby Carver was throwing the ball, but he was aware also that if he played his defensive backs too far back, the Army rushing offense would have huge runs against the Panther line.

Army coach Major Ralph Sasse knew his backfield was deep and talented. The Cadets were constantly substituting, keeping their offense fresh. Greensburg native Pete Kopsak and Richard King were the Army ends that were also important parts of the Cadet offensive machine that Sutherland had to find a way to contain.

It wasn't only the Panther hall-of-fame coach that had to prepare his defense against the pass; Sasse was also concerned, as the Pitt aerial attack had become very dangerous in the previous two weeks with Fats Heller's accurate passes leading to three of Pitt's last four touchdowns. The Army staff was well aware of the Panthers' diversified offensive attack. Their scouts, who had followed Pitt in preparation for the game, reported to the Army coach that the Panther offense was more dangerous than that of Harvard, the lone team to defeat the Cadets.

By Friday, the rain hampered practices for both Pitt and the Army, who were at the Shadyside Academy in Aspinwall, not allowing them to complete the preparation the day before the game. Despite the poor weather, which hampered the game as well with a very cold mist, 65,000 excited fans, the second-biggest crowd ever to witness a football game in Western Pennsylvania, descended on Pitt Stadium on this afternoon. The large throng, which included the 1,450 cadets from West Point, filled the facility to see what would be the turning point of the 1931 campaign for the Panthers.

A massive traffic jam, the likes of which had never been seen in the city, greeted the cadets as the pomp and circumstance was something that riveted the city. The corps arrived in Pittsburgh at approximately 9:45 and paraded down Grant Street not only to the thrill of thousands of local citizens, but to the Pitt band, who was playing Army songs in honor of their guests. Once the Cadets and the massive crowd settled into the stadium, there was an explosion that no one, not only there watching the game, but in the nation would have expected. While many knew Sutherland spent the week preparing to defend against Army's effective passing game, few understood just how well he had schooled his offense to attack the Cadets through the air.

The contest did not begin auspiciously for the Panthers as they not only were held scoreless in the first quarter but lost both starting quarterback Bobby Hogan, who had been injured during practice earlier in the week and only made it through the first five minutes of the game, and Hirshberg, who was ill throughout the week and was pulled out twice, the final time in the third quarter where he collapsed on the bench. Despite the fact that they were without two of their starters, Pitt showed early on that they had a weapon the Army defense could not defend against. Late in what had been a closely fought defensive first quarter, Heller heaved a perfect pass into the arms of Reider, who took it to the Cadet five. Army did keep them out of the end zone, but the die was cast. Sutherland would put the Panthers' national championship hopes on the arm of Heller.

Before the Cadets could breathe a sigh of relief for holding the Panthers off the board, after Pitt got the ball again only to be stopped once again, Rip Collins went back to punt, only to toss a strike to Reider who looked like he was about to be stopped by the Army defensive players who were closing in on the halfback. Suddenly Reider broke through the Cadets and took it the final 30 yards to put Pitt in front 7–0. It was a lead that looked like it would be short-lived when Kilday picked off a pass and took it to the home team's 49-yard line. Stecker immediately turned the ball over to Pitt with a fumble on the first play of the drive, but after stopping the Panthers on their possession, Kopcsak blocked a Collins punt giving the Cadets the ball even closer at the 39.

Unfortunately for Sasse and his squad, they could have been at the one and it wouldn't have mattered; Sutherland had his team playing at an incredible level defensively, constantly stymieing the Army attack. Offensively Pitt became unstoppable, giving themselves several opportunities to score. Unfortunately each time they would threaten, either the Army defense held firm or Pittsburgh turned the ball over, sending the game into the half with the Panthers holding on to their precarious one-touchdown advantage.

The statistical domination continued in the second half as did the turnovers. Kilday picked off a Heller pass after one more effective Pitt drive only to have Steckler give it back with an Army fumble. While Pitt didn't score following the fumble, the punt by Collins that pinned Army deep in their own territory led to one. Unable to move against the stout Pittsburgh defense, the Cadets punted once again only to have it blocked by MacMurdo. The two Panther stars came to the forefront once again soon after the block, this time with Reider connecting with Heller on a pass at the five where the halfback rambled in to increase the Pittsburgh lead to 14 points.

4. 1931: A Quick Rebuilding Process

At that point the Army defense seemed to wilt letting the Panthers drive easily through them not only on the strength of Heller passing to Reider, but also on Reider's legs following several long runs. The Cadet defense would bend but not break continuing to keep the powerful Panther offense out of the end zone. Finally in the fourth quarter, the Cadet defense broke when Heller, running around in the pocket with no receiver open, tossed a pass that seemingly looked like it was to be thrown away. All of the sudden out of nowhere came an unmarked Rocco Cutri, who had replaced Hogan earlier in the contest, snagging the ball and then sprinting into the end zone untouched giving Pitt a 20-0 advantage.

At that point with the game seemingly in hand, Sutherland sent in his reserves, who promptly gave up their initial first down of the game to Army. Despite the fact they lost the opportunity to hold the powerful Army offense without a first down, the reserves did score the final touchdown of the day when Heller connected with Mike Sebastian for a 26-yard touchdown toss making the final score 26-0.

It was a complete destruction of the powerful Army program that the final score could not explain. Pitt racked up 201 yards on the ground and remarkably 293 through the air on ten completions, compared to only 67 total yards and three first downs by the Cadets. Author Harry G. Scott described the rout and the surprising Panther passing attack succinctly in his book on Jock Sutherland when he said, "This completely aerial maneuver, the likes of which had never before been demonstrated by Sutherland, shocked and pleased even the sourest of critics, who heretofore had cried out for deceptions, tricky ball-handling, an open passing game—anything but the conservatism and straight football of the typical power-laden machines that Jock fielded."[14]

It was a brilliantly coached game by Sutherland, who showed his famous sportsmanship afterward saying simply, "I do not think the score tells the real skill of the two teams that competed today. Luck was on our side and one has to have the better of the breaks when up against such a fine team as Army under the direction of Major Sasse."[15]

As conciliatory as the Pitt coach was to his opponents, he had to have known what a superior victory this was. It vaulted them right into the national championship picture as only six major teams remained undefeated in Notre Dame, Northwestern, Tulane, Tennessee, SMU and the east's only unblemished squad, Harvard. They had one game left against the Nebraska Cornhuskers, whom they needed to beat decisively if they hoped to impress the experts that would decide their fate.

Game 9—November 25, 1931, at Pitt Stadium
UNIVERSITY OF NEBRASKA CORNHUSKERS 0
UNIVERSITY OF PITTSBURGH PANTHERS 40

As the 1931 campaign was coming to an end, the University of Pittsburgh Panthers were coming off their best performance of the season against Army. Playing almost a perfect game against the Cadets, the Panthers wished they would have gotten an opportunity to play the Notre Dame Fighting Irish once again, thinking that the results might have been different this time around. Unfortunately for Pitt, they would not get the chance and had to live with the outcome of the Irish contest. To have a shot at winning the eastern championship as well as being considered for national honors, the Panthers would need some help in the final two weeks of the season. First off, for the eastern title they would need Yale to defeat the unbeaten Crimson of Harvard. If that was simple enough, the national championship would be more complex, hoping that either USC or Army beat Notre Dame, Purdue had to top Northwestern and Tulane, and USC had to lose their final contests of the season. Anything other than that scenario and their odds would diminish significantly.

The odds were still long for Pitt, but before any thought of championships could take place they had one huge task at hand: defeat the university of Nebraska Cornhuskers at Pitt Stadium to complete their regular season. While Pitt's rivals from Penn State no longer wanted to compete with the Panthers at Pitt Stadium on Thanksgiving Day, the University still wanted to host a game on the holiday and worked out an agreement with Nebraska to play in 1931. After defeating Pittsburgh in their first encounter in 1921, the Cornhuskers had lost two and tied two with Pitt, including a scoreless tie in Lincoln the year before.

This would be the first time the two schools had played in Pittsburgh since 1927, the last three contests being played at Nebraska, and Jock Sutherland hoped that the home field would give him the advantage he needed to win this important contest decisively. The hall-of-fame coach needed any advantage he could as this Cornhusker squad was anything but a pushover. Coach Dana X. Bible had a fine squad that had wrapped up the Big Six Conference championship the week before after defeating Iowa State at home 23–0.

Nebraska had a tough defense that led them to a 7–1 mark coming into this contest, the only loss being a 19–7 at undefeated Northwestern in the second game of the season. It was a contest where Bible had to start seven sophomores due to injuries. Other than the loss to the Wildcats, the Huskers yielded only 16 points in their seven victories on the way to the conference title. It was a big, physical defense that was as effective defending the pass as it was stopping the run, so Pitt would have quite a challenge repeating their success through the air that they'd had the previous three weeks

Offensively, led by All-American tackle Hugh Rhea, Lawrence Ely and Gail O'Brien, the Cornhuskers fielded a huge line that Pitt's legendary coach felt could cause issues for his squad. While not one of the most effective offenses in the nation, the Nebraska backfield, behind their mammoth line, was still dangerous. Quarterback Bernie Masterson and three Husky runners by the names of Marvin Paul, Everett Kreizinger and one of the best backs in the midwest, George Sauer, were the men that the Panther defense had to be well prepared for.

With the team having ten days in between their final two games, Sutherland gave his squad Monday off following their impressive win against Army for their first weekday off the team had during the season. It was break he felt the squad needed to heal and rest for his final opponents. He was missing two of his starters in the early days of practice for the contest and had hopes they would return for the game. The captain of the team, Eddie Hirshberg, fell ill in the Army game and spent a couple of days in the hospital recovering. He continued his recovery at home, but with the extra time off, he felt he could make it back. Quarterback Bobby Hogan was also sitting out the first few practices, nursing a leg injury that forced him out of the Army game in the first few minutes. He had been reported to only have a slight limp as preparations began and felt the only thing that could keep him out of the lineup was backup Rocco Cutri, who performed admirably in his absence.

As Pitt was putting the final touches on their game plan for Nebraska, the city's two other prominent universities, Carnegie Tech and Duquesne, were preparing for a contest at Pitt Stadium the Saturday before the Panther–Cornhusker tilt in a game to benefit local charities. To do their part, the administration at Pitt chose to donate their portion of the gate receipts against Nebraska to the Allegheny County Emergency Association. It was a generous offer by the school to help out needy citizens as the Depression was worsening.

For the Panthers, the college football gods must have been looking down on them for their good deeds and rewarded them with two of the greatest holiday presents they could have hoped for. A 16–14 upset of Notre Dame by Southern California after the Trojans fell behind 14–0, and more importantly, only a few days after deciding to deemphasize football and athletics in general, Yale upset Harvard 3–0 on All-American Albie Booth's 12-yard dropkick late in the game.

The fortuitous late score by Booth put Pitt in a strong position to capture the championship of the east with a win against Nebraska. It would be a victory that would be a glorious end for the eight successful seniors that graced the Panther roster in their last game at Pitt Stadium. Each started curently and played an important role in the Pitt success since 1929. Lineman Mike Milligan, who was a policeman in Aliquippa in the summer and didn't think he would play his senior season after suffering from appendicitis in the off season; Hart Morris, who regretted the fact he broke his hand during the campaign and just longed to run one more time under one of Rip Collins's punts to "crash the safety man to earth"[16]; Collins, whose favorite moment at the university was the previous week against Army; the humorous Eddie Hirshberg, whose proudest moment was being the captain of this year's squad; the small but fast fullback Jimmy Clark, who seemed frustrated by the fact he couldn't nail down the starting fullback job; center Ralph Daugherty, one of the few bright spots in the Notre Dame contest, yet who was more proud of his teammates that they overcame that discouraging loss to play strongly down the stretch; tackle Jim MacMurdo, who enjoyed his senior season more than anything; and Jess Quatse, who like MacMurdo also felt his final season was his most satisfying, claiming that "if ever anyone enjoyed playing football, it was yours truly these last three months,"[17] would be together for the final time in front of the home crowd on this Thanksgiving Day.

Knowing that the Irish and Crimson lost as well as the fact they were one win away from not only the east title but vaulting themselves into the national championship picture, the senior-laden Panthers burst onto the field, remarkably playing at an intensity level higher than they had against Army. It was as if the field was slanted as the Pitt played most of the contest deep in Nebraska territory. They did so by showing off the incredible depth that had been ineffective against the Irish. Early in the game, superstar half back Paul Reider suffered a painful shoulder injury that saw him spend most of the afternoon on the bench. The injury gave an opportunity for Mike Sebastian to show the 22,000 fans who braved the cold day that he was a star in waiting. The vast difference in the depth of the two clubs was shown when Rhea was also injured necessitating his removal from the game, as the Panthers were able to take advantage of his absence to run roughshod over their opponents.

From all accounts, the Cornhusker defense was physical and hit the Pitt offense hard, but the powerful Panther attack overcame that with very aggressive play of their own. Taking the opening kickoff, the Cornhuskers went through the Pitt defense, passing their way to the Panther 24-yard line where Cutri picked off a pass giving Pitt the ball. While no one knew it at the time, the game was over at this point. The Panthers slowly moved through the Nebraska line before Heller found Hirshberg for 23 yards in Cornhusker territory. Reider and Heller continued to advance the ball when Reider was hurt after a three-yard run. Sebastian took his place without missing a beat as they continued the long drive to the one. Heller finished it with a bolt through the middle and an early 6–0 lead.

When they took the ball back, their combination of tough running and the fortuitous long passing game, that included a 22-yard strike from Heller to Sebastian, brought Pitt to the Cornhusker 18. Sebastian then bolted for 13, setting up Heller's second score of the ball game and a very quick 13-point advantage. The two defenses dug in, although the Panther offense was still moving the ball, and they ended the half with the score still 13–0. With the game much closer than it should have been, Pitt continued to be aggressive in the second half. Hogan, who did not start the contest with his leg injury, came in for Cutri in the third quarter and sparked the attack.

Sebastian took over, running down the field, first for 16 yards on a triple pass then rambled for a 22-yard run to set up Heller's third score with another short burst up the middle, putting Pitt up by 20 thanks to his 18 points. His day wasn't over yet as Sebastian set up another touchdown for him with a 38-yard run. With the ball at the 23, Heller took the handoff and rolled through

In his All-American shirt is Rillton native Jesse Quatse. After his fabulous career at the University of Pittsburgh, Quatse embarked on a three-year NFL career with Green Bay, New York and Pittsburgh. After his career ended, he coached the Pittsburgh Americans of the American Football League in 1937. He died in 1977 at the age of 69.

several Nebraska defenders, breaking tackles every time it looked like they had him stopped for the touchdown jaunt, making the score 27–0 with his fourth touchdown.

The fourth quarter was anti-climactic but did provide Sebastian with his chance to get on the scoreboard as he had yet another long run, this one 22 yards, that set up his four-yard TD run on a reverse to give Pitt a 34-point lead as the fourth quarter was just beginning. Moments later Hogan picked off a Sauer pass and ran it back to the Nebraska 31. Two plays later Heller caught Sebastian in stride, who glided into the end zone for the final tally of the day.

The story the statistics told was exactly the one the scoreboard did, a one-sided dominant victory. Outgaining their opponents 517 yards to 169 as well as beating them in first downs by a 23-to-9 margin, the Pitt offense put on a clinic with depth of power and speed; the Panthers had the victory it needed to put them in the championship hunt. Many experts were singing the praises of Sebastian as he gave a good exhibition of what fans could expect from him in the future. *Pittsburgh Post-Gazette* sports editor Harvey Boyle said simply, "If Mike Sebastian is at all behind Paul Reider and Warren Heller in backfield skill the difference is not noticeable to the casual football fan. He is a young gent of speed and power who has not been seen often enough to suit those who like his dash and sparkle on the field."[18]

It was certainly a perfect way to end the season, putting up more points against what was thought to be one of the best defenses in the country than any opponent had to a Nebraska team at that point in their history. The victory, coupled with the upset of Harvard, gave the Panthers an eastern crown that only weeks ago seemed like an impossibility. To further their hopes in the national picture, undefeated Tennessee was tied by the heavy underdog Wildcats of Kentucky before Army handed Notre Dame its second consecutive defeat and Purdue had turned aside unbeaten Northwestern in their final contest also.

This string of upsets against national powers put Southern California, Tulane and Pitt in the conversation of who would be national champions. Only Tulane had an unblemished record, standing at 10–0–0 after easily defeating LSU to capture their third consecutive Southern Conference championship under coach Bernie Bierman, who would take over the program at Minnesota following the 1931 campaign. They had only one contest left against Washington State.

Each team had a feasible argument for them to become national champions. The Southern California Trojans began the campaign with a devastating loss to St. Mary's before reeling off nine consecutive wins on their way to the

4. 1931: A Quick Rebuilding Process

Pacific Coast Conference championship and a spot in the Rose Bowl. This gave them the easiest shot at the top spot as they would get to choose between the two schools who would play in Pasadena.

An attorney by the name of Conrad Checco came up with the idea of having a contest between Pitt and Tulane in mid–December to see who would earn the honor of the second spot beside the Trojans in the Rose Bowl. The game would have marked the first attempt at a playoff in college football. A game at Pitt Stadium with the proceeds going to charity was one of his proposals, but some schools had objections to such a contest. Eventually the Rose Bowl was settled the way it always had been, with the committee picking the western representative, which in this case was USC, who would have the biggest voice in who would be invited to face them.

While the Panthers were waiting to see if they received the bid, many individuals were given richly deserved awards as the various All-East and All-American teams were announced. The United Press team was among the first, as Daugherty received third-team status while MacMurdo was on the honorable mention squad. As impressive as those were, it was the former Greensburg High star that was given the greatest honor as Quatse was named as the first-team tackle. Quatse was also given the first-team nod with *Collier's Weekly*, the Walter Camp Football Foundation, the All-America Board and *College Humor* magazine to garner the consensus designation as the best right tackle in the country.

The individual awards aside, for Pitt to compete in the Rose Bowl it was simple. If Washington State somehow went to New Orleans and defeated Tulane, the Panthers would travel to Pasadena to play for the national championship, since some selectors had decided to wait until then to pick their champion. Unfortunately Tulane was a brilliant squad and easily defeated the Cougars 28–14 to finish the season undefeated.

There was originally the thought that USC would not want to invite a second consecutive southern team, as Alabama came to the Rose Bowl the season before beating Washington State 24–0, but it was a clear choice once Tulane was able to complete their undefeated campaign.

The Trojans went on to win the Rose Bowl 21–12 over the Green Wave and captured most of the major national champion selections. As in 1929, it was a couple of years later when the Panthers received the recognition they hoped for as Parke E. Davis named them national champions in 1931 when he selected his famed list of champions in the *1933 Spalding Football Guide*. Davis, as was stated in the last chapter, was one of the foremost historians on the game in the country, and his national champions list was considered one of the more legitimate in the country. Because of this fact, the University of Pittsburgh officially recognizes it as a national championship for the school.

Years later, Davis's findings in 1931 were confirmed by two statisticians, Bob Kirlin and Ted Noel's 1st-N-Goal website, when they also named Pittsburgh as the title holders in retrospect with their computer statistical analysis as each tried to calculate who the national champions were in each past season.

Regardless of the fact that they received their longed-for championship in retrospect, it was a special team who knew how to play championship football, coming back to play their best football of the season after a disastrous loss to Notre Dame which helps it go down in the annals of Pitt football as one of the best teams ever to take the field.

National Champions selections made by modern-day analysts are noted "(retrospective)." Players rated as **First Team All-Americans** by a plurality of NCAA-recognized selectors are noted as "(consensus)." Players rated by all NCAA-recognized selectors are noted as "(unanimous)."

1930 Scores

Date	Opponent	Score	Record
9/27	Waynesburg	52–0	1–0–0
10/4	@West Virginia	16–0	2–0–0
10/11	@Western Reserve	52–0	3–0–0
10/18	@Syracuse	14–0	4–0–0
10/25	Notre Dame	19–35	4–1–0
11/1	@Nebraska	0–0	4–1–1
11/8	Carnegie Tech	7–6	5–1–1
11/15	@Ohio State	7–16	5–2–1
11/26	Penn State	19–12	6–2–1
		186–69	

1931 Scores

Date	Opponent	Score	Record
9/26	Miami (OH)	61–0	1–0–0
10/3	@Iowa	20–0	2–0–0
10/10	West Virginia	34–0	3–0–0
10/17	Western Reserve	32–0	4–0–0
10/24	@Notre Dame	12–25	4–1–0
10/31	@Penn State	41–6	5–1–0

Date	Opponent	Score	Record
11/7	Carnegie Tech	14–6	6–1–0
11/14	Army	26–0	7–1–0
11/25	Nebraska	40–0	8–1–0
		280–37	

Selected as National Champions by:
The Spalding Guide (Parke H. Davis Ratings)
Bob Kirlin Ratings (retrospective)*
1st-N-Goal (retrospective)*

*Not Recognized as Official National Championship Selector by University of Pittsburgh.

Selected as First-Team All-American
Jesse Quatse (consensus)

5

1932: The Program Up and Running

The proudest moment for a football coach and school administration when it comes to their college football program is when the program can withstand a series of heavy graduation losses and keep on running at a national championship level. While the rebuilding seasons in the past were successful, it usually was not without issues that took the Panthers out of the national championship race; in 1932 that all changed for legendary Coach Jock Sutherland. Sutherland would have to deal with a combination of losing eight highly successful starters from his 1931 national championship squad as well as an extremely difficult schedule that saw them play no less than seven national powers to close the season, including an anticipated trans-continental matchup against former coach Glenn "Pop" Warner and his Stanford Cardinals. Despite that fact somehow he fashioned a young team that cut through that monstrous schedule undefeated, garnering third trip to Pasadena to play in the Rose Bowl.

The hall-of-fame coach was gaining vast national recognition by the coaching fraternity, and earlier in 1932 Mal Stevens of Yale, president of the organization, had appointed Sutherland chairman of the membership committee of the National Coaches Association. All accolades were deserved for the Panther coach who had proven to be one of the most adept coaches in the country at maintaining his program's excellence. While it's never easy to overcome the losses that Sutherland did after the 1931 campaign, the incredible depth he formulated that season would serve him very well in 1932 although it didn't necessarily seem so in pre-season practice as the varsity and the second team scrimmaged before their opener against Ohio Northern.

5. 1932: The Program Up and Running

Before he agreed to be coach of the University of Pittsburgh in 1915, the school only had a few great moments in football. The moment Glenn "Pop" Warner took the sidelines, the school's became one of nation's best programs. He won his first 30 games and captured three national championships in his first four seasons. Winner of 319 games in his 44-year career, Warner held the record for the most wins in a career until Paul Bryant eclipsed him in 1981.

Led by Mike Nicksick and Heine Weisenbaugh, the reserves bolted out to a 27–0 lead going into the fourth quarter. End Ted Dailey picked up a fumble in the end zone, and Mike Sebastian, who starred as a substitute the previous season on a couple of occasions, did it once again as he replaced Paul Reider in the lineup for the starters and scored the final touchdown in a 27–12 defeat.

As angry as the Scottish coach was at his first team for the humiliating defeat, he had decided to stick with them as he broke camp and returned back to Oakland from Windber where the team had their camp. Three returnees from the previous year, Bobby Hogan, Reider and Warren Heller, led a powerful backfield that included Izzy Weinstock at fullback. As experienced as the backfield was, the line was equally inexperienced, except for Dailey at end. New starters sophomore Robert Hoel and Paul Cuba took over at tackle, and Joe Tormey was at center with Ken Ormiston and Tarciscio Onder, who spent some time starting in 1931 for the injured Hart Morris at guard. At the other end was junior Joe Skladany. Nicknamed Muggsy, Skladany would go from a first-time starter early in 1932 to one of the most revered names in Pitt football history by the time his career ended the following season.

As they were the year before, one of the main strengths of this squad would be its incredible depth, led by Nicksick, Weisenbaugh and Harvey Rooker, who had impressed the coaching staff late in camp. The depth would be important early on as the young sophomore Nicksick would be thrust into the starting lineup for the opener when Heller went down with an injured ankle, and Charley Hartwig would slide into Ormiston's slot at guard when the latter was hurt at camp. With a talented squad of 50 players, Pittsburgh began the season looking to finally convince the nation's experts, except for historian Parke E. Davis who already was aware of their greatness, that the Panthers were the best program in the land.

Game 1—September 24, 1932, at Pitt Stadium
OHIO NORTHERN UNIVERSITY POLAR BEARS   0
UNIVERSITY OF PITTSBURGH PANTHERS   47

Luckily for the Panthers, by the time kickoff came at Pitt Stadium, Heller had recovered from the injuries suffered in camp and took his starting spot at halfback as Pittsburgh was about to take on a very undermanned Polar Bears of Ohio Northern. Ten thousand fans had made their way to the stadium as 17 players touched the ball in the one-sided affair. Ohio State coach Sam Willaman made the trek to Pittsburgh to scout the Panthers for what would be a classic contest between the two schools later in the season. He came away amazed, only muttering, "I see Jock Sutherland has another of this doggone lines."[1]

What turned out to be a rout started off anything but. Early in the first quarter Weinstock fumbled, although he recovered before Heller turned the ball over to the Polar Bears on the next play to give them a first down on the Pitt 22. The Panther defense was incredible this day, surrendering only one first down and a net 74 total yards to their opponents as the Ohio Northern scoring threat would end there. Pitt's offense would not make the same mistakes on consecutive series as Hogan rumbled for 34 yards and Weisenbaugh ripped through the Polar Bear line for 19 yards on three consecutive carries. Heller eventually took it in from 13 yards out for a 7–0 advantage. Moments later after stopping Ohio Northern, Reider sprinted for 34 yards and then Weinstock carried it in the final six to double the Panthers' lead to 14 points. The game quickly turned into a one-sided affair when Heller scored his second of the day from four yards out for the Panthers' third touchdown.

Pitt's reserves continued the onslaught as Jim Simms scored twice and Dick Matesic once to put the final touches on the 47–0 victory. While they had dominated the contest, it could have been worse as the Panthers could have scored on two other occasions when Heller had a 45-yard touchdown jaunt called back because of a clipping call and a Weinstock 33-yard touchdown run was nullified by a Panther offside. Late in the half before Pitt decided to empty their bench, Reider suffered the only injury of the day for the Panthers. After catching a 30-yard pass from Heller and ripping through three Polar Bear defenders for a touchdown, the Pitt captain was kicked in the stomach and had to be carried off the field. The only positive for the day for Ohio Northern came in the third quarter when they held Pitt scoreless, but the game was already out of hand by that point.

With the opening win under their belts, things would be more challenging for the Panthers as they would travel to Morgantown the following week, although their rivals at WVU had to be intimidated with the powerful squad that Sutherland was showing off against Ohio Northern.

Game 2—October 1, 1932, at Mountaineer Field in Morgantown, West Virginia

UNIVERSITY OF PITTSBURGH PANTHERS   40
WEST VIRGINIA UNIVERSITY MOUNTAINEERS   0

In 1932 the Backyard Brawl was a two-week event as Greasy Neale and the Mountaineers of West Virginia took on two of Pittsburgh's three major college football programs to open up the campaign. In the first contest of the season, Elmer Layden's Duquesne University Dukes upset WVU 3–0 at Forbes Field on quarterback Red Sullivan's field goal.

With the upset loss under their belt, a victory was essential to the program, and it hopefully would come against a Pitt team that had outscored them 77–7 in the three victories the Panthers had over West Virginia since a 9–6 Mountaineer upset in 1928. WVU did have the advantage of hosting Pitt at Mountaineer Field where 15,000 raucous fans would be on hand hoping to inspire their hometown team in the contest.

While the home-field advantage was important, the West Virginia hall-of-fame coach would have to play his powerful opponents without two of his top players as end Will Sortet and starting fullback Patsy Slate were doubtful with injuries. Sutherland knew that he might be without team captain Paul Reider and center Joe Tormey, both of whom had been ill during the week, but was confident that the Panthers had a depth advantage that became more prevalent with the experience the reserves received against Ohio Northern. If he had to go without his two starters, halfback Mike Sebastian and center George Shotwell were more than capable replacements. The depth was more than the Mountaineers could handle as West Virginia would not only lose their second consecutive matchup to a Pittsburgh school, but did so in a way that had rarely been seen in this renowned rivalry. Pitt's 40-point victory was the most one-sided victory between the two schools at the time, exceeded only by the 53-point outburst in 1904.

The Mountaineer offense only contributed two first downs against a sturdy Panther defense that had allowed only three in the first two games of the season, and 29 total yards compared to the 419 that the Pitt offense accumulated on the porous WVU defense. Even the home-field advantage that Neale and his squad counted on was lessened by the fact that a bigger-than expected-percentage of the crowd was wearing Pitt blue and gold.

The carnage started early and never let up as the Panthers scored three times in the first quarter. Sebastian and Shotwell did in fact start for Pitt, but it made no difference who was in the lineup as Pittsburgh was in control for 60 minutes. Sebastian put the Panthers on the board first with a 56-yard touchdown run that was set up by pounding runs up the middle by Weinstock and Heller. Pitt soon went up by two touchdowns after Sebastian made a fine punt return to the WVU 33. The next play saw a spectacular open-field run by Heller that saw him sprint into the end zone untouched by the stunned Mountaineer defense.

Trying to get something started by going to the air, West Virginia found themselves losing 14 yards on the next drive before turning it over to the powerful Pitt offense once again. A 19-yard run by the reserve fullback Sebastian set up a 24-yard touchdown sprint by Weinstock to make the score 20–0 as the first period was coming to an end. It was at this point that Sutherland mercifully removed his starting squad. It didn't seem to matter as Henry Weisenbaugh scored twice, the second set up by a magnificent 47-yard interception return by Rocco Cutri, and Frank Gelini tallied one to give the Panthers the dominant 40–0 victory.

For the Mountaineers, despite the fact they were able to fashion a .500 season by going 5–3 the rest of the campaign, the 40-point beating made 1932 a year to forget. For Pitt, the season looked bright as they would continue their magnificent campaign the next week by renewing a Pittsburgh rivalry that had been dormant since 1903 against Duquesne.

Game 3—October 8, 1932, at Pitt Stadium

DUQUESNE UNIVERSITY DUKES 0
UNIVERSITY OF PITTSBURGH PANTHERS 33

Since 1927, Elmer Layden had slowly built the Duquesne University football program from an afterthought among Pittsburgh colleges to the edge of being a competitive program in the major college football division. The proof of that came on October 8, 1932, when they took on the University of Pittsburgh in the first contest the schools played against each other since a 10–6 Dukes triumph 29 years before in 1903. The contest marked a new era in Steel City football that included a third team competing for the city championship. Since 1923, that title was the exclusive possession of either Pitt or Carnegie Tech, who battled through nine close contests, with the Panthers holding a slight 5–4 advantage.

The final game of 1931 actually began the new era when Carnegie Tech and the Dukes had agreed to play in a post-season holiday contest at Pitt Stadium in a charity contest that ended in a dramatic scoreless tie that showed perhaps Layden's squad was ready for the next step. While Carnegie Tech played the Panthers tough in their national championship campaign the year before, they were still a step behind the Pitt as were the Dukes, who would enter the contest a prohibitive favorite despite the fact that Sebastian would replace an injured Reider in the contest for the Panthers.

Duquesne came into the game relatively healthy with only tackle John Donohue sidelined for the contest. Layden replaced him with Steve Sinko, who would be part of a solid line that hopefully would open holes through the Panther defensive wall for their effective backfield that included quarterback Larry Sullivan, halfbacks Al DeLuca and Ben Pawlina, as well as fullback Silvio Zaninelli. It was a group that helped lead the Dukes to an impressive

3–0 start highlighted by a 3–0 upset of the West Virginia Mountaineers in Forbes Field two weeks earlier. For Sutherland, other than Reider's injury, he felt he was coming into this birth of a new rivalry relatively unscathed as he would see Mike Nicksick, who had been out with an infected leg in the first two games, back at his disposal.

Despite the fact that the game didn't seem to be sparking much interest among the Pitt faithful, Duquesne fans were thrilled at the fact their program was finally up to the level that allowed it to schedule the Panthers. Because of the enthusiasm of the Catholic University, 30,000 fans, quite a few of them rooting for the Dukes, entered Pitt Stadium to see if Duquesne had what it took to compete with a national power; they would soon find out they did not.

The Panther hall-of-fame coach didn't feel the need to incorporate a majority of his playbook and used only three or four simple running plays to manhandle his opponents. Despite the limited offense, Pitt outrushed Duquesne 330–42 in what turned out to be a forgettable initial renewal of the soon-to-be-fierce rivalry. From the outset it looked like it would be an easy win for Sutherland and his squad when Sebastian ripped a 56-yard run on the games second offensive play before Heller went off right tackle from 15 yards out to make it 7–0. Two series later with Pitt looking at a third-and-long at their 32, Bobby Hogan found Skladany at the Dukes' 40, who took the ball down to the 11 for a clutch first down. Not long after, Heller busted in from inside the one to increase the Pittsburgh advantage to 13 points as the first quarter was about to come to a close.

At that point Duquesne threatened Pitt twice, the first time all season that a team had a scoring opportunity against the Pitt defense, but both times the Panthers stood firm, holding back the Dukes to keep the score 13–0 at the half.

Pitt continued the pressure in the third quarter, pushing deep into Duquesne territory on a couple of occasions, including at the six when Heller turned the ball over with a fumble, but after some frustration, they eventually capitalized when Sebastian returned a punt 34 yards to the Dukes' six then scored on the next play with a nice run around the right end.

After their third touchdown of the contest, the Dukes had one last scoring threat, moving down to the Panther four before a phenomenal defensive play by Hogan in the end zone halted the drive. At that point Duquesne seemed defeated. With Sutherland putting in his reserves, the Dukes' defense yielded touchdowns to Matesic and Nicksick in the fourth quarter to make the final 33–0.

Even though it was a rout, Sutherland, as usual, was complementary in victory, saying, "If we hadn't got our share of breaks, it might have been a much closer game. I had to get my players 'up there' for Duquesne. That's how much I thought of Elmer Layden's boys. The Dukes had plenty of heart."[2] Truth be told, had the Dukes received the breaks that the Panther coach mentioned, it still would have been a rout. The statistical domination in this game would back that claim. While eventually this became a bitterly fought rivalry, for now it was the third successive tune-up for Pitt as they began the difficult part of their schedule with a contest versus a national power in Army.

Game 4—October 15, 1932, at Michie Stadium in West Point, New York

UNIVERSITY OF PITTSBURGH PANTHERS   18
UNITED STATES MILITARY ACADEMY CADETS 13

In 1931, the University of Pittsburgh and the United States Military Academy met each other on the football field for the first time in the storied histories of both programs. It was a contest between two of the east's premiere teams, one where the Panthers crushed whatever championship hopes the Cadets had 26–0 at Pitt Stadium. This year the two schools would meet in West Point at Michie Stadium and Army had nothing but revenge on their minds.

The game in the previous season, while celebrated in Pittsburgh for the ceremony that comes with hosting a football contest against a service academy, took a backseat to the tragedy that had happened a couple of weeks prior when second-year cadet Richard Sheridan was killed in the Yale game while making a tackle. Army was continuing to heal as they opened the season with two victories, shutting out both Furman and Carleton (MN). The offense was led by one of the most productive backs in the east in Ken Fields as well as quarterback Joe MacWiliams, half back Travis Brown and fullback Tom Kilday.

The Cadets also had another factor on their side to inspire them for a victory against the Panthers. Before the season began, their coach, Lieutenant Colonel Ralph Sasse, announced he would be retiring from the academy at the conclusion of the 1932 campaign. A graduate of the Military Academy and a major in World War I where he led the 301st Tank Battalion, Sasse was named coach after the 1929 season and had led the Cadets to a 19–3–2 mark in two-plus campaigns. While highly successful at both the Army and Mississippi State, where he came out of retirement taking over the program in 1935 and leading them to the Orange Bowl a year later, Sasse unfortunately had to retire from coaching in 1937 when he collapsed and was confined to his home after suffering a nervous breakdown following a 41–0 loss to LSU.

Nonetheless, in 1932 Sasse was one of the best coaches in the game and was looking to lead his team to victory against a phenomenal Pitt club that outscored its first three opponents by a 120–0 margin. Coach Jock Sutherland had a powerful running attack at his disposal that would be enhanced in this game with the return of halfback Paul Reider, who had been out since the first quarter of the opening game against Ohio Northern with an injured leg.

More than 20,000 fans crammed into Michie Stadium to witness one of most intense battles of the year. It was a back-and-forth contest that saw each team take turns dominating a game that went down to its final moments before a winner was decided. Army kept the ball in Pitt territory early in the contest with the Panther defense keeping them out of the end zone each time. After a couple of inept drives in their normal single-wing formation, Sutherland switched them to two wings, which confused Army, as Heller ran through their previously impenetrable defense for 56 yards and the first score of the game. Izzy Weinstock was unable to successfully complete the conversion as Pitt was up 6–0.

Unable to recover, the Panthers took advantage and once again moved down the field against the Cadet defense. After moving into Army territory at the 40, Heller found Hogan for 13 yards to the 27. Looking like the drive would end there after being stopped three consecutive times, Heller completed a long toss in the end zone to his soon-to-be-All-American end Skladany, giving Pitt a 12-point advantage.

In the past, this was usually the point where the Panthers would feel comfortable as the reserves got ready on the sidelines for the play time that usually came with a one-sided victory. Unfortunately for Pitt this was no Ohio Northern, and Army was determined to get back into the game. They once again drove deep into Panther territory only to have a pass picked off by Mike Sebastian. Finally after another stalled Pittsburgh drive, Army moved inside the Pitt ten on the strength of a 19-yard pass from Brown to Fields. Eventually after a few tough runs up the middle, Kilday cut the Pitt lead in half with a one-yard run as the two teams went into the half with the Panthers up 12–6.

In trouble for the first time all season, the Pittsburgh defense allowed a 39-yard Field-to-Kilday completion which put the ball on their 11. A few plays later Kilday gave the Cadets a first down inside the three. Somehow the Panthers bore down, stopping Army four straight times securing their lead, even if it was only temporary. Both offenses were having trouble moving when an inopportune penalty gave the Cadets a chance to take their first lead of the day. A long Army pass fell incomplete when a flag was thrown on Reider for interference, giving their opponents the ball at the seven. Two plays later Fields took the ball in for the score and a 13–12 Army lead.

With their championship dreams on the line, Pitt responded the way champions do. Heller and Skladany came to the rescue again with a 51-yard connection that put the Panthers on the seven. Sebastian roiled around right end to the one where Weinstock finished the job two plays later, but missed his third extra point to put Pittsburgh up by five.

Pitt had two opportunities to put the game away in the fourth quarter but once again was unable to complete the drives. It gave the Cadets one last chance late in the contest to pull out an exciting victory. Fields hit Felix Vidol for 13 yards; then they reversed the connection when Vidol found Fields with a pass that took it to the Panther 23. Fields then ran the ball out of bounds at the 13 as time was running out. Pitt began to once again show what a dominant defense it was, holding the Cadets to a fourth down in the waning seconds. On the final play of the game Fields sent a ball into the end zone into the waiting hands of Vidol, who seemed to be open. Out of nowhere, Joe Tormey came into the play knocking the ball out of Vidol's hands to preserve the thrilling win.

It was as enthralling a win as Sutherland had in his tenure at Pitt, but unfortunately they would have little time to celebrate as they had to prepare for another team who was looking for revenge, with Ohio State visiting Pitt Stadium a week later.

Game 5—October 22, 1932, at Pitt Stadium

OHIO STATE UNIVERSITY BUCKEYES   0
UNIVERSITY OF PITTSBURGH PANTHERS   0

Pitt came into the game against Ohio State at Pitt Stadium as not only arguably the top college football team in the east, but a leading contender in the national championship race following their exciting 18–13 victory over the Army in West Point. It was a confident bunch, which was also something of a concern for Coach Jock Sutherland, who wanted to guard against overconfidence as the team prepared for its important contest against the Buckeyes.

It was the third game between the two schools, the first two split, with the Panthers winning 18–2 in their national championship run in 1929 before losing a year later at Columbus 16–7. Odds were good for the Panthers in this contest that would give them an opportunity to increase their national championship hopes, which is why Sutherland wanted to make sure his squad was taking them seriously.

The Buckeyes had a formidable backfield led by their captain Lew Hinchman, who had been injured but was slated to return to the lineup against Pitt. Despite the fact that they potentially were a high-scoring offense, they had struggled in their first few games. Following a 34–7 win against Ohio Wesleyan, they were held to a single touchdown in a 7–7 tie against Indiana and shut out 14–0 at the hands of the Wolverines of Michigan.

Despite the disappointing 1-1-1 mark, the Buckeyes were considered one of the strongest teams in the Midwest, one capable of pulling the huge upset. Both teams came into this matchup relatively healthy with Ohio State without end Junius Ferrall, who was replaced by Joe Salvaterra, and the Panthers losing right tackle Bob Hoel, which gave Frank "Tiger" Walton the chance to start.

In Pittsburgh's prior game, Army not only figured out how to slow down the powerful Pitt attack but became the first team to find a way to move on their incredible defense. It was a lesson that Coach Sam Willaman would learn well, at least the lesson of stopping the Panthers.

A decent crowd of 30,000 came to Pitt Stadium to see what would be a classic affair. While it did not start out auspiciously, with Paul Reider fumbling the opening kickoff, he recovered it and started one of several drives that saw the Panthers rip through the Buckeye line only to be eventually thwarted by their defense and kept them from crossing the goal line. Offensively Ohio State was dormant in the first half until late in the second quarter when Bill Carroll and Hinchman started finding holes in the Panther defensive wall, taking it to their 22. Hinchman eventually fumbled, turning it over to Pittsburgh which ended the half scoreless.

While Pitt dominated the first half, they were unable to score which almost cost them early in the second half after the Buckeyes took the opening kickoff. Cal Cramer sprinted down the field 21 yards which started a 53-yard drive that eventually stalled deep in Panther territory. Ohio State continued to threaten after taking the punt on the next drive, going down to the Pitt eight before once again the Panthers' defense held firm, again keeping the game scoreless.

The Pitt offense was frustrated for most of the second half, and it appeared the contest would end as a disappointing tie for Pittsburgh, that is until they found a way to come up with one last desperate possession in hopes of saving their unblemished campaign.

With time running out, Hinchman launched a 60-yard punt that pinned Pitt back at their 14-yard line. After a half of inadequate offense in which Ohio State continually frustrated the Panther running attack with a physical defense that also forced Weinstock out of the game with a broken nose, Heller launched a pass to Sebastian, who pulled it in at the 50 and rambled 16 more yards to the 34. The Buckeye defense, which had been dominant for the previous three quarters, was now apprehensive and immediately gave up a 20-yard run to Sebastian which put Pitt at the 14. Ohio State struck back as

Sebastian was sacked for a 12-yard loss, but unfortunately a mistake by the aggressive Buckeye defense cost them dearly on the next play when defensive back Tom Keefe hit Dailey in the end zone before the pass from Sebastian reached him, giving Pitt the ball on the one with 40 seconds left on the interference call.

Pitt had been at this point many times during the season, one huge surge by their offensive line creating a hole for one of their incredible backs and the game would be theirs. Weinstock and Heller were stopped short of the goal, although Ohio State was called for offsides before Heller's attempt. With the ball that deep in their territory, Willaman continued to instruct his defensive team to go offsides, which at that point and time in college football history allowed the clock to run, giving Pitt little time to score. The Buckeye offside ploy proved to be successful, running the clock down as Sebastian failed to score on a third attempt, leaving Pitt with a fourth and inches and seconds left. They decided to pass; Sebastian thought he had completed the winning pass only to see it fall harmlessly to the ground.

The incompletion left Pitt's perfect season blemished with the tie and possibly hurt their shot at a national championship. While they had a difficult schedule that could vault them back into contention with victories the rest of the way, they would now need help in order to keep their hopes alive.

Game 6—October 29, 1932, at Pitt Stadium
University of Notre Dame Fighting Irish 0
University of Pittsburgh Panthers 12

The pieces of what was once a serious national championship appeared to be potentially crumbling for the University of Pittsburgh as the offense seemed to be deserting them as they began the difficult part of a difficult schedule. Against Army they struggled to score three touchdowns; then there was the scoreless tie versus Ohio State, an inferior team who kept Pitt out of the end zone despite the fact that the Panthers threatened on several occasions. The team was in desperate need to play an underdog where they could work on the issues they were having; instead they got one of the greatest programs in the country, one they had never beaten in the University of Notre Dame. The Fighting Irish had gone 4–0–1 in the five meetings versus Pittsburgh at this point, the only blemish being a scoreless tie in 1911.

Heartley "Hunk" Anderson was trying to lead his club back to national championship contention after two discouraging losses to USC and Army to end the 1931 campaign and seemed to be guiding his club in that direction. They had beaten the Haskell Indian Nations School from Kansas and Drake by a combined 135–0 before annihilating Pitt's brethren from the Steel City, Carnegie Tech, 42–0 in South Bend.

So dominant were the Irish that there were rumors Anderson would play his reserves to start the game, which would have been showing a lack of respect to Jock Sutherland and his squad. It was a rumor that Anderson vehemently denied when he said, "I will have the first team, all 11 men in there at kickoff."[3] The Pitt coach may have wished Anderson trotted out the second team, as the backfield of Ray Brancheau, Nick Lukats, George Melinkovich and Chuck Jaskwhich were enough to keep any coach concerned of not only preparing for the Irish but surviving them.

To make matters worse for the Panther hall-of-fame coach, George Shotwell, Bob Hogan and Izzy Weinstock had all been injured, and they were doubtful against Notre Dame. With Hogan still suffering from an injury that occurred in the Army game, Sutherland used sophomore Miller Munjas to start at quarterback while Tormey slid back into his starting spot at center for Shotwell, who had taken over for Tormey when the latter was hurt himself earlier in the year. While not injured, Reider appeared to have lost his spot at halfback to Mike Sebastian, who had been putting together a very productive campaign so far.

With the Panthers hurting, Notre Dame came into a jam-packed Pitt Stadium with 60,000 rabid fans looking on as a 3½-to-1 favorite to end any chance the Panthers had for a national title. From the outset, it looked like the Panthers had little chance to beat the Irish; it just had to hope that the defense found a way to stop the Irish offense from entering the end zone. In the first drive of the game, the Fighting Irish took the ball down to the Pitt 25 before they finally stopped Notre Dame in its tracks taking the ball over on downs.

As the first half unfolded, Pitt was unable to generate any semblance of a scoring threat, while the Irish did manufacture one of their own late in the second quarter, taking it as deep as the Panther 18 before once again being repelled by the bend-but-don't-break Pitt defense. The half ended with both offenses ineffective in a scoreless tie. The third quarter was much like the first two; the only significant circumstance was an injury to Munjas giving way to the also-injured Hogan to play the rest of the contest.

Entering the final period, the Panthers had gone eight quarters without scoring a touchdown since the game-winning score in the third quarter of the Army contest. With the Irish defense making the Pitt offense look inept, the hope of the Pittsburgh fans and alumni was that the Panther defense would continue to hold steady to secure at least a tie; it was at that point that everything changed.

Starting Sebastian turned out to be an incredible move by Sutherland when the junior took the ball at the Irish 46 and looked like he was about to get tackled around right end for no gain before busting through the line. It was at that point he eluded several Irish defenders as he reversed his field, eventually rambling into the end zone to break the Pitt scoreless streak and give the Panthers a hard-fought 6–0 advantage.

Before the exuberant fans had a chance to relax, the Pittsburgh defense put an end to Notre Dame's undefeated season when a pass by Al McGuff was picked off by Dailey at the 40. Dailey took the ball and raced in untouched to put the final touches on the dramatic 12–0 Pitt upset to the joy of the large throng at Pitt Stadium.

The loss devastated Anderson who said simply to the press, "I'm in a hurry, I've nothing to say."[4] Sutherland on the other end was unusually ecstatic over the surprising victory, gushing over his impenetrable defense, saying, "It was one of the finest defensive teams I've ever seen. Every boy played superb football and I'm certainly happy."[5]

It was the signature victory for the Panthers in 1932, who would go into a renewal of a former rivalry against Pennsylvania the next week with the knowledge that after a poor performance against Ohio State, they were now back in the conversation again as the best team in the country.

Game 7—November 5, 1932, at Franklin Field in Philadelphia, Pennsylvania

UNIVERSITY OF PITTSBURGH PANTHERS 19
UNIVERSITY OF PENNSYLVANIA QUAKERS 12

In a week where the country was about to elect Franklin Delano Roosevelt to his first term as president of the United States, two prominent Pennsylvania schools prepared to renew a rivalry that had been dormant for six seasons. As the University of Pittsburgh traveled to Philadelphia to play the University of Pennsylvania Quakers, it was the first time the two teams had met since a 14–0 Panther win in 1925. Between 1915 and 1925 the two teams met every season with the exception of 1924 with Pitt losing only once, a 6–0 defeat in 1923. As the two came into this matchup, they did so as two of the strongest squads in the east.

Pitt had one blemish, a scoreless tie against Ohio State, while the Quakers were undefeated. Coach Harvey Harman was looking to rebuild after they stumbled in 1931 with three losses in the final four games. Penn started out the 1932 campaign with five consecutive victories highlighted with wins against Dartmouth, Lehigh and Navy while yielding only two touchdowns in the process.

Harman had his team focused for this contest that potentially could vault the Quakers firmly into the national championship picture. He made sure his squad was informed of an early season report that the Panthers were considering this nothing more than a breather in the middle of a tough stretch in the schedule.[6] While Pitt had most likely a better backfield, they would be challenged by the fact that the middle of the defensive wall for Penn was among the best in the nation with Stan Sokolis, Roy Eugle and Harry Colehower not only charged with stopping the Panther inside rushing attack, but blowing holes through the Pittsburgh defensive wall on offense.

The gamblers had the game as a toss-up with the Panthers hoping to use the momentum they had gathered against the Irish to continue a streak that had not seen Pitt lose a game since being defeated by Notre Dame on October 24 the previous season. Sutherland's squad was relatively healthy as he decided to once again put Mike Sebastian into the starting lineup over Paul Reider at half back. He also gambled at quarterback where Bobby Hogan was not yet 100 percent, yet Sutherland called on Hogan, even though injured, feeling he would be his best option to begin the game.

Franklin Field was full for this contest as the largest college football crowd in the east in 1932, 70,000, was on hand to see if the Quakers were up to the challenge of remaining undefeated against their toughest foe of the campaign to this point. Statistically, Pitt dominated the contest but had trouble once again finding a way to put the ball in the end zone. Early on they easily drove to the Penn 10-yard line before a fumble by Sebastian put the Panthers at the 20 where the drive stalled. Sebastian turned it over on the Quaker 40 on the next possession as Pitt looked far from sharp. Finally as the first quarter was coming to an end and the second was beginning, Sebastian, Heller and Weinstock began slicing through the formidable Penn defensive line with Heller finally punching it in for the 7–0 lead.

Hogan picked off a pass from the Quakers' George Munger immediately after the touchdown as it looked like Pitt would quickly put away their opponents early on. Unfortunately Sebastian returned the favor, tossing an interception of his own. A 15-yard penalty on their next drive coupled with a blocked punt caused the Panthers to once again give the ball back to Penn deep in their own territory, which turned out to be a costly mistake for Pittsburgh.

Unable to get their offense back on track, Hogan punted a ball which Penn got a hand on, giving the Quakers the ball on the Pitt ten. It was their first true scoring opportunity of the game as Penn was only able to muster up one first down on the Panther defense to this point. Despite the fact Pitt had stopped Penn for a four-yard loss on the first play and had receiver Johnny

Powell covered by three players on the ensuing pass, somehow he incredibly snagged the pass for the touchdown. They missed the extra point but, in a game where their offense had been dominated, they were only down by one.

Sutherland was furious with his starters and sent in his reserves to start the second half as the game turned into a defensive struggle with each team surrendering two interceptions. Finally the reserves rewarded the Pitt coach for his faith. Backup fullback Harry Weisenbaugh pulled in a 46-yard pass to the Penn 14 and a few plays later dragged it in from five yards out to give the Panthers the 13–6 advantage.

Exchanging fumbles following the Pitt touchdown, the Panthers took over at the 50 as Sutherland sent his starters back in the contest. Invigorated, Heller and Sebastian ripped through the Quakers, taking it deep into Penn territory where the two combined on a touchdown pass, after a Pitt holding penalty, into the hands of Sebastian to give what the Panthers thought was an insurmountable 19–6 lead.

As Pitt proved against Army, good teams find ways to win, and the Quakers wanted to prove they were a good team. A spectacular 45-yard run after catching a pass from Penn's Don Kellett put the Quakers within seven. After taking over following a stalled Panther drive, Pennsylvania moved to the Panther 15 as time was running out. Fortunately for the 1,000 Pitt fans that made the cross-state trip to see their team, the Panther defense held, forcing an incomplete pass into the end zone as time ran out to give Pitt the close victory.

While Penn proved it would not be a breather for Pitt, it unfortunately could not prove it was a better team. It was a great win in preparation for a trip to Lincoln, Nebraska, to face the perennial Big Six Conference power from the University of Nebraska as the tie against the Buckeyes was now apparently forgotten by the Panther fans.

Game 8—November 12, 1932, at Memorial Stadium in Lincoln, Nebraska

UNIVERSITY OF PITTSBURGH PANTHERS   0
UNIVERSITY OF NEBRASKA CORNHUSKERS   0

With another Big Six title just about in their possession, Coach Dana X. Bible and his University of Nebraska Cornhuskers had their sights on finally doing something that they had been unable to do since a 10–0 victory in their first meeting in 1921: defeat the University of Pittsburgh Panthers in a football game. Except for the one-sided victory in 1931, it had been a bitterly fought close rivalry despite the fact that Pitt owned a 3–1–2 record against the Cornhuskers. Bible and his squad were quite upset with their performance at Pitt Stadium the year before that saw them lose 40–0 in a game that was probably worse than the score indicated.

They had rolled to a 4–1 early mark with their only defeat being a 7–6 heart-wrenching loss to perennial power Minnesota in their second contest of the season. They looked to use this game as a springboard to a memorable campaign as beating Pitt was one of the main objectives for Bible, the same as it had been in the past few seasons,.

One advantage the Nebraska coach did have other than the home field was the weather. It was a snowy, cold afternoon in Lincoln, and the field at Memorial Stadium was frozen. The conditions, along with the fact that Jock Sutherland felt his team was worn down by its difficult schedule, gave the Pitt coach reason for concern as his team came into the contest. He decided to start his second squad, at least in the first quarter, to guard against his team wearing down in the second half. It gave their captain Paul Reider a chance to start again at halfback, a position he lost to Mike Sebastian after getting hurt early in the season's opener and never was able to regain with the success Sebastian had.

He hoped somehow that his reserves could give him the same spark that they gave him in the third quarter of the Penn contest which hopefully would keep them in contention for the Rose Bowl bid that they were now a favorite to receive. Even though he probably should have been proud of how the team responded to the disappointing tie against Ohio State, Sutherland was trying to guard against overconfidence and was very short when a Nebraska reporter asked him about the potential of playing in Pasadena. "Don't forget we have a game with Nebraska tomorrow and another with Carnegie Tech next week and then comes Stanford," the irritated coach shot back. "And don't forget, too, that we've already played six major games. We are long overdue for the letdown that very seldom overlooks any team. It may hit us any Saturday from now on and when it does, we may not need to worry about that California stuff."[7]

Sutherland's rant proved prophetic as 20,000 frozen Nebraska faithful would witness what might have been that letdown the Panther coach was afraid of. Pitt had played some close games over the course of the season but generally by game's end were at least clearly the dominant team on the field statistically; that did not happen on this afternoon. It wasn't that Nebraska was overly dominant, but they had found a way to force holes in the Pittsburgh defensive line that only Army had figured out during the first seven contests of the season.

The Panther coach incorrectly guessed that the reserves would spark the club, with the Cornhuskers slightly outplaying them. Taking the ball to the Pitt three before being stopped on downs by a great fourth-down deflection by Warren Heller in the end zone and then missing a 31-yard field-goal attempt late in the half to keep the game scoreless which frustrated Bible and his squad as he knew they wouldn't get many more chances to score.

Pitt did have a couple of opportunities in the second half, moving to the Nebraska 11 before the drive ended and then another possession later in the game to the 26, where the Cornhuskers' Bernie Masterson picked off a pass to end a rally, but it would be all the offense could muster as Nebraska surprisingly outgained them 223–183 and had more first downs by a 14–9 count.

The game was unfortunately the letdown that down that Sutherland correctly predicted that does in fact inevitably come for every team. While at least they survived with their undefeated record intact, talk of a certain Rose Bowl bid would now end for the time being, at least until the experts saw how they could compete with Carnegie Tech and Stanford.

Game 9—November 19, 1932, at Pitt Stadium

CARNEGIE TECH TARTANS	0
UNIVERSITY OF PITTSBURGH PANTHERS	6

In a banner week for the city of Pittsburgh, where it was apparent that the state blue laws which prohibited, among other things, games from being played on Sunday would soon be repealed. The importance of that ruling was that it led Art Rooney to buy a professional football team that became the Steelers. More importantly, the fans also had the pleasure of celebrating football of the collegiate variety as Pitt and Carnegie Tech met in their annual clash at Pitt Stadium.

The matchup was not as anticipated as it had been in the past. It was the last city matchup for the legendary Walter Steffen, who while being rumored to be taking over the spot at the University at Chicago, had retired from Carnegie Tech following the season. Except for a 6–6 tie against Washington and Jefferson, they had an undistinguished season to this point, being crushed by the only major opponent they had played, losing to the same Notre Dame team Pitt had beaten earlier in the season, 42–0.

Despite that fact, they still owned a 3–1–2 mark and had a penchant to play the Panthers tough even though they rarely were the better squad. It had been homecoming week on the Tech campus and the team was inspired to end their season with a win against the more powerful University of Pittsburgh squad. Steffen and Waddell came into this game with their star halfback, Bill Spisak, out with a bad elbow and replaced by Tom Coulter, who had never started a game in his college career to that point. The injury would hamper the Tartans' attempt to capture the three city championship trophies from the city of Pittsburgh, the chamber of commerce and the Warner brothers, that were awarded to the winner of the matchup every season.

While Carnegie Tech was not at their best, Jock Sutherland was tinkering with his lineup in order to break the Panthers' offensive slump that they had been on since the shutout victory over Duquesne. Paul Reider again would start over Mike Sebastian, Miller Munjas was replacing Bobby Hogan, while he inserted Jon Meredith and Francis Seigel on the line for Tar Onder and Paul Cuba.

The moves Sutherland made unfortunately did not spark the club, as the malaise the Panther offense had been in continued this afternoon. While the game would be void of offense, the atmosphere was festive among the schools with the bands facing off in a musical battle as well as the enthusiastic student sections from both institutions taking their place in the massive but empty Pitt Stadium as a less-than-enthusiastic college football fan base in Pittsburgh stayed away from this contest, with only 15,000 showing up for the city championship.

Luckily for the Pitt fans, the defense was stellar, although in the first moments of the game they would have to be at the best to make up for a huge turnover by their offense. Advisory coach Steffen and his cohort Tom Wadell, who managed the squad during the week, stunned Sutherland by putting out his reserve line to start the game. Remarkably he then had the first chance to get on the scoreboard. After George Kavel started the game with a fine kickoff return to the Tartan 46, Carnegie Tech punted, pinning Pitt deep in their own territory. A fumbled snap gave the Tartans the ball at the Panther ten where they quickly took it to the five. The Pittsburgh defense held firm, taking over the ball and ending the threat. Reider took advantage of regaining his starting position once again and rambled for 29 yards on two runs to put the ball at the Tech 20 before Steffen and Wadell decided to end the experiment and put in their starting front line which stopped the Panther drive and kept the game scoreless.

Reider seemed to be the only effective runner for the Panthers early on, but unfortunately an aggressive tackle by the Tartans' Bunny Burzio severely hurt his knee, sending him out of the game and putting Sebastian back in the lineup. Sebastian seemed to spark the Panther offense for a while as they moved down to the Tartan 15, but once again, as in the past few games, they were unable to complete the drive, turning it back over to the Tartans.

The game was scoreless at the half as the third quarter started, with the Tartans having one last chance to end the tie. Kavel ripped off a run that looked like it was going the distance but was stopped on a fine tackle at the Pitt 34 which ended the last serious scoring threat in the game for Tech.

Offensively Pitt could do no better, but an opportunistic play on the Panther special teams gave Pittsburgh their best chance to pull the game out. Munjas ripped a long punt that skipped out of Dugger's hands. Panther sophomore Harvey Rooker fell on it at the three. For a moment it looked like the Tech defensive wall would once again thwart Pitt after Heller failed to get in the end zone on three runs, but just when it appeared as if a third scoreless tie was in the cards for the Panthers, Izzy Weinstock ripped through their line for a 6–0 lead. The extra point was blocked, but the six points were all Pitt needed, as an outstanding job of punting kept the Tartans stuck on their side of the field. What was once again supposed to be a one-sided game in the rivalry ended up a bitterly fought affair.

Waddell was upset, hoping that he and Steffen could win this final clash against Pitt that they would be on the sideline for, saying simply, "I'm sorry to lose a game that way, through the recovery of a fumble near our goal line, but I'm proud of those boys."[8] As usual Sutherland was conciliatory, claiming he was proud of his team and that "the Carnegie boys deserve much consideration for the type of ball they offered. They showed a remarkable line and a hard running back in Kavel. I'm certainly glad that game is over."[9]

For the Pitt coach, he perhaps wasn't as proud as he was claiming, knowing he almost lost a game he should have easily won. Somehow he would need to figure out his offensive woes quickly as the final game of the season would be the return of Pop Warner to Pittsburgh as he brought his Stanford squad to the Steel City to face his undefeated team.

Game 10—November 26, 1932, at Pitt Stadium

STANFORD UNIVERSITY CARDINAL   0
UNIVERSITY OF PITTSBURGH PANTHERS   7

As the University of Pittsburgh was coming to an end of its undefeated campaign in 1932, it was doing so in the most spectacular of ways, bringing back the original architect of the championship program that the school currently enjoyed. Glenn Scobey "Pop" Warner was bringing his Stanford club to Pittsburgh to face the Panthers for the first time since a controversial 7–0 victory over Pitt in the 1928 Rose Bowl. Since coming to Palo Alto he had never lost to a club from the east, and since this contest would mark the final game Warner would coach at Stanford, as he would take his seventh and final coaching job in 1933 at Temple University, he didn't intend to exit this contest on the wrong side of the score.

In Warner's return to play his final game at Stanford against his protégé Jock Sutherland, he would not bring one of his better teams. After winning three Pacific Coast Conference championships and a national title in nine years with the Cardinal, the team was on a downward spiral losing three hard-fought contests, combined with a scoreless tie in their annual battle versus Cal to come into this game at 6–3–1.

Despite the unusual slump, and the fact that he came into this contest as an underdog even though his club had never lost to an eastern squad, Warner had a highly talented team led by All-American guard Bill Corbus and tackle Henri LaBorde. They were the important parts of a fine line that opened holes for a backfield that included Ernie Caddell at half back and fullback Phil Baker, who also happened to be one of the best passers in the nation with 6'3" Don Colvin as one of his favorite targets.

It was a dangerous team for Sutherland and his squad to prepare for, especially with the fact that they had do without their captain Paul Reider, who wrestled his starting spot back from Mike Sebastian only to suffer a serious knee injury early in the Carnegie Tech game. It was a sad ending to the career of Reider, as the impressive senior class of him; Warren Heller; Ted Dailey; Joe Tormey; Paul Cuba; Johnny Luch, who had a very quiet senior campaign after a fine junior season; Francis Seigel; Mel Brown; Art Sekay; Rocco Cutri; and George Shindehuette were playing their final contest at Pitt Stadium.

The seniors would have to be at their best to beat Warner and his team, which was essential if they wanted to not only secure the eastern championship from undefeated Colgate, coached by Andy Kerr, who along with Sutherland also learned his craft from Warner as an assistant at Pitt, but also the Rose Bowl bid that went with it.

It was a sunny yet bitterly cold day at Pittsburgh for the intersectional contest that not only drew 35,000 patrons to the stadium, but an impressive array of football coaches that included Ohio's Don Peden; head coach of Minnesota who came at the half, Bernie Bierman; Harvey Harman of Penn; Tom Davies and Herb McCracken, of Rochester and Lafayette respectively, who were both former Pitt All-Americans; Geneva's Howard Harpster, the former Carnegie Tech All-American who was about to take over the program at his alma mater; George Gauthier of Ohio Wesleyan; and local coaches Duquesne's Elmer Layden as well as the Tartans' duo of Walter Steffen and Bob Waddell. Those in attendance were about to not only witness the student defeating the teacher, but him doing so in a dominant manner that was not indicative of the final score. While the defenses on both sides of the field prevailed in this contest, the Panthers were much more magnificent.

Early in the contest, Pitt quickly got on the scoreboard, which proved to be the only points they would need on this day. Taking advantage of the stiff wind that was blowing throughout the stadium, Bobby Hogan pinned the Cardinals deep in their territory with a 65-yard punt. Unable to move on the Panther defense, Stan Anderson muffed his punt, giving Pitt the ball at the Stanford 30. Sebastian and Izzy Weinstock took it to the 14 on two consecutive runs. Corbus, who had a fabulous day, stopped the Panther rushing attack on three consecutive plays before Heller found Dailey, who made a spectacular catch at the two for a first down. Two plays later on the frozen turf, Heller took the ball into the end zone for the game's lone touchdown. Weinstock connected on the extra point to give Pitt the 7–0 lead.

For over three quarters, Hogan kept Stanford in their territory with his spectacular punts, and the Panther defense completely shut down the Cardinal offense allowing no first downs until the fourth quarter when Warner's crew had their only threat of the game. Bill Sim faked a punt at his own 20, running to the 34 for the initial Stanford first down. Stan Anderson then found Gordon Campbell at the 45-yard line before Caddell took a pitch in the open field and looked as if he would ramble in for the tying touchdown, a score that certainly would have bounced the Panthers from Rose Bowl consideration. Luckily Pitt caught up to him at the 25, although it gave the Cardinals their third consecutive first down. Their season on the line, the Panthers bore down and threw Caddell for an 11-yard loss, eventually forcing Stanford to turn the ball over on downs and securing the undefeated season with the impressive victory.

Led by Weinstock's 66 yards and Heller's 64, Pitt outgained the Cardinals 175 to 60 (most of which came on their last-ditch fourth-quarter drive) and first downs 11 to 3. Davies was complementary toward his former teammate, saying "Jock Sutherland certainly has done a wonderful job this year in building the Pitt line. When one considers that he started the campaign with green line material, his work is realized as being all the more remarkable."[10] It was a win that not only kept them undefeated but threw them square in the Rose Bowl picture against the Pacific Coast champion USC Trojans.

Knowing it was down to most likely Colgate or Pitt getting the bid against the presumed western representative Southern California, the two coaches met at midfield for an exchange after the Panther victory. Kerr congratulated the hall-of-fame coach but let him know that even though he was happy for him, he thought Colgate would get the bid. "Congratulations Jock, but I'm taking my team to the coast." Always the sportsman, Sutherland responded by simply saying, "OK Andy if I don't go I'll be glad if you get it."[11]

Unfortunately for the program, it appeared that Colgate had the rumored spot next to the Trojans after their 21–0 win against Brown that ended their campaign 9–0–0, which more impressively saw them outscoring their opponents

264–0, the first eastern team to not allow a point since the Panthers in 1910. Reportedly the Trojans wanted to play Big Ten champion Michigan, but that matchup was unlikely as the conference was opposed to sending its teams to any post-season contest.

A few days after the Stanford victory, it was officially announced that the Trojans got the western bid to Pasadena, as everyone assumed, which reignited the rumors that the Wolverines would be the team of choice if they accepted the bid, which depended on the Big Ten relaxing their stance on post-season games. It was a stance by the conference that had held firm since Ohio State was beaten in the Rose Bowl 21–0 by Cal in 1921. Should the Big Ten deny Michigan, Pitt's advantage over Colgate would be their much tougher schedule during the campaign, although the reports coming out of Los Angeles before the selection were that Colgate was a firm second behind Michigan.

Luckily for Sutherland and his squad, USC and the Rose Bowl committee showed that newspaper reports weren't accurate as they decided that Pitt's impressive schedule, in which they emerged undefeated despite the fact they had two ties, was more impressive than the perfect season Colgate produced against a soft slate. Sutherland and Pitt were ecstatic as their club, which included two consensus All-Americans in Joe Skladany and Heller, who was a unanimous selection, knew that their season would last another game while Kerr and his Red Raiders of Colgate were highly disappointed at their perceived slight. Their athletic director William Reid said simply, "I'm sorry for our sake that we are not going out there."[12]

In the end, almost a month to the day after they were selected, Pitt's enthusiasm was washed away by the Trojans as it had been three years earlier. For the time being, though, the bid was a worthy reward, because while the Panthers may not have been as dominant as they had been in the past, they fought and found ways to win games that they easily might not have and deserved the trip to Pasadena.

National Champions selections made by modern-day analysts are noted "(retrospective)." Players rated as First Team All-Americans by a plurality of NCAA-recognized selectors are noted as "(consensus)." Players rated by all NCAA-recognized selectors are noted as "(unanimous)."

1932 Scores

Date	Opponent	Score	Record
9/24	Ohio Northern	47–0	1–0–0
10/1	@West Virginia	40–0	2–0–0
10/8	Duquesne	33–0	3–0–0

5. 1932: The Program Up and Running

Date	Opponent	Score	Record
10/15	@Army	18–13	4–0–0
10/22	Ohio State	0–0	4–0–1
10/29	Notre Dame	12–0	5–0–1
11/5	@Pennsylvania	19–12	6–0–1
11/12	@Nebraska	0–0	6–0–2
11/19	Carnegie Tech	6–0	7–0–2
11/26	Stanford	7–0	8–0–2
1/1	USC—Rose Bowl	0–35	8–1–2
		182–60	

Selected as First-Team All-Americans
Joe Skladany (consensus)
Warren Heller (unanimous)

6

1933 Rose Bowl: A Rematch Gone Bad

While the University of Pittsburgh had the prize it wanted, even if it was partly because the Big Ten Conference had a rule prohibiting its teams from post-season contests, which eliminated Michigan from Rose Bowl consideration, it would have its eye on an even bigger reward if things worked out on the regular season's final week. Despite the fact they had two scoreless ties to mar an otherwise spectacular campaign, the Panthers would have the opportunity to play for the mythical national championship against the University of Southern California Trojans in the 1933 Rose Bowl if USC could do their part by defeating Notre Dame in its final contest.

A victory by the Trojans would be easier said than done as the late Knute Rockne's last group of varsity players would play its final game in Los Angeles against Southern California. The Fighting Irish had a good season to this point, although not quite up to the campaigns turned in by the legendary coach before his untimely death almost two years earlier. With only a 12–0 loss at Pitt Stadium earlier in the season as the only blemish on their record, Notre Dame had run through their schedule with relative ease beating such powerhouse programs as Carnegie Tech, Army, Northwestern and Kansas, outscoring its opponents by a 255–18 margin.

The University of Southern California hoped to do their part in sending a second undefeated club to the Rose Bowl in what would then be a national championship clash. They had also run through their schedule in a one-sided manner giving up only 13 points in their eight victories, the last of which was their toughest contest in a hard-fought 9–6 win over Washington, a victory that secured the Pacific Coast Conference championship and a spot on January 2 in Pasadena.

Even though the Trojans were undefeated and playing the game at home in front of 100,000 fans at the Memorial Coliseum, a facility that also played host to the recently completed Summer Olympics, they were 10-to-7 underdogs against the Irish in this emotional clash for the Notre Dame seniors.

It was a rainy and unusually cold day in Los Angeles as the Trojans made this game a very forgettable one for the Irish seniors as they easily defeated Notre Dame 13–0. Sophomore quarterback Irvine Warburton handcuffed the Irish defense with not only his running, but his punt returns. Notre Dame threatened to come back with an aggressive passing attack in the fourth quarter, but there was just too little time left as the final Rockne-coached players walked off the drenched field slowly, while USC ran off knowing their chances for a national championship were still very much alive.

It was announced after the Trojan victory that the winner of the contest would be awarded the Rissman National Trophy, awarded by Chicago businessman Jack Rissman, as winners of the national title; the announcement also marked yet another controversy that has plagued college football throughout its history. The trophy had been given in the past to the winner of a mathematical point system that was originated by University of Illinois economics professor Paul Dickinson called the Dickinson System. Before the days of the coaches and writers polls, it was considered one of the most important recognitions of the national championship.

The conflict began when Rissman claimed the Dickinson award hinged on the Notre Dame–USC game; the professor did not agree and awarded his trophy prior to the Rose Bowl to Michigan. Rissman decided at that point to award his trophy to the Pitt–Southern California winner in 1932 and form an 11-man committee going forward for his national champion.

With a shot at the title and a first victory in the Rose Bowl in his sights, Coach Jock Sutherland quickly began to prepare his eastern champions not long after receiving the bid. Even though they had endured a very difficult, physical schedule to end the season, Sutherland's squad was fairly healthy, with only team captain Paul Reider on the sideline as his injured leg was in a cast.

Sutherland rewarded his squad for a job well done with new uniforms for the Rose Bowl and laid out a plan for the long trip west that he hoped would allow his squad to prepare properly. He decided the team would leave on Monday, December 20, and travel to Dallas, before a stop in Tucson, feeling that the trip south first would better help his team to adjust to the warm Southern California climate. Pitt would then arrive in Los Angeles on New Year's Eve for the game that would be played two days later on the second.

Before they would leave for the sunnier Pacific climate, the Panthers had to deal with the much colder unstable Western Pennsylvania one. They began their preparation at the Hunt Armory on campus as the unbearable cold made it difficult to practice outside. Even though they were under cover, the armory wasn't much warmer. Coupled with the fact that Joe Tormey and Izzy Weinstock were excused from practice with illness, Sutherland was not happy with his team's performance as they were not sharp with little time left before they left Pittsburgh. To make matters worse, especially with his team not practicing their best, the hall-of-fame Panther coach had to spend time away from his squad in the early part of December as he first traveled to see the annual Army-Navy game before taking off for Baltimore to take charge of the all–north squad in a college charity all-star game, leaving his assistant coaches to prepare the squad

Hoping to correct their issues before they began their travel, the varsity were scheduled to face a selection of Pitt alumni players at Pitt Stadium if the weather warmed up or at the armory if it remained frigid. The Panthers would play a tough collection of players who were some of Sutherland's greatest over the past few years. The group included Joe Donchess, Jess Quatse, Ray Montgomery, Gibby Welch and Toby Uansa. The alumni would have a playbook similar to USC's to help the varsity in their preparation.

The alumni game was their last chance to practice in Pittsburgh before they took off for the coast as the day after the contest the squad boarded a train just before midnight. They stopped in St. Louis before continuing their trip to Dallas where they would practice at Southern Methodist University. While they expected warmth in Dallas, they got an unusual cold spell in Texas as the club continued to play on the snow-covered fields with an inch of snow falling in the lone-star state. The team seemed weary of the cold and travel as they had their final scrimmage at Ownby Stadium with a curious crowd on hand to see the Panthers. Instead of snow, it was now rain and fog they dealt with as the temperatures had risen on their final day in Dallas.

Soon after the scrimmage, the tired squad got back on the train for Tucson, the city they would call home for ten days before leaving for their final destination. After 25 hours on the train, the team finally arrived in Arizona. Unfortunately they found out on arrival that their ten-day stay in Tucson might be cut short as USC requested their arrival in Pasadena to help promote the game as the ticket sales were less than stellar. If the weather was good, they were expecting only 65,000 in the 84,000-seat facility. The general feeling was that Colgate would have been a much more formidable and salable opponent than Pitt. There was also a fear that it would be another one-sided defeat as it had been in 1930, which also seemed to be keeping fans away.

Sutherland was terse as he exited the train. When asked if he thought this Pitt team was better than the last one to play in the Rose Bowl, he said simply, "You can't compare football teams."[1] The reporters then inquired about whether the practices would be open to the public, to which the Pitt coach shot back, "No. We want privacy and hope that we can get it."[2] Other members of the football staff pointed out that the passing game and the more formidable defense when compared to the 1929 squad gave the Panther squad an advantage this time. The other edge for Pittsburgh as the month was coming to an end was that Reider's leg seemed to be responding to treatment as the team was now as healthy as it had been all year.

While healthy, their good luck pertaining to weather was not on the Panthers' side, as yet another rare snowstorm in a warm climate descended on Tucson. Two inches of snow fell that were preceded by a cold rain, hampering Sutherland's preparation at the University of Arizona, which made the coach even more surly. He thought that the weather was hurting his squad and was considering heading to California early on his own to find suitable conditions.

The team had planned to watch the film of the Southern California–Notre Dame tilt to study the Trojans' tendencies. Afterward he was asked once again by the press about his chances against USC, and once again the frustrated coach ripped into them, saying, "We'll get beat worse than Notre Dame. Our Boys can stand some warmer weather as they are slightly overweight and there is a possibility that we may have to pack up and move on to Pasadena."[3]

Not pleased, the Panther coach took it out on his squad with an intense three-hour practice against USC plays. Joe Skladany was the lone casualty of the tough scrimmage, although luckily the injury was not serious. Sutherland appeared to be very unhappy with his defensive preparations.

With Pitt pushing its starters, USC hall-of-fame coach Howard Jones spent his time working with the reserves while his starters, which considerably outweighed the Panthers' first team, went through a light workout before breaking for Christmas. After the Christmas break Jones was concentrating on his rushing attack led by Gordon Clark and Homer Griffith, feeling that this would be the way to defeat the Panthers rather than through the air.

After a church service and a visit to a dude ranch, which picked up the players' spirits on Christmas Day, Sutherland continued to work the players hard. The practices were now becoming very spirited as the warmer weather was melting off the excess weight that Sutherland had been so concerned about. Instead of frustrated, the players' attitudes reportedly were now fierce and focused, which came as a relief to the Pitt coaching staff. Their legs, which had looked so tired before, were now seemingly fast and in shape.

Unfortunately, just as it looked like things were more positive for the

Jock Sutherland was a student of the great Pop Warner, garnering a first-team All-American mention as a guard in 1917. Never playing a game before entering a contest for the first time at Pitt, Sutherland learned well from his mentor, becoming a head coach for Lafayette where he led the Leopards to a national championship in 1921.

Panthers, three major players were hurt in the tough Sutherland practices as Paul Cuba had what was feared to be a serious leg injury while All-American Warren Heller and halfback Mike Sebastian also suffered injuries. Luckily for the Panthers, Cuba's injury was not serious enough to keep him out of the contest, but the fact that they had been banged up on the long trip to California made the Trojans heavy 12-point favorites as a $10 bet on USC would garner only a $7 return. Jones wanted to make sure his team was not overconfident, ripping into his squad and threatening those who believed the smaller Panthers would be a pushover.

The usually conciliatory Sutherland was not thrilled with the fact his squad was such an underdog and boasted, "I am satisfied with the condition of the entire team. The boys are ready for Southern California."[4] He soon caught himself being boastful and quipped, "I still say Southern California will lick us simply because it has a better club."[5] He may have just been trying to keep his team from overconfidence himself, but his claim unfortunately proved prophetic. Sutherland also decided that the game would be on the shoulders of his starting lineup as he planned to do less substituting, although he also felt that his starting Panthers' backfield, which consisted of Heller; Sebastian, who once again replaced Reider since Sutherland felt the team captain was not sufficiently recovered from his injury to start; Weinstock; and quarterback Bobby Hogan, might not be together in its entirety when it took the field for the opening kickoff on January 2.

Pitt finally arrived in Pasadena on New Year's Day as the organizers of the event blamed the university for being in Tucson rather than in Southern California promoting the game for the lackluster sales, which threatened to leave at least 10,000 seats empty. As the contest began the next day, it was apparent that those who felt this was not an attractive matchup would be correct.

The ticket sales did eventually perk up as football fans in Southern California showed up, with 83,000 patrons almost filling the Rose Bowl to see what would be a dominant performance by the hometown team. After the USC defense stopped Pitt's first drive at the Panther 28 following the opening kickoff, the bruising Trojan running attack took form as Griffith and Clark rambled down the middle of the field through the massive holes opened up by the Trojan offensive line. The ball stood at the Pitt 38 when USC showed off its passing game for one of the few times that afternoon. Griffith took the snap and heaved a long pass into the end zone to Ford Palmer who was covered tightly by Sebastian. Palmer leaped as high as he could and pulled in the pass right over a confused Sebastian to give USC the early 7–0 lead.

Following the early score, the remainder of the first period turned into a defensive struggle with the Panthers having the only real scoring opportunity. After Dailey secured a pass from Sebastian for a first down at their own 46, the Trojans were whistled for an interference call at the USC 35. With Pittsburgh moving down the field, Sebastian, not having his best game by any stretch of the imagination, fumbled the ball on the next play as Palmer fell on it, ending the hopeful drive.

Sutherland changed his earlier strategy of keeping his first team on the field for most of the game as he started to aggressively substitute when the second quarter began. Some of the new players seemed to spark the Panthers as they began their first sustained drive of the contest. Sebastian began it with a completion to the All-American Skladany at the Trojan 49. Two plays later Henry Weisenbaugh muscled through the line for a run up the middle to 23 before the drive sputtered as Heller tossed a pass over the end line giving the ball back to USC at the 20.

Two possessions later Griffith picked off a Heller pass as Warburton and Sparling made Pitt pay for the turnover, ripping through the Pitt line and taking it to the 33. Griffith then advanced the ball to the Panther 20 on two successive runs. With time running out in the half, Skladany made the defensive play of the half, tossing to Griffith for a 24-yard loss as time ran out with the Trojans still holding a precarious one-touchdown lead.

As the second half began, Pitt turnovers, which would crush them as the game went on, came to light once again when Griffith had his second interception of the day, picking off a pass from Heller at his 33-yard line and returned it 34 yards to the Panther 33. Raymond Sparling then continued his fabulous afternoon with first a 10-yard run to the 23 on a reverse before sprinting for nine more. Griffith took the ball to the four where the Panther defense stiffened and took over on downs, albeit for a very short period of time. Once again Sebastian fumbled the ball, which was recovered by Ray Brown who took it to the seven. Three plays later on fourth down, the Pitt defense could hold no more when Ken Bright found Griffith with a flat pass, with Griffith taking it in for a 14–0 lead.

What fading chance Pittsburgh had ended abruptly after a punt that ended the third quarter. With USC seemingly the fresher team at this point of the game, Warburton and Clark rambled through the tiring Panther defensive line, taking the ball from their own 34 to the Pitt 30. Warburton secured the handoff on the next play, and while Pitt was able to rip his shirt off, the Trojan back was not stopped until he reached the 15. After advancing the ball to the five, Pitt once again hoped to stop them as USC had the ball inches away from the line, with a fourth down coming up. Warburton ripped through the line, and all of a sudden it was an insurmountable 21–0 lead.

Rather than mount a stirring comeback, Weinstock fumbled the ensuing kickoff with Palmer picking it up at the 21. Warburton continued to impress the almost sell-out throng with an 11-yard run, then taking a pass from Clark where he rambled untouched through a defeated Panther defense for a 28–0 advantage.

Jones emptied his bench, but it didn't seem to matter as the Pitt starting squad continued to sputter. Following a quick, ineffective drive, the Trojans' Ward Browning blocked a Hogan punt as Southern California secured the ball at the five-yard line. Not long after the block, Richard Barber rambled up the middle to end the scoring for the day and give USC what was at the time the biggest victory in Rose Bowl history with a 35-point victory, breaking the record they set three years earlier against the same Panther squad.

As always Sutherland was a true sportsman at the end of the game, giving the Trojans their due. "It was a smart, aggressive and versatile team. It took advantage of the breaks," the coach stated. "The score was not a real indication of the strength of the two teams for intercepted passes and fumbles played a large part in the scoring spree. They had too much power for us at the guard and tackle positions."[6] An elated Jones said simply, "It was a glorious finish to a great season."[7]

While Pitt took advantage of the trip west by visiting a couple of movie studios after the game, they limped home to Pittsburgh soon after, secure in the knowledge that turnovers or not, they were an inferior squad to the national champion Trojans. Sutherland once again would dejectedly have to focus in the off-season to come up with a plan on how to recover after a third consecutive devastating Rose Bowl defeat and figure out how he could make another run at a national championship.

Box Score 1933 Rose Bowl

Team	1	2	3	4	F
Pittsburgh	0	0	0	0	0
Southern California	7	0	7	21	35

Category	Pitt	USC
Total Yards	193	278
Rushing	132	237
Passing	61	41
First Downs	9	22
Comp/Att/Int	4/11/2	2/4/0
Penalty Yards	15	20
Average Per Punt	32	34

LINEUP

Pitt	Pos	USC
Dailey	LE	Sparling
Cuba	LT	Brown
Hartwig	LG	Rosenberg
Tormey	C	Yonel
Onder	RG	Stevens
Walton	RT	Smith
Skladany	RE	Palmer
Hogan	QB	Griffith
Heller	LH	Erskine
Sebastian	RH	Bright
Weinstock	FB	Clark

7

1933: Close but No Championship

As the University of Pittsburgh football program went through nine excruciating months trying to piece together exactly why they failed so miserably in their national championship quest at the Rose Bowl in January, Coach Jock Sutherland and his squad finally had the opportunity to put it all behind them as they began anew with the beginning of the 1933 campaign. The season was highlighted by a schedule arguably more difficult than the one they just endured. While Pitt would go up against the same difficult intersectional rivals, such as Notre Dame and Nebraska, that they had over the previous few years, they made it increasingly more troublesome by adding national power Minnesota to the tilt.

There were many new faces that dotted the lineup as the varsity first team took the field in their annual scrimmage against the reserves. Generally in the previous few campaigns, the reserve unit showed just how deep Pitt was by not only giving the starters a solid game, but defeating them on a couple of occasions. On this rainy wet afternoon at Pitt Stadium, the second team was anything but competitive. Tailback Heinie Weisenbaugh, who had some impressive moments in 1932 and was hoping to impress the legendary Pitt coach, fumbled twice deep in his own territory which set up two scores by junior Mike Nicksick, running into the end zone each time on a double reverse. Sophomore Hub Randour and Mike Sebastian, who was struggling to secure a spot in the starting backfield, also scored for the varsity to give them a relatively easy 27–0 win.

Whether they could match the success of 1932 or not was questionable, but Pitt still was a talented team and was sure to put a strong team on the field as they prepared for their opening game of the season. At end, the team would feature Harvey Rooker and All-American Joe Skladany, who had been suffering with a painful bruised shoulder. If he was unable to go, Verne Baxter, a sophomore from Oliver High School, was having an outstanding pre-season and would be a worthy replacement. The line, as usual, was the strength of this Panther team as the veteran-laden squad was led by Frank Walton and John Meredeth at tackle, George Shotwell manning center and Tarciscio Onder and Charles Hartwig at guard. As impressive as that group was, any injuries they had would be very easily filled by Bob Hoel and Ken Ormiston.

In the backfield, Sutherland still had decisions to make, but while they may have had no stars, they did seem to have acceptable depth that would be essential with such a tough schedule. Senior Bobby Hogan was the quarterback of the team, with the capable Miller Munjas backing him up. Hogan was never considered to have the most natural talent at the position, but he did have the ability to not only spark the team when it needed it most, but to come through calmly in a crisis situation. The Scot had Howdy O'Dell, Mike Nicksick, Dick Matesic and Mike Sebastian all aggressively competing for the two spots at halfback while Izzy Weistock and Weisenbaugh were going head to head for the starting fullback position.

The squad was talented, but it was not facing an easy opponent as it began its 1933 slate, playing tradition rival Washington and Jefferson. The fans that were paying $6.60 to $26.95 for a season ticket to watch all the Pitt and Carnegie Tech home games at Pitt Stadium would get to see early on whether or not Sutherland had the forces to bring a championship to the Steel City.

Game 1—September 30, 1933, at Pitt Stadium

WASHINGTON AND JEFFERSON COLLEGE PRESIDENTS   0
UNIVERSITY OF PITTSBURGH PANTHERS   9

The 1933 opener at Pitt Stadium would not match the University of Pittsburgh against a low-end minor collegiate football squad that would face the Panthers for the sole purpose of seeing how many yards the third team could muster against an inferior opponent. For Coach Jock Sutherland and the young Panthers, they would play one of their most intense local rivals, the Presidents from Washington and Jefferson College. While Pitt played five local rivals at any given time during this time period, Carnegie Tech, Duquesne, West Virginia, Penn State and W & J, the one against the Presidents was the closest by far. The game in 1933 was the 31st in the rivalry, and it would be the one that broke the tie as the two schools battled to a 14–14–2 mark in the first 30 contests.

Washington and Jefferson had a huge early advantage, capturing eight of the first nine games, but during the Jock Sutherland era, Pitt was 3–1–2. The two schools hadn't played since a 21–0 Panther shutout in 1929, and Coach Hank Day hoped that his veteran squad would surprise the powerful Panthers in this contest. Day had several experienced players on the field, but unfortunately academic ineligibility kept many of their better players off the gridiron for this affair. They had an effective backfield led by quarterback Don Holland, but with the talented veteran Pitt defensive wall in front of them, the Presidents' only hope for victory was if the defense found a way to halt the Pittsburgh offensive attack.

For this contest, the Pitt coach chose to go with his experienced first team to start this campaign, with Nicksick replacing graduated All-American Warren Heller. With the Presidents missing several players due to academic ineligibility and Pitt featuring one of the best 11 in the nation, this contest had all the makings of a mismatch. When rivals such as this get together on the field of play, oftentimes talent differences are negated by inspired play, and on this late-summer afternoon in front of 15,000 surprised fans, that's exactly what happened as the President defense certainly rose to the occasion. It was a contest where the Panthers thoroughly dominated their opponents, outgaining Washington and Jefferson 297 to 147 yards while doubling the Presidents in first downs 16 to 8, but somehow in this game stats meant nothing as the underdogs had many opportunities to emerge victorious.

Early on it looked like Pitt was going to run away with an easy win as they drove down the field on a long drive as the first quarter was coming to an end. After W & J had a possession halted in Pitt territory, the Panthers took over on its own 20-yard line. Sebastian, who was coming off a less-than-stellar Rose Bowl performance, ripped a 31-yard run to put the ball in the Presidents' territory. The only thing that kept the Pitt back out of the end zone was a clutch tackle by Wilson. A few plays later they stood at their opponents' 30 before the W & J defense finally held firm.

Not being able to finish drives is something that had plagued the Panthers since a 19–12 win against Penn the previous season. After the impressive victory, the Pitt offense was limited to only two touchdowns in the final four games of the season and looked like this would be a repeat performance.

Confident, Sutherland started the second quarter by inserting his second squad into the contest and let them try to go for it on fourth down from the 41. Unfortunately Rich Matesic missed on a pass to Robert Timmons and Washington and Jefferson took over on downs. Unable to move from there, the Presidents gave the ball back to Pitt at their 31, which ironically would set up W & J's first scoring opportunity. Weisenbaugh fumbled running around left end which was recovered by Rittersbaugh. The Pitt defense held firm, but Day decided to send out his field-goal squad to see if he could break the ice. Unfortunately Hardy's 31-yard attempt fell short and the game remained scoreless.

After taking the ball to begin the second half, the Presidents pinned Pitt at their own one-yard line on a punt hoping to set up yet another scoring opportunity. Not able to advance the ball out of trouble, Hogan kicked a masterful punt that sent Washington and Jefferson back to its own 24 that seemed to give the Panther defense breathing room. Pitt took the ball once again a few plays later before turnovers would hurt them once more. Halfback Herb Randour fumbled at his own 45, and the Presidents quickly took it to the 11-yard line. Hardy once again attempted a field goal, this one from 20 yards away, and luckily for the Panthers it went wide as the game went into the fourth quarter still scoreless.

As Pitt kept pushing into Washington and Jefferson territory only to come up empty-handed, with about five minutes remaining in the contest, it looked like this game would end up a very disappointing scoreless tie. At that point arguably the team's best player, Skladany, made the play of the game, picking off a lateral at the W & J three. Unfortunately Sebastian gave the ball back on a fumble. Not able to move the ball, W & J punted back to Pitt as the Panther offense took over with time running down. Thanks to a 31-yard completion by reserves Matesic to O'Dell taking it to the Presidents' nine, Sutherland hoped his team would pull this contest out. While they were kept out of the end zone once again, Weinstock finally put the Panthers on the board with under four minutes left with a field goal to give Pitt a 3–0 advantage.

Having one last chance, W & J moved to the 45 before a Weinstock interception all but ended the game. If the interception didn't finish the Presidents, moments later an O'Dell 45-yard touchdown run did, letting the Panthers escape with a hard-fought 9–0 victory.

Even though they were victorious, the game ended with more question about this University of Pittsburgh team than it had answered. With a tough schedule in front of them, those questions would need to be answered sooner rather than later if Pitt had hopes of staying competitive for the any championships.

Game 2—October 7, 1933, at Mountaineer Stadium in Morgantown, West Virginia

| UNIVERSITY OF PITTSBURGH PANTHERS | 21 |
| WEST VIRGINIA UNIVERSITY MOUNTAINEERS | 0 |

When the administration at West Virginia University hired Earle "Greasy" Neale to replace Rat Rodgers before the 1931 campaign, they had envisioned an ascension to the upper echelon of college football, competing for national championships year in and year out just as the University of Pittsburgh had since hiring Pop Warner to lead their program.

The dreams that the Mountaineer faithful had for a championship future never came to fruition. What started out so promising for Neale ended up mired in mediocrity. Things worsened as they began the 1933 campaign. They were held to a scoreless tie by an underdog Washington and Lee squad and then were soundly defeated by Duquesne University the following week 19–7. The only player of note was starting tackle Joe Stydahar, the future 11-year NFL vet and head coach for the Rams and Cardinals, as they prepared to face the powerful University of Pittsburgh. While the situation looked dire for the Mountaineers, Pitt Coach Jock Sutherland was concerned about his own offense that was awful in the opener against Washington and Jefferson. He knew if they didn't become more productive, Neale and his squad could provide the Panthers a much more difficult game than anyone would expect.

Whether because of injury or just a lack of productivity the week before, Sutherland had four starting spots open before the WVU contest. As he contemplated the potential changes from a hotel in Uniontown, where the team stayed the day before the contest, the Panther coach knew at least his team was relatively healthy. The only player that was unable to make the trip was Bobby Timmons, a backup at end who was suffering from an infection in his leg which necessitated him to be admitted to the hospital.

The first position he would look to possibly replace was at end where the starter, Harvey Rooker, was questionable with an injury. Reserve Verne Baxter would be the potential starter if Rooker couldn't go. The other three positions up for grabs were more out of competition than injury. Junior Frank Kutz was pushing senior guard Tar Onder for play time while sophomore Nick Kliskey seemed to impress the coach in practice more than incumbent George Shotwell had. While changes at the aforementioned three positions were not certain, one that seemed to be was at left halfback. Burgettstown's Mike Nicksick had a less-than-stellar performance against W & J and looked to give way to either sophomore Hube Randour or senior Howdy O'Dell to join Mike Sebastian and Izzy Weinstock in the Pitt backfield.

As the team pulled into the Morgantown Country Club hours before the 2:30 kickoff to relax before the game, Sutherland decided to in fact make changes at three positions, with Baxter, O'Dell and Kliskey getting the nods and only the veteran Onder holding on to his starting spot. Onder would get the opportunity to play across from his brother Angelo, who was the starting end for the Mountaineers.

After the Panther defense thwarted the West Virginia offense following the opening kickoff, it looked as if the offensive ills of the past two games would come to light again. Pitt easily moved through the Mountaineers' defensive line to the WVU three. Sebastian took the ball hoping to give Pittsburgh the early lead. Instead of the game's opening score, Sebastian put the ball on the ground with a fumble. Just as West Virginia was about to pounce on the loose ball in the end zone, John Meredith secured it to give the Panthers the early 7–0 lead.

As the first quarter was coming to an end, it looked like the Pitt early advantage would be short-lived when a clutch special team play by West Virginia set them up for what appeared to be an easy score. With Pitt stuck on their 15, Bobby Hogan went back to punt. Senior Romeo McDonald broke in and blocked the punt, then recovered it on the Panther two. While Neale and his squad were excited to be in position to score, they unfortunately were up against one of the toughest defensive units in the country. Onder and Frank Walton overpowered the West Virginia offensive wall and kept the Mountaineers out of the end zone to preserve the 7–0 lead. Early in the second quarter Neale's team once again threatened to score, moving the ball to the Pittsburgh 25 as the Pitt second team struggled, with Sutherland giving his starters a break. They were unable to move it any further as the half ended with the Panther advantage still intact.

WVU had another opportunity to tie the contest on the kickoff to begin the second half, returning it to the 40, but the impenetrable Pitt defense was once again up to the task, stopping the Mountaineers in their tracks and taking the ball back on a punt. Wanting to make the score more comfortable, the Panther backs ripped through West Virginia advancing to the Mountaineer side of the field. After Sebastian tossed a perfect pass to O'Dell at the 17, the two then took turns running the ball to the 10. At that point O'Dell powered through two defenders, taking a third across the goal line to increase the Pitt lead to 14 points. Refusing to give up, the Mountaineers once again took the ball into the Panthers' territory before being halted at the 41 and sending a punt into the end zone.

It was at that point that Pittsburgh all but ended any chance West Virginia had of making this a more competitive contest. With the ball at the 20, reserve halfback Heinie Weisenbaugh took the handoff toward Rooker's end of the field. With the Panther end in front of him, Rooker threw a devastating block at the Mountaineers' Eck Allen, leading the way for Weisenbaugh to saunter into the end zone untouched for the 80-yard dash and a 21–0 lead for Pitt. Neither team was able to cross the goal line the rest of the contest as Pitt returned home with yet another impressive win in the 1933 version of the Backyard Brawl.

For Sutherland, it allowed the stench of the opening contest to be forgotten; for his counterpart, it was the beginning of the end for his tenure in Morgantown. WVU would drop five of their first eight games, tying the three others before winning their final three contests of the season to end 1933 with a disappointing 3–5–3 mark.

The three-game winning streak was not enough to save his job as he was replaced by Charles "Trusty" Tallman following the season. It in effect ended his college head-coaching career as Neale became the backfield coach for Yale over the next seven seasons. Luckily for the hall of famer, his career would take an upswing when he was named the head coach of the Philadelphia Eagles in 1941, leading them to the franchise's first two league championships in 1948 and 1949.

While his coaching career in Philadelphia would help garner a spot for him in Canton, as far as his Backyard Brawl record went, it was not the highlight of his career as he lost all three contests to Sutherland by a combined 95–0 score.

Game 3—October 14, 1933, at Pitt Stadium
UNITED STATES NAVAL ACADEMY MIDSHIPMEN 6
UNIVERSITY OF PITTSBURGH PANTHERS   34

While Navy has been the dominant service academy team in the early part of the 21st century, in the 1930s it was their bitter rivals from the US Military Academy that constantly contended for national honors while the Midshipmen were mediocre at best. Head coach Edgar "Rip" Miller, a member of the famed "Seven Mules" linemen on the legendary 1924 Notre Dame squad, became a very treasured figure in Navy football history. While he was successful first as an assistant coach, then as an administrator in the athletic department, his three-year tenure as head coach was anything but memorable.

Given the post in 1931, Miller's teams were a disappointing 7–11–2 in his first two campaigns, losing both times to Army by a combined 37–7. Losing twice in a one-sided manner to the Cadets is usually a death knell to a Navy coach, but in 1933 Miller would get one last chance to show he could beat their rivals. The Midshipmen began the season with a fine 2–0 start as they prepared to meet the University of Pittsburgh. They had defeated both William and Mary and Mercer in their first two contests, but traveling to the Steel City to face the Panthers would be a much bigger test than their first two opponents gave them.

Despite the fact that many of the experts were calling Pitt the Navy's toughest opponent to this point, one so-called expert gave the Midshipmen the respect as a difficult opponent themselves: Coach Jock Sutherland himself. In an article where he was asked to predict the outcome of the game, the Pitt coach stated that "despite the tendency to make our Pitt boys the favorites, this will be anybody's game. Navy has the best team since 1922 and has not yet had to expose a single card in its hand."[1]

It was certainly a sentiment held by many, including *Pittsburgh Press* sports editor Chester Smith who seemingly understood the talent that this Navy team possessed as the Midshipmen made their first visit to Pitt Stadium since 1916. Smith felt that "save for a brief respite when Centre College comes here in November, the fun is over for Pitt's football team. It ends officially at 2 o'clock this afternoon in the stadium when the kickoff will send the Panthers down the field against Navy."[2]

After two games against less-than-stellar opponents, the Navy contest would begin a stretch that would also see them travel to perennial national powerhouses Minnesota and Notre Dame following this contest. Sutherland hoped that his team would not look ahead to those two games and would focus properly on the task at hand.

The Midshipmen had a dangerous passing attack led by Walter Baumberger, Gordon Chung-Hoon as well as ends Fred Borries and the captain of the team, Hugh Murray. It would be the passing game that Miller hoped would be enough to keep Navy in the game, as he realized that trying to run through the difficult Panther front defensive wall would be impossible.

For Sutherland, he kept the same front line he had used against West Virginia that included center Nick Kliskey, who would be making his second consecutive start over former starter George Shotwell. In the backfield, while he wasn't as efficient a blocker as Nick Nicksick and Hub Randour, Howard O'Dell got the nod to join Weinstock and Sebastian in the starting backfield with what Sutherland felt were superior running skills. The Panthers, as it turned out, did not look ahead to the difficult games in the next two weeks; they had their efforts squarely focused on the team in front of them. Smith put it succinctly when he led off his story on the contest by saying, "A sailor man may have a sweetheart in every port but Pitt had something better—a kick in every play—as the Navy discovered yesterday at the stadium."[3]

A large crowd of 45,000 turned out on this gorgeous October afternoon to see the offensive fireworks that Pitt would display. It didn't start out as a rout for Pittsburgh as Navy held them to a scoreless first quarter. Stuck at their own 13 as the second quarter began, Sebastian started the onslaught when he launched a long pass that found its way into the arms of O'Dell at the Midshipmen's 30-yard line. O'Dell took the ball to the 23 before Weinstock rambled through the middle in the end zone five plays later to give the Panthers an early 7–0 advantage.

While the game eventually turned out to be one-sided, it appeared as the half was ending that Navy was about to tie the score thanks to a fumble by Sebastian which Chung-Hoon recovered. The Midshipman drove to the Pitt eight-yard line where the Panther defense bore down and kept Navy scoreless as the half came to an end.

What chance the Midshipmen had ended quickly in the third quarter after Pitt took the ball over on their first possession of the second half. The now aggressive Panther running attack ripped holes through the Navy defensive line taking the ball to the 30-yard line; Henry Weisenbaugh ran through the wide open gap the Panther line opened for him at that point to give Pitt a 14-point advantage.

After a series of interception by both clubs, Bobby Hogan picked off a pass by Baumberger returning it to the Midshipmen 45. Pitt easily took it to the 19 where O'Dell finished the job rambling past the left side of the Navy line to make it 21–0. Moments later Pitt took a four-touchdown lead as Weisenbaugh picked off a pass from Bolton Rankin and sprinted over the goal line from 40 yards out for a 27–0 lead.

Early in the fourth, Leon Shedlosky bolted in from a foot-out, set up by a 27-yard Randour run to increase the Panthers to a 34-point advantage. Hawaiian-born Chung-Hoon ended the Panthers' string of 11 straight shutout quarters with a seven-yard scamper, finishing the scoring at 34–6. Even though their shutout streak was now over, it came at the hands of the Pitt reserves as, all told, 35 players, a large amount for the time, took the field for Pittsburgh that afternoon.

While the offense was impressive, the defense was the more dominant aspect of the team, holding Navy to 66 total yards and one first down for the contest. It was a thoroughly impressive performance that Sutherland and his program needed before they went into their two-game road trip that would determine whether the Panthers were national championship contenders or just a very good team.

Game 4—October 21, 1933, at Memorial Stadium in Minneapolis, Minnesota

UNIVERSITY OF PITTSBURGH PANTHERS   3
UNIVERSITY OF MINNESOTA GOLDEN GOPHERS   7

To witness the moment when an average program turns into a dynasty in college football is rare. After all, dynasties are not a common occurrence; that's what makes them so special. In the case of the University of Minnesota, they had had some fine moments in the short history of their program, including a 6–0–2 Big Ten co-championship in 1927, but they were rarely mentioned as national championship contenders. As the 1930s began, future hall-of-fame coach Herbert "Fritz" Crisler began his head-coaching career at Minnesota and took the Golden Gophers to a 7–3–0 record in 1931 before leaving for first Princeton and then his more famous tenure at the University of Michigan. When Crisler left, he turned the program over to a man who had been both a basketball and a football coach at Montana, Mississippi State and Tulane, where after mediocre seasons at the former two schools and the first two seasons at Tulane, he led the Green Wave to three Southern Conference championships and a Rose Bowl berth in 1932. That man's name was Bernard W. "Bernie" Bierman.

During his first season with Minnesota in 1932, the Golden Gophers were mired in the bottom half of the Big Ten standings. That coupled with the first three contests a year later, a win against South Dakota State and two consecutive ties versus Indiana and Purdue, not only gave no indication that Bierman was about to embark on the hall-of-fame portion of his career but certainly made Bierman wonder why he left the comforts of New Orleans for the frigid climate of Minneapolis. Bierman was playing one of the country's greatest teams in the fourth contest of the year for the Gophers, Jock Sutherland and the University of Pittsburgh, and while he may not have known it at the time, it was the moment when Minnesota went from an afterthought to a dynasty.

Sutherland himself had no idea this was to be a potential game-changing moment for his opponent; he was just trying to find the right mix to turn his 17-game regular-season unbeaten streak into an 18-game one. He may not have known what was coming, but the *Pittsburgh Press*'s Chester Smith certainly may have. "There was the up and coming Minnesota team bent on proving its ties with Indiana and Purdue were a mistake and that football they play in the Western Conference is good enough to trim the best the East can offer."[4]

The Panther hall-of-fame coach wanted to try and make sure that a team from the midwest understood just how dominant teams from the east were.

Sutherland was concerned with how his quarterback controlled the offense against Navy despite the 34-point output and decided that Miller Munjas would be a better option to start. On the line he feared that incumbent John Meredith was not strong enough to keep the young sophomore-laden defense out of the Pitt backfield, so he inserted Bob Hoel into the starting line for the first time since the Army contest in the fourth week of the 1932 campaign.

In the backfield, Sutherland was thankful for his incredible depth as one of his most dependable performers, Izzy Weinstock, was suffering from an injured leg and wasn't going to be able to take the field against the Golden Gophers. Luckily for Pitt they had Henry Weisenbaugh, who had some of the most exciting touchdown runs early on in 1933, to replace him.

Even though they hoped to be effective offensively, they really needed to make sure the usually stout Pitt defense was playing at their highest level as they would face one of the best young fullbacks in the nation in sophomore Sheldon Beise who was complemented by halfbacks junior Francis Lund and sophomore Julius Alfonse. The youthful Gophers had never hosted a top team from the east, and while they tied their last two opponents, they had outplayed them statistically and hoped that they would be able to get a better result on what turned out to be a windy, bitterly cold day in Minnesota.

It had rained heavily the night before this contest, but the weather, while cold, was at least dry for kickoff. Early on in the contest, the Golden Gophers made a statement that the Panthers would be in for a long day. In the first quarter, to the surprise of the visitors, Minnesota dominated the early play, taking the ball down to the Pitt 14. Many times over the past three games, their opponents had put themselves into scoring position only to be turned all but one time, that being a late irrelevant touchdown by Navy against the Pittsburgh reserve defense. On this occasion the Panthers would give up their first score with their starting squad in the game when Lund tossed a shovel pass to Robert Tenner, who rambled behind his huge line, finding an opening on the right sidelines, and went into the end zone, putting Pitt behind for the first time in 1933, 7–0.

It was at that point the Panthers took control of the game, only to be rebuffed by the two factors that hampered the offense all season, turnovers and incomplete drives. Pittsburgh immediately took the ensuing kickoff, and Sebastian, Weisenbaugh and O'Dell took turns advancing the ball 47 yards downfield to the 20. A tackle of Sebastian in the backfield then a close yet incomplete pass from O'Dell to Sebastian as the ball slipped through the latter's hands kept Pitt off the board.

As the first half went on, Pitt continued to have an advantage statistically, with Weisenbaugh even picking off a pass by Lund to end a Gopher drive.

Despite their continued threats, interceptions by Luch and sophomore Vernal LeVoir kept Pittsburgh off the board. Finally as the second quarter was nearing an end, the Panthers embarked on another drive. O'Dell hit Harvey Rooker with a pass in the strong wind as the end ran the ball to the Gophers' 21. Weinstock, who after originally being ruled out of the contest hobbled onto the field in the second quarter, was given the ball on the next few plays and took it to the five. While it seemed apparent that Pitt would tie the contest, errors once again came to the forefront when a bad snap, that O'Dell luckily pounced on, pushed the Panthers back to the 13. Unable to get in the end zone, Weinstock kicked a field goal that cut the Minnesota lead to four.

With time running out in the half, Pittsburgh almost took the lead, but a 30-yard pass from Dick Matesic to Munjas was short of a touchdown as the gun sounded to end the half with the young Gophers on their heels, hoping they could survive and maintain the lead with 30 minutes left in the game.

The 30,000 frozen fans in Memorial Stadium feared a similar trouncing in the second half as the Panthers had done the week before to the Midshipmen, but it never materialized. Lund took the second half's opening kickoff 60 yards deep in Pitt territory. While the Pittsburgh defense held firm, except for two drives to their own 45, one ending with an interception and one called back on a penalty, the Pitt offense was at a standstill, constantly stuck deep on their side of the field for the entire half without anything close to a scoring threat. Minnesota held on for the close victory that not only vaulted them into the the national championship conversation but was a springboard, as they used the momentum from the win to tie for the conference championship, finishing with an undefeated 4–0–4 mark.

The victory gave this young club the confidence it needed to be a memorable collegiate football dynasty that saw them not only win seven Big Ten titles but three consecutive national championships in the following three seasons. For Pitt, it was another disappointing loss that would cost them a title in 1933. Traveling to Notre Dame the next week, Sutherland had to protect against another defeat that could completely unravel the season that looked so promising.

Game 5—October 28, 1933, at Notre Dame Stadium in South Bend, Indiana

UNIVERSITY OF PITTSBURGH PANTHERS   14
UNIVERSITY OF NOTRE DAME FIGHTING IRISH 0

It had been over two years since the legendary Knute Rockne was tragically killed in a plane crash in an Iowa field and the third season Heartley

"Hunk" Anderson had tried valiantly to replace him. As the years went on, rather than make his own mark on one of the most famous collegiate football programs in the country, his inability to keep the team at the high level the alumni had come to expect proved two things: Rockne was one of the greatest coaches the game had ever known, and Anderson was no Rockne. After going undefeated in his first seven games as the coach of the Fighting Irish in 1931, Notre Dame fell to USC and Army in their final two contests to finish 6–2–1. They followed that up with a 7–2 mark in 1932 that included a 12–0 loss at Pitt Stadium. So far in the third campaign of Anderson's tenure at the school, things were looking dire. A 12–2 victory over Indiana was sandwiched between an opening-day scoreless tie to Kansas at home and a 7–0 loss at Pitt Stadium against Carnegie Tech, a contest that was more one-sided in the Tartans' favor than the score indicated, leaving Notre Dame with an uncharacteristic 1–1–1 mark. Coupled with the Panthers' upset loss to Minnesota the week before, this matchup, which usually had national championship implications, was nothing more than a game to see which program would still have a faint chance at championship honors and which would be uncharacteristically finishing out the season with no hope whatsoever.

Following the pathetic offensive performance against Pitt's neighbors in Oakland, Carnegie Tech, Anderson put his hopes at quarterback on an untested sophomore, Tony Mazziotti, who had relatively little experience coming into this contest but was considered an efficient passer. On top of Mazziotti, the Notre Dame coach added five more sophomores into the Fighting Irish lineup, including end Wayne Miller, tackle Ken Stilley and 235-pound fullback Don Elser, who appeared to be a poor pass defender that might allow Sutherland to take advantage. Anderson knew the players he was adding wouldn't have much experience, but he felt it was necessary. "Our line has lacked drive and we are sacrificing experience to get it," the Irish coach stated.[5]

As the Irish mixed up their lineup, Anderson's counterpart, Pitt Coach Jock Sutherland, certainly had to solve some issues of his own, namely a potentially effective offense who was its own worst enemy early on with turnovers and uncharacteristic stalled drives. One of Sutherland's biggest disappointments had been senior halfback Mike Sebastian. Depending on his experience and talent to lead his squad, Sebastian had begun a penchant for fumbling at the Rose Bowl the year before and had continued to drop the ball through the first four contests in 1933. Sebastian's continual problems had prompted the Panther coach to insert Dick Matesic into the starting lineup at Sebastian's right-halfback spot. Sutherland would have one other issue he would need to make a decision on, whether or not Kliskey was healthy enough to start at center. If the injury would not allow him to go, George Shotwell would be ready to take over. One move on the line that he went with was to give John Meredith his starting spot back at left tackle as Meredith, who lost his starting nod to Bobby Hoel in the Minnesota contest, had an impressive week of practice. The real opportunity in the game would be for Sebastian. When Sutherland would give him the opportunity to play giving Matesic a rest, he would have to prove that he was dependable; Sebastian would do that and more.

Wanting to prove the loss to Minnesota was a fluke, Pitt started out by dominating this game from the outset, although they were unable to score in the first quarter. O'Dell and Matesic continuously ran through the Irish defensive wall, taking it to the Notre Dame 28 on their first series. As had been the case so many times that season, the Panthers turned the ball over on the next play when senior Nick Lukats picked off a Matesic pass. Two possesions later, Pittsburgh had great field position after they pounced on a Mazziotti-fumbled punt return, taking over at the 19. Before too long, after several runs by Matesic and Izzy Weinstock brought the ball to the two, the Irish intercepted another pass, this time by Rocco Schiralli.

Pitt had completely dominated the contest, yet like the week before they had nothing to show for it. Could another heartbreaking loss be on the horizon? Enter Mike Sebastian. After Henry Weisenbaugh picked off a pass of his own at the Pitt 16, Sutherland brought in his fumble-happy star. Sebastian took the ball to the 22 before Weisenbaugh ran for two more to set up a third-and-two. Sebastian took the handoff, ripping through the center of the line. The senior almost tripped over Notre Dame's Ray Brancheau, who later broke his ribs during the contest, which would have ended the play before it began, but Sebastian stayed upright and went downfield, he had Weisenbaugh on one end and O'Dell on the other forming a convoy that took him 76 yards for the touchdown and a 7–0 lead.

The spectacular run put the Fighting Irish on their heels as Pitt wasn't done yet in the second quarter. After a couple of gains on the ensuing kickoff, Lukats went back looking for Wayne Millner. O'Dell stepped in front of the toss and took it to the Notre Dame 38. An invigorated Sebastian snatched an O'Dell toss for 19 yards before Weisenbaugh rambled for 17 more to the two. On the next play, Weisenbaugh muscled through the staunch Irish defensive wall into the end zone for a 14–0 lead. The play deflated Notre Dame and their 25,000 loyal fans who were in the stands on that cold day. The Irish hardly put up a fight the rest of the game, only producing one meaningful drive in the second half when they moved the ball to the Pitt eight before losing it once again on an interception. So dominant were the Panthers in this game that they outgained the Irish 251 to 97 and 13 to 7 in first downs.

The loss was the beginning of the end for the Hunk Anderson era at

South Bend. Notre Dame lost three of the next four games, scoring only seven points in the process. They did muster up a season-ending upset of Army 13–12, but even with the win, the 3–5–1 record was too much to save Anderson's job. For Jock Sutherland it was an impressive victory, one where he seemingly got through to his senior halfback. "I explained to Mike early in the week and again shortly before the game why I wasn't going to start him," the Pitt coached said following the game. "As I sent the varsity onto the field I turned around and saw Mike, and right then I felt sure he was ready to go."[6]

Jock, of course, was correct; Sebastian was ready to go, rambling for 117 yards on 14 carries, leading his team to a victory that put them back on course for yet another run at the national title.

Game 6—November 4, 1933, at Pitt Stadium

CENTRE COLLEGE COLONELS 0
UNIVERSITY OF PITTSBURGH PANTHERS 37

Centre College is a small Presbyterian-related school located in the quaint city of Danville, Kentucky. Founded in 1819, the liberal arts college still exists today and houses over 1,600 students. It's not the kind of place that one would ever associate with major college football, but in 1933 the Colonels found their way to Pitt Stadium to provide what most experts felt was the only so-called breather in the difficult schedule that the University of Pittsburgh endured that season. While today it would be remarkable to see such a small school compete against a national power, in the early part of the 20th century it wasn't rare at all. In fact the Prayin' Colonels, as they were referred to back then, not only played bigger schools, but had their temporary run of fame in the colligate football world. In 1919 they traveled to Charleston, West Virginia, to play the Mountaineers of West Virginia and stunned their hosts 14–6. Five years later they were named champions of the south with a memorable run of victories against Alabama, Tennessee, Kentucky and Georgia in successive weeks.

Even though they still had successful teams, they no longer were competitive among the elite of college football. Their coach, Eddie Kubale, who was a star of that memorable 1924 squad, wanted to use this contest to shake up one of the sports elite programs and put Centre College back in the headlines. Kubale thought that three of his younger players, Barksdale, a 175-pound end; Marks at tackle; and Bartlett at halfback, all sophomores, would give him a better chance to compete against the larger, faster Panthers.

The Prayin' Colonels were 3–2 coming into this game, a record that included an impressive 30–0 shutout victory against Louisville and two narrow defeats, 6–0 to Boston College and 7–6 versus Furman. They had a respected passing attack which they hoped would test the Pitt secondary. Even though they were competitive, the lineup changes that were intended to make them faster also made them lighter, and few gave them a chance to challenge Pittsburgh.

For Pitt, as Coach Jock Sutherland had in the past against apparently undermanned opponents, he had to decide whether to give his starters the nod in the contest, or rest them and see what his reserves would do. In practice during the week, since he had been so impressed with Miller Munjas at quarterback against Notre Dame, he continued to give him the majority of the time with the first team. The only other area of concern was at center where Nick Kliskey was still troubled by an injured shoulder, giving George Shotwell the spot at center. It had only been two weeks earlier that Sutherland felt that Shotwell's less-than-stellar play was hurting his offense and had put Kliskey in the starting lineup. When Kliskey went down with an injury in the Minnesota game, Shotwell took advantage of his opportunity, having one of the best games of his career against the Fighting Irish.

Eventually Sutherland decided on resting 8 of his 11 first-team players, keeping only Izzy Weinstock, Tar Onder and Shotwell in the starting lineup. It was Boy Scout day at Pitt Stadium, as all scouts in the Western Pennsylvania area would be permitted to attend the game free of charge, although what they witnessed in the first quarter gave them reason to wonder if it was worth the effort.

Pitt's reserves gave a halfhearted effort in the opening frame as the Colonels kept the game scoreless for the first 15 minutes. They even had a few opportunities to threaten themselves, but several dropped passes kept Centre from providing more of a scare to the favorited home team. The Colonels did have the best chance to score in the first quarter, getting the ball at the Panther 32 after a poor Hogan punt, then driving to 15 where Barksdale missed on his field-goal attempt to keep the game scoreless. Finally, after a period of ineptitude, Sutherland put starters back in the game, which turned this close affair into the slaughter that most expected.

Bartlett returned the favor for Centre with a bad punt of his own that went out of bounds at his own 39. A 17-yard pass from O'Dell to Skladany highlighted a touchdown drive that culminated with a three-yard scamper by O'Dell, who fumbled the ball into the end zone where Meredith jumped on it to give Pitt a 6–0 lead. Moments later, Onder picked off a pass, returning it to his opponents' 28. After moving to the 15, Weisenbaugh faked a reverse to O'Dell which opened up a gaping hole that Weisenbaugh sauntered into untouched for the score that put the Panthers up by 13 at the half.

Early in the second half Pitt quickly went up by three touchdowns as they had their first sustained drive of the game. Taking the ball at their own 19, Hub Randour ran the ball twice for 26 yards before Dick Matesic found Sebastian on a 30-yard pass setting up a 20-yard jaunt by Nicksick giving Pittsburgh a 19–0 advantage. At this point Centre College was reeling and the Panthers were about to put the game out of reach. With his reserves in, Sutherland's squad went to the air on their next drive. A pair of 11-yard completions set Pitt up deep in the Colonels' territory where Matesic barreled in with a short run to increase the lead to 25 points.

With game out of hand at that point, Matesic found Nicksick for a 40-yard touchdown pass, the final 30 on a fine run by the Panther halfback. Sutherland emptied his bench at that point, and with the back end of the bench in the game, Wilkins, a third-team center, picked off a pass returning it to the seven, where Rector eventually took it in to put the finishing touches on a 37–0 shellacking. So dominant were the Panthers, running for 326 yards, they garnered 529 total yards versus the Prayin' Colonels' 99. It was the tonic Sutherland and his boys needed as they began a three-game tough stretch to end the season, two of the contests against their city rivals.

Game 7—November 11, 1933, at Pitt Stadium

| DUQUESNE UNIVERSITY DUKES | 0 |
| UNIVERSITY OF PITTSBURGH PANTHERS | 7 |

One of the most prevalent streets in Pittsburgh is Forbes Avenue. Named after the famous Brigadier General John Forbes, who led an expedition to overtake Fort Duquesne during the French and Indian War, Forbes Avenue covers approximately a 10-mile stretch from the downtown area of the city to the Oakland section.

Start at 600 Forbes Avenue and you'll find Duquesne University, the largest Catholic University in Pennsylvania, founded in 1878. About three and a half miles further is 6000 Forbes Avenue, the home of Carnegie Mellon University, one of the top academic research institutes in the country established by Andrew Carnegie in 1900. In between is a university that was chartered in 1787 called the Pittsburgh Academy. Later it became the Western University of Pennsylvania before being renamed in 1908 to what it is more famously referred to as today: the University of Pittsburgh.

During the mid–1930s, that 3.53-mile stretch of Forbes Avenue was nirvana to college football fans as each institute fielded one of the best college football teams in the land. While Pitt was one among the elite in the country, Duquesne University checked in with a 52–18–1 mark in a seven-year stretch between 1933 and 1939. They won the 1933 Festival of Palms Game (a precursor to the Orange Bowl) and the 1937 Orange Bowl in a thrilling 13–12 victory against Mississippi State, and were ranked 14th in the nation in 1936 and 10th in 1939. Carnegie Tech struggled a bit more than their Forbes Avenue neighbors during those seven seasons with a 24–31–4 mark, but nonetheless had a magical campaign in 1938. During that special season they not only beat both of their city rivals, but almost upset the eventual national champion TCU Horned Frogs in the Sugar Bowl, finishing the year ranked 6th, two places ahead of the Panthers.

It was 1933 at this point when this three-teamed Pittsburgh rivalry really took hold as the Dukes head coach Elmer Layden finally was able to take the program into the major college level and get the respect of his Steel City brethren. After taking over in 1927, Layden's squad hit a bump in the road in 1931 with a 3–5–3 record, but rebounded at 7–2–1 the following year. The momentum they garnered in 1932 spilled over to 1933, as the team was dominant in their first eight games coming into the Pitt game, winning each one by a combined 147–20 margin. They had beaten two common opponents of Pitt, West Virginia and Washington and Jefferson, in the process.

Pittsburgh was doused with a constant heavy rain during the week as the field crew at Pitt Stadium used a tarp in hopes of keeping the field as dry as possible for the contest. Cold weather was a possibility for the game, which meant that if there was precipitation, the rain threatened to become snow. A wet field would be more apt to hamper the Duquesne offensive attack, which featured speed and an effective passing game.

The practice field on the bluff was a quagmire, but Layden kept his squad working hard in their most important game of the season. The Duquesne coach had two decisions to make for his starting lineup, at quarterback and guard. After practice he decided to insert Joe Cutrona over Frank DeCoster at quarterback and Harry Weinberg at tackle for George Kakasic. By the time Pitt began their final practice of the week, which was just about the time the Dukes were finishing, the rain had in fact turned over to snow as the heavy winds helped produce what was described as close to blizzard-type conditions. Nonetheless Sutherland wanted to make sure his team was completely ready, so the Panthers continued to practice in the horrendous conditions.

Luckily by game time, while the weather would be less than stellar, the tarp had kept the field in decent condition. A crowd of 50,000 to 60,000 was expected in what would be the largest of the year at the stadium. The two clubs would not only invite the members of the Veterans of Foreign War to witness the contest, but would entertain the huge crowd with a game between young middle school teams from Shadyside and Arnold. It was a festive atmosphere which unfortunately looked like it would be the last between the two schools, at least for a couple of years. The contract called for games to be played through 1934, but Pitt had a chance to add USC to their slate at Pitt Stadium and chose to drop the Dukes rather than Westminster. When asked, the Panther athletic director W. Don Harrison explained that he made the move because the Dukes had become so successful and they needed an easy game to break up what promised to be a brutal schedule, which is why they opted to keep the small Western Pennsylvania school instead. If this was the last game they would play against each other for the foreseeable future, Layden and his team wanted to show the Panthers who was the best team in Pittsburgh. While the high majority of experts felt that Pitt would show Duquesne it was them, the strong Duquesne club wanted nothing more than to show the experts they were wrong.

The game-time climate was as bad as both clubs feared, with a tough, stiff wind and a downpour that lasted almost a half hour and then turned to sleet as the temperatures became colder. The poor conditions did not deter the 60,000 excited fans who were treated to a physical, tough contest. Unfortunately for the Dukes' offense, they were going up against one of the most impressive defenses in the country as they were held to a mere 87 yards and one first down. Duquesne never moved any closer to the end zone than the Panther 22-yard line, although they had the only true scoring opportunity of the first half when Armand Niccolai barely missed a 43-yard field goal.

As impenetrable as the Pitt stop troops were, the Dukes were almost their equals in the first half, keeping the game scoreless at the end of the first half. As close as the game was at that point, the powerful Panther rushing attack would take control of the contest in the third quarter. Three times Pitt looked like they were going to score, and each time their neighbors found a way to keep them off the board. The first drive saw O'Dell hit Skladany for a 20-yard gain to the Dukes' 30. After a penalty which negated a 15-yard pass from Matesic to Skladany, Duquesne held firm, stopping the Panthers in their tracks. Immediately afterward, halfback Art Strutt fumbled the ball, which was recovered by the soon-to-be two-time-All-American Skladany, giving Pitt the ball at the 26. The Panthers ripped through the Duke offensive line on several runs as they stood at the six, close to taking the lead, but once again Layden's troops were able to keep Pitt out of the end zone, and remarkably, despite their dominance, the Panthers still were scoreless. Finally a poor punt by the Dukes' Zaninelli gave them one last opportunity. After once again failing to score, Izzy Weinstock lined up for a field goal that hoped to give the Panthers the points to get them the victory on this blustery day. His attempt failed as it looked like somehow Duquesne would escape with a tie.

Getting the ball back a fourth time, Pitt would not let the opportunity go awry again. After another poor Dukes punt, O'Dell connected with Matesic who rambled to the Duquesne 17. After three runs by Weinstock and Matesic that put the ball at the seven, the Dukes' defense could hold no more as the Panther line opened a huge hole that Weinstock danced through untouched to the goal line, which allowed Pitt to finally take a well-deserved 7–0 lead.

With the field worsening, Duquesne could muster up no other threats as the Panthers held on for the close victory. A dejected Layden went across the field to shake hands first with Skladany, then as he was about to congratulate Sutherland, the Panther coach stopped by to admonish one of the referees, which delayed the post-game handshake until the two met in the locker room.

While the two schools would eventually decide to renew the series again in 1936, it would be the last contest in which Layden and Sutherland would face each other as Steel City rivals. The next time the two would meet on the gridiron was in 1934. At that point his success at Duquesne coupled with the demise of his alma mater led the former Dukes coach to accept the job at Notre Dame. Layden would exact revenge in 1935 when the Irish defeated the Panthers 9–6.

For the time being, though, Duquesne's undefeated run had ended at the hands of Pitt, who continued their faint hopes for a championship with a contest against the difficult Cornhuskers of Nebraska.

Game 8—November 18, 1933, at Pitt Stadium

UNIVERSITY OF NEBRASKA CORNHUSKERS 0
UNIVERSITY OF PITTSBURGH PANTHERS 6

Since coming to the University of Nebraska in 1929, coach Dana X. Bible had wonderful success, capturing three Big Six Conference championships and usually was considered one of the Midwest's elite programs each year in his tenure. There were few disappointments that came out of the program during his era, except for the fact that he had never beaten Coach Jock Sutherland and the University of Pittsburgh.

The high-water mark for Bible against Pitt was two scoreless ties in 1930 and 1932. The scoreless ties were wrapped around a 12–7 defeat in 1929 and a 40–0 shellacking two years later. So inept had they been offensively against Pitt that it had been three years since they scored a touchdown against them. Even though they had been ineffective against Pitt, Bible's Cornhuskers in 1933 were perhaps the best squad he had to date. They had won their first six games in relatively easy fashion and had all but captured yet another conference championship. A victory over the Panthers would certainly put Nebraska squarely in the forefront as favorites for the national championship.

It was a powerful team led by a deep line that included ends Bruce Kilbourne; Lee Penney, who was out against Pitt after suffering a broken shoulder the week before; and John Roby; guards Warren DeBus and Clair Bishop; tackles Gail O'Brien, Walt Pflum, and Russ Thompson; and centers Franklin Meier and Elmer Hubka. The talented group was impressive, opening holes for a backfield that included Bernie Masterson, George Sauer, Hubert Boswell Jack Miller and Bud Parsons. This group helped Nebraska outscore their first six opponents by a combined 109–7 margin. Bible knew that a victory would open up many exciting options for the Huskers. "We have too much at stake today and next Saturday against Iowa to even think of the Tournament of Roses or the Chicago National Championship game. If we get by Pitt today and Iowa next week, we'll have plenty of time to consider any invitations that may come to us for post-season games."[7]

The matchup, along with the Minnesota–Michigan tilt, was considered the premiere contest of the week, one that had piqued the interest of Chicago publisher John W. Murray, who had come up with the idea of staging a national championship game at Soldier Field in Chicago on December 9. Murray came to Pitt Stadium for this contest with the thought of making the winner one of the favorites to receive one of the bids.

Before their loss to the Panthers the week before, Duquesne had been almost assured one of the spots had they defeated Pitt. "We were in strong favor of Duquesne as one of the teams," Murray conceded. "Our committee had watched them closely and had decided to issue the initiation if the Layden team had gone through unbeaten."[8] While the Dukes were now the top contender to face Miami (FL) in the Battle of the Palms in Miami, a precursor to the Orange Bowl, and not being considered for the Chicago contest, the winner of this game became a serious contender for the matchup in the Windy City.

The importance of this game was not lost on the Panthers' hall-of-fame coach. Sutherland understood that his team would have to give a great effort to win this game and was considered an underdog. "While I am hoping for a Pitt victory, I fully realize it would be an upset. Nebraska can't be anything but a favorite in this game."[9] With everything that was on the line for the Cornhuskers, it was equally important for the Panthers, who would have an outside for a Rose Bowl spot along with the national championship contest.

Sutherland had a few decisions in his starting lineup before the contest. He kept George Shotwell at center, who was playing well now after a questionable first half of the year, while also inserting Mike Sebastian, who was injured in the first half of the Duquesne game and didn't practice during the week, at halfback and Bob Timmons, who was considered a more effective receiver, at end for Harvey Rooker.

As had been the case for much of the season, the Panther attack went up and down the field, but more times than not they were unable to come up with the score that would have made a close game a more comfortable lead that the statistics dictated it should. Pitt completely controlled the game from the beginning, outgaining their guests 354 to 125, including a 276-to-50 advantage on the ground, but was unable to win the game until the final quarter.

Actually, Pitt could have begun the victory parade with the first half coming to an end if not for an incredible miscalculation by the referees. After coming close in the first quarter when Skladany just missed a pass in the end zone, Sebastian, who had been knocked out three times only to refuse to leave the game, helped lead the Panthers from the Nebraska 27 to just outside the 2 when the officials brought out the chain to see if it was a first down. The ball was a half yard short as the officials signaled for the Nebraska offense to come on the field. The problem was that it should have been the fourth down, giving Pitt one more shot with 50 seconds left in the half. The mistake was not corrected, and the two teams exited the field mired in a scoreless tie.

In the second half, the Panthers once again took the ball to the Huskers' two on the strength of three pass completions, but once again the Nebraska defense toughened stopping O'Dell for no gain and Hogan to one yard after a short completion to keep Pitt scoreless. The following series after halting the Cornhuskers, the Panthers once again had a great opportunity, but a field-goal attempt from Izzy Weinstock sailed wide to keep Nebraska's hopes of at least a tie alive

Finally in the last period when a 30-yard sprint from reserve halfback Heinie Weisenbaugh put them inside the Nebraska ten one last time, Pitt finally was able to complete a drive. After two more runs by Weisenbaugh and one by Leon Shedlosky, Pitt stood at the two with a fourth down and the opportunities for a victory waning. Forsaking the field-goal attempt, Shedlosky took the snap and sent a pass to Mike Nicksick, who snagged it for the score that finally put the Panthers in front 6–0. Weinstock's point after was blocked, but the disappointing crowd of 20,000 were still invigorated by the touchdown.

Seeing their national championship season wilting away, Nebraska made one last push for victory, completing three passes to advance to the Pitt 45. Fortunately for their opponents an interception by Miller Munjas ended the Huskers' final attempt for victory. While Pitt made one more threat following a 22-yard run by Shedlosky, the two teams would score no more, with the Panthers holding on to the exciting 6–0 victory.

As it turned out, neither team was invited to a post-season game, but the loss crushed the Nebraska championship hopes as they finished second to Michigan in the year-end Dickinson statistical rankings, one of the most respected national championship barometers during the time period.

Game 9—November 30, 1933, at Pitt Stadium

| CARNEGIE TECH TARTANS | 0 |
| UNIVERSITY OF PITTSBURGH PANTHERS | 16 |

Perhaps the greatest player who ever stepped on the gridiron for Carnegie Tech's longtime coach Walter Steffen was quarterback Howard Harpster. Harpster, who remains one of the, if not the, greatest player ever to strap on a uniform for the Tartans, had a football intelligence equal to none as a player. In probably the seminal game of the program's history against a heavily favored Notre Dame Fighting Irish squad coached by the great Knute Rockne in 1928, Harpster called a quarterback sneak on a third-and-15 that went for 35 yards in the one-sided 27–7 upset of the Irish. That play along with many others during that memorable campaign helped him become not only a first-team All-American but initiated his election to the Collegiate Hall of Fame in 1956.

After his brilliant football career, the hall of famer took over the program at Geneva College in nearby Beaver Falls. Harpster was a huge success at the small campus leading the Golden Tornadoes to an impressive 22–6–2 mark in three seasons. When Steffen resigned following the 1932 campaign, it was only natural that his alma mater would choose him to continue the success that Steffen had enjoyed for 19 seasons.

As Thanksgiving Day approached, the day when he would lead his team on the field at Pitt Stadium for his first encounter with his neighbors, the Tartans were having a fine season. The squad stood at 4–2–2, losing only to national power Purdue 17–7 and NYU 7–0, while holding Michigan State to a scoreless tie and defeating the same team from South Bend 7–0 at Pitt Stadium, which he led to such an impressive victory as a player. So impressive was his defense that except for the two losses, they kept their other six opponents scoreless.

Former Pitt captain Luby DiMeolo, who at the time was the line coach for NYU, told his alma mater that the Tech line was the best he had seen since the 1928 Panther squad that allowed only 15 points. With the thought that he was facing perhaps the stiffest test of the year for his offense, Sutherland decide that he would insert the man they called the "Flying Dutchman," Heinie

Weisenbaugh, to fullback, replacing Izzy Weinstock. Weisenbaugh had led the Panthers in scoring to this point and had some of the most spectacular runs during the season. While probably not as physical as Weinstock and not his equal blocking, Weisenbaugh gave the Panthers a dangerous triple threat out of the backfield with Mike Sebastian and Howdy O'Dell.

For Carnegie Tech, as successful as Harpster had been in his first season at his alma mater, he knew the Panthers were the toughest team he was facing during the season and wanted to make sure he was putting his most effective team on the field. He decided to put sophomores Steve Trbovich at center, Bill Spisak at quarterback and Steve Terebus at left halfback in the starting lineup for the contest. Each playing in their first year of varsity, Terebus looked to be the best of the trio as the experts considered him not only an exceptional passer but a strong physical runner, which the Carnegie Tech coach hoped would lead his squad over the next two seasons.

The tough Tartan front wall were confident they could keep the Panthers from cracking the scoreboard. They insisted that if Pitt was to be successful offensively, it would have to be through the air; the seniors on the Pitt club had other ideas. For Bob Timmons, Frank Walton, Bobby Hogan, Joe Skladany, Tar Onder, O'Dell and Sebastian, it was the last time they would take the field at Pitt Stadium, and they wanted to make sure the anticipated 40,000 fans on hand that day would remember just which team was the national power.

After winning the city championships for four straight seasons, Pitt made sure early on that Carnegie Tech knew they were correct and incorrect at the same time. Pitt would in fact beat them by air, but they would also beat them on the ground and with their special teams. In short, the Panthers dominated them every way they could. The Tartans had their only two serious scoring threats in the first quarter. Bunny Burzio blocked a Hogan punt five minutes into the contest, taking over at the Panther 17. The Pitt defense held and Tech missed a field goal wide right from 27 yards out. The next series, the fumbles that had plagued Sebastian all season came to light again when he turned it over at the 29. Once again the Panthers forced a field-goal attempt, this one from 42 yards out. The ball barely reached the goal line as the game remained scoreless. It was at this point that Pitt inserted their dominance.

They began to get physical and sent two of the Tartans' best players back to the locker room as Lib Lewis fractured his finger and Burzio, who had been suffering during the campaign with broken ribs, reinjured them and could not go on. After a couple more series, Pitt was the beneficiary of a poor punt as the Panthers took over at the Tartan 45. Weisenbaugh made Sutherland look like a genius for making him a starter, rolling over the supposed Carnegie Tech impenetrable line for runs of none, 7 and 17 yards to set his team up 12 yards from pay dirt. Three plays later from the nine, O'Dell found Hogan at the two, where the Pitt quarterback barreled into the Tartans' Angie Bevevino and rambled into the end zone to give the Panthers the 7–0 lead.

The seven-point advantage held up through the remainder of the first half as the defense started the second half by continuing to frustrate Harpster's offense. After Walton cost the Panthers a scoring opportunity early in the third period with a holding call, he more than made up for it defensively on the next series. With the ball at the ten, Spisak took the handoff and tried to pick up ground around his left end. Walton ripped through the line and took down the Tech quarterback in his own end zone for a safety to increase the Pitt lead to nine.

Wanting to make up for his own mistake, Spisak continually busted through the Panther defense, which also included what was described as a brilliant run of 25 yards, in hopes of cutting the Pittsburgh lead and giving Carnegie Tech an opportunity to win its first city championship since 1928. Unfortunately for the Tartans, the benched Weinstock wanted to show his worth and picked off an errant Bevevino pass at the 40 and brought it back to the Tech 19. Weinstock wasn't done and reeled off an 11-yard run. After an offside call against the Tartans, the senior fullback muscled through that Carnegie Tech line for the final score of the game and the season for Pitt, giving the Panthers an impressive 16–0 victory.

As Pitt waited to see if the big victory would lead to any opportunity for them to play in the post-season, the All-American selections began to roll in as Skladany was named to his second consecutive first-team selection while Walton, Sebastian and Weinstock all were given honorable-mention honors. The Panthers were still alive for the Rose Bowl spot as the opponent of Stanford University, who was representing the west. Rumors had it that the three finalists for the spot were Pitt, Nebraska and Alabama, with Columbia and Princeton having an outside shot. Michigan was considered as one of the top teams in the country and would be a natural choice to face Stanford as they had been selected national champions by the Dickinson ratings, but the Big Ten still prohibited their teams from playing in the post-season, so luckily for the rest of the group they were not an option.

Unfortunately for Pitt, the underdog Lions of Columbia somehow were the team that the Cardinals selected for them to meet in Pasadena, passing over the more established programs that were deemed as being a more difficult test for them. Their former coach Pop Warner, who was now with Temple, was perplexed by the decision, claiming, "If they are looking for a real team to go to the Rose Bowl, pick Pitt or Nebraska."[10]

As it turned out, Pitt was considered a formidable foe for Stanford, but their poor performances in past Rose Bowls seemed to be the deciding factor in them not being chosen. An unnamed correspondent from the West Coast explained that "Pitt, though unbeaten in the east and stopped only by Minnesota, is out of the picture. The Panthers have lost too often in Pasadena."[11]

Despite the fact that they were without a post-season spot, whether deserved or not, Pitt enjoyed a fine season that saw them ranked fourth in the Dickinson poll. It would be a precursor for what would be a memorable championship season in 1934, even though it would be a title that nine decades later would turn out to be a very controversial one.

*National Champions selections made by modern-day analysts are noted "(retrospective)." Players rated as **First Team All-Americans** by a plurality of NCAA-recognized selectors are noted as "(consensus)." Players rated by all NCAA-recognized selectors are noted as "(unanimous)."*

1933 Scores

Date	Opponent	Score	Record
9/30	Washington and Jefferson	9–0	1–0–0
10/7	@West Virginia	21–0	2–0–0
10/14	Navy	34–6	3–0–0
10/21	@Minnesota	3–7	3–1–0
10/28	@Notre Dame	14–0	4–1–0
11/4	Centre	37–0	5–1–0
11/11	Duquesne	7–0	6–1–0
11/18	Nebraska	6–0	7–1–0
11/30	Carnegie Tech	16–0	8–1–0
		147–13	

Selected as National Champions by:
Bob Kirlin Ratings (retrospective)*

Not Recognized as Official National Championship Selector by University of Pittsburgh.

Selected as First-Team All-American
Joe Skladany (consensus)

8

1934: A Forgotten Title

It's not that the University of Pittsburgh Panthers in 1934 didn't deserve to be recognized as the school's sixth national championship squad. After all, they came through one of the most difficult schedules in the nation with only one defeat, a 13–7 loss to the Minnesota Golden Gophers, as they finally solved whatever offensive issues they had suffered over the previous two seasons winning eight very one-sided games in that tough slate. Pitt had the stars and the performances to be recognized as champions; the only problem with the recognized national champions during the pre–Associated Press poll era was that most were recognized years later, as were the first six Panther champions.

In the late summer of 1967, in the wake of the bitter controversy over whether or not Michigan State or Notre Dame should have been named champions (they both claimed the title), the legendary Dan Jenkins and *Sports Illustrated* magazine decided to set the record straight as far as which teams could rightfully lay claim to the various championships in the history of the sport.

In the early part of the 20th century, there were many people and organizations that proclaimed a national champion, not unlike the numerous computer polls in today's game. The difference was that precious few sports fans really put much stock in them. Jenkins, in his always entertaining style, put it best when he said, "Somebody like Casper Whitney in *Harper's Weekly* or J. Parmly Paret in *Outing* looked at the records of Yale, Harvard, Princeton and Penn, quickly deciphered which one had out-groped Columbia Law School by the biggest margin, and boldly proclaimed them the mythical national champion. Nobody argued about it, preoccupied as most people were with striking for an eight-hour work day and wondering where Khartoum was. Nobody even cared. You told a man that your school was No. 1 some 80 years ago and all he said was, 'that's swell but, excuse me, I got to go invent the airplane.'"[1]

By 1967, after Ara Parsheghian sat on the ball to preserve a 10–10 tie against the second-ranked Spartans of Michigan State to secure his portion of the national title, people most definitely cared. *Sports Illustrated* researched every possible champion there was between 1924 and 1966, and low and behold banners were raised at hundreds of colleges throughout the nation proclaiming their championships.

At the University of Pittsburgh, thanks to football historian Parke Davis and the research *Sports Illustrated* did uncovering his list of champions that was published first in the 1934 *Spalding Football Guide*, they were able to proudly raise the banners in 1915, 1916, 1918, 1929, 1931 and 1934, with all but 1916 and 1918 coming specifically from Davis's ratings. While the first five titles were undisputed, the championship in 1934 is the one that came into question.

The university claims that it relies on the article for its national championships, saying in its media guide that *Sports Illustrated* "researched the first and only complete and wholly accurate list ever compiled of college football's mythical national champions."[2] The article by Jenkins is considered perhaps the most important research in the history of the sport, although one question that comes to the forefront is the last two years on Davis's list. In 1934 the article has Minnesota, Pittsburgh and Alabama sharing the championship according to the historian, with Princeton and Minnesota capturing it a year later. The problem is that Parke H. Davis passed away in June of 1934 before the college football season began, bringing into question the validity of his last two championships. The website Tiptop25, which attempts to rate the top 25 collegiate teams throughout the history of the sport, says about Pitt's claim to the 1934 championship, "Curiously, Pitt also claims an MNC (mythical national championship) for 1934, even though they lost to 8–0 Minnesota, and no organization listed in the NCAA Records Book, human or computer, selected them for this season. Their media guide lists Parke Davis as the selector who chose them for 1934, but he died in June of 1934, before the season had even started. Whoops."[3]

The website is correct, as neither the NCAA Football Records book, nor one of the premiere collegiate football history websites, the College Football Data Warehouse, www.cfbdatawarehouse.com, do list a champion selected by Davis after 1933, thus leaving Pitt with no claims to a national title in 1934 in two of the most renowned portals for college football history in today's media.

Despite what appeared to be a lapse in the research, Jenkins stood by the researchers who came out with this groundbreaking list for *Sports Illustrated*.

Jenkins, who is a renowned college football historian himself as well as the listed official historian of the National Football Foundation, the organization that runs the College Football Hall of Fame, took a look at the original article and the editing notes that went with it. He stated in an e-mail that he was aware of Davis's death in 1934 and he was certain that he had information that either an associate or family member made the selection on Davis's behalf after his death. He also stated that the fact-checkers at *Sports Illustrated* were very good in those days and that there was a red check next to the Davis selections in 1934 and 1935, meaning they were accurate. Jenkins went on further to say that, "moreover, one of the top editors was a man named Jack Tibby, who was a football nut—and a Pitt grad—and he would have approved it."[4] As much of an authority as Jenkins is on the game, it was conceivable that someone did make the selection for Davis and that the list is accurate despite Davis's death.

As it turned out, Jenkins's faith was rewarded. Upon further review in the *1936 Spalding Guide*, the publishers of the book continued to choose national champions two years after Davis passed away. While the Panthers are listed in their media guide as the choice of Davis in 1934, it was in fact the publishers of the guide that Davis worked for who chose Pitt as the best football team in the country. Regardless of the technicalities of who selected them champions, the Panthers began their 1934 campaign with some question marks that only the traditional depth of a Jock Sutherland team could answer.

To help improve their depth, the school raised the yearly stipend to $480 before the season, after dropping to $400 in 1933. The cut in 1933 wasn't retroactive, which meant that whoever was on the team in 1932 was still getting $650. The large amount allowed the players who were making the $650 in many instances to get married and support their families on the stipend. They were referred to as "the married man's team."[5] This fact was reported and caused many accusations of professionalism among the teams on Pitt's schedule. Wanting to quell the uproar, the administration decided that no Pitt athlete could be married. Regardless of any change, the stipend had given Sutherland the ammunition he needed to compete for the national championship.

As Sutherland prepared for what would be a championship campaign, the *Pittsburgh Press* ran a contest with fans telling of their favorite moments in Pitt football history, with the winner to receive season tickets at the stadium. Mike Sebastian's electrifying run against Notre Dame in 1932 and the long clutch punt by quarterback Bobby Hogan in the same game were the clear winners. Sebastian, save some fumbling issues in his senior season, and Hogan provided Pitt aficionados with many thrills over their careers, but both had graduated, forcing Sutherland to find replacements for each in his backfield.

With the team getting ready for its opener against Washington and Jefferson, the Panther coach had to restructure his backfield. Statistically Pitt had been impressive over the last year and a half offensively, but due to turnovers or just ineptitude as far as finishing drives, they often struggled to score. Sutherland felt he had the makings of a more dynamic backfield with Miller Munjas getting a full season as the starting quarterback, joined by standouts Izzy Weinstock and Heinie Weisenbaugh as well as Mike Nicksick. Future star Bob Larue, as well as Leon Shedlosky, would provide Pitt with very capable backups should they become necessary.

The line the Panthers employed had good experience, although they had yet to prove if they were as talented as the crew from the previous season. Harvey Rooker and Verne Baxter were extended the starting spots for the opener at end, with Bob Hoel and Art Detzel at tackle, George Shotwell at center and Ken Ormiston and Doc Hartwig, who was named as the team captain, at the guard spots.

It seemed like the Panthers certainly had the talent to continue to be a successful team, but they would have a tough challenge in the opener against W & J, who gave Pitt all they could handle a year earlier.

Game 1—September 29, 1934, at Pitt Stadium
WASHINGTON AND JEFFERSON COLLEGE PRESIDENTS   6
UNIVERSITY OF PITTSBURGH PANTHERS   26

In the previous season, the University of Pittsburgh opened their 1933 campaign against the Washington and Jefferson Presidents hoping to send a message to the rest of the college football world that the Panthers would be a dominant team. As it turned out, fullback Bill King ripped through the Panther defensive line in a manner that no one else on their schedule even approached. What was a tight 9–0 Pitt victory could have easily turned out to be one of the most embarrassing upsets the program had endured in the Jock Sutherland era.

Unfortunately for the Presidents, King hurt his knee that afternoon, and what looked like it could be a very promising campaign for the small school ended up being one of the worst in the history of the program. After victories against Waynesburg and Xavier in the next three games, W & J lost five of their last six games, with only a scoreless tie against Carnegie Tech going somewhat in their favor. They finished the season 2–7–1, scoring only 20 points in those final six agonizing contests.

Luckily for third-year coach Leroy "Hank" Day, King was healthy again and would join the effective backfield of Holland, Rosso, Malcolm, and

McBurney to hopefully complete what they couldn't do in 1933 and hand the Panthers their first defeat in the series since the 10–0 victory during Sutherland's first season in command of his alma mater in 1924. Day had a veteran team in 1934 and hoped that his players could now master what was a complex offensive system for the time and have a successful season with it.

For Sutherland, while he originally thought to combine Weinstock and Weisenbaugh in the starting backfield, his main concern was whether or not he was comfortable with two fullbacks starting and was going back and forth between combining them or throwing LaRue or Shedlosky into the mix at right halfback, thus keeping Weisenbaugh on the bench to spell Weinstock.

Whatever he decided, the Pitt coach wanted his squad to relax before their opener and sent them, along with the teams from Carnegie Tech and Duquesne, to the Pittsburgh Pirates (Steelers) contest against the Philadelphia Eagles at Forbes Field on Wednesday evening as guests of Art Rooney three days before their opener.

With his team well rested and hopefully focused much more than they were on the Presidents in 1933, the Panther coach made his final decision the day before the contest, choosing to insert Greensburg sophomore LaRue into the starting lineup at halfback with Weisenbaugh on the bench. Having too much depth in the backfield is a problem most coaches would love to have, including Sutherland. By putting the sophomore at halfback, Sutherland would also have the luxury of incredible speed, much better than he had the year before, to send against his opponents.

The speed and depth would pay big dividends for Pitt in their opener as a driving rainstorm not only drenched the 15,000 fans who attended as well as both teams, but turned the usually good Pitt Stadium turf into a quagmire. The conditions contributed to a scoreless first quarter in which the Panthers threatened twice but came up empty both times, once on a halted drive and once due to a fumble by Shedlosky.

Finally after the game looked to be a repeat of the unusually close contest a year ago, Weisenbaugh, despite starting the game on the bench, showed the fans that he was nonetheless an important part of the team when he broke through what had been an impressive Washington and Jefferson defensive line and sprinted 43 yards for the opening touchdown. Once the Panthers were on the scoreboard, they were confident they could make the contest a rout. After holding W & J on the next series, they took over at midfield after LaRue's 20-yard return. LaRue then showed the Pitt faithful what a success he would be in his career when he sprinted around the right end to the 35. Hub Randour took it to the 18 before runs by Weinstock and LaRue as well as a pass com-

After taking over for his mentor Pop Warner in 1924, coach Jock Sutherland (center, flanked by an unidentified assistant coach and a player) took the University of Pittsburgh to another level with a 110-20-12 mark that included four Rose Bowl appearances, eight eastern championships and five national championships. His career with the Panthers ended suddenly after the 1938 campaign, when Chancellor John Bowman and Athletic Director Jimmy Hagan forced their new restrictive policies on the program.

pletion put the ball at the Presidents' one. Weinstock barreled in on the next play to give Pittsburgh a 13–0 lead at the half.

Pitt was looking confident and wanted to put the game away early in the third as they drove far on the two series of the half, once inside their opponent's 25-yard line and the second to the 17. The Presidents stopped the Panther attack on both occasions and would turn what looked like a blowout into a tight contest after an electric run by Washington and Jefferson's Don Craft. Starting at their own 13, Craft, a sophomore from nearby Sharon, took the ball, running quickly to his right before he broke into the open. The fans rose to their feet as the sophomore had a clear line to the end zone. As Craft inched closer he was about to do something that no W & J player had since their victory in 1924: score. Exhausted he finally went over the goal line to cut the Panther lead to seven. Unfortunately, the 87-yard run would account for more than half of the Presidents' 163 on that day. In fact, when you factor in a run by Rosso for 33 yards and one by Myers for 11, that meant that the rest of the team accounted for only 42 yards and one first down the rest of the way as the Pitt defense made sure W & J got no closer.

While the Panther defense made sure they did their part, the Pitt attack showed that they would also be effective the rest of the way. Immediately after the Craft touchdown, The Panthers ran the ball for 55 yards on five plays, putting it at the ten. Weinstock took over from there, powering it the final yards on three carries for Pitt's third rushing touchdown of the day.

Finally, with the outcome no longer in doubt, the Panther offense continued the onslaught. Randour rambled for 40 of Pitt's 361 yards rushing on the day before Shedlosky took it the final 26 yards two plays later, making it 26–6, which turned out to be the final score.

The Panthers, as it turned out, had a much more pleasant opener than they did the year before. It was a good tune-up, as they hoped the game in Morgantown would be next week also, before they had to play two of the nation's elite teams in USC and Minnesota.

Game 2—October 6, 1934, at Mountaineer Stadium in Morgantown, West Virginia

UNIVERSITY OF PITTSBURGH PANTHERS   27
WEST VIRGINIA UNIVERSITY MOUNTAINEERS   6

Much had been hoped for the football program at West Virginia University when they tabbed Earle "Greasy" Neale to be their head coach following the six-year run of Ira Errett "Rat" Rodgers. After all, Neale had done the impossible, not only leading the tiny Washington and Jefferson Presidents to the Rose Bowl in 1922, but pulling off one of the greatest upsets in the game's history when he tied the powerful California Golden Bears in a scoreless encounter. It was hoped he could do the same for the Mountaineer faithful when tabbed to be their head coach in 1931; he unfortunately came nowhere near that level and was let go following a very disappointing 3–5–3 mark in 1933. With its eyes still on competing for national honors on a year-in-and-year-out basis, the administration at WVU went back to the past for one of their own, an All-American end in 1923 who was considered one of the best players ever to don the school colors for the Mountaineers: Tariff, West Virginia, native Charles "Trusty" Tallman.

After a successful run as both football and basketball coach at another West Virginia school, Marshall, Tallman became an elected member of the West Virginia legislature before returning to his alma mater in search of greater glory for the university. While considered the greatest end at the time to play for West Virginia, Tallman was impressed with the group of players that WVU had in 1934. Angelo Onder (the brother of former Pitt guard Tar Onder) and Charlie Goodwin were two very talented athletic ends who were a very pivotal part of the Mountaineers' two victories in their first two contests of the campaign, a 19–0 win the opener against West Virginia Wesleyan before a 7–0 upset of the Duquesne University Dukes at Forbes Field the week before.

In the backfield the Mountaineers employed two of the lightest halfbacks in the country, although they were extremely fast, in Eck Allen and Jimmy Scott. Allen had been a quarterback under Neale and was considered not an extremely tough football player who was subject to injuries. Tallman had turned him into a halfback, and he arguably was the best player on the field, certainly against the Dukes. In the Wesleyan game, Allen went to the bench after a minor injury, and the 150-pound Scott entered the contest to show his effectiveness. Despite the fact he was so light, Scott showed an unusual toughness, ripping impressive runs up the middle. Tallman had hoped to use his impressive offensive position players as well as the momentum of his first two victories as the Mountaineer coach to defeat his rivals from the University of Pittsburgh, just like he had done in his senior season at WVU 13–7 in 1923.

Since that victory 11 years earlier, the Mountaineers had only beaten their rivals one other time, a 9–6 defeat in 1928, losing the other nine contests most decisively. Panther veteran Coach Jock Sutherland knew that this version of West Virginia would certainly be a formidable one and that they had a very impressive defensive line that was capable of frustrating his rushing attack, which was why Sutherland had his offense sharpening up their passing skills hoping to defeat the Mountaineers through the air.

The experts concluded that despite the fact WVU had their best talent in the decade to this point, Pitt most likely had the superior team. They were a faster and more athletic squad, which was more important than the perceived advantage West Virginia had with their powerful line. While favorites, one thing would possibly hamper their way to a second consecutive victory, a driving rain that was expected in Morgantown by game time. Rain can be the great equalizer when defending against a faster team, but luckily for Sutherland, the Panthers' talent superseded the weather as his team gave yet another impressive performance.

The game looked eerily like the opener against W & J. The Panther defense held the Mountaineer offense to a mere three first downs as the Pitt offense embarrassed the supposedly tough WVU defensive line at will in front of 20,000 disappointed fans at Mountaineer Field. The only difference between this contest and the one against the Presidents was that the Panthers scored early, grabbing the lead in the first quarter, sparing their fans the fruitless drives they witnessed in the opening frame at Pitt Stadium the week before. End Harvey Rooker showed his opponents, who thought they had the better talent at the position, who the superior end was. Halfback Mike Nicksick tossed a pass to the Pitt receiver who took the ball at his own 47. As three Mountaineer defenders were descending upon him, Rooker broke through the tackles where he found open field all the way to the end zone to give Pitt the early lead 7-0.

After reserve halfback Leon Shedlosky scored in the second quarter to give Pitt a 14-0 advantage at the half, West Virginia fought back, dominating the third. Quarterback George Allen led the way with a long pass completion to George Heath which put the Mountaineers inside the Pittsburgh ten-yard line. Immediately after, Allen broke several tackles, scoring WVU's only touchdown of the game, temporarily cutting into the Panther lead at 14-6.

It was a momentary lapse as the Pitt offense reestablished control in the final frame as Izzy Weinstock and Vern Baxter each scored, putting the finishing touches on a one-sided 27-6 victory to give the Panthers a 2-0 record.

Unfortunately for the Mountaineers, the Pitt loss brought them back to reality as they struggled the rest of the season, finishing with a 6-4 mark against a less-than-stellar slate. For Pitt it was an important victory as it gave them momentum going into a contest against the team that subjected them to embarrassing defeats in their past two Rose Bowl encounters, the Southern California Trojans, a week later at Pitt Stadium.

Game 3—October 13, 1934, at Pitt Stadium
University of Southern California Trojans 6
University of Pittsburgh Panthers 20

As successful as Jock Sutherland had been in his college coaching career, especially at his alma mater, he did have one opponent that no matter how hard he tried and how well he prepared his team he just could not overcome. That opponent was Howard Jones and the Southern California Trojans. To say playing USC was a nightmare for Pitt was perhaps an understatement; it had in fact been hellish. They not only beat the Panthers in their two Rose Bowl encounters in 1930 and 1933, but had done so in a record-setting manner, inflicting decisive margins such as no one had seen in the history of the game.

Was it because the Panthers had to take a tiring cross-country trip to get to Pasadena while the Trojans had a relatively short jaunt to play in the game? Alabama, Washington and Jefferson and Columbia as well as others who made a similar trip only to come away victorious would beg to differ.

A big part of their lack of success may just have come from the fact that the USC Trojans in the late 1920s and early 1930s were among the greatest college football teams ever to grace the gridiron. They won five Pacific Coast Conference titles in a six-year period that included back-to-back national championships in 1931 and 1932. The 47–14 and 35–0 defeats of Pitt in the Rose Bowl not only gave them national recognition, but while the Panthers were later given recognition as champions in 1929 by Parke Davis, the losses cost Pitt's unanimous recognition.

The question begged to be asked: why would the Panthers give up a date with local rival Duquesne to bring their nemesis to Pittsburgh? Did they feel that with USC traveling east it would allow them a measure of revenge? Perhaps, but whatever prompted them to schedule the team that brought them so many forgettable moments, Pitt fans would come in droves to see this important contest.

While the travel USC had to endure did fall in Pittsburgh's favor, they also had to be pleased that Southern California had an unusual regular-season loss the week before after so much sustained success. Following three successive wins to start the 1934 campaign, the Trojans hosted the Cougars of Washington State and were clearly outplayed in a 19–0 defeat.

Despite the fact that Pitt had some advantages in this contest, the fact that the Trojans had so severely beaten them had to be the biggest advantage of all. While having beaten Pitt so easily in the past, USC coach Howard Jones was nonetheless livid at the fact that the Trojans were so roundly defeated by the Cougars and wanted to make sure they were focused on the task at hand.

The hall-of-fame USC coach had felt that his line played poorly and needed to improve greatly against the Panthers.

Other than the line, there were other thoughts on why Southern California lost. The student newspaper, the *Daily Trojan*, made the claim that the influence of the stars in Hollywood, where the team had become stars themselves, had affected their concentration on the field. Before finishing their trip in Pittsburgh, Southern Cal had stopped in Kansas City where Jones had put them through a brutal workout. After the workout it was stated that "the team had little to say on the charges they were largely a group of Hollywood struck boys who were as toys in the clutches of the film queens and the movie magnates."[6] The charge seemed to make the squad surly as Jones continued to work them hard. Team captain Julie Bescos just told the press when confronted about the claim, "We can't worry about that now, but tell them just to wait until tomorrow."[7]

The Panthers on the other end were all business and had practiced well during the week following their two impressive season-opening victories. Usually Sutherland liked to tinker with his lineup early in the season, but since the starting 11 had been so effective, the Pitt coach decided to keep them in for this important contest.

Jones, whose team was also disappointing against a less-than-stellar Pacific squad, winning only 6–0, had made significant changes in their starting 11. He moved Calvin Clemens from right halfback to the left guard before deciding he was better off at the former position as well as moving Haskell Wotkyns from fullback to quarterback. On the line, Elwood Jorgenson shifted from right to left tackle and Art Dittberner from guard to tackle. He demoted Herbert Tatsch while promoting end Hueston Harper and center Gil Kuhn to the starting squad.

The USC coaches hoped the changes would ease the ongoing controversy that continued to be the talk of the town. In Chester Smith's column the day of the game, he abused Pitt's opponents in his opening paragraph: "So the Trojans have gone Hollywood eh? The tackles crave to be cuddled by Garbo, Ann Harding coos the guards, it's a big evening with the ends and centers step out with Crawford and the fullbacks—well, you'd think Mae West would be the gal for the fullbacks, or have I gotten my directions mixed?"[8]

Questioning their manhood as all seemed to be doing was either going to inspire the Trojans to live up to their potential and crush Pitt yet again, or contribute to their continued downfall. Luckily for the Panthers and the 55,000 fans that packed into Pitt Stadium, Southern California was anything but inspired.

Unlike the trips to California, this game, while clear and sunny, was played on a brisk, windy day in Pittsburgh. Pitt dominated from the opening kickoff as they were led by quarterback Miller Munjas's effective punting. Early in the game, Munjas pinned USC deep in their own territory. Pitt took the ball back at midfield and quickly moved to the 20 before turning the ball over on downs. On the next play Bill Howard fumbled, and Munjas pounced on it. Southern California was called for two offside penalties before Nicksick took the ball ten yards to the one. Finally the burly Izzy Weinstock took the ball into the end zone for the Panthers' first lead they ever had against USC, 7–0.

The lead held until the second quarter when Pitt took over at their own 31 after a punt by Clemens. Heinie Weisenbaugh, who came into the game for Bobby LaRue, rambled 31 yards on the first play to the opponents' 39. Weisenbaugh's one-man show on this drive continued as he found Baxter with a 14-yard completion then two plays later took the ball through the line before cutting to his right into the open for a 22-yard touchdown run and a surprising 13-point advantage.

The Panthers found themselves deep in Southern California territory once again in the second quarter, but just when it appeared that Pitt was about to put the game away, the Trojans' defense held. With a rout averted, the USC offense was about to break through. After a quick first down, Irv Warburton ran for 16 yards. Two plays later Warburton found Clemens with a 40-yard pass that took Southern Cal inside the Panther ten to the eight-yard line. Finally the two combined again in the far corner of the end zone to give the Trojans the momentum as the teams went into the locker room with USC now only behind by a touchdown.

The third period seemed to find the Trojans firmly in control as several big plays put them in position to tie the game. A 39-yard pass from Warburton to Bob Fuhrer set up one scoring threat, while a Panther fumble set up another. Each time the Trojans got close, the tough Panther defense rose to the occasion and kept them off the scoreboard. As USC was moving the ball once again, Baxter made the defensive play of the game, stopping fullback Inkey for an eight-yard loss to stop the momentum. Inkey seemed shaken and shanked the punt for only 11 yards, giving Pitt not only great field position but the momentum they had lost the period before.

The Panthers took little time to turn this contest from a close game to a comfortable Pittsburgh lead. On the next play the defensive star turned into an offensive one as Baxter pulled in a long pass, diving over the goal line for the touchdown that put Pitt comfortably in front 20–6. The Trojans threatened on a couple of occasions in the fourth quarter, getting as far as the Panther 22 before turning the ball over on a fumble, but was unable to score as Pitt hung on for the impressive victory.

It was a contest that gave Pitt the measure of revenge they had longed for for so many years against the Trojans. The win would also hopefully inspire them against the Golden Gophers of Minnesota a week later, the same Gophers that cost them a shot at a national championship in 1933. For USC it was the beginning of the end of their dynasty. Whether true or not, the rumors seemed to have gotten the best of them as they went on to win only one more game the rest of the season, tumbling to a 4–6–1 mark.

Game 4—October 20, 1934, at Pitt Stadium

UNIVERSITY OF MINNESOTA GOLDEN GOPHERS 13
UNIVERSITY OF PITTSBURGH PANTHERS 7

It was a game for the ages, two of the country's best teams, both of whom would claim the national championship at year's end, facing off at Pitt Stadium on a fall afternoon. The winner would have a clear road to eventually being named the undisputed best team in the nation, with the loser left to dwell on what might have been. To say this game was important was a great understatement; it was as important a contest as there was in 1934, and those who had the honor of witnessing it would agree it lived up to its hype.

There was incredible talent on the field for this memorable matchup. On the Pitt sidelines stood Charles Hartwig, George Shotwell and Izzy Weinstock, all of whom would achieve All-American status by year's end, as well as Art Detzel and Ave Daniell, both of whom would be named first-team All-Americans once each over the next two years, respectively. For the Golden Gophers, Butch Larson, Pug Lund, and Ed Widseth, each becoming two-time first All-American in their careers, were in the field along with Sheldon Beise, Bill Bevan, Bob Tenner and Dick Smith, all four making at least one first-team All-American squad. The twelve first-team All-Americans on the field at the same time was a feat that certainly was a once-in-a-lifetime occurrence, especially in the era of single-platoon football.

Minnesota had an experienced and deep team that hadn't lost a game since the final contest of the 1932 campaign when they lost to Michigan 3–0. The Gophers were a healthy squad and had won two very one-sided contests to start the season against North Dakota State and Nebraska, and coach Bernie Bierman decided to stay with the same starting squad that had led them to the two impressive victories. Bierman employed a single wing that saw the left halfback and the fullback as the focus of the offense. For Minnesota that meant two-time All-American and team captain Lund and future All-American Beise would get the bulk of the carries, a problem for the Panther defense.

Pitt was not as lucky as the Golden Gophers. End Verne Baxter, who was the star of the USC victory, was suffering from the flu and his status for the game was very questionable. The Panthers were very thin at the position with only Karl Seifert available as a replacement. While basically healthy other than Baxter, Sutherland was considering replacing Weinstock in the starting lineup with Heinie Weisenbaugh. Even though Weinstock was a superior defender and tough runner inside, Weisenbaugh was a quicker, more dangerous runner. Sutherland eventually decided to keep his backfield intact by keeping Weinstock with LaRue and Munjas, but Baxter was still too ill to play and would not play. On the line, the Pitt coach did have one correction at the last minute, replacing Art Denzel at right tackle with Stanley Olejniczak.

To gain revenge for the defeat Minnesota administered Pitt the year before that cost them a shot at the national championship, they would have to come up with a different strategy than they used the week before against Southern California. The Trojans were a bigger, more physical team on the line, while the Gophers were a faster, more athletic club on the front wall and would create a challenge for Pitt.

It was an unusually warm October day in Pittsburgh as 65,000 fans jammed Pitt Stadium. The nation looked forward to listening to the contest, but unfortunately the Panther athletic office decided not to allow a national broadcast of the game just as they had the week before against USC. Unfortunately, those in attendance would be left to tell the tale of this classic contest.

From the outset, the game was a defensive battle, with the teams playing a contest of field positions as the punters became the most important part of the offense. The Golden Gophers looked as if they were feeling out their opponents, employing a strategy of one-play plunges and a punt since Munjas had done a wonderful job pinning them deep in their territory with his punting.

Weinstock, proving he was also an offensive threat, gave Pitt one of two scoring opportunities early on, the first with a 30-yard run that put the ball deep in their opponents' territory before an interception by Lund gave the ball back to Minnesota. The Panthers had another chance soon after when Harvey Rooker pounced on Lund's fumble at the Gopher 16. Pitt pushed inside the five, but Minnesota's Bill Bevan almost single handedly stopped the Pitt attack with four successive tackles, helping the Gophers to take over the ball at the two.

As the first half was coming to an end, the Panthers got a third scoring opportunity, one that happened quickly. At their own 36-yard line, Weinstock took the ball around end for nine yards before sending a lateral to Mike Nicksick who rambled through the Minnesota defense for the final 55 yards and the touchdown that gave Pitt a 7–0 lead, one that they took into the locker room.

Pitt was dominating play, and they could see a potential national championship if they could hold on in the second half. As the third period wound down, while held scoreless, the huge, quick Minnesota backfield was tiring the Panthers' defense; still, the Panthers almost never gave up a lead, especially late in the game, and as the third quarter was coming to an end, their seven-point lead held up.

Late in the quarter Munjas fumbled at his own two, recovering it and then launching a 60-yard punt. Lund returned the punt, fumbled into the arms of LaRue who was then battered by Dale Rennebohm, forcing another fumble which was picked up by Frank Larsen and returned to the Panther 45. Early in the fourth, the Golden Gophers drove the ball to the 22 where reserve halfback Julius Alfonse took it around right end and sprinted to the end zone. After 45 minutes of being soundly beaten, Minnesota had remarkably tied the game at seven.

The game remained tied until the five-minute mark when the Gophers took over at the Pitt 46 after a LaRue punt. It was at this point that Stanley Kostka took over. He and Lund threw several completions leading the Gophers downfield. Finally after they reached the Panther 18, the Pitt defense appeared to have stiffened holding them to a fourth-and-five. Kostka faked a run, then lateraled it to Glen Seidel who pitched it to Lund. Lund took the ball and threw it to Tenner who had broken free in the end zone for the game-winning score.

Pitt had one last chance but could not mount a serious threat, turning it over to the Gophers, who ran out the clock for the come-from-behind 13–7. With the victory, Minnesota was able to win the rest of their games, capturing the national championship with a second consecutive undefeated season. For the Panthers, they had to go back to the drawing board and come up with a way to rebound in the face of a very difficult remaining schedule as they had the year before following another disappointing loss to the Gophers.

Game 5—October 27, 1934, at Taggart Stadium in New Wilmington, Pennsylvania
UNIVERSITY OF PITTSBURGH PANTHERS 30
WESTMINSTER COLLEGE TITANS 0

When the University of Pittsburgh replaced local rival Duquesne University on their schedule with Westminster in 1934 so they could play Southern California, many Pittsburgh-area collegiate football fans were critical of the maneuver, thinking that the school quickly ended what was becoming a fine city rivalry. The school decided to make the change feeling that putting Westminster on the docket would give them what would be described as a breather after severely difficult games against Southern Cal and Minnesota. As it turned out the athletic administration at Pitt knew exactly what they were doing as a game against a lesser football team is exactly what the Panthers needed following their disappointing 13–7 loss to the Golden Gophers of Minnesota.

The last time the two schools met was in 1926 when the Panthers crushed the Titans 88–0 and co-coaches Bill and Tom Gilbane did not entertain any thoughts that Westminster could challenge Pitt, much less defeat them. The two were twins and also were important cogs on three of the greatest teams ever fielded at Brown University. Bill had been a fullback and team captain as well as a fine baseball player and wrestler at the school while Tom was a center/linebacker and was the starting center in the annual east/west all-star game in 1933. Both were inducted into the Brown Hall of Fame in 1971 and 1973 respectively, but for the time being they faced their most difficult challenge in their short history as head coaches.

They had a solid squad for a small school. The Titans' backfield of quarterback Bob Arrowsmith, halfbacks Ray Sweeney and Jack Laraway and big fullback Bill Staples were effective against schools their size, but certainly were not the class of the Panthers and posed not much of a threat. The Gilbanes decided that they would go with the squad that had started for the better part of the new season, with the plan to give the reserves a good bit of playing time that would help prepare them for the second half of the season, especially the matchup the following week against undefeated Grove City.

For Panther Coach Jock Sutherland it was a chance for him to have his starters recover from the beating the Gophers inflicted on them the week before as well as give his reserves an opportunity they had yet to get in the first four contests. On the line, Ken Ormiston severely hurt his legs and would definitely be out for the contest. During practice in the week leading up to the Westminster contest, Ormiston suffered with a laceration of his shin and what was described as a bad charley horse on his other. While Ormiston would not start due to injury, the rest of the starting squad, except for Izzy Weinstock who got the nod at fullback, would get most of the afternoon off to make sure they were healthy for the game the following week against the Fighting Irish of Notre Dame.

In the backfield, Bobby McClure and 200-pound Arnie Greene would get most of the time at quarterback while Hub Randour and Leon Shedlosky would join McClure and Weinstock in the backfield. At end, Vincent Sites and Wilkins hoped to give Pitt more experience at a position that was extremely thin with effective performances, while there would be a new collection of linemen to start that included sophomore Averill Daniell, who two years later would become one of the most revered offensive linemen in school history as a consensus first-team All-American on their 1936 national championship squad.

Even though Westminster would give a better performance against this Panther squad in front of a full house of 10,000 fans at Taggart Stadium than they did eight years before, the Pitt reserves nonetheless gave a great account of themselves in this contest. From the beginning the game appeared to be a mismatch. The only starter Sutherland left in, the tough-running Weinstock, showed the talent disparity early in the first quarter. Two plays into the contest he took a handoff at his own 35-yard line and rambled through the Titan defense until he crossed the goal line, giving the Panthers a very quick 6–0 advantage.

It would be only a few moments later when Pitt doubled their lead as they took the ball in their own territory and then muscled downfield through an overmatched Westminster defensive wall with Weinstock barreling through from a yard out to give Pittsburgh a twelve-point lead, a lead they held on to until early in the second quarter.

With his bench now firmly in control of the game, Arrowsmith punted to Pitt as the quarter began with Shedlosky returning it to the Titan 44. On the next play Randour ripped through the right side of the line and rolled to the outside where he went down the sideline on his way to a touchdown and an 18–0 lead which, despite the fact that the Pitt offense was in the Westminster side of the field for the remainder of the quarter, was the score as the half came to an end.

Pitt continued to control the contest in the third quarter, but unfortunately they continually failed to complete their drives, keeping the lead at 18 points. Finally as the period was coming to an end they were able to tack on their fourth touchdown of the afternoon. After starting at the Westminster 49, Shedlosky took the ball to the 35 before Randour once again showed his talent, taking the ball off left tackle, reversing his ground and breaking into the open for his second long touchdown run of the day, increasing the Panther advantage to 24–0.

Wanting to make sure his starters were sharp for the Notre Dame encounter in their next game, Sutherland put in his top squad as Pitt took the ball to begin the final quarter. Taking the ball at the Titan 45 after another less-than-stellar punt, Mike Nicksick rambled for ten yards before taking a pitch the remaining 35 yards for the final score of the game. Perhaps the only issue for the Panthers was the fact they missed all five extra-point conversions in the 30–0 victory.

Despite the fact that the special teams were an issue, Pitt had the win it needed in hopes of regaining its confidence for the second half of the season. As it turned out, not playing a difficult opponent in Duquesne after the USC and Minnesota clashes turned out to be a stroke of genius by the athletic department as the Panthers were now ready to assault their final four opponents of the season.

Game 6—November 3, 1934, at Pitt Stadium
UNIVERSITY OF NOTRE DAME FIGHTING IRISH 0
UNIVERSITY OF PITTSBURGH PANTHERS   19

When the University of Pittsburgh canceled their game against Duquesne University so they could play a lesser opponent following two very difficult games, fans assumed that meant they wouldn't see the Dukes' successful coach Elmer Layden. While Duquesne in fact did not appear on the schedule in 1934, Layden did make a trip to Pitt Stadium as he took his alma mater, Notre Dame, into battle against the Panthers on the first Saturday of November in Pittsburgh.

After a successful run at Duquesne, the Fighting Irish had called their former player back to South Bend to lead them out of the state of mediocrity that coach Hunk Anderson had them in after taking over the program following Knute Rockne's untimely death in the spring of 1931. Layden was a member of the school's legendary Four Horsemen backfield and had done a marvelous job taking Duquesne from the ranks of a small college program to that of a major football team capable of competing on a national level. He led the school to a 10–1 mark in 1933 that included a victory over a tough Miami (FL) squad 33–7 in the Festival of Palms, a preamble to the Orange Bowl. He would have a much more challenging job in turning around the fortunes of a former national power in Notre Dame.

While not geographically close, the rivalry between these two schools was nonetheless as intense as the one they had against Carnegie Tech. Of course anytime you played Notre Dame, you played the tradition, the ghost of Knute Rockne, the four national championships won in 1919, 1925, 1929 and 1930. It was a lot to take in, and fans across America, as well as in Pittsburgh, certainly understood that and appreciated it, especially when their favorite teams defeated the Irish.

The lore of the Irish tradition is something that Layden certainly understood. He was a member of arguably the most well-known backfields in the history of the game, the legendary "Four Horsemen of Notre Dame" along with Jim Crowley, Harry Stuhldreher and Don Miller. His career at Notre Dame culminated in his selection as an All-American in 1924 as well as a memorable performance in the 1925 Rose Bowl where he returned two interceptions for touchdowns in the Irish's 27–10 defeat of Stanford. Layden was also aware of the passion of the Steel City football fans in his seven-year tenure as coach of the Dukes. The Irish coach also understood that while he had such a rich tradition on his side, the school had been shut out by the Panthers over the last two seasons and was even held scoreless in a 7–0 loss to Carnegie Tech on this same Pitt Stadium turf in 1933.

Through all the difficult memories in Pittsburgh for Notre Dame since Rockne passed away, Layden was off to a great start in South Bend following a close opening-day loss to Texas 7–6. They had defeated the Big Ten's Purdue and Wisconsin soundly while also gaining a measure of revenge against the Tartans with a 13–0 win. Even though they were 3–1, this contest against Pitt represented the first time the Irish played outside of South Bend and would go a long way toward showing whether Notre Dame had sufficiently recovered from the disappointing 3–5–1 record the year before or whether the former Duquesne coach still had his work cut out for him.

If Layden was confident with the Fighting Irish three-game win streak, he didn't show it as he met the Pittsburgh media when he got off the train. "The football scouts say we are playing under wraps because they haven't seen anything. Well, the joke is on them. We haven't anything to show. But we will try to make it interesting."[9]

Both teams seemed relatively healthy as they entered the contest, with many members of each team having experience playing in this rivalry. While not to the level of the Four Horsemen, the Notre Dame backfield, consisting of George Melinkovich, Fred Carideo, Bud Bonar and Andy Pilney, was nonetheless effective and gave Jock Sutherland reason to worry. The Panther hall-of-fame mentor was set with his lineup except for end where he was tinkering with going with either Verne Baxter, who was recovering from a bout with the flu, and Vincent Sites at end, with the Pitt coach eventually sticking with Baxter.

As it turned out Layden wasn't kidding and Sutherland did have nothing to worry about as the Panther defense played their best game of the season, putting the squad right back in the national championship picture. As had been the case for most of the season, Pitt spent a lot of time in its opponent's side of the field in the first quarter, going as far as the Notre Dame five in this one, only to come up scoreless each time.

While the Panther offense had been impressive, albeit scoreless, it was their special teams that broke the ice midway in the second quarter. Halfback Leon Shedlosky, who was given the moniker of "slant nose" by his teammates, grabbed a punt by Notre Dame's Bill Shakespeare, the man who is famous in Pittsburgh Steeler lore as the first player ever taken by the franchise in an NFL draft, chosen by the Pirates, the name of the Steelers until 1940, as the third pick in the first round. Shedlosky made a mockery of the Irish players who tried to stop him. He broke through no less than six Notre Dame tacklers before running into open field right past the goal line for a 6–0 lead that held up through the end of the first half. It was a half of football that was so thoroughly dominated by the Panthers' defense that the Irish offense only made it past midfield once, and that was only to the 46.

As the Irish came out for the second half hoping for a change in their fortunes, the Panthers quickly showed it would be nothing but the same. After swapping punts with Pitt still having the advantage in field position, the Panthers took over the ball at their own 35 as LaRue pounced on his own fumble and quickly went down the field. LaRue, Nicksick and Weinstock methodically burst through the middle of the Notre Dame line until they reached their opponents' 46. At that point Nicksick took a handoff slashing behind left tackle before cutting back as he saw open field. Finally at the ten, Shakespeare seemed to have stopped the Pitt halfback before Nicksick broke the tackle and continued toward the end zone where Pittsburgh increased their lead to 13–0. After the score, Weinstock, who was not having a great year kicking, converted on the extra point.

After being frustrated for the better part of three and a half quarters, Notre Dame finally had their first serious scoring threats in the middle of the fourth quarter on the heels of one big play. Andy Pilney tossed a pass to Marty Peters that covered 46 yards, giving the Irish a first down at the Panther 46, their deepest penetration of the game. Right as it looked like they'd slice the Panther lead in half, Pilney was intercepted by Weisenbaugh, who returned it to the Notre Dame 32. On the first play following the pickoff, Shedlosky muscled through four tacklers, rumbling to the three-yard line. Afterward, Nicksick promptly went over right tackle for Pitt's third and final score in the 19–0 shutout.

It was as dominant a victory as Pitt had in the season so far, ruining Layden's return to the Steel City. The Irish, while soon to be back in the national spotlight, were still not quite ready yet to resume their championship runs, but Pitt was as they used this game as a springboard to a strong second half.

Game 7—November 10, 1934, at Memorial Stadium in Lincoln, Nebraska

UNIVERSITY OF PITTSBURGH PANTHERS   25
UNIVERSITY OF NEBRASKA CORNHUSKERS   6

Superman had kryptonite as his chief weakness; no matter how superhuman he was, kryptonite would always be able to nullify his power. For Coach Dana X. Bible and the University of Nebraska Cornhuskers football team, the team coached by Jock Sutherland, the University of Pittsburgh Panthers, was their kryptonite.

Since taking over the program in 1929, Bible had built the Cornhuskers into one of the most powerful football programs in the Midwest. The team never had a losing season under his direction and had only lost four games in the previous three seasons, capturing the Big Six championship each time. While the 23-4-1 record during that time period was certainly impressive, the 0-2-1 mark against Pitt certainly wasn't. It was an embarrassment of futility for sure, while 40-0 in 1931 was humiliating, the 6-0 defeat by the Panthers in 1933 most likely cost Bible and his troops the school's first recognized national championship. Even though it looked like there would be no national championship on the line for either squad in this matchup, thanks to the Minnesota Golden Gophers, it was nonetheless an opportunity for Nebraska to settle an old score and try to finally overcome their kryptonite.

The Cornhuskers were enjoying another fine season coming into this contest with a 4-1 record, but it was very apparent that they weren't as dominant as their 1933 squad had been. A 20-0 shutout loss to Minnesota in the season's second week and three very close victories against Iowa, Oklahoma and Iowa State by a total of eight points, three clubs that they had beaten by a margin of 30 points the year before, showed that Nebraska had seemingly taken a step backward. A revenge victory against Pittsburgh would certainly change the perception that this was a disappointing season in Lincoln.

Bible had a very young team at his disposal with a starting squad that featured an abundance of sophomores. Their backfield was led by two first-year players, Lloyd Cardwell, who was considered a potential All-American by the experts of the day, and Sam Francis. Their young and relatively inexperienced offensive line, led by senior center Franklin Meier, had potential as they weighed a combined average 235 pounds, one of the largest groups ever to hit the gridiron in the history of the sport at that point in time. The Cornhusker passing game was still a work in progress but was slowly beginning to become effective as their sophomore end, Lester McDonald, was showing exceptional promise himself.

Nebraska's excited fan base knew what an opportunity this game was to showcase their young team and showed their enthusiasm very aggressively. The contest was sold out with a record attendance almost guaranteed to Memorial Stadium as Lincoln had been host to several pep rallies and parades to spur on their home team. Over 25,000 students at the university signed a petition imploring the Cornhuskers to "kindly tear the Panther from limb to limb."[10]

It was a level of passion that the school had rarely seen before, and the hope was it would inspire the team to rise above what was perceived as a superior opponent. Sutherland wanted to make sure his club would not fall victim to the hype. While Pitt dominated the Fighting Irish of Notre Dame the week before, they did so without completing a pass, so Sutherland really wanted to work on that aspect of the offense and spent quite a bit of time during the week working with Mike Nicksick on his passing skills. He also wanted more explosiveness to his running game and decided to replace the bigger Izzy Weinstock at fullback over the quicker Heinie Weisenbaugh. He also was toying with the idea of inserting Leon Shedlosky, who was phenomenal against Notre Dame, for Bobby LaRue, who was suffering from a badly bruised shin which he hurt the week before.

Luckily for the team, LaRue had sufficiently recovered by game time and did end up starting as the Panthers took the field with a record 35,000 fans in Memorial Stadium on hand. Pitt stepped onto the gridiron in white shirts for the first time in 1934, choosing to discard the jerseys that they wore in the Minnesota game as the players refused to put them on. It was a symbol for sure, but one that proved to be stronger than the Nebraska petition of victory as Pittsburgh continued the momentum they acquired against the Irish the week before. The defense proved to be too much for the huge Nebraska line to handle as Nicksick showed that the hard work he put in at practice during the week was about to pay off.

They were in control of this matchup from the onset, and after a short first-quarter touchdown by Nicksick put Pitt ahead 6–0, the Panthers showed this large throng they would be in for a long afternoon before the first half ended. After driving deep in Nebraska territory on the heels of a 28-yard scamper by Nicksick, the Cornhusker defense stopped Pittsburgh, forcing a punt that pinned Nebraska near the end zone. The Pitt defense did the same as a poor Cornhusker punt set up the Panthers in excellent field position once again. Nicksick, Shedlosky and Weinstock complemented each other with savage blocks and effective runs that advanced the ball to their opponents' 11. The Pitt halfback then rolled around on an end run and ran the final 11 yards for his second touchdown of the game and a 12–0 halftime lead.

As the second half began, Nicksick's one-man show continued. He took the kickoff 27 yards to the Husker 49, and a play later Weinstock and Nicksick combining for one of the most spectacular runs of the campaign. Weinstock took the handoff into the line where he appeared to be stopped by the beefy Nebraska line. As he was going down, the fullback saw Nicksick and lateraled the ball to him. Nicksick ripped through the line into the open and sprinted in the rest of the way for an 18-point advantage.

If it wasn't apparent at this point that the Cornhuskers weren't coming back to tear the Panthers from limb to limb, Nicksick soon made sure it was. Taking over at their own 39, Weinstock promptly ripped through a huge hole in the now feeble Nebraska front wall. He looked like he could possibly take it the whole way until the secondary caught up to him. At that point he handed it to Nicksick who ran to the Husker 15. Immediately afterward Weinstock lateraled the ball once again to the day's star who went 13 yards to the two. One play later the left halfback bulled into the end zone, tying Warren Heller's school record that was set three years earlier against the same Nebraska club, with his fourth score to make the score 24–0. Like the week before, the only weakness Pitt showed was in its kicking game. Weinstock had missed the previous three attempts, so Sutherland inserted Ken Ormiston, who finally converted on one to give Pittsburgh the 25–0 advantage.

Nebraska did score a late touchdown on a pass from Henry Bauer to Ray Toman, but it was after Sutherland had emptied his bench with his second- and third-team players. Making it 25–6 was nice, but it couldn't mask the utter domination the Panthers had leveled against the Cornhuskers on this day. With the win they became the first team to win two games in Memorial Stadium against Nebraska in the 11-year history of the facility and also broke their home undefeated streak that had lasted since a 10–9 loss against Kansas State in 1930. The statistics did not lie: 287 yards rushing against the Huskers' 90, 391 yards of total offense versus Nebraska's 249, 17 first downs while holding the home team to 8, the majority of the Cornhuskers' yards and first downs coming when the game was all but decided.

In the end, the excitement of the Husker fans and players could not overcome something stronger: the kryptonite in the form of Mike Nicksick that Sutherland threw at them to continue Pitt's dominance over their midwestern rivals.

Game 8—November 17, 1934, at Thompson Stadium in Annapolis, Maryland

UNIVERSITY OF PITTSBURGH PANTHERS   31
THE UNITED STATES NAVAL ACADEMY MIDSHIPMEN   7

There had been no better reclamation project in college football during the 1934 college football campaign than that of the United States Naval Academy and their new coach Lieutenant Thomas J. "Tom" Hamilton. After a 5–4–1 season in 1933 in the final year of Rip Miller's disappointing three-year tenure at the academy, the athletic department called on one of its former sons, Hamilton, to see if he could lead the school back to the prominence it enjoyed only eight years before in 1926 when the Midshipmen had a 9–0–1 mark while being named national champions on several rankings.

One of the stars on that memorable 1926 squad was Hamilton himself. An All-American halfback with the academy, the coach led the nation in field goals that season and launched a dropkick that tied the 1926 Army-Navy classic 21–21. Eventually rising to the position of rear admiral, Hamilton's resume in the armed serves was much more impressive than his gridiron career. One of his most enduring contributions to the service was founding the Navy's V-5 Pre-flight Training Program during World War II that was vital to the war effort. He also served on the USS *Enterprise* and was part of several invasions that included the Philippines and Iwo Jima.

While his time in the service would eventually be legendary and historic, at this point in time he was the first-time 28-year-old head coach of the Navy Midshipmen, and his team was undefeated as they were about to host the University of Pittsburgh with a legitimate shot at the national championship if they emerged victorious.

After a 3–0 start, they upset Columbia and beat Pennsylvania on successive weekend road games, which forced the experts to take notice. The Midshipmen won an easy game against Washington and Lee the following week before a stunning 10–6 victory over the Fighting Irish of Notre Dame at Cleveland. The win gave them a perfect 7–0 going into the final two games of the season against Pitt and their bitter rivals from the United States Military Academy. Sweep those two games and Navy would have completed one of the most remarkable turnaround campaigns in the history of the game at that time.

Despite the fact that the Panthers were the favorites, they would still have to come up with a strategy to stop a very fast backfield that was led by Fred Borries, who had developed into an effective passer. Borries was joined by sophomores Tom King and Rich Pratt at halfback and senior fullback Charlie Clark. Navy was a weak team up the middle, but they had very effective tackles that helped open holes for their backs.

Luckily for Pitt they were relatively healthy again except for end Verne Baxter, who had a couple of issues during the season, this week being an injured knee that made him doubtful for the contest. Backup Karl Seifert was also sidelined, which left the starting spot to third-string junior Vincent Sites. The only other changes in the starting lineup Sutherland brought to Annapolis was giving the starting spot at fullback to Izzy Weinstock, who had an impressive performance at Nebraska the previous week. The Scottish coach also decided to take backup tackles Gene Stoughton and James Scarfpin on the trip with the team, replacing John Valenti and Vincent Hanley, both of whom didn't travel with the squad.

The team stayed in the nation's capital the night before the game before traveling to Thompson Stadium, but when they got to the stadium, they found out just how much the game had roused the interest of the community. Twenty-five thousand tickets had been sold for the contest which filled every seat in the small facility. So high was the interest that scalpers were reportedly receiving $50 per ticket, which was an outrageous amount for the time.

It was a perfect day for football, seasonably cool with blue skies and little to no wind as Pitt ran on the field for the second week in a row wearing their white jerseys. The shirts proved to be a good-luck charm for the team as they controlled every aspect of the game from the opening whistle. The Panther offensive line continually outmuscled their opponents as the team went on five impressive drives, three of which covered over 75 yards including the opening possession in which Pitt started at the 20-yard line. Sutherland's game plan was to take advantage of the Midshipmen's deficiencies in the middle and at the ends. Mike Nicksick, Bobby LaRue and Weinstock took turns going through gaping holes in the Navy line which led to a long, sustained drive that the fullback ended with a shirt burst up the middle from inside the five as the Panthers took the early six-point lead.

Before Navy had time to breathe, Pitt took the ball again, continuing the onslaught in the first quarter. The team once again went on a long drive, the highlight of which was a 24-yard run by Nicksick, taking the ball to the 11-yard line. At that point LaRue took the handoff and sprinted around right end untouched into the end zone as what was supposed to be Navy's coming-out party turned into a clear statement that the Panthers were making for national championship honors.

For a short period of time in the second quarter, the Midshipmen made a close game of it after Borries completed a 57-yard pass to Tom King that put the ball on the Pittsburgh eight. On the next play Borries took a lateral and found King for the touchdown to cut the advantage to five at the half.

Just when it seemed like the Midshipmen's hopes were on the rise, the Panther offense quickly doused them as the second half began. Starting at their own 45, Pitt quickly took the ball downfield as Nicksick rambled for 11 and Weinstock for 17 then 16 yards and past the goal line, restoring their two-touchdown lead. Navy seemed defeated as the game entered its final 15 minutes. Sutherland emptied his bench, but it didn't seem to matter as Hub Randour had three substantial runs, the most impressive being a 36-yard one to the Midshipmen 15. One play later it was 24–7 when Randour finished the drive with a touchdown run that all but ended Navy's championship hopes.

Unfortunately for the home team, the Panthers were not done when Leon Shedlosky first ran the ball 48 yards, only to be called back after a holding penalty. It didn't matter as the next play he went 61 yards to the 13 where Borries made a touchdown-saving tackle. Two plays later Shedlosky finished the onslaught with a nine-yard sprint. When Weisenbaugh connected on the only point after of the game for Pitt, it made the final score 31–7.

Hamilton would eventually go on to a successful hall of fame career as an athletic director not only at Navy but at the University of Pittsburgh between 1949 and 1959 where he helped lead them to Gator and Sugar Bowl bids (he also spent two seasons as the Panthers' head coach in 1951 and 1954). As good as his career was, he never came close to leading a team to a national championship again as while Navy defeated Army the next week 3–0 to finish the season 8–1, their title hopes were now gone at the hands of the University of Pittsburgh.

Game 9—November 29, 1934, at Pitt Stadium

CARNEGIE TECH TARTANS 0
UNIVERSITY OF PITTSBURGH PANTHERS 20

It had been a disappointing year for Pitt's close neighbors in the Oakland section of Pittsburgh, the Carnegie Tech Tartans. As the year before, the defense for former Tartan legend and current coach Howard Harpster was very physical and effective; the offense on the other hand had spent the season nonexistent. It was not as if the season was a total loss. They came into this contest with a 4–4 mark that included victories over Geneva, Miami (FL), NYU and their cross-town rivals, Duquesne University. While the victories were certainly impressive, the wins came due to their stout defense as the offense could only muster 29 points in the four games. The losses came at the expense of some of the best programs in the country, including Michigan State, Notre Dame, Purdue and Temple. In those games the ineffective offense produced exactly six points. Despite the fact that the campaign wasn't a total loss, the chance that they could somehow defeat the University of Pittsburgh was remote indeed.

The Tartans came into the contest healthy but certainly had no reason to expect much from their backfield that included Joe Mihm, Bill Carlson, Willie Spisak and Freddy Lehman. Their outstanding line of Dutch Croft,

Cliff Doloway, Nestor Henrion, Fred Kelley and Steve Trbovich hoped to stall the aggressive Panther attack. The one hope that the Tartan fans had in their upset attempt was that Pitt would come into this game extremely overconfident after their remarkable wins against Notre Dame, Nebraska and Navy. Sutherland would counteract that possibility with the help of his seniors, perhaps the greatest senior class of his tenure at the school to that point.

Harvey Rooker, Karl Seifert, Bob Hoel, Stan Olejniczak, Doc Hartwig, Ken Ormiston, George Shotwell, Miller Munjas, Mike Nicksick, Heinie Weisenbaugh and Izzy Weinstock would march on the turf at Pitt Stadium for one final time in hopes of not only securing the city championship yet again for the school, but an eastern title as well as a potential Rose Bowl berth, not to mention a slim chance for a national championship.

No one knew the success and potential of this senior squad better than the man that recruited them, Coach Jock Sutherland. While grateful for the efforts they gave to him and the team, he knew come game's end, especially if Pitt was not able to secure a Rose Bowl bid, that their time at the school would be over and he would miss witnessing their performances. "No matter what the score is at the end of tomorrow's game, I will not be one of the happiest men in Pittsburgh," the coach lamented. "I will be saying goodbye and good luck to entirely too many fine boys, boys with whom it has been my privilege to work for the past four years."[11] Yes, Thanksgiving Day in 1934 would certainly be a memorable day for Sutherland and the Pitt Panthers as either the day they finished off one of the most powerful seasons in the program's history, or one where Tech would administer an extremely devastating defeat that would turn this senior class's last performance into a nightmare.

As it turned out, the Tartans' defense proved more formidable than just about anyone else the Panthers faced during the season, and Mihm was incredible, punting with an average of 46.5 yards on 12 punts. Unfortunately for the underdogs, though, the Pitt defense proved to be as impenetrable as they ever had been under the hall-of-fame coach. They yielded only 36 yards for the whole holiday afternoon, permitting Tech a mere first down.

What little chance Carnegie Tech had ended quickly in the first quarter as the Panthers scored all the points they would need when the inept Tartan offense turned the ball over. Spisak fumbled and Nicksick pounced on it at the opponents' 23. An offside penalty put the ball at the 18 before Weinstock took the ball to the nine. Bobby LaRue fumbled the ball on the next play losing 11 yards, but another defensive offside nullified what was a clutch defensive play. Instead of the third-and-12, Pitt stood with a first down at the four. Two plays later, the Panther fullback muscled over the goal line for a 7–0 lead. While Sutherland's boys did threaten once in the second quarter, the

Tartans held and the score remained a one-touchdown lead for Pitt as the half ended.

The Tech defense continued to be strong as the second half began, although they were losing the battle of field position as Munjas pinned them back with a long punt into the end zone. It wouldn't be long before Pitt extended their lead to two touchdowns. Turnovers can be death to a team in football as the Tartans would quickly find out in this contest. Douglas fumbled the ball on the initial play of the drive as the ball went bouncing toward the Panther goal line. Trbovich tried to pick it up for Carnegie Tech but failed in the attempt. Finally Hartwig covered it at the three where two runs later Weinstock had his second touchdown of the game as he also connected on his second conversion, an unusual occurrence for Pittsburgh in 1934, increasing their lead to 14–0.

It didn't matter whether the lead was 2–0 or 50–0 with the way the Pitt defense was playing on this day; there was no chance that the Tartans could win. Knowing he had the easy win, Sutherland freely substituted as the fourth quarter began. It didn't seem to matter, though, as the Panthers went on their only sustained scoring drive of the game. After Leon Shedlosky returned a punt to the Carnegie 48, Hub Randour found Arnold Greene with a 14-yard pass. Shedlosky rambled for 19 yards on the next play where he was sent to the sidelines with a vicious tackle by Terebus. After a two-yard run by Weisenbaugh, Randour ended the scoring for the day with a 13-yard sprint around left end to make it 20–0.

With time running out, Sutherland reinserted his seniors for one last experience at the stadium. They almost made the most of it on the last play of the game when a double lateral found its way into the arms of right guard Ken Ormiston who completed the spectacular 36-yard play just short of the end zone. It didn't matter, though; the 20–0 victory put an exclamation point on what had been a fantastic end to the season after the disheartening loss to Minnesota. They were named champions of the east and finished second in the Dickinson poll, only .32 of a point behind the Gophers, right in front of Navy, the team they crushed only a week and a half before.

Any thought of Rose Bowl dreams were squashed quickly after the victory when it was announced that the western champions from Stanford would meet the undefeated Alabama Crimson Tide, who were chosen over Pitt, Colgate and Temple. The disappointment was at least tempered by the fact that three Panthers would be given the honor of being named first-team All-Americans. Hartwig and Shotwell were consensus choices at guard and center respectively, while Weinstock was given the nod at fullback by the Newspaper Editors Association and the North American Newspaper Alliance.

8. 1934: A Forgotten Title

It was frustrating, though, for Sutherland and his squad, complete with the knowledge that a fourth-quarter meltdown against the Gophers cost them what would have certainly been a unanimous selection as national champions. While it may have helped that the *Spalding Guide* had chosen them as best in the land along with Minnesota, it certainly was fitting that the school chose to recognize their incredible efforts 33 years later as an official champion, a title that was disputed until verified in 2014, and one that now can comfortably be celebrated into the future, never to be forgotten again.

National Champions *selections made by modern-day analysts are noted "(retrospective)." Players rated as* **First Team All-Americans** *by a plurality of NCAA-recognized selectors are noted as "(consensus)." Players rated by all NCAA-recognized selectors are noted as "(unanimous)."*

1934 Scores

Date	Opponent	Score	Record
9/29	Washington and Jefferson	26–6	1–0–0
10/6	@West Virginia	27–6	2–0–0
10/13	Southern California	20–6	3–0–0
10/20	Minnesota	7–13	3–1–0
10/27	@Westminster	30–0	4–1–0
11/3	Notre Dame	19–0	5–1–0
11/10	@Nebraska	25–6	6–1–0
11/18	@Navy	31–7	7–1–0
11/29	Carnegie Tech	20–0	8–1–0
		205–44	

Selected as National Champions by:
The Spalding Guide

Selected as First-Team All-Americans
Charles Hartwig (consensus)
George Shotwell (consensus)
Izzy Weinstock

9

1936: Everything for Football

As the University of Pittsburgh Panthers embarked on the 1935 campaign, they did so with the knowledge that they had lost quite a few players to graduation after one of the most successful three-year runs in the history of the program. It made no difference, though; the Panthers and Coach Jock Sutherland would just reload without missing a beat.

It was a mostly new starting lineup that Sutherland used that year, but as the season went on the team grew. They beat the usual cast of characters to begin the campaign, topping Waynesburg, W & J and West Virginia without being challenged. The next week they suffered their only loss of the season when Elmer Layden finally defeated Pitt, leading his Notre Dame Fighting Irish to a 9–6 victory. Scoreless ties to Fordham and Carnegie Tech were the only other blemishes on an otherwise fine 7–1–2 season that included a season-ending 12–7 win in Los Angeles against Southern California.

It was a great way to end the season as the new group of recruits in 1935 and 1936 began what perhaps was the best two seasons in Sutherland's tenure. It didn't matter what season it was or who the players were; the two common factors of Sutherland-led teams were that they were a deep team and they played a tough defense that was very difficult to score upon. It was the result of a system with the teamwork of Sutherland's coaching and the support of a group of boosters called the Golden Panthers that produced nothing but victories and championships.

The Golden Panthers did what they could to get the best possible players to the university. The leader of the group was a man by the name of Jim Marks, who was the football coach at Kiski Prep. The organization was singularly focused on making Pitt one of the strongest programs in the country; they even had a lighthearted motto printed on their official stationary: "Not one cent for the Chancellor—Everything for Football."[1]

Known as the College of the North, the organization not only helped recruit the best players but made sure that if it was better grades the kids needed or they needed to build strength or were just too young, they found them a home in either Saltsburg or Bellefonte Academy to receive whatever they needed to be a future Panther. If the player was poor, they provided suits or clothes. The Golden Panthers also helped set the players up with successful careers after their time at Pitt was done.

To say the Panther football players of the era were well taken care of was an understatement; they were among the best taken care of in the nation, prompting other schools to criticize them for turning their players into professionals. The claims, while hypocritical, as many who complained also subsidized players, weren't unfounded; as stated before, the players were well compensated for their commitment to the team.

It was a perfect combination for winning and allowed the program to be the best in the east consistently as they had not been defeated by an eastern team since a 6–0 loss to Carnegie Tech in 1928. It was also a system that began to unravel after the team's seventh national championship season in 1936. For the meantime everything was status quo as Sutherland was concentrating on putting together yet another powerful team in hopes of continuing the dynasty.

The philosophy used throughout the years by Sutherland and his band of recruiters was to build a deep team, one that would play in the first and third quarters and the other in the second and fourth with equal production. They had been successful in their endeavor for the better part of Sutherland's tenure, and 1936 would be no different.

Arnold Greene had been a bigger-than-average backup quarterback weighing in at 200 pounds for the Panthers over the past couple of seasons. As the pre-season workouts went on, Greene seemed to finally be showing the promise that the coaches had hoped for him as he looked ready to take over a more expansive role in the offense. On the line it appeared that Averell Daniell had done enough to supplant George Delich from the right tackle spot.

Perhaps the main surprise from the camp was the emergence of a sophomore halfback who was the son of a movie theater owner from Elkins, West Virginia. Marshall Goldberg was heavily recruited out of high school as Pitt won the recruiting battle from Notre Dame for his services, claiming later in his life that he chose Pittsburgh because "in those days a Goldberg at Notre Dame would have been a big thing," as he referred to a Jewish back playing for a Catholic school.[2] He was a versatile athlete in Elkins captaining his football, basketball and track teams, and Sutherland hoped he would be able to translate that success for the Panthers. Luckily for the hall-of-fame coach, he would be able to do that and more. Lineman Steve Petro, a sophomore in 1936 who got his first shot to start in the 1937 Rose Bowl, didn't even realize that Goldberg was a player when he first saw him at training camp. "He was there about two or three days before I realized he was a football player, I thought he was a manager he was such a small person."[3]

With a potential sophomore star in his backfield, Sutherland seemed a little more indecisive about his starting lineup than he had in the past, and the time before the opening tilt against Ohio Wesleyan was growing short. At fullback he was at a loss with who to start, though Bill Stapulis held a small edge as the week was coming to an end because he impressed the coach with his conditioning. On the line, one of the main competitions was at center, where Don Hensley and Henry Adams were battling for the starting spot at center. One of the few areas he was settled was at end, where Bill Daddio and Frank Souchak held down the spots. Regardless of who eventually started, one thing was for sure, Sutherland and the Golden Panthers had done their jobs, as 1936 was going to be a season to remember.

Game 1—September 26, 1936, at Pitt Stadium

OHIO WESLEYAN UNIVERSITY BATTLING BISHOPS	0
UNIVERSITY OF PITTSBURGH PANTHERS	53

Legends don't always begin with a bang; sometimes they ease into their place in history. With the special players, when they play their first game, it's as if they had been there all along. For Tony Dorsett, in his initial game of his college career as a freshman, he had his first 100-yard contest against Georgia in 1973. In their battle versus the Battling Bishops of Ohio Wesleyan to open the 1936 campaign, Coach Jock Sutherland had another future Panther legend at his disposal, one that he decided to start against his undermanned opponents. The decision would prove fortuitous as sophomore Marshall Goldberg gave the Panther fans a taste of things to come as he helped ignite a powerful offense in his first varsity game that made quick work of their Buckeye opponents.

It wasn't that Sutherland ever had a fear that Ohio Wesleyan was a legitimate foe that was making him so indecisive about his starting lineup, but with such a vast array of talent at his disposal he was just trying to get the right mix to see what they could do together. What he did was forge together an effective backfield that would be very dangerous for opponents the rest of the campaign.

With an unknown teammate looking on, Coach Sutherland speaks with Marshall Goldberg (left) who had an amazing career at the school, ending with a record 1,957 yards rushing that stood as the school mark until Tony Dorsett broke it in 1974.

Led by the sophomore Goldberg at left halfback, the Panther coach inserted Stapulis at fullback, who had the edge as pre-season camp was ending; the veteran Bobby LaRue at right halfback; and Pitt's future head coach who would lead them to the Sugar Bowl in 1956, quarterback John Michelosen.

With their dynamic duo of Frank Souchak and Bill Daddio at end, the interior Panther line to begin the 1936 campaign was made up of the following. At tackle stood George Delich and Tony Matisi with Bill Glassford and Dante DalleTezze at guard; as center Don Hensley would anchor the line. While Delich may have gotten the nod over Averill Daniell for this contest because of Daniell's less-than-stellar practice habits the week before the game, before too long Daniell understood Sutherland's message and would become the strength of the offensive line.

While seemingly outclassed, the Battling Bishops of Ohio Wesleyan were not strangers to upsetting major college football foes. They had several wins over the years against schools that were a class above them. In 1927, the Bishops helped open the University of Michigan's legendary Michigan Stadium with a 33–0 loss in the first game ever at the facility. A year later coach George Gauthier brought his squad once again to Ann Arbor and pulled one of the sport's greatest upsets with a 17–7 victory. The win proved to be the highlight for Gauthier, who spent 26 years as the Bishops' coach after a one-year stint at Michigan Agricultural (later known as Michigan State). "No one who was there will ever forget—that little band of Battling Bishops against the mighty Wolves. A special train-load of faculty, alumni and students went along for the dedication game. We were nervous in the unfinished dressing rooms. With a half-hour to go to game time someone started singing, and soon the locker room rang with close harmony college songs. We were relaxed, and we were ready. After the first few minutes, a player coming off the field told me: 'They're not too tough, coach. We can take them,'" the coach remembered.[4]

While Gauthier had some big wins in his career, odds were certainly against him in this one. He had two effective players in his backfield with John Heinlen at quarterback and Harold Hulsbeck at fullback, but they certainly were not the equal of the Panthers' backfield. Nineteen thousand fans showed up for the opener, and the proof of Pitt's superiority was apparent from the opening kickoff.

The Panthers notched two touchdowns in the first quarter and three more in the second. So dominant was Pittsburgh that they even converted on four of five extra points on the first half, an area of the Panthers that had been their Achilles' heel over the years. They ran through Ohio Wesleyan at will, led by Goldberg in his first varsity game. He started off the affair with a short touchdown before his initial spectacular moment in a Panther uniform. The sophomore took a handoff from his own 24 and rambled through the Battling Bishop defenders, breaking tackles before finding an opening. Goldberg didn't stop until he saw the end zone 76 yards later giving Pitt a 14–0 lead.

He was one of the most sought-after Pitt recruits in ages and showed his talent with several long runs before being pulled by Sutherland by the half. The Panthers notched three more scores in the second half as John Wood scored twice and sophomore Harold Stebbins once, with single touchdowns by Bobby LaRue, Leo Malarkey and Frank Patrick in the 53–0 win. Remarkably the score wasn't indicative of Pitt's supremacy on this day as they outgained the Bishops 801–44 as the defense held Gauthier's squad to a mere two first downs.

It was an incredible performance by the blue and gold, but as well as they played, it was Goldberg that stole the show. "The speedy Jewish boy looks like the best broken field runner since the days of Toby Uansa and he seems destined to move into the select group of outstanding left half backs which includes such great ones as Gibby Welch and Tommy Davies. In addition to his elusiveness and a swell change of pace which completely fooled the Battling Bishops, Marshall has the drive of a fullback when he is cornered and must call on pure power to brush past would-be tacklers."[5]

As it turned out, Goldberg would be that and much more, eventually becoming a more renowned back than Welch and Davies. Goldberg would go on to become the single greatest running back and arguably Pitt's greatest offensive player until an Aliquippa native by the name of Tony Dorsett set foot on Pitt Stadium 37 years later, and it all started on this day, with a spectacular performance against Ohio Wesleyan.

Game 2—October 3, 1936, at Pitt Stadium
WEST VIRGINIA UNIVERSITY MOUNTAINEERS   0
UNIVERSITY OF PITTSBURGH PANTHERS   34

After a decent start to his tenure at West Virginia University with a 6–4 mark in 1934, Charles "Trusty" Tallman's Mountaineers had gone in reverse with a 3–4–2 record a year later. WVU seemed to be rebounding at the start of the 1936 campaign, beating Waynesburg 7–0 in the opening contest before a 40–6 dismantling of Cincinnati a week later. Coming off their impressive thrashing of Ohio Wesleyan in the opener 53–0, Coach Jock Sutherland and the University of Pittsburgh Panthers knew that they would have a much tougher go of it against the Mountaineers, the final contest before they took on their first national power of the season: the Ohio State Buckeyes.

To improve the program, Tallman knew he needed to be successful recruiting in the fertile football hills of Western Pennsylvania and felt he was making inroads in that endeavor. Spud DeAngelis, Dave Volkin, Harold Lorenz and Alex Atty all were from the area and hoped to help take West Virginia to a new level. As well as his Western Pennsylvania recruits, the Mountaineer coach was also excited about his passing attack which performed exceptionally against the Bearcats. Junior halfback Kelly Moran and end Babe Barna led the way, combining for three touchdown passes against Cincinnati. Tallman hoped they could be as effective against the Pitt defensive backfield. Quarterback Harold Lorenz, halfback Glenn Carder and fullback Sam Audia rounded out the dangerous West Virginia backfield.

For the Panthers, it was time to get serious about the season, and Sutherland wanted to get the message to his players that they needed to play hard from the first day of practice to game time. Before the opening contest against the Battling Bishops, three of his projected starters for the season, fullback Frank Patrick, future All-American tackle Averill Daniell and quarterback

Arnold Greene, were on the bench when the game started due to their poor practice habits. Bill Stapulis, George Delich and future Pitt coach John Michelosen all received surprising starts and did well in the demolition of the Bishops. Seemingly all three who were benched got the message clearly and recaptured their spots for the important game against the Mountaineers. Sutherland decided on making one more switch before the game. He inserted Henry Adams, who had struggled the first two seasons despite his promise as a recruit, to the center spot replacing Don Hensley.

With Patrick back in his spot at fullback, it gave Sutherland perhaps the deepest backfield in his tenure at Pitt. His starting crew that included Greene, Patrick, Marshall Goldberg and Bobby LaRue were more than capably backed up by Stapulis, Michelosen, John Wood and Harold Stebbins. It would be this group of runners that would help the Panthers to a big victory in the 1936 version of the Backyard Brawl, crushing Tallman's hopes of an upset in the process.

The game was scoreless after the first period giving the Mountaineers a hope that turned out to be a farce. Sutherland knew his backfield was explosive. As it turned out, a ninth back in the incredible arsenal would turn out to be the star. Leo Malarkey was a product of the incredible recruiting that Sutherland and the Golden Panthers did in Western Pennsylvania. The McDonald, Pennsylvania, native, who kept in shape running to Carnegie and back, went from an afterthought to the star of the afternoon in front of 21,000 at Pitt Stadium as he led Pittsburgh on their first scoring drive of the afternoon. With the ball at the WVU 46, Stebbins sprinted 36 yards to the 10. Three plays later Malarkey pushed it over the goal line carrying some Mountaineer defensemen on his back to give Pitt the 7–0 lead.

West Virginia drove into Panther territory the next series, but the defense stiffened and took over on downs at the 31. Their confidence rising with every play, the Panthers easily went to their 48 before LaRue found Fabian Hoffman wide open behind a surprised WVU secondary for the 52-yard completion and a 14-point lead as the half came to an end.

It was apparent at that point that Sutherland had little to worry about as the two-touchdown advantage seemed to be perfectly safe. Instead of sitting on it, Malarkey stretched the Pitt advantage to three touchdowns quickly as the second half began. As the Panthers started at their 20, the McDonald native found a huge hole, bursting through it and not stopping until he had his second score of the day.

Tallman's troops were desperate to try and make the game competitive and decided to force the offense through the air. Moran went back to pass and tossed it off Daniell's hands, who was having a phenomenal defensive effort against the Mountaineers. After the ball hit the All-American's hands it went into those of Tony Matisi. Matisi took it the final 33 yards for the defensive touchdown, and what was a rout now turned into an embarrassment.

Before the third quarter was over, the Panthers put the finishing touches on the impressive 34–0 shutout when Matisi threw a classic block which gave Malarkey another huge hole as the halfback waltzed in for his third touchdown on this memorable afternoon. Sutherland gave his little-used reserves plenty of playing time in the last quarter of the contest, but WVU was still unable to get in the end zone.

It was a devastating loss for Tallman. Despite the fact they won their next four contests against less-than-marginal programs, the coach lost his final three contests to finish at 6–4, losing his job in the process. For Pitt, it was happier times as they began the toughest part of their schedule with an impressive victory, one where they showed their future opponents that there was no back they could concentrate on to stop as there were nine interchangeable backs that could make a Saturday afternoon a miserable experience for all who tried to contain them.

Game 3—October 10, 1936, at Ohio Stadium in Columbus, Ohio

UNIVERSITY OF PITTSBURGH PANTHERS 6
OHIO STATE UNIVERSITY BUCKEYES 0

One of the hallmarks of Coach Jock Sutherland's tenure at the University of Pittsburgh was his schedule, which would begin with an easy tilt or two before giving way to one of the, if not the, most difficult schedules in the nation. Following one-sided wins over Ohio Wesleyan and West Virginia, Sutherland took his squad to Columbus, Ohio, to face an estimated 80,000 fans and the defending Big Ten–champion Ohio State Buckeyes.

Led by coach Francis A. Schmidt, the Buckeyes finished tied with the Minnesota Golden Gophers in 1935 for the conference title and seventh in the nation on the Dickinson ratings. With only an 18–13 upset loss to the Fighting Irish of Notre Dame to mar an otherwise excellent season, Ohio State ran through a phenomenal 7–1 campaign that culminated with a 38–0 annihilation of their bitter rivals from Michigan. It was the year before that Schmidt etched his name in Ohio State football when he uttered a memorable statement talking about chances over the Wolverines, claiming that they "put their pants on one leg at a time same as everybody else."[6] The statement gave rise to the legendary gold-pants club where each Ohio State football player receives a gold-pants charm every time they defeat the Wolverines.

Following their exceptional campaign, Schmidt's crew began the 1936 season with a rout of NYU 60–0. With their impressive talent, coupled with the home-field advantage and their large, passionate home crowd, the experts installed the Buckeyes as a 7-to-5 favorite to beat the Panthers. They did so despite the fact that Pittsburgh had two impressive wins themselves to open the season. The gamblers felt that NYU was a much tougher opponent than either that the Panthers faced and the Buckeyes should be able to prevail at home.

Ohio State had suffered only one injury in the opener with right tackle Charlie Gales as the only player who would not be able to go against Pitt due to the tendon he pulled against the Violets. Their explosive backfield, who hoped to run roughshod over the Panther defense, included one of the best backs in the Big Ten, quarterback Tippy Dye, as well as halfbacks Bill Booth and John Bettridge and fullback Jim McDonald. Dye had propelled an offense that averaged close to 30 points a game during their conference championship season and were expected to do the same this year.

Luckily for the Panthers, they came into the contest as healthy as the Buckeyes were. Only left end Paul Shaw, who was out with an injured leg, would not be available for Ohio State. It made no difference to Sutherland as he had Bill Daddio as a more-than-capable replacement. Frank Souchak had suffered an injured shoulder earlier in the season but was expected to be healthy for this matchup, and lineman Dante DalleTezze had a cut above his eye received against WVU the week before but was also expected to play. The Panther coach was impressed at the cordial treatment he had received by the home team prior to the match in Columbus, but he assured players and fans alike, "We'll try to make ourselves the most unpleasant guests the Buckeyes have had."[7]

While the attendance was less than the 80,000 expected, 71,000 still showed up, including 12,000 from Pittsburgh to see the most anticipated college football game that weekend. The Pitt defense had been thoroughly impenetrable during the season to that point, but hadn't met an attack as successful as the Buckeyes had been. As it turned out, it should have been Ohio State saying that they had not met a defense as difficult as the Panthers. Pittsburgh thoroughly frustrated their impressive opponents, only permitting a net total of 30 yards for the home team. Unfortunately for Sutherland, while his offense proved to be superior, the Buckeye defense was equally tough, holding Pitt scoreless for the first three quarters.

While Ohio State never crossed the Panther 43-yard line and their vaunted backfield was limited to six yards rushing, Pitt had their first scoring chance on their first drive of the game. Following what looked like a promising Buckeye drive that ended quickly at their own 11-yard line thanks to an offside penalty and an aggressive Pittsburgh defensive line, Ohio State punted the ball to midfield. Marshall Goldberg and Bobby Larue ran the ball to the 30

A first-team All-American end in 1937, Frank Souchak's athletic career was more notable following his career at Pitt. After one season with Pittsburgh in the NFL, Souchak went on to greater fame as an amateur golfer where he won several local tournaments as well as the 1967 Bing Crosby Pro-Am with his brother Mike. Souchak's greatest moment came in the 1953 U.S. Open at Oakmont where he was in second place after the first day and finished ninth as low amateur for the tournament.

before Frank Patrick rambled 12 yards to the 18. Not throwing a forward pass for the entire game, Pitt continued to power through the Buckeye defense until they reached the four. Ohio State stood firm at that point and held Pitt without a score, taking the ball over on downs to keep the game scoreless.

Penalties and a bend-but-don't-break defense, as well as the fact that there was a very difficult wind that was strongly gusting against the Panthers in the second quarter, held Pittsburgh off the scoreboard for the remainder of the first half. Ohio State began the third quarter all of a sudden seemingly in control of the game. It wasn't that they were moving the ball better—they were not—but their defense had dug in with the wind at their backs as the Buckeyes were beginning to win the field position battle. Finally as the quarter was coming to a close, the Pitt offense was finally on the move again, taking it to the Ohio State 33. They couldn't complete the drive, but as the fourth quarter was about to begin, the Panthers once again would have the wind advantage, and with it the hopes of the winning drive.

Even with the gusts blowing behind them, the Panthers were still unable to score midway through the fourth, as it seemed more apparent the game would end in a disappointing tie. They had driven to the Buckeye 35 with six minutes remaining when a sophomore from Williamsport, Pennsylvania, made the play of the game that would allow Pitt to remain undefeated. Harold Stebbins took the ball, cut toward the right sideline and sprinted toward the end zone with the Panther lineman continually mowing down their opponents. John Chickerneo made the clutch block that sent Stebbins into the end zone for the game's lone touchdown.

With under six minutes left, Ohio State tried in vain to tie the game, but unfortunately for the scarlet and gray, the contest's final scoring threat came on a drive by the Panthers as they ran through the now-deflated Buckeye line, ending up at their four-yard line as time expired.

Sutherland was impressed by the performance, giving credit to fullback Bill Stapulis and his line for their inspired performances in the win. The team was now 3–0 without allowing a touchdown. Both the win and scoreless streak would end a week later, but for now, they were intact as Pitt celebrated beating a fellow national power.

Game 4—October 17, 1936, at Pitt Stadium

DUQUESNE UNIVERSITY DUKES 7
UNIVERSITY OF PITTSBURGH PANTHERS 0

It was supposed to be the coronation for the University of Pittsburgh's football team in 1936, the day they legitimized their national championship hopes against their up-and-coming yet underdog neighbors from Forbes Avenue, Duquesne University. The schedule would certainly get more difficult, but it was nothing that the experts figured the Panthers couldn't handle on their way to the title. After all they were 3–0, including a victory over a national power, Ohio State, not only keeping their opponents from scoring, but none of the first three teams they faced even came close to scoring. This was the game where Pitt became the unabashed best team in the nation, and seemingly every confident player on their team knew it. Unfortunately for Coach Jock Sutherland, the Panthers were overconfident, and sometimes difficult moments happen to the overconfident. In reality it did turn out to be the greatest day in the program's history; the problem was it wasn't Pittsburgh that was celebrating. It was the men from the Bluff that would celebrate a victory for the ages.

John "Clipper" Smith headed the program at Duquesne in 1936 as the school had taken a significant step up to major college status with its football team. They had enjoyed nominal success, defeating schools such as West Virginia, Washington and Jefferson, Carnegie Tech, Oklahoma A & M (soon to change their name to Oklahoma State in 1957) and Miami (FL), whom they defeated in the 1933 Palm Festival, the precursor to the Orange Bowl. The problem was that none of these programs were considered national powers at the time the Dukes defeated them. They had yet to have their defining moment.

Following a 10–1 mark in 1933, the architect of the program, Elmer Layden, left to revive his alma mater at Notre Dame. First Joe Bach, then Christy Flanagan did a fine job maintaining their winning ways, but they had fallen back a bit from their high-water mark in 1933. The administration at Duquesne wanted to get the program back on an upward swing so they used the same philosophy they had when they brought Layden aboard in 1927—hiring a former Notre Dame All-American who was taught the game by the legendary Knute Rockne: Clipper Smith. The former guard was named All-American in 1927 and coached North Carolina State unsuccessfully in two of the three seasons he was there between 1931 and 1933. Smith was named line coach for the Dukes in 1935 before assuming the mantle of head coach a year later.

There was a different feel in 1936 for Duquesne. Like the Panthers, they had reeled off three successive victories without allowing a point. They outscored Waynesburg, Rice and Geneva 61–0 in the contests but were still considered a sizeable underdog against Sutherland's squad. Center Mike Basrak, who would be named a first-team All-American by season's end, anchored an aggressive line, while end Ernie Hefferle and quarterback Boyd Brumbaugh, who would take a backseat to Frank Zoppetti as the starter on this afternoon, were the spark plugs of the offense during the memorable campaign.

While the team looked impressive, the Dukes had two injuries that potentially could hamper their efforts against Pitt, with halfback Beto Vairo, who was their top punter, suffering a ruptured blood vessel in his ankle, and fullback Johnny Karrs had sprained his back during practice before the game. They were both reported as available for the game but would not start; nor were they completely healthy by game time. Smith decided that George Matsik would take Vairo's spot while Ken Bechtloff would start for Karrs.

The two injuries in his backfield made Duquesne's chances even longer, especially considering the fact that the Panthers would come into this contest with the same starting squad intact that dominated Ohio State the week before. The only two spots he was contemplating as game time approached was whether Arnold Greene or Jon Michelosen would start at quarterback, and at center where he was deciding between Henry Adams and Don Hensley. One change Sutherland did decide on early was at fullback where Bill Stapulis got a shot to start after his impressive performance against the Buckeyes.

While there was a talent differential and Duquesne had some important injuries, the Dukes were the defending city champions on the basis of Pitt's tie against Carnegie Tech and their defeat of the Tartans, although 1936 marked the first time all three city opponents would play against each other in a single season for a true Pittsburgh title. Despite their 1935 Steel City championship, Pitt hadn't lost to an eastern foe for eight seasons and was 3–1 against the Dukes, their only loss being a 10–6 defeat 33 years before in 1903, the last time Duquesne scored against the Panthers.

Only 25,000 fans came to the game, a far cry from the 50,000 that the experts had predicted. The sparse crowd was treated to a punting contest in the first quarter before Pitt took over at the 48. After a four-yard run by Bobby LaRue, sophomore Marshall Goldberg took the team to the Dukes' 22 on two successive runs. Eventually they advanced it to the 13 before the drive stalled, one yard short of a first down.

After they took over, the Dukes quickly advanced to the 42 on runs by Brumbaugh and Vairo, but a holding penalty stopped the drive, forcing a punt deep into Pitt territory. Unable to advance, Duquesne returned a short Stapulis punt to the Panther 30. Brumbaugh then rambled for a first down at the 20. Moving to the 12 as the second quarter began, the injured Karrs fumbled the ball where Fabian Hoffman picked it up. The game returned to a punting contest again after the two threats as Smith inserted Matsik into the game for Vairo which would soon prove to be a very fortuitous substitution. After Stapulis launched a punt which was downed at their own 22, Brumbaugh ran the ball twice to the 29; at that point several streaks were about to end. Matsik took the ball around left end where the play looked like it was about to end as he was about to be stopped by the stout Pitt defensive wall. Somehow the Matsik broke thorough the line as his offensive line pushed away the Panther defenders. As the goal line approached, LaRue was the only Pitt defender left with a chance to preserve the scoreless tie. He couldn't catch the Duquesne back as Matsik did something no other Dukes player had done since early in the 20th century: score against a Panther team. Brumbaugh converted on the extra point as the Dukes took a 7–0 lead.

Pittsburgh quickly came back after picking up a fumble on the Dukes' 28 when Boyd Brumbaugh dropped the ball in what was becoming a badly rain-soaked turf on this wet afternoon. Led by Frank Patrick, the Panthers took the ball to the six before Leo Malarkey fumbled himself, with Duquesne picking it up at the two. They ran out the half and remarkably took the touchdown advantage into the locker room.

Pitt had been in this situation before, and coupled with the fact that Matsik broke his finger after his impressive run and would not return, as well as Vairo, who left the game with what was a bad knee injury, they had to feel good about their chances in the second half. Unfortunately for the Panther faithful, the Dukes' defense would be just as magnificent in the second half.

The bad weather kept both offenses in check until the middle of the fourth quarter when the Panthers had one last chance to tie the game and keep their undefeated season intact. With the ball near midfield, Goldberg ran the ball 26 yards to the Duquesne 29. With the game on the line, Zoppetti made the defensive play of the game, picking off a LaRue pass to end the threat at the 21.

At that point the game was just about over. Pitt took the ball at their own 45 late in the fourth quarter but only stood at midfield as the clock ran out; with it went the Panthers' eight-year unbeaten streak against eastern teams and severely diminished their national championship hopes. Sutherland was distraught that his team's overconfidence cost them the game. "I tried to tell those boys what to expect. They wouldn't take me seriously though. Duquesne looked better than I've seen them play before. They deserved to win, no doubt about that," the hall-of-fame coach lamented.[8]

After the game, the Dukes were elated. The administration even extended Smith's contract as a thank-you for the school's signature victory. While the Dukes eventually won the city championship with a 13–0 win against the Tartans and captured the Orange Bowl championship after a thrilling 13–12 victory over Mississippi State, overconfidence got the best of them, costing them a shot at the national title. Following their big win, they immediately lost the next two games as West Virginia Wesleyan and Detroit upset them, putting a damper on the school's big victory.

For the Panthers, it was a lesson well learned as their chances for a national championship would rise again as their season went on. While their day against the Dukes was forgettable, the biggest day in the program's history at that point was only a few months away.

Game 5—October 24, 1936, at Pitt Stadium
UNIVERSITY OF NOTRE DAME FIGHTING IRISH 0
UNIVERSITY OF PITTSBURGH PANTHERS 26

The odds were stacked against the University of Pittsburgh as they prepared to play the University of Notre Dame on an October afternoon in the Steel City in 1936. They were coming off their first loss against an eastern foe in eight seasons when they were beaten by the Duquesne Dukes, and had suffered quite a few injuries in the process. To make matters worse the Fighting Irish had won three games in a row, including a 27–0 shutout against Wisconsin the week before in South Bend. Coach Elmer Layden even had the advantage of beating the Panthers the year before 9–6, handing Pitt its only defeat of the season. Yes, it looked like a tough day for Coach Jock Sutherland and his team. The only problem for Notre Dame was that Pitt's normally emotionless coach and his team were an angry group of Panthers, and in the 1930s, when these Panthers were angry, they rarely came away defeated.

When Notre Dame reached Pittsburgh the day before the game, they brought 35 healthy players with them, a luxury Sutherland did not have. Besides the win against the Badgers, they had also gotten the best of Washington (MO) and Carnegie Tech in the opener. Led by an explosive backfield of Andy Puplis at quarterback, Bob Wilkie and Vic Wojchihovski at halfback and Larry Danbom at fullback, the Irish had rolled up 62 points in their first three contests. They knew, though, that the tough Pitt defense, which yielded a mere touchdown in four games, would be a true measure of how good they were. The one thing that was going against them for this game was that it was their first venture outside South Bend, and if nothing else, Pitt had the home-field advantage.

What Pitt didn't have was four of their starters. Bobby LaRue, Bill Glassford, Frank Souchak and Paul Shaw were injured and doubtful for the contest which led Sutherland to consider a lineup where six of his 11 players would be sophomores. For most schools that would be a scary endeavor; for the Panthers, though, they had Sutherland and his band of Golden Panthers rounding up talent, so replacing four starters wasn't as daunting a task. Sophomores Walter Raskowski, Albin Lezouski, Fabian Hoffman and quarterback John

Chickerneo were all being considered to join Bill Daddio and Marshall Goldberg on the first team.

After the huge upset, many thought that an irritated Sutherland would have pushed his squad with extreme workouts to prepare for Notre Dame, constantly reminding his club of its embarrassing defeat. Instead he made it business as usual, knowing his team was more than embarrassed for its subpar performance against its undermanned opponents. In fact, he didn't even show up for practice. Ave Daniell remembered that "after we had played Duquesne and got beat, 7–0, Jock didn't even come to practice but we had Notre Dame coming up the following Saturday. He didn't even come to practice; the assistant coaches carried the ball. He didn't say a word in the dressing room. He disciplined us. We went out and beat the pants off Notre Dame. He knew what he was doing."[9]

They would have the biggest crowd behind them since the Irish crushed Pitt 35–19 at Pitt Stadium in 1930, the last time they faced the legendary Knute Rockne. A sold-out throng of 75,000 was expected as ticket sales for the game were stopped by the university a few days before the game. So popular was the ticket that there was a rash of counterfeit tickets that were making their rounds in the city as the officials at the school warned patrons to be careful they weren't buying the fake versions.

It was such a sought-after ticket not only because two of the nation's elite programs were facing off, but also because rumor had it that this might be the final game between these two schools in Pittsburgh for the foreseeable future. It was being reported that the game in 1937 at South Bend would be the last in the rivalry, although Layden did his best to dispel the rumors, claiming that the schools were working to extend their agreement. Unfortu-

Ave Daniell was a walk-on tackle who remarkably was eventually named as a first-team All-American for the University of Pittsburgh his senior season in 1936. Called by coach Jock Sutherland one of the smartest tackles who played for him, Daniell was elected to the College Football Hall of Fame in 1975.

nately for college football fans, the rumors proved to be true as Notre Dame, as well as most of the Big Ten schools, decided they did not want to schedule Pitt as long as they participated in paying their players such a generous amount; therefore, while they did finish out their contract with a 1937 tilt in South Bend, this would be the last contest between the two schools at Pitt Stadium for seven seasons. It was a game, though, that Panther aficionados would long remember.

It was a perfect warm October day at the sold-out facility as the fans and the players alike would turn feisty as the day went on. While injured, LaRue and Glassford found their way onto the field and would be a big part of the success on this afternoon. Midway in the first quarter, Pitt had their first scoring opportunity of the game as they quickly pushed the ball to their own 46. At that point their incredible sophomore back, Goldberg, who was celebrating his 18th birthday, took the handoff and went 23 yards to the Notre Dame 31. On the next play he went 13 more, setting up a field-goal attempt by Daddio at the 22. The fellow sophomore missed the kick as Notre Dame luckily kept the game scoreless.

The game turned into a battle of field positions as the punters took over. Finally as the second quarter was reaching its midway point, the Panthers took over at their 34, and Pitt would use this drive to establish the dominance it would show for the remainder of the game. Goldberg, Bill Stapulis and Harold Stebbins took advantage of the holes their line was opening in the Irish defensive line. Slowly the team went down the field ending up at the Notre Dame 27. Goldberg then ran over the right side of the Irish wall to take it to the 17. Four plays later Stapulis muscled the ball to the two. The fullback ended the drive with a jaunt to the left as he easily went in for the first score of the game and a 7–0 Panther lead.

At that point Pitt took control that it would not relinquish when LaRue took the ball 67 yards to the three with seconds left in the half. The Irish kept their faint hopes alive, stopping the Panthers before they scored again, as the clock ran out. It didn't matter, as before the second half was too old, they would put the game out of hand. Goldberg took the kickoff 45 yards to the Irish 40. Stapulis sprinted 40 yards on the next play to apparently put Pitt up be two touchdowns, but the ball was brought back on a holding penalty. Two plays later Stapulis found Hoffman with a pass at the 20. Hoffman caught the ball and ran down the sideline over the goal line giving Pitt a quick 13-point advantage.

The Panther defense had been at its best all day, so the two-touchdown lead seemed to be more than enough. Notre Dame had their only scoring threat of the game in the fourth quarter moving to the Panther 18 on the heels of the two first downs they had in the ball game, but the drive was halted when Bill McCarthy threw the ball over the end line giving Pitt possession at their 20. LaRue quickly gave the Panthers outstanding field position at the Irish 40 with a 40-yard run. They moved to the 26 when the frustration of the Notre Dame players came to the surface. Chuck O'Reilly hit a Pitt player and was given a roughing penalty, putting the ball at the 13. Thinking his quarterback was kicked out of the game, Layden ran onto the field and grabbed a referee, prompting the police to come out thinking there would be a fight. Peace was once again restored as Goldberg eventually made it 20–0 with a one-yard burst that sent the sellout crowd to their feet cheering for their hometown team.

With the game officially out of hand, John Wood, who was perhaps the fastest player on the team, picked off a George Kovalcik pass and ran 46 yards for the final touchdown late in the fourth quarter for the 26–0 shutout victory. Wood said a few days after the game that he actually had set up a play with Tony Matisi where if he intercepted a ball, he'd run right behind Matisi hopefully for a score. Matisi wasn't there at first, but when he finally spotted him, Matisi screamed for him to go as he went right behind his cohort who leveled a few Irish players, leading Wood into the end zone as he had promised.

Before the contest, the experts felt that Notre Dame would continue to be a national championship contender with a victory over an injured Panther squad that seemingly was out of the title chase. Hours later when the final whistle blew, the Irish knew they should never underestimate a Jock Sutherland–coached squad as the dominant win put Pitt back in the championship spotlight.

Game 6 — October 31, 1936, at the Polo Grounds in New York, New York

UNIVERSITY OF PITTSBURGH PANTHERS	0
FORDHAM UNIVERSITY RAMS	0

In the 21st century, to hear that the University of Pittsburgh was facing Fordham University, immediately thoughts would be of a pre-season basketball contest where Coach Jamie Dixon was looking for an easy win. Never would one have thought of a football game that had national championship implications. In the 1930s, though, Fordham and Pitt were on top of the college football world, and after a breathtaking scoreless tie in 1935, the two teams would meet once again, a burgeoning rivalry that while brief would be one of the most memorable in the history of the sport.

After an upset loss to their neighbors from Duquesne, the Panthers had vaulted themselves back into the national championship conversation with a one-sided shutout of Notre Dame. The Rams of Fordham also were one of the few teams that could join them, thanks to a vaunted line that has been known in the history of the sport as one of college football's best. The competition they had played early on was not among the most difficult. They had forged a 4–0 mark coming into this contest, but two of their first three victories came at the hands of lower-level schools in Franklin and Marshall as well as Waynesburg. Out of the 128 points the offense would score in 1936, 86 of them came against these two lesser opponents. A 7–0 victory against SMU in the season's second week gave them some legitimacy, and a one-point 7–6 win when St. Mary's came to New York took it one step further, giving them title aspirations.

Coach Jim Crowley was a member of the legendary Four Horsemen backfield for Knute Rockne and the Notre Dame Fighting Irish in the early 1920s and knew what it took to be a champion. He took over a successful Fordham program in 1933 from Frank Cavanaugh, who had built his winning teams with a dynamic line called the Seven Blocks of Granite. The powerful line led the Rams to a 15–1–2 mark in 1929 and 1930. Rather than create a new roadmap to victory, Crowley borrowed the same strategy as he built his own version of the Seven Blocks of Granite, a group of players that would surpass and become more remembered than their predecessors: Al Babartsky, Joe Bernard, John Druze, Ed Franco, Jim Hayes, Harry Jacunski, Mike Kochel, Leo Paquin, Nat Pierce, Alex Wojciechowicz and a man who would be more renowned as the greatest coach in the history of the NFL, Vince Lombardi. The group led by Wojciechowicz and Lombardi had an impressive 12–1–3 mark in 1936 and 1937 with eight shutouts. They would need every ounce of talent, though, to stop what had become a devastating Panther offensive attack. Crowley felt that they would be successful, calling his magnificent defense "the best defensive bunch I had ever seen."[10]

That great defensive group had their eyes firmly focused on the Panthers' superb sophomore Marshall Goldberg, who had earned the nickname "Mad Marshall" or the "Elkins Eel" during his phenomenal first campaign in a blue-and-gold uniform. Crowley knew if he could stop Goldberg, it would hamper the Panthers' offense. They also could follow the game plan the Dukes used when they did just that, shut down the Panthers.

Pitt was healthier than they were against the Irish, although fullback Frank Patrick and Tony Matisi, who had injured his leg, were questionable and not anticipating much time on the field. Coach Jock Sutherland decided that his starting lineup was so impressive against the Irish, he would use the same group in front of 57,000 at the Polo Grounds for this important game that just might decide the eastern region champion and the spot in the Rose Bowl that came with it.

In the game, the Panthers would prove Crowley wrong on one aspect: it was them and not the Rams that had the best defense on the field that day. It was Pitt who was the best as they kept Fordham out of the end zone for their fourth shutout in five games. The Ram coach was correct, though, in the thought that if they bottled up Goldberg, they would be able to stop the vaunted Pitt attack; they did that and more.

As impenetrable as the Seven Blocks of Granite were offensively, the Panthers found a chink in their armor, constantly attacking the right side of their line to limit the Fordham attack to 180 yards and only one venture past the Panthers' 40-yard line. The game was nothing short of a field position battle in the first half, with a Goldberg 26-yard run being the only significant gain in the opening two quarters.

LaRue gave the Panthers some hope as the third quarter began, rambling with the opening kickoff 41 yards as he appeared to be headed toward the end zone with the contest's first score. Unfortunately, as he passed midfield the Rams caught up with him, putting him down at that point. They were unable to advance any further, but it became obvious that Pitt was the better team on the field.

After a quick three-and-out by the Rams, Pittsburgh started again at midfield, but this time they were intent on powering through the tiring Fordham defense. Goldberg; Patrick, who played well despite his injuries; and LaRue led them to the 25. At that point the latter two advanced to the 12. Following a couple of short runs, Goldberg sprinted to the three where the Panthers stood with a fourth-and-one. Sutherland had an important decision to make: kick a field goal, pass for either a first down or touchdown, or

From the first time he stepped on the gridiron for the University of Pittsburgh, Marshall Goldberg showed Panther fans he was something special. The Elkins, West Virginia, native impressively ran for 203 yards in his first varsity game which was a 53–0 rout of Ohio Wesleyan at Pitt Stadium in 1936.

power it through the Blocks of Granite. Field goals were far from a sure thing in that era, and the Panthers had tried to go through the air twice before in clutch situations only to see the ball end up in the enemies' hands. Journalist Dan Jenkins stated that when talking to a football fan of the era, the fan said about Sutherland, "All Jock knows how to do is run the fullback up the tackle's ass."[11] It was true that Sutherland was conservative in his offensive approach, but the fan wasn't quite correct in this instance. He ran LaRue, a halfback not a fullback, up the tackles ass. Fordham quickly surrounded him and tackled him short of the sticks.

With the game remaining scoreless, Pitt had one more opportunity in the final quarter as they had the ball at the Fordham 40. Trying to go against his conservative patterns, John Urban went back to toss a pass to John Wood. Unfortunately the pass went into the waiting arms of the Rams' Waitkoski. Not only was Pitt's last chance to score now thrown out the window, but Fordham had the ball. The Panther defense held and even was able to enter Fordham territory again, but that was as close as they got.

As time was running out, the Rams threw a scare into Sutherland with a 26-yard ramble by Joe Dulkie, but that drive eventually went the way of all other drives in this contest when John Lock slipped on fourth down and fell to the turf. What had appeared like a sure first down ended with Pitt taking over. The clock soon struck zero as these two schools remarkably battled to a scoreless tie for the second consecutive year.

It was a disappointing end and would put the Panthers under extreme pressure in their final three contests as they knew one more tie or loss would all but end their Rose Bowl hopes for this talented team.

Game 7—November 7, 1936, at Pitt Stadium
PENN STATE UNIVERSITY NITTANY LIONS 7
UNIVERSITY OF PITTSBURGH PANTHERS 34

To grasp just how long Joe Paterno coached at Penn State, one needs only to compare how many coaches had walked the sideline at Penn State since 1930 and how many coached at their opponents' on this day, the University of Pittsburgh. At Pitt between 1930 and 2011 when Paterno resigned under controversial circumstances, 22 men were called upon to lead the program; at Penn State there were but four. The first of the four, who took over in 1930, was the one that originally made the program relevant, Bob Higgins.

Three-time All-American at the alma mater for which he now coached, Higgins would eventually lead the Nittany Lions out of mediocrity to a place among the elite of college football. Seven years into his tenure, though, the school was still struggling. They had finished .500 on two occasions with 4-4 marks, but struggled below .500 in the other campaigns.

The 1936 season was proving to be more of the same for Penn State as they were about to meet their rivals from the western side of the state. After an opening win against Muhlenberg, they lost three consecutive games against Villanova, Lehigh and Cornell before a home victory against Syracuse. The odds that they could turn heir fortunes around against Pitt were long indeed.

Even though they played a close contest against the Panthers in 1935, their first game against them since 1931, losing 9–0, it was a young Pitt team that seemingly had matured. The other two factors were that despite the dominance Penn State would eventually have against Pitt, they were inferior at this point. They had lost 11 straight games since back-to-back scoreless ties in 1920 and 1921 and were 1–17–2 between 1913 and 1935. To make matters worse, the Panthers were coming off a scoreless tie against Fordham which put their eastern championship and Rose Bowl hopes in peril, so the odds that Sutherland would take it easy on the Lions were long indeed.

Before the contest began, the experts were giving Penn State a chance to at least compete with the Panthers, feeling that a victory over Syracuse plus the fact they were getting some injured players back, which included sophomore halfback Johnny Patrick, would spur the Lions to a good performance. Patrick, a Pittsburgh boy from Schenley High School and Kiski, had been Higgins's only sophomore to start in the season opener, but was hurt against Muhlenberg and hadn't played since. He joined a starting backfield that also included Frank O'Hara, Sammy Donato, and Tom Silvano. They would run behind a line anchored by center Chuck Cherundolo, a player who was better known in Pittsburgh sports history as the greatest center the Steelers had prior to the Chuck Noll era.

As had been the case in the past couple of weeks, Sutherland was grateful for the incredible depth he and the Golden Panthers had recruited, as he had talented reserves for Bill Glassford and Dante DalleTezze, who were both doubtful for the contest, as well as Bobby LaRue, who had been banged up by Fordham. Without two important members of his line in the starting lineup as well as his senior half back, Sutherland chose three sophomores, halfback Harold Stebbins, Walter Raskowski and Albin Lezouski, to replace them. That left the Panthers with seven sophomores in their first team with Fabian Hoffman and Bill Daddio at the ends and quarterback John Chickerneo and halfback Marshall Goldberg joining them.

It was a perfect fall day for football as 19,000 fans descended on Pitt Stadium to watch this cross-state rivalry. While the game eventually was a one-sided affair, for the better part of the contest it was a fiercely fought, close game. Penn State looked like it had the firepower to destroy the Panther's season early when a fake punt by Patrick turned out to be a 35-yard run that set up the Nittany Lions on the Pitt 30. Patrick fumbled on the next play turning it back to the Panthers when Don Hensley fell on it ending the threat. It would be one of six fumbles that Penn State would have this day, four of them ending up in the Panthers' hands.

On the next series, Patrick put the ball on the ground again as Daddio picked it up, giving the Panthers their first real scoring threat of the contest, taking over at the Lions 25. With the second quarter now beginning, Pitt was in position to take the lead and quickly took advantage. On third down Goldberg found Bill Stebbins at the two-yard line with a perfect slant. Stebbins easily crossed the goal line to give the Panthers the seven-point lead.

The score inspired Pitt as they had no less than four chances to score in the second quarter. Two of the opportunities were stunted by Panther fumbles of their own as following a 38-yard run by Johnny Urban, which put Pittsburgh at six, he then lost the ball with O'Hara picking it up. Pitt then advanced the ball to the Lions' 19 following a poor punt, then losing it when a Stebbins fumble was recovered by Patrick. Two more times Pitt came close, but a great Penn State secondary helped stop the Panther passing attack, keeping the lead at seven as the teams went into the locker room at the half.

Frustrated with so many chances going awry and the fact that the Nittany Lions' Harry Harrison took the opening kickoff of the second half 49 yards, setting up Penn State with tremendous field position, Pitt went on its first sustained drive of the game when they took the ball at the 20 following a punt. Goldberg ripped a 45-yard run through the Penn State defense that put the ball at the 35. Goldberg and Frank Patrick then burst through the reeling Lion defense until they took it to the one. Penn State gambled that Goldberg would get the ball at that point and attacked him. Unfortunately Patrick got the handoff and danced into the end zone for a 14–0 lead.

Sutherland was pleased with the drive and felt the game was now in hand as he sent out his reserves on defense to get them some experience on the field. This proved to be a grave error as Penn State quickly got back in the contest. Returning the ensuing kickoff 35 yards, Penn State moved to the Pitt 46. A quick strike passing offense then came to light with Wendell "Windy" Wear connecting with Henry Adams for 33 yards, then Harrison snuck behind the Panther secondary and was wide open in the end zone. Wear saw him and easily put it into Harrison's hands to make the score 14–7.

Remarkably what looked like a rout was now a one-touchdown game. After Duquesne, Fordham, and now this, Sutherland and his squad were angry and decided to show Penn State exactly who the better team was in the fourth quarter. It was a statement that would speak loudly for this young club. Stebbins started the onslaught with a 39-yard run that put the ball at the Lions' 32. Led by a 15-yard ramble by Goldberg, the ball was now at the four where Stebbins gave Pitt back its two-touchdown lead with a four-yard gallop.

Soon after, a 44-yard touchdown run by Urban after the Panther picked up a Patrick fumble doused whatever hope the Lions had at that point. With Penn State now reeling, Sutherland did not allow Pitt to let up and made what was a close game the one-sided affair they had hoped when Leo Malarkey found a wide-open John Wood in the end zone from 25 yards away to make the final 34–7.

It was a powerful display that the Panthers knew they needed to open the eyes of the college football world as it gave them the momentum they hoped for with a trip to Lincoln, Nebraska, the next week to take on the Cornhuskers.

Game 8—November 14, 1936, at Memorial Stadium in Lincoln, Nebraska

UNIVERSITY OF PITTSBURGH PANTHERS   19
UNIVERSITY OF NEBRASKA CORNHUSKERS   6

The dictionary describes the term "monkey on your back" as a burdensome problem, situation, or responsibility; a personal affliction or hindrance. Since 1929, for Coach Dana X. Bible and the Nebraska Cornhuskers, Pitt had been that monkey on their back.

Bible had led the University of Nebraska Cornhuskers, taking them to the upper echelon of the college football world. Coming into the 1936 campaign, the Cornhuskers had an impressive 43–11–7 under Bible's tutelage and five Big Six Conference titles. As 1936 was coming to a close, so was Bible's tenure at Nebraska. A year later he would take control of the program at the University of Texas. Bible certainly had a wonderful career in Lincoln, Nebraska, one that would be a big reason he was eventually elected to the College Football Hall of Fame in 1951. There was only one regret in his eight seasons with the Cornhuskers; to this point he had never beaten Jock Sutherland and the University of Pittsburgh. As it would turn out, this would be his last chance, being outscored 108–13 in the seven encounters between the two schools.

As had been the case in the past, the Cornhuskers came into this contest with momentum. A 7–0 loss to the eventual national champion Minnesota Golden Gophers in the season's second week was their only blemish in a 5–1 season. Except for Indiana, whom they beat 13–9, they rolled over the rest of their schedule in an easy manner and had all but wrapped up another conference title. Getting this particular monkey off their backs with a victory would give Nebraska a legitimate shot at the national title; a loss would make it just another good season. For Pitt, they knew they had to win their final two games impressively to get a shot at the Rose Bowl and would come out focused to continue their personal stranglehold on this proud program.

The Nebraska loss to Minnesota was particularly upsetting. They had battled the defending national champions evenly for the entire game. With under a minute left, the game was scoreless when Cornhusker halfback Sam Francis went back to punt from his two-yard line. Francis, who was the 1937 NCAA shot-put champion as well as finishing fourth in the 1936 Summer Olympics at Berlin, launched a magnificent punt. They went too aggressively after the returner, who lateraled the ball to a teammate. With Nebraska defenders all going toward the original returner, the Gophers waltzed into the end zone for the victory.

This was a chance for reclamation, and they would try to do so with one of, if not the, best middle lines in college football. Sophomore center Charles Brock and guards Ken McGinnis and Bob Mehring were as difficult a front three as Marshall Goldberg and company would face all season. The solid middle wall gave Sutherland great concern—so much that he was considering a heavy air attack in order to loosen up the middle of their defense.

As good as their defense was, the Cornhuskers' backfield would also give the Panther coach reason for pause. Lloyd Cardwell and Francis were two of the best running backs in the land, two that would certainly test a Pitt defense that had only given up two touchdowns in the season, one with their reserves in.

Sutherland had drilled his team aggressively while in Pittsburgh and then at Stagg Field in Chicago where they stopped on their way to Lincoln. Bill Glassford had been on the sideline for the previous two games with a bad knee, but while he probably would be limited, he seemed to be ready to get back into action. He would rotate with Walter Raskowski and Dante DalleTezze, giving the Panthers a devastating guard combo themselves.

Pitt also had one of the best fullback combinations in the country with Frank Patrick and Bill Stapulis. In this contest Patrick, who had been injured himself earlier in the season, would have to go it alone when Sutherland decided to keep Stapulis in Pittsburgh to take care of his injured shoulder. His backfield would be helped, though, with the return of Bobby LaRue, who had sat out the week before recovering from injuries suffered in the scoreless tie with Fordham.

Enthusiasm was high in Nebraska. The hotels were full of Husker fans as Memorial Stadium was sold out on what would be a cold yet clear day. The Cornhuskers were healthy and a five-to-four betting favorite as the experts dismissed the fact they were playing the team who had dominated them so. Sutherland and his squad would soon show what a mistake that had been.

With his deficiency at fullback due to Stapulis's injury, Sutherland made one maneuver that would turn out to be very fortuitous; he inserted backup quarterback Arnold Greene at fullback to help spell Patrick. Greene had always been considered big for a quarterback, and his size would pay off in this game.

The game started out innocently enough as both teams battled to a scoreless first period, but as the second quarter began, the Cornhuskers looked like they finally figured out how to break the Panther jinx. Pitt actually had the first chance, driving inside the Cornhusker 30, but Bill Daddio missed the field goal from 30 yards out, which set the stage for Cardwell. The speedy Nebraska back sprinted 42 yards on the next play; the only thing holding him from a touchdown was a fine running tackle by Johnny Urban. While the Pitt defense held stopping that drive, they would not be so successful on the next one.

Cardwell returned a Patrick punt 35 yards to the Panther 35. After a few runs by Francis which took the ball to the 20, he took a handoff and went back to pass. Cardwell was covered by three Pitt defenseman in the end zone, but all three failed to disrupt the toss as the Nebraska halfback pulled it in to give the Huskers a 6–0 lead.

Like the week before when the Nittany Lions cut the Pitt lead to a single touchdown and appeared to have the momentum, the Panthers began to take control. With less than four minutes left before the half, the wind picked up and forced a poor Nebraska punt which Pittsburgh picked up at the Husker 44. Greene then sent a 30-yard pass to the 14. A few plays later the ball sat at the two-yard line where the former quarterback muscled through the tough Nebraska line, carrying a few defenders into the end zone to tie the score.

There was now 1:10 remaining in the half as Pitt had a chance to take the lead when the Cornhuskers' John Howell fumbled the ensuing kickoff at the 30 as Tony Matisi pounced on it. Sutherland wanted to go to the air more in the game, and that he did on this series as Johnny Wood connected with Daddio at the 11 and then Greene tossed one to John Michelosen at the four with time enough for one play. Urban used that last play well, going around left end for the touchdown that gave Pitt the 12–6 lead as the half ended.

The two touchdowns seemed to break the backs of the Huskers as it seemed like no matter what happened, the Panthers always had the answers. In the third quarter they spent most of the time dominating play as their offense created more scoring chances. Unfortunately for Sutherland, they couldn't complete them, and the two teams entered the fourth quarter with the visitors still holding on to a precarious six-point advantage.

It seemed like Pitt would finally put the game away on the first drive of the quarter after two runs by Goldberg totaling 52 yards helped set them up at the 10. Unable to move any further, Sutherland wanted to make it a two-score game, sending Frank Souchak in for the short field goal. Already missing a field-goal attempt as well as the two extra points, it obviously wasn't a good day for Pittsburgh kickers, which Souchak proved once again as his attempt was blocked, giving Nebraska one last chance. Their chance ended quickly when Francis fumbled at the 14 as Elmer Merkovsky pulled it for the Panthers, all but ending the contest. Goldberg and Stebbins took turns moving Pitt to the three where the burly Greene once again embarrassed the vaunted Nebraska line, pummeling through them into the end zone which gave Pitt the impressive 19–6 win.

The game wasn't as close as the score indicated, with the Panthers outgaining their opponents 330–109, but the bottom line was Bible failed once again to beat his hall-of-fame foe. Years later after he moved to Texas, Bible wrote to Sutherland and said, "Jock, I just have the highest regard for you, but I wanted so much to have one victory before I left Nebraska. Your teams were always a little too good."[12] Pitt always seemed to be a little better, just enough to keep the monkey on Dana X. Bible's back.

Game 9—November 26, 1936, at Pitt Stadium

CARNEGIE TECH TARTANS	14
UNIVERSITY OF PITTSBURGH PANTHERS	31

Usually when these two neighbors separated by less than a mile in the Oakland section of Pittsburgh met in their annual gridiron clash, the title of Pittsburgh collegiate football champion was on the line. The previous season in 1935 when Carnegie Tech battled Pitt to a scoreless tie, Duquesne won the crown on the basis of their 7–0 defeat of the Tartans. This season, the Dukes swept their Steel City foes with a 13–0 shutout of Carnegie Tech and a 7–0 upset of the Panthers to clinch the title before these two teams met. While there was no city championship on the line, fortunately for the University of Pittsburgh there was something a little bigger to play for: a shot at the eastern championship with the Rose Bowl bid that possibly came with it.

While two years later Tech would transform into a national power, at this point in time they were a young club who showed potential but weren't able to transform it to the win/loss column. They were 2–4 with close losses at the hands of Michigan State and Duquesne. While the offense continually struggled, with only 28 points to their credit defensively they were improving weekly. The problem with playing the Panthers, though, was the fact they had arguably the best defense in the country, allowing only 20 points in their eight games. If Las Vegas sports experts were in vogue in 1936, there would most certainly be odds set that Carnegie Tech would be shut out.

To make matters worse for the Tartans, their star right tackle, Joe Slaminko, who got his first varsity start against Pitt in 1935 and was a huge reason they stalled the Panther attack, would not be able to play because of a bad leg injury he suffered against the Dukes. Nicknamed Lil Abner, Slaminko's injury gave way to Wayne Yeknich, who hoped to be able to replicate Slaminko's success. The injury gave Harspter reason to consider changes in his line. He had several options to reshuffle his starters including shifting his starting left tackle Earl Hudson to the right side so he could move the captain of the team, Nestor Henrion, from left guard back to left tackle where he played the year before. In the backfield the Tech coach kept his starting quarterback and fullback, Coleman Kopcsak and Jack Lee, in the starting lineup, but changed his halfbacks, giving Jerry Rosenthal and Freddy Lehman the shot over the two sophomores he had used the week before.

On the other side of the gridiron, Jock Sutherland made two maneuvers. The first was to reinsert Bill Glassford on the first team as he felt his knee had sufficiently recovered. The other was to replace John Chickerneo at quarterback with John Michelosen, not because Chickerneo's play had suffered, but because Michelosen was considered a more effective defensive back. Sutherland felt the Tartans would be aggressive with their passing game and that Michelosen gave them a better chance to win.

The talent level was much greater at Pittsburgh, but as game time approached a controversy that would eventually bring down the dynasty that Sutherland had built began to surface. The student paper at the University of Nebraska called for the school to end the series between the Panthers and the Cornhuskers. They claimed that they wanted Nebraska to play only schools that "resort to clean, wholesome, amateur practices."[13] Their coach, Dana X. Bible, defended the way Pitt played, claiming they were a clean team and that the relations between the two schools "are most pleasant."[14] While the coach completely supported Sutherland, he never actually addressed the issue that the students were concerned with, that the football program at the University of Pittsburgh was not following the amateur principles that they felt the sportsmen at the time should.

Sutherland angrily quipped, "I might be a biased judge of my own sportsmanship. I suggest you ask other coaches whose teams we have played during my 18 years of coaching."[15] Some of the assertions that the paper made were that Pitt practiced year round and held summer training camp, both considered against the proper practices for a collegiate squad. They also did claim that the Panthers played dirty against the Cornhuskers in their recent game, but none of those accusations would be as important an issue in the future as was the stipend the school gave the football team.

Regardless of the distraction, Pitt remained focused on the task at hand as a larger-than-anticipated crowd at Pitt Stadium of 40,000 people showed up to see the contest. Harpster decided against moving around his line and kept sophomore Manuel Zawacki at right halfback instead of Rosenthal. He did make one unexpected change, inserting Leo Napotnik at fullback for Lee. The changes Harpster made would make them more competitive than the experts felt they'd be; unfortunately they were not able to contain sophomore Marshall Goldberg, which would prove to be the undoing of their upset attempt on this cold, windy winter afternoon as the snow swirled around the stadium.

Carnegie Tech showed Pitt just how difficult a game it would be on the first drive when they advanced the ball from their own 25 to the Panther 17 before the Pitt defense finally dug in to keep the game scoreless. The Pittsburgh offense was just as effective on the following possession, but unlike the Tartans, they were able to get on the scoreboard with a 23-yard field goal by Bill Daddio to give Pitt a 3–0 lead.

As the second quarter began, Pitt increased their lead to ten points thanks to Goldberg. The sophomore took a handoff and then swung around the right end, sprinting through the Tartan secondary past the goal line for the first touchdown of the day. The big play for the Panthers would be the main ingredient of their attack on this cold afternoon, which would continue as they tried to make the game a rout. Arnold Greene, the huge quarterback that Sutherland felt was more suited for fullback, muscled through the center of the Tech line and didn't stop until he reached their nine-yard line for a 53-yard scamper. Two plays later Bobby LaRue easily scored from the three, giving the Panthers what they thought to be an insurmountable 17–0 lead.

It had been four years since the Tartans had scored a touchdown against their city rivals, and while it appeared that the streak would continue, Carnegie Tech finally broke the ice with a half minute left in the half. Looking badly beaten, the ineffective Tech offense turned things around and methodically went through the vaunted Panther defense until Jerry Matelan, who had been hampered with injuries during the season, rambled in from 19 yards out to cut the Pitt lead to ten points as the teams went into the locker room at the half.

As the second half began, the momentum Carnegie Tech acquired late in the second quarter continued as what once looked like a rout was quickly becoming a close encounter. Just as Pitt had quickly built a 17-point lead with the big play, the Tartans used one of their own, making the score 17–14, when Matelan heaved a 54-yard pass to the end zone into the hands of Kellar for the score. The 40,000 fans were stunned as the Panthers' post-season hopes were now in serious jeopardy.

Marshall Goldberg would eventually go on to be one of the greatest players in the program's history, but in 1936 he was a young impressive sophomore who was about to take the squad's Rose Bowl hopes on his back. After LaRue took the kickoff at the 13, the Elkins, West Virginia, native caught a long lateral from his fellow halfback and went down the sideline, bringing the frigid Panther fans to their feet as he easily scored on the 87-yard run to all but put the game out of reach 24–14.

At that point the Tartans had folded. Hoping to keep the game close, Pitt once again made it a rout when first George Delich recovered a Matelan punt at the Tech 17 before Goldberg scored his third touchdown of the game with a six-yard jaunt making the final 31–14. Despite the fact that the game statistically was closer than the scoreboard showed, with the Panthers holding a slight 270–238 advantage in total yards, Goldberg would not let Sutherland and his team be denied. With the Washington Huskies defeating Washington State 40–0 to capture the Pacific Coast Conference title, there was hope around the Panther program that they would be the club selected to face the Huskies.

Not long after the game ended, Averill Daniell and Marshall Goldberg joined fellow Pittsburgh player Mike Basrak from Duquesne on the all-eastern squad. Eventually Daniell would be honored as consensus All-American while Glassford, whose candidacy was hurt by his knee injury, nonetheless had impressed enough experts that he was voted as a first-team All-American by the International News Service. Daddio and Goldberg, who finished the season with a team high of 861 yards on only 106 carries, were impressive as sophomores, but neither achieved first team recognition, with Daddio taking a spot on the third-team Associated Press squad. Alongside the All-Eastern team selection, Goldberg was named on the first-team All-Jewish squad with Robert Goodman of Duquesne and Carnegie Tech's Maurice Patt.

As nice as the individual honors were, the first of the team honors came through, which bolstered the Panthers' Rose Bowl hopes. Sutherland and his squad were awarded a new trophy that eventually would become symbolic of the best college football team in the northeast, capturing the initial Lambert Trophy. It gave the Panthers more choices than they originally counted on. There were rumors that they were given a bid to the Sugar Bowl to face the Louisiana State Tigers. While AD Don Harrison did not confirm the bid, he did insinuate they would accept it if it was given.

If Pitt in fact was going to New Orleans, it was now rumored that the Alabama Crimson Tide, who rolled to an undefeated 8–0–1 mark in 1936, would take the spot opposite Washington in the Rose Bowl. Either matchup would have been great for the school as LSU was second in the Associated Press poll and the Huskies were fifth. As it turned out, the Washington players did not want to force a rematch with Alabama, who defeated the Huskies 20–19 in the 1925 Rose Bowl. They told their coach they wanted the Panthers, feeling they were the best opponent out there.

Because of the team's sentiment, Pitt now vaulted to the top of the Rose Bowl's wish list with Alabama, Navy and LSU as potential choices. Harrison denied that Pitt had received any bids as the Rose Bowl committee was waiting for Husky coach Jimmy Phelan to arrive in California to discuss the matter. Unfortunately his plane was grounded in Portland due to fog and the committee, while hoping he'd arrive, was set on making their decision by the end of the day with or without him.

Finally, despite the fact that there were several writers who protested the potential selection of a team that they felt wasn't good enough to play in Pasadena, Pitt was given the news they longed to hear; they would play the Washington Huskies in the Rose Bowl. There were several deciding factors that went in their favor. Alongside their selection as Lambert Trophy winners, their loss to the Dukes was discounted when Duquesne received a bid to the Orange Bowl against Mississippi State. It was stated that because Pittsburgh and Seattle had similar climates, neither would have a weather advantage in Pasadena. While the latter claim might have been a minor one, there were two other factors in play that perhaps helped them be successful in their quest. The first was that Washington president Dr. Lee Paul Sieg was a former dean at Pitt and a big fan of their football team, and probably most important, the players wanted Pitt as their opponent.

As it turned out, the Panthers were considered a better financial choice to the bowl as the committee felt an eastern team would be able to sell tickets better than a southern team. In fact, rumor had it that if Fordham wasn't upset by NYU in the season's final contest, they would have received the bid over Pitt and the southern schools.

Regardless of why they were there, this once disappointing campaign was now a memorable one, a fact that was heightened when they were chosen as national champions by William Boand, who combined some of the better mathematical ratings there were at the time, including the popular Dickinson System, to come up with a champion that was published yearly in the *Illustrated Football Annual*. They were also picked as the best team in the land by the *Football Thesaurus* and Esso Gas.

9. 1936: Everything for Football

Further proof that the Panthers were the best team in 1936 came later on when computer rankings, as well as other posthumous electors, came in vogue, as selectors such as Bob Kirlin, Earl Jenssen and the College Researchers Association pegged Pitt as the best in the land. It was a wonderful end to such a strange season, one where a sophomore-laden squad would only get better, making a college football nation fearful of what it would soon experience in 1937.

*National Champions selections made by modern-day analysts are noted "(retrospective)." Players rated as **First Team All-Americans** by a plurality of NCAA-recognized selectors are noted as "(consensus)." Players rated by all NCAA-recognized selectors are noted as "(unanimous)."*

1935 Scores

Date	Opponent	Score	Record
9/28	Waynesburg	14–0	1–0–0
10/5	@Washington and Jefferson	35–0	2–0–0
10/12	West Virginia	24–6	3–0–0
10/19	@Notre Dame	6–9	3–1–0
10/26	Penn State	9–0	4–1–0
11/2	@Fordham	0–0	4–1–1
11/9	Army	29–6	5–1–1
11/16	Nebraska	6–0	6–1–1
11/28	Carnegie Tech	0–0	6–1–2
12/14	@Southern California	12–7	7–1–2
		135–28	

Selected as First-Team All-American
Art Detzel

1936 Scores

Date	Opponent	Score	Record
9/26	Ohio Wesleyan	53–0	1–0–0
10/3	West Virginia	34–0	2–0–0
10/10	@Ohio State	6–0	3–0–0
10/17	Duquesne	0–7	3–1–0
10/24	Notre Dame	26–0	4–1–0
10/31	@Fordham	0–0	4–1–1
11/7	Penn State	34–7	5–1–1

Date	Opponent	Score	Record
11/14	@Nebraska	19–6	6-1-1
11/26	Carnegie Tech	31–14	7-1-1
1/1	Washington-Rose Bowl	21–0	8-1-1
		224–34	

Selected as National Champions by:
Illustrated Football Annual—Boand System
The Football Thesaurus
1st-N-Goal (retrospective)*
Angelo Louisa (retrospective)*
Bob Kirlin (retrospective)*
College Football Researchers Association (retrospective)*
Earl Jenssen (retrospective)*
Esso Gas*
Houlgate System (retrospective)*
Jim Koger (retrospective)*
Patrick Premo (retrospective)*

Not Recognized as Official National Championship Selector by University of Pittsburgh.

Selected as First-Team All-Americans
Averell Daniell (consensus)
William Glassford

10

1937 Rose Bowl: Pitt's Greatest Day

After a roller-coaster season that culminated with the eastern college football championship as well as a spot next to Washington in the Rose Bowl, Pitt began to set its sights not only figuring out the logistics of their trip, but on how to break the three-game Rose Bowl losing streak that had been the thorn in the side of what had been an otherwise incredible football program. The last two losses against the Southern California Trojans in Pasadena had been particularly upsetting to Panther Coach Jock Sutherland. Defeats of 47–14 and 35–0 represented the two most embarrassing conquests against Sutherland in his impressive 13-year tenure at his alma mater. The need to try and come up with different approaches to the game was imperative for Sutherland and his staff.

The first and most basic thing was to change the way they traveled to Pasadena. In the past, they would make several stops on the way to California and arrive for the game only a couple of days prior to kickoff. Sutherland and graduate manager Jimmy Hagan decided they would depart on December 16, the day that the school began its Christmas break. After a quick stop in Albuquerque, they anticipated arriving three days later and would train in Arrowhead Springs, about 60 miles outside Los Angeles. It was the same plan the team used when they defeated the USC Trojans in 1935, 12–7.

Before they left looking for greater glory, the campus had a pep rally at Soldiers and Sailors Hall to not only wish the football team good luck, but to watch Coach Sutherland receive the first Lambert Trophy, awarded to the best college football team in the northeast. The rally was not only broadcast over KDKA radio, but attended by over 2,000 students and the band.

Pictured above is the 1937 Rose Bowl where the University of Pittsburgh defeated the University of Washington 21-0 for their first Rose Bowl win in four tries. Pitt, in the lighter helmets, had been defeated by the two largest margins in the game's history by USC in 1930 and 1933 before finally earning their first victory which helped propel them to the 1936 national championship.

Critics in Los Angeles were continually pounding the selection of the Panthers for the Rose Bowl, feeling that Alabama or Louisiana State would have been more worthy choices for such a prominent game. While they may have had better records, neither school had a chance for the bids as Washington was against inviting a southern team, since Alabama was there in 1934, nor did they want a team from Texas after SMU played the year before. As stated earlier, Fordham had the bid sewn up; they only had to defeat their New York City brethren NYU. News of the early bid was probably the worst thing for coach Jim Crowley and his team.

While 4-3-1, the Violets were not of Fordham's caliber, losing 60-0 to Ohio State and 14-6 to Carnegie Tech, and were prohibitive underdogs when they met. The main thing the school was known for in a football manner was that the figure on top of the Heisman Trophy was modeled after their bruising fullback Ed Smith, who played for the school between 1933 and 1935. After the Rams were upset 7–6, the Huskies were still set on playing the best team in the east and Pitt just happened to be that team.

Along with being the Lambert Trophy winners, the Panthers also happened to be among the youngest teams in the land. The starting squad consisted of mostly sophomores and averaged 21 years and 2 months of age, the youngest Rose Bowl team ever at that point in time. It was a deep team with probably the most potential talent of any in the successful tenure of Jock Sutherland. While joy of traveling the country and then visiting Hollywood might have been on the minds of their predecessors who were defeated in the Rose Bowl, these team seemed focused on the task at hand: to win.

The team finally boarded its train with a party of 66 excited Panther players, coaches and administrators in tow looking to make history in Pasadena. Sutherland was informed by team physician Ralph Shanor that the team was almost 100 percent healthy, with no illness and few lingering injuries, which prompted the normally placid coach to a joyful mood. He was also extremely pleased with their enthusiastic attitude and excitedly exclaimed, "This team of ours is anxious to play football. I've never seen better spirit on any squad that has gone west."[1] The one injury that was reported was to their captain, halfback Bobby LaRue. Before Pitt departed for the coast, LaRue pulled a muscle in his leg in a scrimmage. While concerned, the Rose Bowl would be his last performance in a blue-and-gold uniform, and he was determined to play.

It was an enthusiastic squad, one that Ohio State coach Francis Schmidt felt had the best line he had come across in his years with the Buckeyes. "There is not a weak spot in the forward wall and Coach Sutherland is able to substitute his men frequently without any appreciable weakening."[2] University of Chicago coach Francis Powers, while not playing Pitt in 1936, nonetheless felt that the depth they had in their backfield was incredible, perhaps too deep for the Huskies to control.

As the Panthers arrived in Albuquerque, they put their backfield depth on display, including a healthy fullback Bill Stapulis, at the University of New Mexico football stadium as the squad practiced there before heading to Los Angeles the following day. While he was out with a shoulder injury, former quarterback Arnold Greene did a magnificent job in his absence which gave Sutherland some problems in his rotation. Throughout most of the season Frankie Patrick and Bill Stapulis provided one of the most dynamic fullback combinations in the country; Greene played as well if not better than the duo in his short time at fullback. It was a good problem to have.

While Pitt was still traveling, Washington set up home base at their own university before settling at Santa Barbara Junior College. They were showing an incredible amount of confidence in their chances against the champions of the east. Coach Jimmy Phelan was in his seventh season at the helm of the Huskies, and despite the fact that he promised a title in two years, he had finally reached pinnacle he had with Purdue in 1929, his final season with the Boilermakers, when they captured the Big Ten title. For the Huskies, 1936 represented the university's fourth Pacific Coast Conference championship and their first since 1925 in a year that was very similar to their opponents at Pittsburgh.

The Huskies had finished the season rated fifth in the Associated Press poll, losing only the season opener to top-ranked Minnesota 14–7 and tying Stanford 14–14 seven weeks later. In the remaining games, Washington showed almost as impressive a defense as the Panthers had during the season, allowing a single touchdown in a 19–7 victory over Oregon State. The remaining six victories were all shutouts with the team outscoring their opponents in those contests 108–0. The future hall-of-fame coach boasted a fine backfield that included Jim Cain, Byron Haines and Ed Nowogroski and Frank Waskowitz, who were their most efficient passers.

Washington's chance to defeat Pitt almost certainly would come with their passing attack, which was considered very aggressive and wide open for the time. Nowogroski had four targets at end, all of which were at least six feet tall, Bud Douglas, Dick Johnson, Carl Matronic and 18-year-old, 6'3" Coburn Grabenhorst.

As Pitt finally pulled into Arrowhead Springs, they did so with Sutherland intent on working his team hard, before letting up toward game time. The team seemed exhausted with constant train stops and a brutal practice schedule on their last two ventures to Pasadena. This year with the shortened trip the players seemed more refreshed. LaRue was still hobbled with his pulled muscle as Harold Stebbins was taking his place in practice, but there were two switches that Sutherland was considering that had nothing to do with injuries, replacing Dante DelleTezze with sophomore Albin Lezouski at left guard and Don Hensley for Henry Adams at center.

While Sutherland continued to be thoroughly pleased with their efforts and attitudes, the writers in Los Angeles had their doubts, claiming that while they were big, they may not be nimble enough to compete with the Huskies. Maxwell Stiles of the *Los Angeles Examiner* stated that "the Pittsburgh team has enormous piano legs, the kind of legs that are not moved out of the way ... outrun and outpassed but not shoved around." He further went on to be uncomplimentary about their passing game. "Their passing was off color and receivers as butter-fingered as any group of men that ever came west. They perform as if they've never seen a football thrown in the air before."[3] Braven

Dyer of the *Los Angeles Times* was equally unimpressed. "I am not sure about Pitt. The players are big enough, but they will be outweighed by Washington in the line and this is Washington's great strength."[4]

The criticism helped Washington be declared as ten-to-nine favorites in the early line before the game. The lack of respect also seemed to be inspiring the Panthers as their practices continued to be crisp. The team was also given a lift as LaRue started practicing. Even though he wouldn't be 100 percent until after Christmas, it was a sign that he would be ready for game time.

As positive as Sutherland was, Phelan was the opposite. When asked how his team was coming along, the normally positive, jovial coach replied tersely, "We're right where we were last September. Our timing looks like a clock that has lost its works, our wind is bad, our legs are tired and when we throw forward passes, someone has to look for the ball, the receivers haven't the faintest idea where it is."[5] While it may have been nothing more than a smoke screen, Phelan sounded very much like Sutherland, who was anything but jovial and outgoing, did on his last trip to Pasadena, and the Pitt coach definitely wasn't throwing a smoke screen back then.

As Christmas approached, LaRue appeared to be healed and ready to go, but Phelan would not be so lucky as one of his main reserves in the backfield, Al Gruver, broke two ribs in practice and would not be ready for the game; it was something sure to sully the Husky coach's mood even more. Regardless of the injuries, the two teams had done all the preparation they could and were ready to take the field in front of 87,000 excited college football fans, having to turn away another 50,000, proving that the committee's thought that an eastern team would be more apt to fill the mammoth bowl than a team from the south correct.

Not only was New Year's Day 1937 an opportunity for retribution for the Panthers, but it happened to be potentially the greatest day for Pittsburgh collegiate football fans as Duquesne took on Mississippi State in the Orange Bowl. While the Dukes would do their part with a dramatic 13–12 victory, Pitt began their quest in Pasadena happy that the rain that had plagued Southern California during the week had subsided. In his final game for the Panthers, LaRue led the team onto the field and met the Huskies' captain, their fine center John Wiatrak, at the center of the field.

The two teams took to their respective sidelines, but only one bolted onto the field with a fierceness that had been lacking in their past Rose Bowl excursions. Pitt came out angry, angry at the lack of respect by the local media, angry at their past performances, perhaps even angry that they weren't able to defeat the Dukes and Fordham, two teams they felt they had superior talent to. Whatever drove them, they were about to show the college football world just how impressive they were. On the other side were the Washington Huskies, hell-bent on showing that Phelan's concern before the contest was not an issue.

Those who wondered if LaRue would be able to play were about to find out quickly that the senior was anything but injured; he was about to give the finest performance he had in a Panther uniform. After a short ineffective drive by the Huskies, Pitt took over at its 45. LaRue had a short run before Marshall Goldberg shot to his left for 12. The senior then took a direct snap and rolled behind the left tackle. The aggressive Panthers, who were thought to be big but immobile by the Los Angeles media, showed them how quick and powerful they could be, bowling over the defenders as LaRue ran around a defender toward the sideline then broke into the open and rambled 30 yards to the Husky ten. Four plays later from the one, the Pitt front wall pushed back Washington a yard into the end zone as Patrick rolled behind center for the easy touchdown. Daddio made the conversion as Pitt did something it wasn't used to in their past two Rose Bowl excursions: take the lead.

The Panthers maintained their 7–0 advantage at the end of one as Sutherland opted to put his reserves in to start the second quarter as he had done so many times in the past. The Husky offense came to life against the second team, crossing midfield for the first time that afternoon. The drive eventually bogged down, but Washington had new momentum and hoped they could tie the contest before the half. This wasn't their day, though, as Pitt continued to dominate the tough Husky defense going to their opponents' 21 on the strength of a 21-yard Stepulis run and long sprints by Stebbins and Johnny Urban, but gave their opponents new life when senior Frank Waskowitz intercepted a pass.

Once again Washington went on the attack as their vaunted passing game was riddling the Pitt secondary. Again with the reserves on defense, the Huskies successfully drove to the Panther 18. Seeing enough, the Panther coach inserted his first squad and promptly stopped three straight Washington passes with an aggressive rush that allowed the Huskies no chance for a completion to take over at the 18. If there was a turning point in the ball game, it happened there.

Late in the first half with time running out and Washington with the ball, sophomore Steve Petro, getting the chance to start the first varsity game of his career, intercepted a wayward Husky pass. It didn't matter that the speedy Johnny Wood gave it right back to Washington with an interception toss of his own on a long pass deep in the Huskies' end of the field; the clock had run out in the first half as Pitt was about to come out in the third quarter and put an exclamation point to the end of their Pasadena nightmares.

While the Huskies did have one more chance, falling on a Goldberg punt inside the Panther 30 at the 29 early in the third quarter, Hensley immediately gave it back to Pitt with a clutch pickoff. Not wanting to let what had been an inferior Washington team back into the game, Pitt went on their longest sustained drive of the afternoon to all but give the Panthers the Rose Bowl championship.

With the ball at their own 25, LaRue continued his mastery over the Washington defense. He took the handoff up the middle, sprinted through two Washington defenders ten yards downfield, and almost was tripped another six yards later before once again finding open field. He sprinted until he was caught from behind by Nowogroski at the 32 with a 43-yard scamper. Now with the Husky defense on their heels, Patrick went for 19 before LaRue bolted for ten more to the three-yard line. As the afternoon shadows in Pasadena were covering half the field, the now seemingly defeated PCC champions were bowled over by the Panther line as Patrick waltzed into the end zone to give Pitt the two-touchdown lead.

Washington at that point had no fight left in them; the only question was whether or not the Panthers would run up the score in the fourth quarter as USC had done to them the last time they were in this position. They almost made it three touchdowns late in the third when they recovered a fumble at the 21, but unfortunately they could not get past the 12 and gave it back to the Huskies.

While the game seemed all but over, Pitt saved their best play for last when Bill Daddio, who had been Sutherland's iron man all game, playing 54 minutes, made not only the play of the game but one of the most spectacular in the program's history. With Washington on the Pitt 37-yard line after once again getting the best of the Panther reserves, Sutherland called on his first team to stop the drive in its tracks, they did that and more.

Haines sent a lateral back that Tony Matisi tipped as he hit Haines. The ball fell into Daddio's hands as he sped downfield with the Huskies in pursuit. Running with a wall of interference behind him, Daddio was never challenged as he crossed the goal line with the nearest Washington defender 13 yards away. The tired sophomore, who was so exhausted he had to be helped off the field after the contest, then successfully hit his third successive extra point to end what was the greatest day in the program's history to that point, exercising whatever demons that had troubled them in this classic facility for their first bowl victory.

With such a young team, Rose Bowl victories seemed to be a very possible reality in the near future. No one would have any reason to think that this would be their last bowl victory for 39 years. Unfortunately while this was such a wonderful moment for the team, conflicts that happened earlier in the

Bill Daddio was one of the fastest players to play for Jock Sutherland during his tenure at Pitt. A two-time All-American in 1937 and 1938, the highlight of Daddio's career came in the Panthers' lone Rose Bowl win in 1937 when he intercepted a deflection and ran 71 yards for the touchdown that put the icing on the cake of Pitt's 21–0 win over Washington.

week would begin a down slide that would quickly see this powerhouse crumble a short three years later.

Academic and financial reform was quickly coming to the university, who was getting tired of the complaints from other schools. Washington players had received $100 in expenses for the trip to the Rose Bowl while the Panthers were given nothing by Athletic Director Don Harrison, who wanted to start controlling the stipends players received. Wanting to at least give them spending money, Sutherland and his staff gave them what was reported as $17 apiece out of their own pockets; as it turned out according to Goldberg, it was much less. "Jock sold some bonds he had and the other coaches threw some money into a pool. They gave us each $2, all they had. Then the bowl people took us out to the Santa Anita race track for an outing. Big deal," the star halfback remembered years later. "Two dollars at a race track. So we all threw in a dollar to make pools to bet. And tapped out quickly. You know what it's like to stand around a race track with no money?"[6] Later on there were what proved to be erroneous reports that the two teams spilt $12,000 after the game, a false rumor that even years later the players emotionally denied.

The players were as irritated with the development as the coaches were. They were frustrated that the Huskies were given $100 for expenses on top of new suits they received for the official bowl reception. "We got nothing," Goldberg angrily recalled. "Except a sweater and a pair of pants. When we showed up for a reception with them, imagine how we felt."[7]

While things had become increasingly tense between the two, this predicament at the Rose Bowl set off an argument that would put the future of the program at risk. Harrison reportedly told the Pitt coach, "I made you, now I'll break you."[8]

It was an ugly end to a wonderful game. For the time being, though, there was celebration as the Pitt students met their conquering heroes parading downtown with the band to Pennsylvania Station. There would be more championship moments in the next year and a half, but the dynasty unfortunately began to fall in earnest on that day, what should have been their greatest day.

Box Score 1937 Rose Bowl

Team	1	2	3	4	F
Pittsburgh	7	0	7	7	21
Washington	0	0	0	0	0

Category	Pitt	Washington
Total Yards	294	146
Rushing	243	48
Passing	51	98
First Downs	11	8
Comp/Att/Int	2/4/2	7/17/3
Penalty Yards	20	0
Average Per Punt	43	29

LINE UP

Pitt	Pos	Washington
Daddio	LE	Johnson
Matisi	LT	Markov
Glassford	LG	Starcevich
Hensley	C	Wiatrak
Petro	RG	Slivinski
Daniell	RT	Bond
Hoffman	RE	Peters
Michelosen	QB	Newton
Goldberg	LH	Cain
Larue	RH	Johnson
Patrick	FB	Nowogroski

11

1937: The Troubled Championship

It should have been the best of times at the University of Pittsburgh. They captured their first Rose Bowl championship and were recognized in some corners as national champions, as well as being the first holders of the Lambert Trophy, emblematic of the best college football team in the northeast. More important than any of that was the fact that they had a great core of sophomores on the 1936 squad who were entering their junior seasons with the Panthers. No other sophomore class in the country even came close to the talent Coach Jock Sutherland possessed with his crew in 1936. It would only get better in 1937.

On the field it certainly did get better with an undefeated team that was universally acclaimed as the best in the land; off the field was another case as the core of the program was coming undone. For years Sutherland and his program relied on the stipends the school provided his players as well as the financial and recruiting support of the Golden Panther booster club to get the best players in the area. It provided him with an unmatched combination of talent and depth, making life miserable for the teams that played Pitt on Saturday afternoons.

As the years went on the criticisms by scribes and opposing schools alike of Pitt's method of aggressively paying players started to become a thorn in the side of Chancellor John Bowman. Universities such as Notre Dame and several Big Ten schools were ending their relationship with Pitt as long as these practices still existed. The situation worsened as Athletic Director Don Harrison and Sutherland, who had a strained relationship at best over the years, were embroiled in an argument at the Rose Bowl over the fact that Harrison did not give the players spending money for their trip and Sutherland and his coaches decided to dig into their own pockets and give money to make up for it.

It was now apparent that these two men could not exist together at the same school and one would have to go. Knowing that Sutherland would not be fired, Harrison resigned as the scheduling duties were turned over to the successful Panther coach who asked the administration for input into the schedule that would include veto power even after a new AD was named. While it seemed like a victory for the football team and its coach, as it turned out, it was not. The hall-of-fame coach was eventually given restrictions on the other things he was doing outside of football to supplement his income, such as writing football columns for the *Pittsburgh Press*, appearing on the radio as well as his various endorsements.

Bowman decided to name a former player who was one of the stars of the 1927 team that went to the Rose Bowl, Graduate Manager of Athletics Jimmy Hagan, to the position over Sutherland. While a former player for the coach that he would now oversee, Hagan's philosophy for reform was aligned more with the administration than with his coach as he had a plan to alter the subsidies that the school paid its players that would potentially hurt the future of the program. Pitt's stipend program would remain similar, but have one important change. Starting with the incoming freshman class in 1937, the players would still get $48 a month plus tuition, but would now have to work two hours a day to earn their stipend, a similar program that some of the other schools who were criticizing the Panthers were using. By working every day to earn the money, it would take the players off the practice field, potentially hurting the preparation time Sutherland needed to properly drill his squad. Hagan also want to end the perception that Pitt was a one-sport school and wanted to invest more money into the other programs. While the Hagan Plan was set in place, Coach Sutherland claimed he was not told of the plan until he read it in a newspaper. Their relationship was further strained when Hagan wanted to end the veto power that the coach had over the schedules and have the full control himself, which he received from the administration.

It was not a good situation for the coach and his squad by any stretch of the imagination, but they nonetheless began preparation for their season as September began and hoped that they could put all this behind them and focus on their goal of a national championship.

When one talks of impressive talent returning on a college football team in 1937, they would have to look no further than the University of Pittsburgh Panthers to see who had the unabashed best. Linemen such as Henry Adams;

Bill Daddio, one of the stars of the Rose Bowl; George Delich; Don Hensley; Fabian Hoffman; Albin Lezouski; Tony Matisi; Elmer Merkovsky; Walter Raskowski; Frank Souchak; and Steve Petro, who got his first varsity start in Pasadena, all were experienced contributors to the Panthers' national championship season the year before.

As impressive as that was, the group in the backfield was even moreso. Captain Bobby LaRue, who saved his best performance for last in the Rose Bowl, was the only significant absence. Harold Stebbins, John Urban and superstar Marshall Goldberg returned at halfback. The incredible duo of Frank Patrick and Bill Stapulis were back at fullback while junior John Chickerneo and future Panther coach, senior John Michelosen, returned to quarterback the club.

It was true that no one in the country could match this incredible talent, but whether or not Sutherland could get them to reach their potential amidst the turmoil surrounding the program was still in question. Pitt aficionados need only look at what happened in 1982 after issues arose between the administration and then coach Jackie Sherrill, which caused him to resign. He turned the program over to Foge Fazio, who had the best group of returning players and seemed the odds-on choice for a national championship. The season failed to produce a successful campaign, which is what all too many times happens when turmoil meets successful young collegiate players. The difference here was that Sutherland did not resign because of the issues—at least not yet—and he would find a way to keep his players sheltered from the issues and focused on the task at hand.

With a game against Ohio Wesleyan to open the season, the college football nation would be able to see clearly that this dangerous group of Panthers was indeed ready to reach their potential.

Game 1—September 25, 1937, at Pitt Stadium
Ohio Wesleyan University Battling Bishops 0
University of Pittsburgh Panthers 59

Almost a year to the day earlier, the Marshall Goldberg era began at the University of Pittsburgh against these same Battling Bishops of Ohio Wesleyan. On that late summer afternoon at Pitt Stadium, 19,000 fans were treated to a view of the future when the highly recruited sophomore halfback ran for four touchdowns while helping the Pitt offense amass 801 yards in the 53–0 whitewash. With so many dangerous backs available from the 1936 campaign for this game, the odds of another sophomore making such a dynamic debut were remote indeed. The hallmark of the great Panther teams of the era was great depth that was the result of superior recruiting. The superior recruiting allowed yet another sophomore to make a memorable debut.

The new star of the Panther backfield, and one that became a pivotal part of what would become the famed "Dream Backfield" of 1938, was 165-pound halfback Dick Cassiano. Cassiano was not a typical Panther of the era, as his hometown was Albany, New York, and not one of the small towns in Western Pennsylvania where most had come from. He also was a player that could make both the administration, who was hungry to improve the academic reputation of the school as well as stop the criticism of the semi-professionalism of its football players, and Coach Sutherland, who demanded excellence on the field, happy.

The young sophomore captured the Charles D. Wettach Award, given for academic excellence among all Pitt athletes, for achieving in his freshman year what would have been today a 4.0 GPA. While the academics would have been pleased that a student of his caliber was on the field, by game's end the defenders for the Battling Bishops were anything but happy he entered the gridiron.

Eventually Cassiano would go on to be a sixth-round draft choice of the Green Bay Packers in 1940 and would be traded to the Brooklyn Dodgers football team, where he ran for 84 yards and snagged two touchdown passes playing for Sutherland in his first season as an NFL coach. For now, though, his career was all in front of him, and Ohio Wesleyan was what he was preparing for.

The Battling Bishops were a poor secondary college football team at this point in their existence. They had a colorful history and boasted such American sporting legends as Lynn St. John, Fielding H. Yost and Branch Rickey as coaches who directed the program over the years. They had a memorable upset victory against Michigan in 1928 and captured a couple of Buckeye Conference crowns under head coach George Gauthier, who would ably lead the Bishops for 26 seasons.

These were not good years, though, for Ohio Wesleyan. After being annihilated by the Panthers a year ago, they finished with a poor 1–6–2 mark and would do no better the next two, finishing 2–7 and 1–9 in 1937 and 1938. They were led by fullback Pat Brooks and tackle Mike Caputo, who both would play an inspired game against Pitt, but it was apparent from the first play just how outmanned they were.

All in all Sutherland got the opportunity to play all 56 Panthers on this unusually hot September day, but it was his starting crew that looked as impressive as the one that took the field in Pasadena almost ten months earlier. At the ends were Daddio and Souchak which surrounded an interior line of Matisi

11. 1937: The Troubled Championship

and Delich at tackle, Raskowski and Petro at guard, with Adams rounding out the crew at center. Pitt's explosive backfield included Goldberg and Stebbins at halfback with Michelosen at quarterback and Patrick at fullback.

So dominant were the Panthers that it took only one play to bring the crowd of 19,677 to their feet and take the lead in the game. After kicking off to the Bishops, Goldberg showed he was also an adept defensive player, as he picked off a pass and returned it 55 yards to give Pitt an extremely quick lead.

By the end of the first quarter, the Panthers were leading 13–0, which prompted Sutherland to empty his bench; enter Cassiano. Like Goldberg a year ago, the Albany native wasted little time to show the fans and team alike how talented he was. He took his first handoff up the middle and ripped through the Battling Bishop defense for a 48-yard run, waltzing into the end zone to give Pitt the 20–0 advantage. As time was running out in the half, Cassiano showed his skills as a receiver, snagging a pass from backup halfback Larry Peace with five seconds left to send Pitt into the locker room with a 27-point lead.

If Ohio Wesleyan thought the second half would be less painful, they were sorely mistaken thanks to Cassiano. Showing that he was extremely well rounded, the sophomore began the scoring spree from his 34-yard line, bolting 66 yards for his third score of the day. Remarkably he would account for a fourth touchdown a third different way with a 26-yard scoring toss to John Dickerson.

In 1988, Pittsburgh Penguins superstar Mario Lemieux had a unique record when he scored five goals for the Penguins five different ways, the only player in NHL history to do so; in the fourth quarter Cassiano gave the football version of Lemieux's achievement when he intercepted a wayward Ohio Wesleyan pass and ran it in from 46 yards out for his fourth touchdown. It was a remarkable performance as he accounted for 225 of the team's 638 yards in total offense and was involved in five of the nine touchdowns, getting them four different ways. Fullbacks Patrick, scoring twice, and Stapulis accounted for the other three touchdowns in the 59–0 demolition.

It was just what the program needed after so much off-the-field mayhem in the off-season. Cassiano was also what Sutherland needed to show the nation that his very strong team just became even stronger.

Game 2—October 2, 1937, at Mountaineer Field in Morgantown, West Virginia

UNIVERSITY OF PITTSBURGH PANTHERS   20
WEST VIRGINIA UNIVERSITY MOUNTAINEERS   0

In 1928, the West Virginia University Mountaineers defeated Jock Sutherland's University of Pittsburgh Panthers 9–6. It was a monumental upset that proved to be a vast exception rather than the rule in the Backyard Brawl during the Sutherland era. The other 12 times the two teams faced each other, the Panthers won each time, crushing their local rivals by a 315–49 margin. Four coaches came and four coaches went in that time period, each unable to take the Mountaineers to the elite level that Pitt enjoyed. Chares "Trusty" Tallman was the last to make the attempt, but a 15–12–2 mark in three years was not what the administration imagined. Tallman was replaced following the 1936 campaign, turning the reins of the program over to Marshall "Little Sleepy" Glenn.

A quarterback on that WVU squad that defeated Sutherland in 1928, Glenn had been coaching the Mountaineer basketball team since 1933 and was called upon to see if he could do what the other coaches failed to. Glenn was the ultimate leader, captaining both the basketball and football teams and leading them to a combined 53–29–6 record in his career as a player. A doctor, who practiced medicine until he was killed by injuries suffered in an auto accident in 1980, Glenn was also known in West Virginia lore for opening a famous golf course on farmland he purchased named Sleepy Hollow. While he would continue to give to the state he loved so dearly after his career as a coach, in 1937 his career was just beginning, and after a win over West Virginia Wesleyan 14–0 in the opener, he set his sights on breaking whatever hold Pitt and their hall-of-fame coach had on them.

The Mountaineers didn't think they had the talent to compete with a team the likes of the Panthers, but they were a very physical team and hoped that would work in their favor. They had a very solid line with Richard Dolly and Murino DeAngelis at the ends, Albert Baisi and Paul Hodges at tackle, guards Alex Atty and Dave Volkin as well as center Olan Hendrick. The backfield was young with potential, led by a highly recruited sophomore halfback from Uniontown named Harry Clark. Sam Audia at fullback and Tony Rapaswick joined Clark in the backfield along with Kelly Moran. By starting Moran, Glenn was tipping his hand with his intention to pass against the Pitt secondary, feeling that as good as the Panther defensive line was, it would be West Virginia's only chance to score, something they had only done twice in the previous seven meetings in the rivalry.

It was a proper fear to have as the interior line of Tony Matisi, George Delich, Walter Raskowski, Dante DelleTazze and Don Hensley, as well as two of the best ends in the country in Bill Daddio and Frank Souchak, shut down many of the best offenses the nation had to offer over the last year. WVU was certainly not an offense of the ilk that Pitt had faced in recent seasons, which helped explain why the Panthers were prohibitive favorites despite the fact that they would be on the road for the first time.

Playing in Morgantown gave Pitt junior halfback Marshall Goldberg an opportunity to play in front of friends and family for the first time. He would do so in a backfield that would see one unique change. Joining quarterback John Michelosen, fullback Frank Patrick and Goldberg in the backfield was Bill Stapulis. Normally a fullback, Stapulis got the opportunity to play halfback the week before against Ohio Wesleyan and was exceptional. The move for the senior was necessitated by the fact that Harold Stebbins had suffered minor injuries in the opener and wasn't fully recovered. While Stebbins was questionable for the contest, Sutherland had to be heartened by the fact that the starting end from last season, Fabian Hoffman, had returned to the team after spending time on a cruise that took him around the world. It was questionable whether or not Hoffman had practiced enough for Sutherland's tastes to play in this contest, but if he was ready it would be another devastating weapon in the Panther arsenal.

While the game was important in the minds of Pitt fans and students alike, the controversial subject of whether or not to compensate their football players seemed to be there too. There was a poll published in the student paper, *The Pitt News*, on the subject. The results were mixed. The students overwhelmingly were in support of the subsidies by a 72 percent to 28 percent margin which seemingly would lead one to believe they wanted the status quo to continue. Strangely enough, when asked if the interest in the sport would remain as high if the sport was rehabilitated and stipends were ended, 54 percent responded positively. Whatever the responses were, the controversy was just beginning and would intensify. The coach had been good at keeping his players' minds off it, though, and unfortunately for the Mountaineers, he did so wonderfully on this afternoon, at least in the second half. The first half saw the aggressive West Virginia defense keep the explosive yet overconfident Panther offense in check.

The game started innocently enough when Goldberg quickly showed his home state how magnificent he was when he took the opening kickoff 78 yards with a sparkling run to his opponents' 22. They barreled to the WVU one as it looked like the blowout that most had expected would come quickly. Somehow the tough Mountaineer line stopped Pitt and took over on downs. The pattern became common in the first half as the Panthers would often drive deep and then come away with no points. It happened again on the next drive following a poor punt that set up the vaunted Pittsburgh offense at the West Virginia 30. This time they were stopped at the six when their opponents tackled Stebbins, who was healthy enough to play, on fourth down.

Finally, following two disappointing drives, the Panthers took the ball in great position again as a poor Moan punt went out at the 45. An eight-yard return by Stapulis and a WVU penalty set Pitt up at the 33. After a four-yard run, reserve halfback Johnny Urban went up the middle before cutting to the left sideline into open field. He kept running until he ended up in the end zone with the game's first touchdown and a seven-point advantage. Instead of using this as a wakeup call, the Mountaineers' defense toughened and held the Panthers off the scoreboard through the rest of the half.

Sutherland was livid and did not hold back at halftime letting his players know how disappointed he was. The coach knew that overconfidence was at the forefront and was blunt in his post-game comments. "This scare today might do Pitt some good. I haven't been able to talk to these boys all season long, that is until between halves after West Virginia had tossed us around the first two quarters." Sutherland further went on to explain, "There are too many persons telling our boys what good football players they are. They didn't show it this afternoon."[1] At least they didn't show it until the fourth quarter.

Irritated at the lackadaisical performance by his first squad, Sutherland inserted his reserves and dissected the Mountaineer defense on an 81-yard drive. The trio of Stapulis, Stebbins and the previous week's hero Dick Cassiano methodically ran the ball through a tiring WVU line. Led by a 15-yard sprint by Cassiano and a 12-yard burst by Stebbins, Pitt eventually ended up at the West Virginia 21. John Chickerneo then put the ball into Stebbins' stomach as he went over left tackle and through the WVU defense for the touchdown that made the score 13–0.

The valiant effort by West Virginia would now give way to the deeper, stronger Panthers. On the next possession, Cassiano rambled for 40 yards before sophomore guard Mike Gussie and Hendrick made a touchdown-saving tackle. With the ball now at the 16, Stebbins sprinted for two eight-yard runs, the second for the score that gave Pitt the 20–0 advantage that put the game away.

Wanting to at least score to show the Panthers they would not fold, WVU took advantage of a clipping penalty that was called after Stebbins scored, which forced Pitt to kick off from the 25. The Mountaineers started at midfield and, led by a 25-yard Moran-to-Clark connection, West Virginia found themselves at the two with a first down. Three plays later they still were not in the end zone. Finally, on fourth down, Clark took the handoff and went toward his right end. It looked like the WVU end pushed the Pitt line enough to score a touchdown. Right as he was about to get in, Clark was knocked hard by the Panther defense and fumbled. Cassiano fell on it in the end zone ending the Mountaineers' only true threat.

The game finally ended as Glenn and his squad used the confidence they acquired in this contest to seemingly turn the corner. They won seven of their final eight contests which included a 7–6 victory against Texas Tech in the Sun Bowl, the only bump in the road being a 6–6 tie against Georgetown. The Panthers on the other hand had the look of a defeated team. With a revenge match against Duquesne on the horizon, the team needed to find a way to quickly recover their swagger.

Game 3—October 9, 1937, at Pitt Stadium

DUQUESNE UNIVERSITY DUKES 0
UNIVERSITY OF PITTSBURGH PANTHERS 6

Celebrating a national championship in 1936, the Pitt Panthers had a lot to be proud of for their performance the year before. Champions of the eastern region to boot, it was as if they had achieved all the goals a college football team could. In the city of Pittsburgh in the 1930s, there were three schools playing major college football, and they all played fiercely for championship of Pittsburgh. For the University of Pittsburgh, it was the one title they did not claim that special season.

A 7–0 upset loss to the Duquesne Dukes was not only the lone defeat in their slate but, when coupled with the Dukes' win over Carnegie Tech, it was they who captured the trophy emblematic of the best college football team in the Steel City. It was something that stayed in the minds of the returning Pitt players for almost a full calendar year. So angry were the Pitt players that years later when asked about it, the anger in All-American Ave Daniell's voice was still very apparent.

For John "Clipper" Smith and the Dukes, the win over Pitt was a springboard that sent the school into the upper echelon of major college football teams. Finishing 14th in the final Associated Press poll, Duquesne finished the regular season 7–2, which garnered them a spot in the Orange Bowl against Mississippi State. The Dukes put an exclamation point on their memorable campaign with an exciting 13–12 victory. Down 12–7 late in the game, halfback Boyd Brumbaugh tossed a desperation pass which found end Ernie Hefferle. Hefferle made a magnificent run to complete the 72-yard touchdown play and give the team the victory.

The 1937 season had been a continuation of the same for Duquesne as they opened the season with a lopsided victory over Waynesburg before gaining revenge for the 2–0 upset defeat the year before by West Virginia Wesleyan, thoroughly beating them 39–0 in the rematch. While momentum seemed to continue on the side of the Dukes, especially with the lackadaisical performance against West Virginia by the Panthers coming into this contest, they also entered Pitt Stadium as a team who was not healthy.

The team's two superb halfbacks, George Matsik and Boyd Brumbaugh, as well as fullback Johnny Karrs and guard Art Amann, were all suffering from various injuries. The two halfbacks were the key to the Duquesne attack, and their injuries created concern for Smith. Matsik had been hurt the previous week against Wesleyan while Brumbaugh was reportedly underweight and lacking the quickness that had made him such a special player the year before. Even though the coach expected both his star halfbacks to play, he knew he had good replacements in Geno Onder and Vince McKeeta to insert in case either would be unable to play.

The Panthers were not without injuries themselves which would test their incredible depth, especially at center where both Henry Adams and Don Hensley were nicked up. If neither could go, Bob Dannies would get the call to anchor the front line. In the backfield, halfback Harold Stebbins, who had an outstanding game against West Virginia, and fullback Frank Patrick were nursing injuries. The backfield injuries would not cause the problems they were having at center as Sutherland possessed numerous backs that seemed almost interchangeable, except of course for Marshall Goldberg who was among the best in the country.

As kickoff came close, both coaches revealed their simplistic strategies for victory. Clipper Smith hoped to break either Matsik or Brumbaugh for quick long runs, as Matsik had the year before in the upset win, and then go into a defensive shell, running the clock for the win. Sutherland wanted to do the opposite, score early and score often as he feared Duquesne was too dangerous if he scored and then sat on it.

Whatever strategies they had come up with before the game, neither would come to fruition in front of the 55,000 fans that showed up at Pitt Stadium on a rainy afternoon to see these two Pittsburgh college football titans play. Stebbins, Brumbaugh, and Matsik did start the contest, but Bill Stapulis manned his old spot at fullback replacing the injured Patrick while Hensley was healthy enough to get the nod at center. Sutherland did make one change in his backfield that was not necessitated by injury; he played John Chickerneo at quarterback, whom he felt was a better offensive player over John Michelosen, the better player defensively.

Before the game began, a controversial statement by a member of the Duquesne faculty at a pep rally set fire to what was already a combustible rivalry. Philosophy teacher Reverend Thomas Jones told the group of 2,000 students that "Duquesne football players will be out there fighting because they love their school. The Pitt team will be out there fighting too, but only for their week's paychecks," in reference to the claims that Pitt players were nothing more than semi-professionals.[2] While Father Jones eventually was relieved of his faculty position because of the comments, there was some hypocrisy with his statements as the Dukes players received tuition, books, meals, room and board and clothing free as well as $15 spending money a month. Despite the fact that Pitt players received tuition and books free, the $48.50 a month had to pay for room, board and clothing, which the Duquesne players already received.

On the field, the contest turned out to be an exact reverse of the 1936 matchup, with Pitt employing the Dukes' strategy rather than the one Sutherland had hoped to utilize before game time. Instead of Matsik being the star, it would be the Panthers' future two-time All-American Goldberg that would bring the fans to their feet with a magnificent run.

Before Goldberg would quickly turn the tide, Duquesne took the opening kick to their own 37 and looked like they would start off as quickly as they did the year before. Matsik and Brumbaugh looked anything but injured, with the former running for 17 yards before Brumbaugh muscled through five Pittsburgh defenders for another 12 to the Pitt 30. Finally the Panthers' defense stopped Duquesne, who punted the ball through the end zone, giving the home team the ball at their 20.

The first time the Pitt offense touched the ball, Stebbins ran for three yards, then Chickerneo took the snap and placed it into the hands of Goldberg. The Elkins, West Virginia, native broke to his left and then stepped through a few Duquesne defenders until he made it to the 35. At that point he looked like he was past any interference that came his way and seemingly had a clear shot into the end zone. Toward the end of his run two Dukes had finally caught up to Goldberg, and it looked like they would keep him from scoring. The junior halfback then cut sharply to his right and went around them for the score. While end Frank Souchak's extra-point attempt went wide, the touchdown seemed to not only destroy the quick-strike-then-sit-back approach Smith had hoped for, but Sutherland appeared like his score-and-don't-stop strategy was going to work just fine.

At that point a combination of a stouthearted Duquesne defensive wall and the futility of a Pitt offense that was inept for three quarters against the Mountaineers destroyed every opportunity the Panthers had to score as penalties and turnovers made what might have been a one-sided contest into a muddy defensive battle.

The game quickly turned into a battle of field position as the defenses were getting very physical, as were the fans in the stands, where several fights broke out between the followers of the two bitter rivals. As the first quarter ended, it appeared as if the Panthers would break through again, when Stebbins and Goldberg ran for 20 and 14 yards respectively to put Pitt at midfield. As he had done so effectively in the past, the Pitt coach put his second team in to start the second quarter; unlike most of those times, this group substitution didn't work out well. The offense quickly was stopped, then the Dukes took over at the 46 on a blocked punt. It was the last excitement of an otherwise mundane first half as the two teams went into the locker room with Pitt clinging on to their slim lead.

Wanting to once again put this city battle away, Stebbins, Goldberg and Johnny Urban took the squad from midfield as the third quarter began, down to the Duquesne seven, running through gaping holes in the Dukes' line. Again they couldn't take advantage and were at the six with a fourth-and-goal. Urban took the handoff around left end and looked like he would finally lead the team to another score. He unfortunately was pushed out at the one, with the Dukes once again taking over on downs.

While the Panther defense kept the Dukes off the board, the Pitt offense continually threatened, one time going to the 19 before being stopped by the Dukes, then a blocked punt gave them the ball at 12. Sophomore Dick Cassiano took it on the next play to the six before Lawrence Peace fumbled, with Ted Grabinski of Duquesne falling on it at the 12.

It was getting late, and while the Panthers were inept offensively since Goldberg's magnificent run, the defense were making sure they'd win the game for the Panthers as they had been continually frustrating the Dukes for most of the game. It was at that point Frank Souchak lost his head and punched a Duquesne player. He was assessed with what was called a half-the-distance-to-the-goal penalty, this one worth 42 yards, which gave Duquesne the ball at the Pitt 44. Cassiano saved the day for Pittsburgh the next play when he picked off a Brumbaugh pass at the 32.

Stopped in their tracks, there were under two minutes left when Michelosen went back to punt from his 20. The snap was high and the ball was slippery as the future Pitt coach fumbled it and then fell on the ball at the 20. Brumbaugh went up the middle to the 18 before the Dukes were given a five-yard penalty for excessive time-outs when Smith tried to get Matsik into the game. The star of the 1937 Orange Bowl game then hit Karrs with a nine-yard pass to the 14. The crowd and players alike were tense as the clock was quickly counting down. Senior Paul Shaw made the defensive play of the game, sacking Karrs with a 10-yard loss; then, under pressure, Brumbaugh threw the ball out of the end zone as Pitt took over and ran out the remaining 30 seconds to secure the tough win.

While it wasn't a well-played offensive game, which gave Sutherland concern for his contest against Fordham in New York the following week, it was a better result than the year before which gave the undefeated Panthers the upper hand in the title that had alluded them for two years: the city of Pittsburgh championship.

Game 4—October 16, 1937, at the Polo Grounds in New York, New York

| UNIVERSITY OF PITTSBURGH PANTHERS | 0 |
| FORDHAM UNIVERSITY RAMS | 0 |

There are many oddities in sports history, things so unique that they stand the test of time. For the University of Pittsburgh's football program, there have been many unique things associated with the team: the first radio broadcast ever of a college football game in 1921 against West Virginia, and they were the first college football team in the country to wear numbers, which they donned in 1908. Of all the things that have happened in this program's proud history, perhaps the one of the most memorable was a series of games it played against one of the other national powers in the country during the mid- to late 1930s: the Fordham University Rams.

What made this series of games truly unique was not just the fact that they were all played at the legendary Polo Grounds in Harlem, but for three consecutive seasons between 1935 and 1937, no one scored—not a touchdown, field goal or safety. While scoring was not at the premium in the 1930s that it is in the game of the 21st century, two national powers with explosive offenses not scoring once in three seasons is as rare as Duquesne and Carnegie-Mellon (formerly Carnegie Tech) competing for a football national championship today.

After two consecutive scoreless ties in 1935 and 1936, the two teams came into this contest undefeated and unscored upon. Pitt ran through their three opponents, outscoring them 83–0, while Fordham shut out both Franklin and Marshall and Waynesburg by a combined 114–0 margin. Fordham coach Jim Crowley was a much more boastful sort than Jock Sutherland and told the press very confidently, "I think we have a very good chance to win. I am sure we have an offense that will hit harder and oftener than any Pitt has seen before and I'm banking on the line to stop the Panthers."[3] Sutherland in his placid yet sportsmanlike manner said simply, "I'm hoping to see Goldberg's face peering through the scrimmage line once or twice during the afternoon."[4]

Crowley had one of the best lines in the country, the famed "Seven Blocks of Granite," that included John Druze, Al Barbarsky, Joe Benard, Alex Wojciechowicz, Mike Kochel, Ed Franco and Harry Jacunski, although Crowley inserted Paul Berezney for Benard at the start of the contest. While they were among the best lines in the history of the sport, the chances for an upset over the Panthers, who were 2½-to-1 favorite in the contest, rested with their young backfield. Sophomores Angelo Fortunato, Steve Kalzo and Dom Principe led a backfield that had helped the Rams average 57 points per game and hoped the combination could give the impenetrable Pittsburgh defense trouble all afternoon.

Sutherland was not as confident as Crowley for a reason; he had two major injuries that would certainly hamper his chance to break the two-year scoreless tie. With the depth Pitt had, there weren't many players who couldn't be replaced with a talented player that was in reserve. There was one such exception on the 1937 squad and that was Marshall Goldberg. Unfortunately for Sutherland, Goldberg was one of the players that was injured before the game. Despite the fact the coach expected to play him, the junior halfback had a sprained instep and a charley horse. The other player who was questionable was end Bill Daddio. Worse off than Goldberg, Daddio had injured his leg so severely that he couldn't straighten it and hadn't practiced during the week. Sutherland anticipated using Frank Souchak and Fabian Hoffman at the end, with the hopes of inserting Daddio at some point. Outside of injuries, the Panther coach decided to keep Chickereno at quarterback and replace Dante DalleTezze at right guard with Steve Petro while giving Frank Patrick back his spot at fullback as he seemed fully recovered from an injury he suffered earlier in the season.

It was a cold, dry day at the Polo Grounds. The dry turf was hoped to be amiable for scoring; as history will remember about this game, though, it didn't matter if it was on astro-turf or on a muddy quagmire, the streak of scoreless games would go to three. Fifty-two thousand fans jammed the home of the New York Giants baseball team, and while the game was scoreless, they were treated to a contest that was at least statistically dominated by the Panthers. They outgained the Rams 195–110, yielding only four first downs, but eight lost fumbles including five by Harold "Curly" Stebbins, and had an apparent touchdown by Goldberg that was nullified by a holding call late in the first half. It was an offensive pattern that was consistent with what Sutherland had seen against West Virginia and Duquesne.

While three times the turnovers led to field-goal opportunities for the Rams, unfortunately for Fordham, three times their captain Druze couldn't capitalize on the opportunity. Desperate for a score of any kind, even Sutherland uncharacteristically sent his team in for a 24-yard field-goal attempt rather than his normal strategy of going for a touchdown on fourth down. The attempt by the injured Daddio went awry to keep the game scoreless.

A sign of things to come came on the first play of the game when Stebbins lost a fumble on his own 20 which would have been the team's ninth turnover, but luckily a Fordham penalty negated the fumble. The Rams missed a golden opportunity to score with the penalty, but got another one toward the end of the first quarter when Johnny Urban dropped the ball after a 15-yard run at the 25. The Rams moved no further, prompting the first of Druze's missed field goals.

Opportunities were rare the remainder of the first half until late in the second quarter when Stebbins returned a punt 35 yards to the 40. Led by a 10-yard run by Patrick, who then fumbled the ball forward which was recovered by Pitt's Bob Dannies at the 17, the Panthers eventually moved inside the ten. It was at that point Goldberg took the ball to his right and found a hole that led him to the end zone to end the futile scoreless streak after almost ten quarters of play. While the Panthers celebrated, referee W.T. Halloran explained why there was such a big hole for Goldberg when he tossed a flag for a 15-yard holding penalty against Pitt, negating the score. With only seconds left, they couldn't push it over a second time, so the only score in the three-year rivalry was for naught as the teams exited the field at the half scoreless. The negated touchdown by Goldberg was the closest either would come to scoring again.

The Panthers had one last chance offensively to break the tie early in the fourth. The Fordham defense appeared to be tiring as the Panthers' Urban helped lead Pitt to the Rams' 40 with long runs through some nice holes that his line was making in the Blocks of Granite. After an 18-yard sprint by Urban, Stebbins got the ball and promptly gave it away one last time. This time Wojciehowicz picked it up to stop Pitt once again.

While they would get no closer offensively, defensively Stebbins had a chance to turn this miserable day into a heroic one when he put his arms around an errant Woitkoski pass with no one between him and the end zone. Unfortunately this wasn't Stebbins's day because the ball fell to the ground as it had done so many times for him during this fruitless endeavor.

So as history will tell us, the game ended scoreless for the third straight year. The three games have been written about for years since, telling the tale of an oddity that has become a legend for the ages, one that would finally end a year later with both teams finally getting on the scoreboard, and the Panthers emerging victorious. As it turned out the legendary scoreless streak that ended a year later would be Sutherland's last great day as the Panther coach; soon after, the dynasty would come tumbling down.

Game 5—October 23, 1937, at Pitt Stadium
UNIVERSITY OF WISCONSIN BADGERS   0
UNIVERSITY OF PITTSBURGH PANTHERS   21

As the 1937 season unfolded for the University of Pittsburgh, Coach Jock Sutherland must have felt he was playing the ghost of Knute Rockne week in and week out. Out of the ten games Pitt would play that season, three of the contests would be against teams run by members of the famed Four Horsemen backfield that was coached by Rockne between 1922 and 1924.

The Panthers had just come off a third consecutive scoreless tie against Jim Crowley's Fordham Rams and would face Elmer Layden's Notre Dame Fighting Irish two weeks later. Don Miller, whom Rockne felt was his best open-field runner, never became a head coach, instead running the backfields for both Georgia Tech and Ohio State between 1925 and 1932, which left only Harry Stuhldreher for Sutherland to play. That opportunity came against the University of Wisconsin following the Fordham game. Stuhldreher, the quarterback of the famed quartet, was a three-time All-American, who while from Massillon, Ohio, graduated from the nearby Kiski School in Saltsburg. The quarterback manned the sidelines successfully for Villanova, compiling a 65–25–9 mark in 11 seasons before taking over as head coach and athletic director at Wisconsin in 1936.

Trying to resurrect a program that had fallen on hard times, Stuhldreher struggled his first season with a 2–6–0 mark, but seemed to have finally turned things in the right direction in 1937 as he was about to meet Pitt. The team had reeled off four consecutive victories to start the season against South Dakota State, Marquette, Chicago and Iowa, outscoring their opponents 84–6 in the process. The four victories were one more than they had amassed over the previous two seasons, and the game against Pittsburgh would be a true barometer of exactly how far they had come.

Their offense had been dynamic in the first four contests as Stuhldreher chose quarterback Vin Garvey, Bill Schmitz, Roy Nerlin and Howard Weiss as his foursome to try and crack the end zone against the Panther defense for the first time this season and would have a very impressive runner by the name of Bronko Malesevich in reserve at quarterback if he needed a spark. He unfortunately would be without his starting quarterback Ervin Windwood, who injured his knee against Chicago and was still in a cast as game time approached, but he was very confident in his duo of Garvey and Malesevich.

At Wisconsin, Stuhldreher ran the Notre Dame offense that he learned from Rockne, but he was concerned his offensive line, especially at center, wouldn't be big and physical enough for the Panthers. His starter, Neil Pohl, was only 183 pounds, so he was considering playing Jack Murray, who was substantially bigger at 210. The Badgers had a very effective passing offense, but the Pitt coach felt their method of attack would be on the ground as the Panthers employed probably one of the finest defensive backfields in the country, allowing only 12 completions in 62 attempts at that point of the season.

Sutherland had what on paper appeared to be a well-balanced attack, with Dick Cassiano rushing for 236 yards for a 14.8 per carry average, Bill Stapulis at 227 yards with a 6.3 average and Marshall Goldberg coming in with 221 yards and a 6.0 average. All told they had run for 943 yards in four games while giving up only 217. In looking at the stats it would be stunning to know that Pitt had not scored in seven quarters despite running up big statistical advantages over Duquesne and Fordham. The Panther coach considered starting Bob Dannies at center in place of Don Hensley and was going through his line tinkering with other potential changes to try and figure out a solution to his recent offensive woes. Despite the fact he fumbled five times against Fordham, Harold Stebbins would be in the starting lineup when the teams entered Pitt Stadium for the contest.

It was a hellish day in the stadium for the 31,000 fans, as heavy winds, rain and snow dampened the crowd, as did the fact that it was announced before the contest that the university would embrace the Hagan Plan in a more aggressive way than anyone could have imagined. To many, despite the fact that the administration thought they could still compete at the national level, it signaled an end in the near future of the dynasty Pitt football had built since Pop Warner took over the program. The changes would be sweeping and installed over the next couple of seasons, ending the subsidies for athletics at the school. It put a dark cloud over what was a dynamic victory by the Panthers and the end of their offensive slump.

The other part of the Hagan Plan, other than the fact the players would now have to work for their money and Sutherland would be restricted on the money he made in his non-football activities, was that in an attempt to make other sports more important on campus and football less, the schedule starting in 1940 would include no more than eight games. Coaches would no longer be held responsible for winning and losing, but would also lose any say-so in making the schedules. Any statements made by the coaches must go through the university's publicity department first. All teams would now have to practice on campus, which eliminated Sutherland's Camp Hamilton, which he used two weeks before the season began to get his team ready for the campaign. The most restrictive of the new policies was that coaches were not allowed to scout or talk to a prospective player off campus; any contact between recruits and coaches had to happen if a player visited campus on his own accord.

Hagan claimed that even though some of the criticisms from other schools were oftentimes unfounded, they were hurting the university and not just in athletics, and he wanted to make sure they would end once and for all. He said that even though he was confident Sutherland would keep the program competitive, the importance of football needed to be lessened. "A football game is no longer a game when teams as powerful as ours run rough-shod over teams of schools which under normal conditions do not attract an abundance of football material."[5]

It appeared that the school would limit its schedule to easier eastern opponents and end the scheduling of stronger national powers in various regions of the country. If that was the case, more restrictive subsidy rules coupled with a schedule against similar eastern schools who were deemphasizing football, Sutherland might have stayed; in reality the administration kept the tough national powers on their schedule which turned out to be a bad mix for a winning program.

Most of these issues would affect the program years later; for the time being they were playing a tough Midwestern on a rainy day as Pitt's turnover issues continued, losing six balls as a part of seven turnovers. Luckily, though, when the Panthers weren't fumbling the ball, they were running over the Badger defense, turning what was thought to be a closer game into a one-sided affair.

Goldberg, feeling healthier, gave Pitt a decided advantage early on, scoring on a seven-yard end run in the first quarter to break the scoreless streak and give the Panthers an early 7–0 lead. They threatened to make it two touchdowns after a 76-yard run by Stebbins put them on the Badger 10, but after Larry Peace appeared to score at that point, an offside penalty nullified the score, which never came afterward as Pitt turned it over on downs. The rest of the half continued on the same path, the Panthers going up and down the field, but turnovers and not finishing drives kept the score at 7–0.

A game that was closer than it should have been was opened up a bit for Pittsburgh as Goldberg scored early in the second half. He took the ball at the 36-yard line, then using his incredible change of speed was able to sprint past the Wisconsin defenders as he rambled in from 64 yards out, giving Pittsburgh the two-touchdown lead.

Goldberg was the leader for the day at that point with 125 yards on ten carries. He gave way to Cassiano who made his own incredible run before the third quarter ended, muscling through the tired Badger defensive wall, then breaking into the open field for a 70-yard touchdown run that increased the Pitt advantage to 21 points. It gave the sophomore from Albany 142 yards on the day.

Despite the fact that Sutherland still may have had concerns about the team's turnovers, it was tempered by the fact that his team crushed a quality opponent, running for 491 net yards to the Badgers' 126. Turnovers in the big picture would be a minor annoyance; the Hagan Plan, which eventually would become much more restrictive than the athletic director announced on that day, became a much larger one to the Panthers' hall-of-fame coach.

Game 6—October 30, 1937, at Pitt Stadium

CARNEGIE TECH TARTANS   14
UNIVERSITY OF PITTSBURGH PANTHERS 25

Unable to revive the fallen program at his alma mater, Howard Harpster parted ways with Carnegie Tech following the 1936 campaign. Instead of a former alumnus, the administration at the college decided to peg a former star from their neighbors in Oakland for a man who could get the job done: that man was former University of Pittsburgh All-American tackle Bill Kern. A former NFL player with the Green Bay Packers in 1929 and 1930, Kern had been an assistant under Jock Sutherland in 1936 before taking over the Tartans, and while a year later he would bring Tech to heights they had not imagined, right now they were a struggling program that had lost three of their four games going into this Oakland rivalry. He brought with him several other former Sutherland players for his coaching staff that included Eddie Baker, Joe Skladany and Frank Kutz.

Despite the fact they were 1–3, the program at Carnegie Tech was growing and was better than their record indicated. They had lost three close games against quality opponents: 18–14 to NYU and 7–0 to both Purdue and Temple. The team they did defeat was the Fighting Irish of Notre Dame at Pitt Stadium two weeks before this game. While strung with several injuries during the season, the advantage the Tartans had against the Panthers was that no one was more familiar with his opponent than Kern, and no one would know how to beat them but him. There was one thing Kern was becoming aware of on a negative end, something his Panther brethren were learning: the football deemphasis. They began deemphasizing the program before the season began, and by the end of the 1930s, Carnegie Tech would be in full retreat from major college football, which chased Kern to WVU. In the long run it was much worse than what the Panthers faced now.

Even though he had to be devastated following the announcement of the Hagan Plan the week before, Sutherland was a good soldier for the university, saying simply, "I am a Pitt man. The University to me is something far bigger than any single individual—something more than those who are not Pitt men can realize. For this reason, if no other, I appreciate the position of the Chancellor the Athletic Council and the athletic department in their efforts to put us on a plane which is comparable to the best in intercollegiate athletics."[6] While many supported it at the time, including one of the former rivals, Washington and Jefferson College, who had deemphasized in 1933, there were two former Pitt players, namely Izzy Weinstock and Frank Walton, who bluntly stated that it wouldn't work as long as other schools were still subsidizing players, a stance which Sutherland soon came to realize.

That battle was one to be fought down the road; the one against Carnegie Tech for a chance to reclaim the city title was the one that Sutherland was concentrating on at the time. After three difficult losses, in two of which, against NYU and Temple, the Tartans were the better team statistically, Kern was looking at using several sophomores to supplement an injured crew, although the coach would luckily get back star fullback Whitey Lee, who was injured in the opener against NYU. They also would have Pete Moroz, Ray Carnelly and Coleman Kopcsak in the backfield and hoped the turnovers that had plagued the Panthers the past few weeks would give the group an opportunity to take advantage and lead Tech to the upset.

Pitt was relatively healthy for this contest, although Sutherland decided to give his star halfback Marshall Goldberg, who had been hobbled by injuries to his leg all season, the day off in favor of sophomore Dick Cassiano, who was having a fabulous season to this point. He also sat end Bill Daddio to start the contest in favor of Paul Shaw. If it appeared like Sutherland wasn't taking Carnegie Tech seriously, by the end of the first half, he would be reminded of just how tough they were.

Once again Sutherland's offensive machine could not stop fumbling, losing six against the Tartans on this warm, sunny fall afternoon in front of 37,000 cheering fans. Despite the fact that turnovers would turn what should have been a rout into this tightly fought, close game, the Panthers took advantage of a blocked punt to take an early lead. Deep in Pitt territory, they blocked a Tech punt with George Delich falling on the ball at the four. A couple of plays later, Frank Patrick muscled into the end zone for a six-point Panther lead.

Try as they might, Pitt could not hold on to the ball, and a fumble by Stebbins at their own 21 gave the Tartans great field position. Five teams tried, most with better pedigrees than the Tartans, and five teams had failed to score against the staunch Panther defense so far in 1937. The streak would end as Tech used a trick play to put Pittsburgh behind for the first time all season in the second quarter. Leo Napotnik gave it to Moroz on a reverse, who sent a pass over the goal line to a wide-open Howarth, who cradled in the pass for the touchdown. Kopcsak kicked the extra point, and remarkably Carnegie

Tech had a 7–6 second-quarter lead. Frank Souchak gave Pitt a 9–7 advantage to end the half with a 25-yard field goal, but despite that fact and that the Tartans lost Carnelly for the game with a broken nose and possible concussion, this contest was a much tighter battle than anyone could have imagined.

Frustrated at the close game against a seemingly inferior foe, the Panthers started the second half aggressively on their first successful sustained drive of the game. Starting at their own 22 to begin the third quarter, the Pitt line was ripping gaping holes in the Tartans' defensive wall. Led by 27- and 18-yard runs by Patrick, Pitt quickly moved to the one-foot line in nine plays. The fullback ended the drive that he almost single-handedly led with a bolt up the middle to increase that Pitt lead to nine. One series later as Tech was punting deep in their own territory, the snap went over the punter Lee's head. He covered the ball in the end zone with the Pittsburgh defenders falling on him for a safety and an 18–7 lead.

With the game now in the fourth quarter looking like it had already been decided, Carnegie Tech desperately passed the ball in hopes of catching Pitt off guard. The Panther pass defense was one of the best in the country as Johnny Urban proved by picking off a pass at midfield. While they didn't score on that drive, a Bill Stapulis punt put the Tartans once again stuck deep in their own territory. A poor punt by Lee gave Pitt excellent field position. Wanting to show he was an offensive threat too, Urban launched a pass to Ed Spotovich in the corner of the end zone, making it 25–7.

With one minute left, Tech was able to once again score as they passed their way down the field, but it was too little, too late as the Panthers were able to hold on for a 25–14 victory, giving them the city championship that they had lost to Duquesne the past two seasons.

Sutherland went over to midfield to congratulate the great job his protégé did against him, and out of respect, the team's acting captain John Michelosen took the game ball into the Tartans' locker room and presented it to his former assistant coach. It was a touch of sportsmanship celebrating a great rivalry that because of football deemphasis would be eliminated in the not-too-distant future.

Game 7—November 5, 1937, at Notre Dame Stadium in South Bend, Indiana

UNIVERSITY OF PITTSBURGH PANTHERS   21
UNIVERSITY OF NOTRE DAME FIGHTING IRISH   6

They were one of the reasons that the administration at the University of Pittsburgh rushed toward deemphasis: the University of Notre Dame. Wanting to distance themselves from a team they felt were nothing more than semi-professionals, Notre Dame ended the series that had become such a classic. Over the previous seven seasons, Pitt had a slight 4–3 advantage and wanted to make sure that they would punish the Irish as a going-away present.

While many felt the Irish had one of the best teams in the country following their 9–7 victory over Navy and 7–6 upset win at Minnesota which left them at 3-1-1, they were challenged offensively, scoring only 44 points in their five contests. The experts felt that Elmer Layden's backfield was on the verge of greatness after the victory against the Gophers. Halfback John McCarthy was considered an explosive runner, and quarterback Andy Puplis was one of the most effective at his position in the country.

Even though the potential was there for a good offensive team, the strength of this squad was definitely on its defensive line. Center Pat McCarty was considered one of the top defensive players in college football, with Leonard Skoglund; Chuck Sweeney, who blocked the extra-point against Minnesota that preserved their victory; Ed Beiner; Alex Shelogg; Joe Ruetz; and Joe Kuharich combining to make a formidable wall. The group yielded a mere three touchdowns and was probably the best defensive team that the Panthers had faced at this point of the season.

Offensively, Layden felt that his best chance to win might be through the air, as Carnegie Tech showed the week before by throwing for the only two touchdowns that Pitt had yielded all season. Despite the fact the Tartans appeared to be successful through the air, the second touchdown came on the final series of the game when the Panthers had most of their lower reserves in the game. The team actually had been very effective as a pass defense all season, with an opportunistic defensive backfield and an aggressive rush led by Tony Matisi and ends Frank Souchak, Fabian Hoffman, and Bill Daddio, who missed the Carnegie Tech game and was questionable in this contest with an injured leg.

Halfback Marshall Goldberg also missed the game against Carnegie Tech, suffering from injuries to his leg as well, but Sutherland was confident that his star halfback would be healthy against the Irish. While confident about Goldberg, he was less so about his other injured starters, end Paul Shaw and quarterback John Chickerneo, who was hurt against the Tartans and was listed as a co-starter for the contest with John Michelosen because of it.

It was a rainy, cold afternoon as 56,000 fans jammed into Notre Dame Stadium to see the final version of this rivalry, which was reignited six years later in 1943 when the Panthers were just a shell of themselves. Shaw was healthy enough to start opposite of Souchak as the script for this game followed the ones that plagued Pitt on more than one occasion throughout the season, an offense driving up and down the field to no avail, relying on their tremendous defense to make up for the offensive inefficiencies.

Pitt threatened several times in the first half but were unable to finish the drives with a touchdown. Defensively they did what many thought they'd do against the unspectacular Irish offense, never allowing them to cross midfield in the first 30 minutes. As was said before, Layden felt his chance to win was through the air, and it only took one play for the Irish to show that.

After moving the ball to the 50, Frank Patrick made the mistake of the game when he botched a punt that went less than a yard before it was recovered by Notre Dame. After a two-yard run, McCarthy took the next snap and found Puplis in the open downfield. The quarterback hauled in the pass and ran through and around five Pitt defenders into the end zone with the stunning first touchdown of the game. The Panthers were irritated that they had completely dominated their opponents yet were in danger of losing this final contest of the series. Champions find a way to win when it appears that their chances are dim, and Pitt was about to show that they were not only champions, but arguably the best team in the history of the program.

Notre Dame was tiring as the momentum they acquired from their score began to falter. They were able to temporarily bottle up Pitt's offense after the touchdown, but as the fourth began the Panther offense was about to have their best quarter of the season when they needed it most. Goldberg ran the last play of the third quarter 18 yards into Notre Dame territory. The play was nullified with a clipping call against Pitt. Instead of frustrating the Panthers even further, Goldberg went to the air, tossing a long pass to Hoffman, who pulled it in at the 30. Hoffman sprinted to the sideline before he was thrown out at the five by Puplis. Two plays later Patrick made up for his poor punt by ripping through the Notre Dame line for the touchdown that gave the rejuvenated Panthers a 7–6 lead.

The Irish defense was reeling as Pitt continued to dominate on the next series. Notre Dame's line was no match for the Panthers as the running backs were taking turns with long runs. Five plays into the drive that started on their 33, Patrick went up the middle for 15 yards to the Irish 26. The fullback went the same way with the handoff on the next play, and when the Notre Dame defense followed, he pitched it to Stebbins who cut the opposite way into the clear with no defenders in sight for the touchdown and an eight-point advantage.

With the game seemingly over as time was running out, the Panthers turned what was only 15 minutes earlier a deficit into a rout. Following a Stebbins interception, which he returned to the Notre Dame 42, Goldberg went 21 yards with a reverse, setting up a spectacular 21-yard off tackle by

Patrick who bolted into the end zone with an Irish defender hanging on his back.

Scoring three touchdowns in the final quarter against one of the best teams in the country made most experts take notice, considering Pitt now the best team in the country. They now had Pitt as the favorite over Alabama to return to Pasadena to defend their Rose Bowl championship. With Nebraska, Penn State and Duke ahead of them on the schedule, they had a chance to distance themselves from any contenders for the national crown.

Game 8—November 13, 1937, at Pitt Stadium
UNIVERSITY OF NEBRASKA CORNHUSKERS   7
UNIVERSITY OF PITTSBURGH PANTHERS   13

For years, Nebraska and its coach, Dana X. Bible, were at the mercy of Pitt's Coach Jock Sutherland's for ten straight seasons, losing seven and playing to three scoreless ties against the Panthers. Despite the fact that they usually came into the game as one of the best teams in the nation, Pitt would generally quiet their fans and destroy their hopes for a national championship. Though Sutherland broke their hearts on a yearly basis, Bible was a staunch supporter of Sutherland and the university when the University of Nebraska student newspaper called on the coach and the program to end its relations with Pitt, not only because it felt the team was too physical, but that it did not display the proper sportsmanship by paying its players so much money. Following his wonderful career at Nebraska, Bible went off to Texas to turn around the fortunes of the Longhorns. In his place to continue the success he built at Nebraska was former Army Cadet Lawrence "Biff" Jones.

A tackle for the United States Military Academy who graduated in 1917, Jones became a lieutenant of field artillery, serving in France during World War I. A few years after serving in the army, Jones returned to his alma mater to head its football program in 1926, leading them to a 30–8–2 mark in four seasons. While there he also smartly hired a young man by the name of Earl "Red" Blaik as an assistant coach who would lead them to greater glory in the 1940s and 1950s. In 1932, Jones continued to show what a successful coach he was, taking the job at LSU and winning the Southern Conference championship the first season and fashioning a spectacular 20–5–6 record before moving on to Oklahoma in 1935 and then accepting the post with the Cornhuskers two years later.

In his initial season, he was undefeated coming into this contest, upsetting the University of Minnesota in the opener 14–9 and tying Kansas and Oklahoma as they were on their way to another Big Six Conference championship.

Defeating Pitt, as it always had been, would show the bowl committees and national experts alike that the Cornhuskers were one of the best teams in the country. They would do so with a relatively healthy team as their staunch defensive line was led by their captain and Latrobe native Fred Shirey. Joining Shirey was tackle Ted Doyle and guards Bob Mehring and Lowell English, with one of the best centers in the country anchoring the group, Charles Brock.

While their defense appeared to be the strength of the team, the offense had struggled since their first two wins against Minnesota and Iowa State. They had scored only four touchdowns in their previous four contests, and their backfield of John Howell, Harris Andrews, Ed Dodd and Bill Callihan potentially could have a very difficult time against the Panthers' defense, which had been among the best in the country.

With Nebraska appearing at 100 percent, Sutherland had some concerns with injuries on his squad. Luckily for him, Marshall Goldberg was healthy, but Harold "Curly" Stebbins was doubtful with injuries he suffered in the Notre Dame contest as Johnny Urban was slated to get the start. End Bill Daddio still would be unable to play, hurting his leg earlier in the season, and was thought to be out until the finale against Duke.

With Pitt coming ever so close to being recognized universally as national champions, a feat that, while others had named them champions in previous seasons, had eluded Sutherland in his tenure with the Panthers, 71,267, the largest crowd to witness a football game in the city of Pittsburgh, turned out to witness this contest. It had rained the day before and continued with a light shower in the morning, but by kickoff the precipitation had stopped and the field was in good shape.

The script for the first half was eerily similar to what the Panthers' offense had done all season—run up and down the field on their opponents only to come away with no points. Pitt had kept the Huskers on their side of the field the first half while driving deep into Nebraska territory twice, once losing the ball on an interception of a Bill Stapulis pass, the second with Dodd picking off a toss by Dick Cassiano in the end zone as time ran out in the second quarter.

For the game, the Pitt defense did not yield a single yard to the outmatched Cornhuskers, permitting negative nine yards, but as it did in the third quarter against the Irish, not taking advantage of so many opportunities hurt Pitt as Nebraska stunningly took the lead in the third quarter. Stapulis lifted a punt from his 20-yard line, and Dodd took it at his 40. His line set up a perfect wall for him and he sprinted freely until he reached the five, where it looked like Goldberg might tackle him. Dodd was able to elude the junior halfback as he crossed the goal line for a 7–0 lead.

Like the Irish, the Cornhuskers had but 15 minutes to keep the Panthers from their date with destiny and an undefeated season. Also in a similar manner to what happened in the Notre Dame contest, Pitt showed Nebraska the spirit of a champion. Starting at the 20 late in the third period, Goldberg totaled 39 yards in two carries to put Pittsburgh at the Husker 35 as the fourth quarter began. Pitt then slowly moved toward the ten as Goldberg and the injured Stebbins took turns going 25 yards in six carries. Frank Patrick and Stebbins took it to the one where the Panther starting fullback, Patrick, barreled through the tough Nebraska line to bring Pitt within a point at 7–6. Unfortunately Frank Souchak's extra point bounced off the upright as the Cornhuskers held on to their lead. Another poor development for Sutherland was the fact that Goldberg was reinjured on the drive and hobbled to the sideline, out for the game.

Despite the fact Goldberg was gone, the momentum now swung in their favor as the Panthers quickly resumed their attack when Al Lezouski jumped on a fumble by Nebraska's Bill Anderson at the Husker 33. They had blown several opportunities in this contest but did not want to leave this one to chance. Stapulis took the ball on the first play from the scrimmage and muscled through the Nebraska defense, up the middle for 20 yards to the 13. Cassiano and Stebbins ran the ball to the three where Stapulis gave Pitt the lead with a touchdown run that sent the jam-packed stadium to their feet with the Panthers taking their first lead of the game 13–7.

Nebraska was unable to move the ball for the previous three quarters and would not begin now as time ran out Jones learned what Bible had learned so many times before him: Pitt was the school's Achilles' heel, once again keeping Nebraska from the upper echelon.

Game 9—November 20, 1937, at Pitt Stadium
PENN STATE UNIVERSITY NITTANY LIONS 7
UNIVERSITY OF PITTSBURGH PANTHERS 28

It had been a long and sometimes painful run for former three-time All-American Bob Higgins, who had been trying desperately to make his alma mater at Penn State relevant in football again. He took over the program in 1930 with hopes of being able to compete with the likes of the University of Pittsburgh, whom he was taking on this afternoon at Pitt Stadium, and through his first six seasons at the school, he seemed no closer to his goal.

Higgins was a mere 21–33–3 in the time period coming off a lackluster 3–5 campaign in 1936. He had never finished over .500 in his tenure to that point, but as the 1937 campaign was unfolding, that streak had come to an end as the Nittany Lions seemed to have finally turned the corner. Penn State was 5–2 coming into their final contest of the season that included impressive wins against Bucknell, Penn and Maryland. To go 6–2 would take an effort of monumental proportions as they were facing arguably the best team in the nation.

As it was for Nebraska the week before, Coach Jock Sutherland and the Pitt Panthers had been the Nittany Lions' own personal mountain to climb, and it had been a mountain that seemingly grew with the years. Not since 1919 had the Lions gotten the best of the Panthers. They battled Pitt to two memorable scoreless ties in 1920 and 1921, but since then, for the most part it had been a series of embarrassing battles. Losing 12 consecutive games while scoring only 51 points in the process, the series had gotten so one-sided that Penn State ended the series after a 41–0 loss in 1931 for three seasons before renewing it in 1935. That season Higgins and his squad almost pulled off a miraculous upset before losing 9–0, but Pitt restored order the following year with a 34–7 shellacking. With his newfound success in Happy Valley, coupled with the Panthers' offensive woes in the latter half of the season, Penn State fans had real hope in 1937.

The strongest lineup in Higgins's tenure at State College at that point of his career definitely had a Western Pennsylvania flare to it. It included a strong line with Greensburg native Paul Enders at center; Schenley High School alum Jack Economos and Joe Peel at guard; Dan DeMarino, also from Greensburg, and W.T. Ellwood at tackle; Spike Alter and Monongahela's Alex Barantovich at end; and a backfield that included Altoona native Lloyd Ickes, Mount Pleasant's Steve Rollins, Dick Skemp from Scottsdale and A.J. Giannantionio.

As good as the above crew was, they were not the equal of the Panthers, who would be inspired today as 19 seniors, including such impressive contributors as Frank Souchak, Bill Stapulis, Frank Patrick, John Michelosen, Tony Matisi, Don Hensley, Henry Adams, Ted Schmitt, George Delich, Dante DalleTezze and Johnny Urban, would see their last action at Pitt Stadium.

The group was impressive indeed as two of them were honored before the contest when the Associated Press released their 1937 potential All-American list that they would choose their annual team from with Matisi and Souchak joining junior halfback Marshall Goldberg and fellow junior Albin Lezouski on the list.

Even with an honored list of All-American candidates at their disposal, the team had not played to their potential the last few weeks. Injuries to Goldberg and end Bill Daddio had truly hurt their cause; unfortunately for the Lions, both came back healthy on this day with a vengeance.

It was a snowy, cold afternoon at Pitt Stadium with a swirling wind as

A two-time All-American at the University of Pittsburgh, Marshall Goldberg also had the honor of being the only player in football history to finish in the top three in the Heisman Trophy voting twice, with a third-place finish in 1937 and as runner-up a year later.

23,000 frozen fans were on hand to watch what turned out to be an onslaught from the beginning. Goldberg made a great case for himself as an All-American with perhaps his best performance of the season. Not wanting to make it an unexpected battle despite the fact they had superior stats, as they had against Notre Dame, Carnegie Tech and Nebraska, Pitt scored early in the first half and often.

After appearing sluggish in the early part of the first quarter, the Panthers started a drive on their own 45, with Goldberg leading the way downfield. The Elkins, West Virginia, native rambled for 26 yards on two carries putting it inside the Lions' ten. The Panthers did not fritter away this scoring opportunity, with Patrick ramming through the overwhelmed Penn State line for a 7–0 early lead.

Now that the momentum was clearly on its side as well as the field position, Pitt started its next drive inside Nittany Lions territory at the 46. The one-man show continued with Goldberg leading a second impressive drive with his first touchdown of the day as the Panthers put a stranglehold on the contest with a two-touchdown advantage. Giving Goldberg a rest in the second quarter, Sutherland inserted his dangerous backup into the contest, Dick Cassiano. The Albany, New York, sophomore continued the offensive show as he sprinted for a 78-yard run into the end zone as Pitt exited the field at the half with a 21-point lead.

Unfortunately, as the third quarter began, the turnover issues that had plagued Pitt for most of the second half of the season came into play in the third, when a Penn State punt bounced of the leg of DelleTezze into the hands of the Lions' Barantovich at the 24. On the next play Wendell Wear found Alter free for the long touchdown to cut the advantage to 21–7. It was a lone positive moment for the Nittany Lions as Pittsburgh would not falter against their rivals, starting on a final scoring drive in the last quarter. Once again Penn State gave the Panthers excellent field position to start a possession as an invigorated Goldberg capped the 54-yard drive with a seven-yard jaunt into the end zone through a huge hole created by his effective line, making the final score 28–7.

It was a disappointing ending to what had been a fine season for the Lions. Better times were ahead for both Higgins and his program as the winning would soon come, as would an end to the dominance the University of Pittsburgh had on his school. For the time being, though, they had fallen victim to what was arguably the greatest team Sutherland had produced in his time at Pitt.

Game 10—November 27, 1937, at Duke Stadium in Durham, North Carolina

UNIVERSITY OF PITTSBURGH PANTHERS 10
DUKE UNIVERSITY BLUE DEVILS   0

On October 5, 1929, early in Coach Jock Sutherland's first national championship season, he took on former teammate Jimmy DeHart's Duke Blue Devils squad in Durham, North Carolina, to open their new stadium. It was an inauspicious debut for the facility as the powerful Panthers crushed the home team 52–7. Two years later DeHart was out at the school, and the Blue Devils would have to wait eight long years for their revenge.

A season later, a young Wallace Wade would take over and make the program a winning one. He was so impressive that in 1967, the field that the 1929 Pitt squad opened in such a dominant manner was renamed in his honor. In 1937 he finally gave his school the opportunity for that long-awaited revenge as he and the Devils wanted to destroy the Panthers' undefeated season as the 1937 campaign came to an end.

At 45 years old, Wade had a phenomenal hall-of-fame career at that point, capturing three national championships at Alabama in his first coaching job before taking over the Blue Devils program. From the beginning he turned Duke into winners, capturing three Southern Conference championships within his first six seasons as his club was ranked 11th in the final Associated Press poll in 1936.

Winning two Rose Bowl titles in his time at Alabama and tying one in 1926, the Brown alum was trying to do the same thing at Duke and felt it could begin by defeating arguably the best team in the country. The 1937 campaign had been a particularly effective one for his squad. They came into this final contest with a 7–1–1 mark, with a disappointing home loss to North Carolina 14–6 and a scoreless tie to the Tennessee Volunteers as the only blemishes in a wonderful season.

Their offense had been explosive at times, racking up 67 points against Wake Forest and 43 versus Washington and Lee with two of the most explosive halfbacks in the country, a duo that could rival the Pittsburgh twosome of Marshall Goldberg and Harold Stebbins. Eric Tipton led the team with 565 yards, but he was a distinct second when it came to excitement; that title went to the speedy halfback Elmore Hackney. He averaged 6.1 yards in his 79 carries, many in an electric manner. As good as he was as halfback, the Durham Dasher, as he was known, may have been even better returning punts. Led by memorable returns of 72 yards against the Tar Heels and 55 versus North Carolina State, Hackney averaged 15 yards a return, prompting Sutherland to instruct his punters to kick away from him.

While Duke may have had a slight advantage in their starting backfield, the Panthers had a huge edge in their depth and line. The combination of Bill Daddio, Frank Souchak, Fabian Hoffman, Toni Matisi, Ted Schmitt, George Delich, Albin Lezouski, Steve Petro, Dante DelleTezze, Don Hensley and Henry Adams had not permitted one touchdown on the ground through the nine games they had played so far. Five of the six scores had been through the air, two when the game was well out of hand, and the other one was on a punt return by Nebraska, the manner of scoring in which Wade hoped to get his team on the scoreboard.

As it turned out, the Blue Devils' defense was almost the equivalent of their more talented opponents, finding a way to do what no other defense had:

completely stop Goldberg. While he was able to garner two long runs, the junior halfback was stopped for negative yards 12 times during the game.

Despite the fact that the soon-to-be All-American was rendered useless, his counterpart with the Blue Devils almost single-handedly gave the Panthers the win. As the first quarter was coming to an end, Frank Patrick did what Sutherland had hoped he wouldn't: punt directly to Hackney. Inexplicably the star halfback fumbled at the 20 with Souchak picking up the loose ball. The Blue Devil defense rose to the challenge allowing only five yards and three carries, but Souchak made sure Pitt would not come away scoreless as he booted a field goal to give the Panthers a 3–0 lead with five seconds left in the first.

The odds that Hackney would bobble a second punt were long indeed, but that's exactly what would happen when Bill Stapulis surprisingly punted to the Durham Dasher with eight minutes left in the half. Hackney looked up to pull in the punt at his own 13, dropping the ball in his tracks. The Panthers' reserve end Ed Spotovich pounced on it, giving Pittsburgh a tremendous scoring opportunity. Sutherland had his second-team offense in at that point as Dick Cassiano took the handoff and ran away from the middle of the Duke line. He sprinted toward the ride sidelines as his own offensive line began to plow down Blue Devil defenders in their way. The sophomore waltzed into the end zone for the final score of the game before the first half ended.

The second half was nothing more than a battle of field position. Duke threatened twice, but the Panthers' tough defense kept them out of the end zone for their fifth shutout of the season. While they gained 237 yards on the ground to the Blue Devils' 60, they were outgained by their opponents 66 to five through the air, despite the fact that the Blue Devils only completed five of 21 passes thrown.

It was a satisfying end to the season as Pitt completed their first unbeaten season since a 6–0–2 mark in 1920. Of course they still were favored to have one game left, a spot in the Rose Bowl against the University of California Bears. They were challenged for the spot by Alabama and Fordham, but it seemed from everything that was reported that the Bears wanted to play the best in the land, and to them that was the Panthers.

While they were waiting for the bid that all expected to come, several members of the squad were given All-American mentions. Lezouski was named second-team guard on the Associated Press squad while Daddio and Souchak each garnered first-team mentions at end. The two most decorated players were consensus first-team picks Matisi and Goldberg. When being chosen to the first-team Associated Press squad, the AP said that Matisi "made good the adage that a football team is as good as its tackles,"[7] and that Goldberg was "a strong all-around back, probably the best climax runner of the season."[8]

National championship honors would soon come as they were selected as the country's best football by the top two sources, the Associated Press poll and the Dickinson system as well as the Boand, Litkenhous and Williamson systems to go with the *Football Thesaurus*. It was the first truly universal respect as the nation's best team in the phenomenal career of Sutherland. Despite the fact that football deemphasis was coming in force to the University of Pittsburgh, times were good and the bowl bids certainly were about to flow. They would have their choice of any bowl they wanted; it was just a matter of time to see where they would go with their second consecutive Lambert Trophy, symbolic of the best team in the east, in hand. It all seemed so perfect; unfortunately, the bitterness of the 1936 Rose Bowl issues, where the team had no spending money, was about to come back and grow into an even bigger controversy.

According to Athletic Director Jimmy Hagan, he had two invitations plus an anticipated bid to the Rose Bowl as he let the team vote on which it wanted to go to, reportedly without telling Sutherland first. "We had invitations from the Sugar Bowl and the Cotton Bowl which we wanted to place before the boys, so we tossed in the Rose Bowl for consideration too," the AD stated.[9]

What should have been a simple thing, where to play, turned into a set of demands. It was reported that they wanted to be compensated for their trip with expense money: $100–$200 was the reported figure. The players also wanted all team members to make the trip instead of keeping some of the third- and fourth-team reserves in Pittsburgh as they had the year before, plus they wanted a reported two-week vacation after the bowl game. One of the other issues that seemed to irritate the players was that Sutherland wasn't part of the meeting or the vote.

It was something that Hagan admitted, Sutherland not knowing about the bid or vote, but said it wasn't on purpose, claiming he had tried to contact Sutherland, to no avail. According to the *Pittsburgh Post-Gazette*, the coach was in his office at the time, not far from Hagan. "In the storm meeting attended by the players the pros and cons of the proposed trip were gone over, and while the players argued, in his office sat Dr. Jock Sutherland either unaware of the meeting or an uninvited figure."[10]

The players decided to vote to turn down all bids. The vote created conflict and was not a strong majority by any stretch of the imagination as it was turned down by a reported 16–15 margin, with the seniors being the group that was most upset with the bowl issues the year before and the fact their coach wasn't consulted this time around. They thought that if the coach was given an opinion on the matter, he would have given the players a united front one way or the other. The vote angered Hagan and business manager John Weber who curtly said, "The University did not and will not call a second meeting of the football players," meaning that the case was closed and the school wouldn't give in to the players' demands, who would therefore stay home for the holidays.

Sutherland tried to be respectful as always, saying simply, "I did not know the meeting to vote on post-season bids was being held yesterday. However I believe that decision should be left up to the players themselves. I have not talked to any of the boys about the matter at all."[11] Later on, the administration and the players tried to deny that it had been about expenses to lessen the poor public relations that were coming with the vote, but the bitterness not only over the previous season's Rose Bowl issues but also the seeming lack of respect for the coach and the Hagan Plan that was about to end their dynasty.

In the end, what should have been their greatest moment turned into a troubled championship. The bitterness among all would deepen in 1938 rather than coming to an understanding. The greatest season in the program's history would become the last in their dynasty as the Hagan Plan would begin to strip the program of its legendary depth a season later costing one of its best senior classes a third title in a row.

*National Champions selections made by modern-day analysts are noted "(retrospective)." Players rated as **First Team All-Americans** by a plurality of NCAA-recognized selectors are noted as "(consensus)." Players rated by all NCAA-recognized selectors are noted as "(unanimous)."*

1937 SCORES

Date	Opponent	Score	Record
9/25	Ohio Wesleyan	59–0	1–0–0
10/2	@West Virginia	20–0	2–0–0
10/9	Duquesne	6–0	3–0–0
10/16	@Fordham	0–0	3–0–1
10/23	Wisconsin	21–0	4–0–1
10/30	Carnegie Tech	25–14	5–0–1
11/5	@Notre Dame	21–6	6–0–1
11/13	Nebraska	13–7	7–0–1
11/20	Penn State	28–7	8–0–1
11/27	@Duke	10–0	9–0–1
		203–34	

Selected as National Champions by:
The Associated Press
Illustrated Football Annual—Boand System
The Football Thesaurus
Dickinson System
Litkenhous System
Williamson System
1st-N-Goal (retrospective)*
Angelo Louisa (retrospective)*
Bob Kirlin (retrospective)*
College Football Researchers Association (retrospective)*
Earl Jenssen (retrospective)*
Billingsley Report (retrospective)*
Houlgate System (retrospective)*
Jim Koger (retrospective)*
Patrick Premo (retrospective)*
Bill Libby (retrospective)*
Bob Royce (retrospective)*
Century Football Index (retrospective)*
College Football USA (retrospective)*
George Trevor (retrospective)*
Harry Frye (retrospective)*
James Howell (retrospective)*
James Whalen (retrospective)*
Loren Maxwell (retrospective)*
Massey Ratings (retrospective)*
National Championship Foundation (retrospective)*
Poling System (retrospective)*
Sagarin Ratings (retrospective)*
What's What (retrospective)*

*Not Recognized as Official National Championship Selector by University of Pittsburgh.

Selected as First-Team All-Americans
Tony Matisi (consensus)
Marshall Goldberg (consensus)
Frank Souchak
Bill Daddio

Heisman Trophy Top-10 Voting
Marshall Goldberg—Third Place

12

The End of the Glory Days

To say Chancellor John Bowman was upset about the football players' decision to turn down a bid to several bowls the preceding season would be an understatement. It was an embarrassing moment for the university that was trying to change its academic reputation by deemphasizing football. The Hagan Plan that new athletic director Jimmy Hagan had instituted to bring the football program under control was tough enough; Code Bowman would make it impossible for the football program to compete as a successful major college football team.

Bowman decided he would tighten the noose around the program by taking away the $300 payments of their tuition unless they worked even more hours a day to pay for it starting with the 1938 freshman class. What had previously required them to work two hours a day would now be three to five on top of their studies and football responsibilities. The student-athletes would also be required to move along with their class if they wanted to be eligible to play, which, while an understandable requirement from an academic standpoint, in major college football at the time was almost a death knell. Grades had never been a requirement in the past and would send some of the better football players, who might not have been academically sound, to other schools. Bowman also officially cut the schedule to eight games and mandated that football practice not start before September 10. The Pitt chancellor originally wanted to adopt the stricter Big Ten student-athlete requirements in hopes of one day being included in the conference; he ended up doing that and much more.

For Sutherland's part, he did support the program except for one aspect; he felt that if you were going to make such wide sweeping changes, it had to be combined with an easing up of the schedule. He felt that it made no sense to take a team with secondary talent year in and year out and make them face the best subsidized teams in the country. "I know that it is unfair and even dangerous to de-emphasize without also de-emphasizing the schedules. I consider it unfair to send other men's sons out to play without proper talent and without even a chance to win. It would be as unwise to put minor league players into heavy major league competition."[1]

The conflicts would come to a head within the next 12 months, but for now the Panther coach would have to prepare his men for the 1938 campaign, a season where they were the odds-on favorite for a third consecutive national championship. He had a wonderful senior class that had been the best of his career, a group knowing nothing but winning titles. Pitt had a deep, dynamic backfield, one that necessitated an unselfish change by Marshall Goldberg so Sutherland could have his best four backs in the game at once. The All-American and third-place finisher in the Heisman Trophy race moved to fullback in 1938, allowing the talented Dick Cassiano to join Goldberg, Harold "Curly" Stebbins and quarterback John Chickerneo, forming what was referred to nationwide as the "Dream Backfield."

It was a dominant group that some felt was better than the legendary "Four Horsemen" of Notre Dame in the mid–1920s. Probably the most underrated was Stebbins. Goldberg said of Stebbins, "He was quick and big, and he was very strong. Every time he got the ball, he wanted to make a touchdown. He was also a very warm person, kind and gentle."[2] Fordham coach Jim Crowley, a member of the Four Horsemen, remembered that Stebbins "runs like a thief and can pass uncommonly well when called upon."[3]

It was a group that led the Panthers to five dynamic victories to begin the season. The Dream Backfield had solved their offensive issues from 1937 as the team ran over West Virginia, Temple, Duquesne, Wisconsin and SMU by a combined 134–19 margin, never being threatened as they hosted another national power, ninth-ranked Fordham University, at Pitt Stadium for the first time. Pitt was now ranked number one in the nation as they were about to play a team that battled the Panthers to three consecutive scoreless ties the previous three campaigns at the Polo Grounds in Harlem. It was a series that became a legendary one in college football history; hopefully Pittsburgh would find a way not only to score, but to finally defeat Crowley and his squad.

A record crowd of 75,587 jammed Pitt Stadium to see this intriguing matchup as Bill Daddio finally ended the 12-quarter scoreless streak with a field goal in the first to give Pitt a 3–0 lead. History dictated that the three points would win the game, but surprisingly it would not; the field goal was only the beginning as a scoring spree would soon ensue. The Rams' Don

In 74 years, Pitt Stadium played host to many memorable games including the one pictured above when a record crowd watched the Panthers finally defeat Fordham in 1938, 24–13, after playing the Rams to three straight scoreless ties. After being the home to Pitt football, track, and soccer; the Pittsburgh Steelers; and even the Panther basketball team, who played in an arena underneath the stadium between 1926 and 1951, the administration decided to demolish the facility and move the football team first to Three Rivers Stadium in 2000, then the Heinz Field a year later.

Principe gave Fordham the halftime lead 7–3 with a short one-yard run, a score that would remain until the final period. In the fourth the backfield was at its best as Cassiano scored once and Goldberg twice to spur the Panthers to the impressive 24–13 victory.

Universally acclaimed as the best team in the nation with their 6–0–0 mark against a difficult schedule, the fans and experts alike now had to wonder if Pitt would turn down another bowl bid after an undefeated season. As it turned out, another Pittsburgh school would not receive a bowl bid, with the Hagan Plan showing its first effect on the program. With the more restrictive plan costing the team a recruiting class of talented freshman in 1937, the depth that had been the hallmark of the program was now challenged. After Stebbins returned the opening kickoff for a touchdown against Carnegie Tech to give Pitt a 7–0 lead, Goldberg was injured and taken from the game the next series. With no capable backups, coupled with a strong Carnegie Tech team that would finish sixth in the Associated Press poll while taking the Lambert Trophy and the city championship from the Panthers, the Tartans defeated Pitt 20–10. It was the first loss for Pitt since the 7–0 upset at the hands of Duquesne in 1936.

They rebounded with defeats of Nebraska and Penn State to rise to fifth in the poll, but in the season finale against the undefeated and unscored-upon Duke Blue Devils in Durham, North Carolina, in the midst of an unusual snowstorm as well as being without Goldberg once again for the majority of the game, the Panthers fell for their second loss of the year. It was a disappointing end to the season that saw them ranked eighth in the final poll. Ironically the win against Fordham, which was thought to be the high point of a potential national championship season, proved to be the final shining moment in the hall-of-fame tenure of Jock Sutherland.

The situation was about to become combustible. First it was reported at the end of the season that none of the freshman, who were required to pay the $300 tuition or work to pay it off, had done either. When asked why it hadn't been done, the group of players stated that they were told by assistant athletic director Walter Good that the paper they signed agreeing to Code Bowman was nothing more than a façade as was the code. They were also told they would not be expected to pay the tuition. It was another embarrassing situation for Bowman, who came down hard on the freshmen, demanding payment.

Being informed that Bowman's policies were nothing more than a joke once again caused a huge issue, prompting the freshmen to make demands of the chancellor. They asked for free tuition, shorter working hours, not being penalized for vacation, and finally repealing the part of Code Bowman that took scholarships away from athletes. The joke among the press was that the freshmen should join the CIO, a federation of unions headed by John L. Lewis, and have him take up their case to the administration.

The public backlash against the administration was firm and furious. They came off looking as if this was about removing Sutherland from the job and the school he loved. The administration recanted and gave the freshmen their 1938 tuition free, but they were told that in the future they would either be responsible to pay the tuition or work for it. In private, it was reported by some that Bowman had given them the impression that he had recanted on charging tuition for all four years, which was denied by the administration. The alumni committee, which was convened to find out what happened in the situation, came to the conclusion that Good had indeed given them the wrong impression. It also came up that Bowman had led them to believe that the tuition would be paid by the alumni to help the university not look so foolish. With the angry administration now claiming that they would indeed have to pay or work for their tuition the final three years, the the players were confused and not really sure what was to happen going forward. This controversy caused other prospective recruits to reconsider Pitt and spend their four years at other universities or colleges.

Finally in early March of 1939, everything came to a head as Sutherland and the administration, including Bowman, met to try and work out the issues. One issue that came out before the meeting was that the administration hired Big Ten commissioner Major John Griffith to oversee the athletic department and make sure it was adhering to the Big Ten student athlete policies. Again this was done without informing Sutherland, which further caused division.

In the meetings at the beginning of the month, Bowman thought that the coach and he had come to an understanding of their differences and that Sutherland "seemed to be in complete accord with the stricter amateur code and the policy against public dispersion of scholarships to football players."[4] In fact the coach had not come to that conclusion. He had turned down a lucrative offer from Mississippi State with the hopes of remaining at his alma mater, the school he so loved. He would support Code Bowman, but only if Bowman relented to playing a schedule at the lower collegiate level where Pitt would be able to compete with the talent they were allowed to have.

Bowman felt that they could have stricter policies and compete at the same level they always had. As time would tell, Sutherland's belief that this was a recipe for disaster would come to fruition. He had no choice in his own mind but to resign, which he did on March 6, 1939. The coach stated in his resignation letter, "I am in favor of good standards, however, the present system of athletic administration has resulted in conditions which for me are intolerable."[5]

The outburst by the city and alumni was very one-sided toward Sutherland. The *Pitt News* wrote that "Chancellor Bowman built a building [referring to the Cathedral of Learning]. Dr. Sutherland built Pitt."[6] A small student strike took place, but it was to no avail. Jock Sutherland was now gone from the university, and Pitt's place among the nation's elite football teams was gone.

The college he turned into a dynasty did quickly go into decay in 1939. Pitt started the season 3–0 with impressive victories over Washington, West Virginia and Duke. They were rated number one in the Associated Press poll after the third week and Bowman and his crew felt this was an affirmation that their system would work and allow them to play major college ball. They lost four of their final six games that season and went on to record only three winning seasons in the next 15 years until a protégé of Sutherland's, John Michelosen, was hired and led a resurgence for the university in football with what he learned from his hall-of-fame coach.

Although the turn of events was not what all involved had hoped, if Bowman had adopted what Sutherland had proposed, taking the university's football program to a secondary level, history tells us that the program would have remained in that position even today. It doesn't mean that the chancellor was correct in trying to seemingly force his hall-of-fame coach out of his position and blindly lead the program into a schedule it had no business playing against, but in retrospect had he catered to his coach, Pitt fans would have been robbed of Michelosen's venture back into bowl games, the surprising 1963 squad and their legendary national championship in 1976.

After Sutherland was unceremoniously forced from his job, he eventually took his coaching act to the National Football League where he remarkably took two moribund teams, the Brooklyn Dodgers and the Pittsburgh Steelers, and turned them around into winners. In fact, in 1947 he led the Steelers to their only post-season in the history of the franchise until Chuck Noll returned them there 25 years later in 1972. Unfortunately his best season in the NFL turned out to be his last. On a scouting trip he was found confused beside his car in Kentucky and was thought originally to be suffering from exhaustion. It turned out to be a malignant brain tumor. The hall-of-fame coach died on April 11, 1948, after surgery to remove the tumor. It was a sad ending to what had been such a magical combination for so many seasons, building what was the greatest dynasty this city has even known.

12. The End of the Glory Days

National Champions selections made by modern-day analysts are noted "(retrospective)." Players rated as **First Team All-Americans** by a plurality of NCAA-recognized selectors are noted as "(consensus)." Players rated by all NCAA-recognized selectors are noted as "(unanimous)."

1938 SCORES

Date	Opponent	Score	Record
9/24	West Virginia	19–0	1-0-0
10/1	@Temple	28–6	2-0-0
10/8	Duquesne	27–0	3-0-0
10/15	@Wisconsin	26–6	4-0-0
10/22	SMU	34–7	5-0-0
10/29	Fordham	24–13	6-0-0
11/5	Carnegie Tech	10–20	6-1-0
11/12	@Nebraska	19–0	7-1-0
11/19	Penn State	26–0	8-1-0
11/26	@Duke	0–7	8-2-0
		213–59	

Selected as National Champions by:
Patrick Premo (retrospective)*

*Not Recognized as Official National Championship Selector by University of Pittsburgh.

Selected as First-Team All-Americans
Marshall Goldberg (consensus)
Bill Daddio

Heisman Trophy Top 10 Voting
Marshall Goldberg—Second Place

Appendix

Panthers under Sutherland Who Played in the NFL

Name	Years Played	NFL Teams
Henry Adams	1939	Chicago Cardinals
Jim Bond	1926	Brooklyn
Jesse Brown	1926	Pottsville
Dick Cassiano	1940	Brooklyn
Ralph Chase	1926	Akron
John Chickerneo	1942	New York Giants
Paul Collins	1932–1935	Boston Redskins
Paul Cuba	1933–1935	Philadelphia
Bill Daddio	1941–1942, 1946	Chicago Cardinals, Buffalo
Ted Dailey	1933	Pittsburgh
Averill Daniell	1937	Green Bay, Brooklyn
Marshall Goldberg	1939–1942, 1946–1948	Chicago Cardinals
Milo Gwosden	1925	Buffalo
Warren Heller	1934–1936	Pittsburgh
Bob Hoel	1935, 1937–1938	Pittsburgh, Chicago Cardinals
Frank Hood	1933	Pittsburgh
Bill Kern	1929–1930	Green Bay
Ben Kish	1940–1941, 1943–1949	Brooklyn, Pitt-Phil Steagles, Philadelphia
Frank Kristufek	1940–1941	Brooklyn
Jim MacMurdo	1932–1937	Boston Redskins, Philadelphia
Ed Matesic	1934–1936	Philadelphia, Pittsburgh

Name	Years Played	NFL Teams
Tony Matisi	1938	Detroit
Elmer Merkovsky	1944–1946	Chicago Cardinals, Pittsburgh
Mike Nixon (Nicksick)	1935, 1942	Pittsburgh, Brooklyn
Stan Olenjiniczak	1935	Pittsburgh
Tom Parkinson	1931	Staten Island
Larry Peace	1941	Brooklyn
Steve Petro	1940–1941	Brooklyn
Jesse Quatse	1933–1935	Green Bay, Pittsburgh, New York Giants
Andy Salata	1929–1930	Orange, Newark
Ted Schmitt	1938–1940	Philadelphia
Mike Sebastian	1935	Philadelphia, Pittsburgh, Boston Redskins
Vinnie Sites	1936–1938	Pittsburgh
Joe Skladany	1934	Pittsburgh
Frank Souchak	1939	Pittsburgh
Bob Thurbon	1943–1944, 1946	Phil-Pitt Steagles, Chic, Pitt Carpitts, Buffalo (AFFC)
Frank Walton	1934, 1944–1945	Boston Redskins, Washington
Izzy Weinstock	1935, 1937–1938	Philadelphia, Pittsburgh
Henry Weisenbaugh	1935–1936	Pittsburgh, Boston Redskins
Gibby Welch	1928–1929	New York Yankees, Providence
Zonar Wissinger	1926	Pottsville
Jim Woodruff	1926, 1929	Chicago Cardinals, Buffalo

SUTHERLAND IN COLLEGE

Year	Team	W	L	T	Pct	Achievements
1919	Lafayette	6	2	0	.750	
1920	Lafayette	5	3	0	.625	
1921	Lafayette	9	0	0	1.000	National Champions
1922	Lafayette	7	2	0	.778	
1923	Lafayette	6	1	2	.778	
1924	Pittsburgh	5	3	1	.611	
1925	Pittsburgh	8	1	0	.889	Eastern Champions
1926	Pittsburgh	5	2	1	.688	
1927	Pittsburgh	8	1	1	.850	Eastern Champions, Rose Bowl
1928	Pittsburgh	6	2	1	.722	

Year	Team	W	L	T	Pct	Achievements
1929	Pittsburgh	9	1	0	.900	National Champions, Eastern Champions, Rose Bowl
1930	Pittsburgh	6	2	1	.722	
1931	Pittsburgh	8	1	0	.889	National Champions, Eastern Champions
1932	Pittsburgh	8	1	2	.818	Eastern Champions, Rose Bowl
1933	Pittsburgh	8	1	0	.889	
1934	Pittsburgh	8	1	0	.889	National Champions, Eastern Champions
1935	Pittsburgh	7	1	2	.800	
1936	Pittsburgh	8	1	1	.850	National Champions, Lambert Trophy Winners, Rose Bowl
1937	Pittsburgh	9	0	1	.950	National Champions, Lambert Trophy Winners
1938	Pittsburgh	8	2	0	.800	
Totals		144	28	14	.812	

Sutherland in the NFL

Year	Team	W	L	T	Pct	Playoffs
1940	Brooklyn	8	3	0	.727	None
1941	Brooklyn	7	4	0	.636	None
1946	Pittsburgh	5	5	1	.500	None
1947	Pittsburgh	8	4	0	.667	East Division Championship L—Philadelphia 21–0
Totals		28	16	1	.636	

College Hall of Fame Members Under Sutherland

Jock Sutherland
Averell Daniell
Joe Donchess
Marshall Goldberg
Joe Skladany

Notes

Introduction

1. David Finoli and Chris Fletcher, *Steel City Gridirons* (Pittsburgh: Towers Maguire, 2006), 259.

Chapter 1

1. Buffalo Sports Hall of Fame Website, "Glenn 'Pop' Warner, Football Innovator," http://buffalosportshallfame.com/member/glenn-pop-warner.
2. Ralph Davis, "Farewell Pop Warner," *Pittsburgh Press*, 30 November 1923, 32.
3. Max E. Hannum, "Panthers Lose to Lafayette Gridders," *Pittsburgh Press*, 5 October 1924, 2.
4. Max E. Hannum, "Legality of Stanford's Touchdown Questioned," *Pittsburgh Press*, 3 January 1928, 26.
5. Ibid.

Chapter 2

1. "The Redoubtable Dr. Sutherland," The Steelers Nation UK, http://www.steelersuk.com/history/forties/1946%20jock%20sutherland.html.
2. *Paths of Glory: 100 Years of Pitt Football* (Pittsburgh: Ross Sports Productions, 1993).
3. Ibid.
4. "Sutherland May Make Changes in Panther Lineup," *Pittsburgh Press*, 25 September 1929, 38.
5. John Sikes, "Pitt's Grid Builder," *Pittsburgh Press*, 6 November 1929, 32.
6. Ibid.
7. Quoteland.com, http://www.quoteland.com/author/Pop-Warner-Quotes/8547.
8. Max E. Hannum, "Pitt to Aid Duke Eleven Dedicate New Stadium Today," *Pittsburgh Press*, 5 October 1929, 18.
9. "Pitt's Hopes at Stake in Duke Game on Saturday," *Pittsburgh Press*, 29 September 1929, sec. 2, 3.
10. Max E. Hannum, "Panthers Favored over West Virginians," *Pittsburgh Press*, 12 October 1929, 19.
11. Knute Rockne, "Rockne Picks Outcome of Saturday's Battles," *Pittsburgh Press*, 18 October 1929, 63.
12. Max E. Hannum, "Pitt Only Big District Team with Clean Slate," *Pittsburgh Press*, 21 October 1929, 34.
13. Associated Press, "National Grid Honors Hanging in Balance," *Washington Observer*, 21 October 1929, 12.
14. George Kirksey, "Eastern Teams Record Better," *Pittsburgh Press*, 5 November 1929, 33.
15. John Sikes, "Pitt's Grid Builder," *Pittsburgh Press*, 6 November 1929, 32.
16. Max E. Hannum, "Tech Victory Would Be Upset," *Pittsburgh Press*, 12 November 1929, 34.
17. Max E. Hannum, "Carnegie Fears Pan-

ther Power," *Pittsburgh Press*, 13 November 1929, 33.

18. Ralph Davis, "Date of Pitt-State Game to Be Changed," *Pittsburgh Press*, 13 November 1929, 33.

19. "New Leadership for a New Era," Penn State Libraries website, http://www.libraries.psu.edu/psul/digital/pshistory/bezilla/new era.html.

20. Dan Jenkins, "This Year the Fight Will Be in the Open," *Sports Illustrated*, 11 September 1967, 33.

Chapter 3

1. Ralph Davis, "Pitt's Coast Trip Still Uncertain," *Pittsburgh Press*, 27 November 1929, 33.

2. Max Hannum, "Panthers Work Hard for Sellout Game on Coast," *Pittsburgh Press*, 19 December 1929, 37.

3. Ralph Davis, "Panthers Facing Big Job in West," *Pittsburgh Press*, 24 December 1929, 7.

4. "Signs as Coach for Five Years," *Pittsburgh Press*, 26 December 1929, 16.

5. Associated Press, "Pitt Eleven Loses on Coast, 47 to 14," *New York Times*, 2 January 1930.

Chapter 4

1. Ralph Davis, "Sutherland Squad Stages Great Rally," *Pittsburgh Press*, 26 October 1930, 33.

2. Lester Biederman, "Panthers Overwhelm Miami in Opener 61 to 0," *Pittsburgh Press*, 27 September 1931, sports sec., 1.

3. Knute Rockne, "Gridiron Glory, 100 + Years of Iowa Football," *Iowalum.com Magazine*, 2009.

4. George Kirksey, "Twelve Vets Remain for Iowa Outfit," *Pittsburgh Press*, 24 September 1931, 27.

5. Jack Sell, "Pitt among Eastern Football Leaders," *Pittsburgh Post-Gazette*, 12 October 1931, 14.

6. Herbert Friedman and Ada Friedman, "The Legacy of the Rockne Crash," *Aeroplane Magazine*, May 2001.

7. United Press, "Hold Rockne's Funeral in South Bend," *Pittsburgh Press*, 1 April 1931, 28.

8. Lester Biederman, "Steffen to Rejoin Tartans Tomorrow," *Pittsburgh Press*, 29 October 1931, 29.

9. "Pitt Lineup for State," *Pittsburgh Post-Gazette*, 28 October 1931, 14.

10. Harvey J. Boyle, "Mirrors of Sport," *Pittsburgh Post-Gazette*, 2 November 1931, 17.

11. "Feared Kebe and Heinzer Not Able to Play Saturday," *Pittsburgh Post-Gazette*, 3 November 1931, 14.

12. Ibid.

13. Associated Press "Expect Army to Complete Season's Gridiron Program," *Pittsburgh Post-Gazette*, 27 October 1931, 16.

14. Harry G. Scott, *Jock Sutherland: Architect of Men* (New York: Banner Books, 1954), 151.

15. Ibid., 153.

16. Jack Sell, "Now that Football Days at Pitt Are Ended," *Pittsburgh Post-Gazette*, 9 December 1931, 15.

17. Ibid.

18. Harvey Boyle, "Mirrors of Sport," *Pittsburgh Post-Gazette*, 27 November 1931, 19.

Chapter 5

1. Chester Smith, "Pitt Beats Ohio Northern in Opener, 47–0," *Pittsburgh Press*, 25 September 1932, sports sec., 4.

2. Chester Smith, "Pitt Overpowers Duquesne for 33–0 Win," *Pittsburgh Press*, 9 October 1932, sports sec., 1.

3. Jack Sell, "65,000 to See Panther, Irish Clash Today," *Pittsburgh Post-Gazette*, 29 October 1932, 16.

4. Lester Biederman, "Panthers Surprise Irish, 12–0," *Pittsburgh Press*, 30 October 1932, sports sec., 3.

5. Ibid.

6. "70,000 to See Powerful Grid Rivals Clash," *Pittsburgh Post-Gazette*, 5 November 1932, 18.

7. Chester Smith, "The Village Smithy," *Pittsburgh Press*, 12 November 1932, 9.

8. Chester Smith, "Pitt Defeats Tech in City Game, 6–0," *Pittsburgh Press*, 20 November 1932, sports sec., 5.

9. Ibid.

10. Tom Davies, "Pitt Defense Marvelous," *Pittsburgh Press*, 27 November 1932, sports sec., 3.

11. Chester Smith, "Pitt Defeats Stanford 7–0 in Last Game," *Pittsburgh Press*, 27 November 1932, 1.
12. "Red Raiders Disappointed," *Pittsburgh Press*, 2 December 1932, 45.

Chapter 6

1. "Panthers' Stay in Arizona Town Could be Cut Short," *Pittsburgh Post-Gazette*, 22 December 1932, 14.
2. Ibid.
3. Associated Press, "Panthers Study Southern California Plays," *Pittsburgh Post-Gazette*, 23 December 1932, 14.
4. Associated Press, "Sutherland Declares Panthers Ready," *Pittsburgh Post-Gazette*, 30 December 1932, 12.
5. Ibid.
6. Associated Press, "Sutherland Says S. California National Champs," *Pittsburgh Post-Gazette*, 3 January 1933, 1.
7. Ibid.

Chapter 7

1. Jock Sutherland, "Reserves Will Win for Dukes," *Pittsburgh Press*, 13 October 1933, 41.
2. Chester Smith, "Hard-Fought Game from Start Seen," *Pittsburgh Press*, 14 October 1933, 8.
3. Chester Smith, "Tars Unable to Cope with Pitt Attack," *Pittsburgh Press*, 15 October 1933, 16.
4. Chester Smith, "Biting Wind, Cold Greets Pitt Eleven," *Pittsburgh Press*, 20 October 1933, 41.
5. Chester Smith, "Pitt Faces Chance to Square Notre Dame Series, Panthers Installed as Favorites," *Pittsburgh Press*, 28 October 1933, 7.
6. Jock Sutherland, "Jock Says Panthers Were Right for Game," *Pittsburgh Press*, 29 October 1933, 19.
7. Claire Burcky, "Nebraska Tries to Hurdle Pitt on Way to Title," *Pittsburgh Press*, November 1933, 7.
8. Claire Burcky, "Panthers Face Chance at Chicago Title Game," *Pittsburgh Press*, 17 November 1933, 48.
9. Jock Sutherland, "Sutherland Says Huskers Hold Edge over Panthers," *Pittsburgh Press*, 17 November 1933, 48.
10. Unites Press, "Pop States Pitt Is Best in East," *Pittsburgh Press*, 5 December 1933, 26.
11. Chester Smith, "Sun's Back in the Sky as Baseball Owners Meet," *Pittsburgh Press*, 10 December 1933, 18.

Chapter 8

1. Dan Jenkins, "This Year the Fight Will Be in the Open," *Sports Illustrated*, 11 September 1967, 35.
2. Greg Trietley, "Pitt Can Claim Nine Titles," PittNewswww, 6 September 2011.
3. Tiptop25.com, 1934 College Football National Championship, http://tiptop25.com/champ1934.html.
4. E-mail from Dan Jenkins to the author.
5. David Finoli and Chris Fletcher, *Steel City Gridirons* (Pittsburgh: Towers Maguire, 2006), 261.
6. Robert Strother, "Trojans, Eyes on Panthers, Shun Editorial Blast," *Pittsburgh Press*, 12 October 1934, 45.
7. Ibid.
8. Chester Smith, "The Village Smithy," *Pittsburgh Press*, 12 November 1934, 7.
9. Claire Burcky, "Light Drill Today Ends Preparation for Panthers," *Pittsburgh Press*, 2 November 1934, 50.
10. Chester Smith, "Nebraska Hopes to End Pitt Drought Today," *Pittsburgh Press*, 10 November 1934, 7.
11. Jock Sutherland, "It's Hard to Take," *Pittsburgh Press*, 28 November 1934, 14.

Chapter 9

1. Jim O'Brien and Marty Wolfson, *Hail to Pitt* (Pittsburgh: Wolfson, 1982), 86.
2. Ira Berkow, "Marshall Goldberg, 88, Who Led 2 Teams to Football Titles, Dies," *New York Times*, 7 April 2006.
3. *Paths of Glory: 100 Years of Pitt Football*, VHS (Pittsburgh: Ross Sports Productions, 1993).
4. "Victory over Michigan Gauthier's Big Moment," *Portsmouth Times*, 14 August 1964.
5. "Local Elevens Start Season in True Form," *Pittsburgh Post Gazette*, 28 September 1936, 16.

6. "Gold Pants Club," Ohio State Online Library: Michigan vs. Ohio State Section, http://library.osu.edu/projects/OSUvs-Michigan/gold_pants_club.html.
7. Jock Sutherland, "We're Ready! We'll Do Our Best! I Hope We Win—Jock," *Pittsburgh Press*, 10 October 1936, 7.
8. Chester Smith, "Great Duke Win Rocks Grid World," *Pittsburgh Press*, 18 October 1936, 20.
9. *Paths of Glory: 100 Years of Pitt Football*, VHS (Pittsburgh: Ross Sports Productions, 1993).
10. Chester Smith, "Stop Panther Ace! Cry of Fordham," *Pittsburgh Press*, 30 October 1936, 49.
11. Quote in correspondence between the author and Dan Jenkins.
12. Harry G. Scott, *Jock Sutherland: Architect of Men* (New York: Banner Books, 1954), 159.
13. "Bible Indignant over Attack at Student Paper," *Pittsburgh Post-Gazette*, 25 November 1936, 20.
14. Ibid.
15. Ibid.

Chapter 10

1. Chester Smith, "Pitt Boys All in Swell Condition, They'll Reach Enemy Line Saturday," *Pittsburgh Press*, 17 December 1937, 38.
2. Chester Smith, "A Couple Fellows Warn the Huskies," *Pittsburgh Press*, 18 December 1937, 56.
3. Chester Smith, "West Critics Proclaim Pitt Cause as Hopeless after Seeing Team Work," *Pittsburgh Press*, 21 December 1937, 35.
4. Ibid.
5. Chester Smith, "Phelan Sings Blues; Seems He's Worried," *Pittsburgh Press*, 23 December 1937, 28.
6. William Wallace, "College Football; This Pitt Backfield Is Still a Dream," *New York Times*, 15 October 1994.
7. Ibid.
8. Jim O'Brien and Marty Wolfson, *Hail to Pitt* (Pittsburgh: Wolfson, 1982), 95.

Chapter 11

1. Jock Sutherland, "Jock Displeased," *Pittsburgh Press*, 3 October 1937, 25.
2. "Time Recalls Pitt Incident," *Pittsburgh Press*, 24 October 1937, 17.
3. Chester Smith, "Sophomore Backs Hold Rams Hopes," *Pittsburgh Press*, 16 October 1937, 11.
4. Ibid.
5. Chester Smith, "Hagan Plan Given Full Endorsement," *Pittsburgh Press*, 24 October 1937, 17.
6. "Sutherland Approves New Athletic Program," *Pittsburgh Press*, 25 October 1937, 35.
7. "Pittsburgh and Fordham Get Two Places Apiece," *Milwaukee Journal*, 28 November 1937, 18.
8. Ibid.
9. Associated Press, "No Cash, No Rose Bowl, Pitt Players Ultimatum," *Milwaukee Journal*, 30 November 1937, 12.
10. Harvey Boyle, "Panther Players Vote to Refuse Rose Bowl Bid," *Pittsburgh Post Gazette*, 29 November 1937, 1.
11. Harvey Boyle, "Panther Players Vote to Refuse Rose Bowl Bid," *Pittsburgh Post Gazette*, 29 November 1937, 40.

Chapter 12

1. Harry G. Scott, *Jock Sutherland: Architect of Men* (New York: Exposition Press, 1954), 190.
2. Frank Reeves, "Harold 'Curly' Stebbins/Part of Panthers 'Dream Backfield,'" *Pittsburgh Post Gazette*, 3 September 2002.
3. Ibid.
4. Francis Wallace, "The Football Factory Explodes," in *Pitt Football History*, edited by Mike Bynum, Larry Eldridge, Jr., and Sam Scullio, Jr. (Nashville, TN: Athlon Sports Communications, 1994), 76.
5. Ibid.
6. Ibid., 77.

Bibliography

Media Guides

Allegheny College 2013 Football Media Guide.
Army 2013 Football Fact Book.
Centre College 2013 Football Media Guide.
Duquesne University 2013 Virtual Football Media Guide.
Fordham University 2013 Football Media Guide.
Navy 2013 Football Media Guide.
Ohio State University 2013 Football Media Guide.
Ohio Wesleyan 2013 Football Media Guide.
University of Iowa 2013 Football Media Guide.
University of Minnesota 2013 Football Media Guide.
University of Notre Dame 2013 Football Media Guide.
University of Pennsylvania 2013 Football Fact Book.
University of Pittsburgh 2013 Media Guide.
University of Southern California 2013 Football Media Guide.
Washington and Jefferson College 2013 Football Fact Book.
West Virginia University 2013 Football Fact Book.
Westminster College 2013 Football Media Guide.

Books

Anderson, Lars. *Carlisle vs. Army*. New York: Random House, 2008.
Finoli, David, and Fletcher Christopher. *The Steel City 500*. Seattle: Createspace Publishing, 2013.
Finoli, David, and Fletcher Christopher. *Steel City Gridirons*. Pittsburgh: Maguire-Towers, 2006.
O'Brien, Jim, and Marty Wolfson. *Hail to Pitt*. Pittsburgh: Wolfson, 1982.
Okeson, W.R., ed. *1933 Spalding Official Intercollegiate Football Guide*. New York: American Sports Publishing, 1933.
Okeson, W.R., ed. *1934 Spalding Official Intercollegiate Football Guide*. New York: American Sports Publishing, 1934.
Okeson, W.R., ed. *1936 Spalding Official Intercollegiate Football Guide*. New York: American Sports Publishing, 1936.
Panaccio, Tim. *Beast of the East*. West Point, NY: Leisure Press, 1982.
Scott, Harry G. *Jock Sutherland: Architect of Men*. New York: Banner Books, 1954.

Newspapers and Periodicals

TheDailyGopher.com
Iowalum.com magazine
The Milwaukee Journal
The New York Times
The Pittsburgh Post-Gazette
The Pittsburgh Press
The Pittsburgh Record: The University of Pittsburgh Alumni Newsletter
The St. Petersburg Times

Bibliography

The Washington Observer
The Youngstown Vindicator

Websites

BaseballReference.com
Buffalo Sports Hall of Fame website
CantonMcKinley.com
Centre College official website
College Football Data Warehouse website
CollegeFootballReference.com
Digital Pitt Library
Football Reference.com
Fordham Digital Library
Huskers.com: The University of Nebraska athletic website
IrishLegends.com
LostLetterman.com
National Football Foundation website
Notre Dame official website
Ohio State University Online Library
Ohio Wesleyan athletic website
Penn State University Libraries website
PittNews.com
Sports Illustrated Vault website
SteelerNationUK.com
Tiptop25.com
University of Pittsburgh website

Index

Adams, Henry 178, 182, 188, 198, 212, 220, 223, 228, 245, 248, 261
Alexander, Bill 15
Alfonse, Julius 131, 161
Alger, Horatio 31
Allen, Eck 127, 154
Allen, George 155
Alter, Spike 245, 247
Amann, Art 228
Anderson, Bill 244
Anderson, Heartley "Hunk" 65, 66, 99–101, 133–135, 164
Anderson, Stan 109
Andrews, Harris 243
Angelo Louisa Ratings 208, 252
Anthony, Frank 50
Arbelbide, Garrett 46, 50
Armentrout, Murray 72, 73
Arrowsmith, Bob 162, 163
Associated Press 26, 40, 147, 205, 206, 212, 227, 245, 248, 249, 252, 256, 258
Atty, Alex 181, 224
Audia, Sam 181, 224

Babartsky, Al 194
Bach, Joe 187
Baird, George 45
Baisi, Albert 224
Baker, Eddie 15–17, 19, 22, 23, 25, 31, 33, 34, 37, 39, 44, 50, 237
Baker, Phil 108
Barksdale (Centre) 135, 136
Barna, Babe 181
Barragar, Nathan 46, 50
Barratt, Fred 29, 30

Bartlett (Centre) 135, 136
Bartrugg, Eddie 22
Basrak, Mike 187, 205
Bauer, Henry 169
Baumberger, Walter 128, 129
Baxter, Verne 122, 125, 126, 150, 155, 158–160, 165, 170
Beaver White Committee 41
Bechtloff, Ken 188
Behnke, William 24
Beiner, Ed 240
Beise, Sheldon 131, 159
Berezney, Paul 232
Bernard, Joe 194
Bescos, Julius 157
Bettridge, John 184
Bevan, Bill 159, 160
Bevivino, Angelo 74
Bezdek, Hugo 38–41, 69
Bible, Dana X. 24, 25, 80, 103–105, 140, 141, 167, 199, 202, 203, 242, 244
Biederman, Lester 55
Bierman, Bernie 84, 108, 130, 159
Bill Libby Ratings 252
Billingsley Report 252
Bing Crosby Pro-Am 185
Bishop, Clair 141
Blaik, Earl "Red" 242
Boand System 208, 252
Bob Royce Ratings 252
Bonar, Bud 165
Bond, Chuck 218
Bond, Jim 261
Booth, Albie 81
Booth, Bill 184

270

Index 271

Booth, Dick 7
Borries, Fred 128, 170, 171
Boswell, Hubert 141
Bowman, John 1, 2, 3, 4, 6, 76, 152, 219, 220, 253, 256, 257, 258
Boyle, Harvey J. 71, 84
Bradley, Omar 76
Brancheau, Ray 66, 100, 134
Bright, Ken 118, 120
Brock, Charles 200, 243
Brooks, Pat 222
Brown, Everett 120
Brown, Jesse 261
Brown, Mel 55, 58, 108
Brown, Ray 118
Brown, Travis 95, 96
Browning, Ward 119
Brumbaugh, Boyd 187–189, 227–230
Bryan, Bill 18
Bryant, Paul 89
Buie, Sam 20–22
Burzio, Bunny 106, 144
Butler (W&J) 33
Byers, Walter 1

Caddell, Ernie 108, 109
Cain, Jim 212, 218
Callihan, Bill 243
Camp Hamilton 235
Campbell, Bill 109
Caputo, Mike 222
Carder, Glenn 181
Cardwell, Lloyd 167, 200, 201
Carideo, Fred 165
Carlson, Bill 172
Carlson, HC 44
Carnegie Foundation 27
Carnelly, Ray 238, 239
Carroll, Bill 98
Cartwright, Wilbur 54, 55
Carver, Bobby 76, 77
Cassiano, Dick 222, 223, 226, 230, 235, 236, 238, 243, 244, 247, 249, 254, 256, 261
Cathedral of Learning 1, 258
Cavanaugh, Frank 194
Century Football Index 252
Charles D. Wettach Award 222
Chase, Ralph 10, 261
Cherundolo, Chuck 197
Chickerneo, John 186, 191, 197, 203, 221, 226, 228, 229, 240, 254, 261
Chung-Hoon, George 128, 129
Clark, Charlie 170
Clark, Gordon 115, 117, 118, 120
Clark, Harry 224, 226

Clark, James 23, 28, 37, 58–61, 63, 67, 70, 73, 74, 76, 77, 82
Clark, Johnny 53
Clemens, Calvin 157, 158
Code Bowman 253, 256, 257
Colehower, Harry 102
College Football Hall of Fame 13, 29, 34, 63, 149, 191, 199
College Football USA 252
College Researchers Association 207, 208
Collins, George 69
Collins, Paul "Rip" 19, 23, 25, 29, 49, 50, 53, 60, 63, 69, 78, 82, 261
Colvin, Don 108
Conn, Donald 69, 71
Corbus, Bill 108, 109
Coulter, Tom 105
Craft, Don 153
Cramer, Cal 98
Crisler, Herb "Fritz" 130
Croft, Dutch 172
Crowley, Jim 165, 234, 254
Cuba, Paul 90, 106, 108, 116, 120, 261
Curry, Tom 69
Cutri, Rocco 63, 66, 70, 71, 79, 81–83, 93, 108
Cutrona, Joe 137

Daddio, Bill 178, 179, 184, 191, 192, 197, 198, 201, 204, 205, 212, 215, 216, 218, 221, 222, 224, 232, 238, 240, 243, 245, 248, 249, 252, 254, 259, 261
Dailey, Ted 90, 99, 101, 108, 109, 117, 120, 261
Daily Trojan 157
DalleTezze, Dante 179, 184, 197, 200, 232, 245
Danbom, Larry 190
Daniell, Ave 13, 159, 163, 177, 179, 181, 182, 191, 205, 208, 218, 227, 261, 263
Dannies, Bob 228, 233, 235
Daugherty, Ralph 16, 17, 26, 29, 31, 50, 52, 82, 85
Davies, Tom 108, 109, 181
Davis, Parke H. 41, 42, 43, 49, 85, 86, 87, 90, 148, 149, 156
Davis, Ralph 4, 38, 44
Day, Hank 123–125, 128, 150, 151
DeAngelis, Murino "Spud" 181, 224
DeBus, Warren 141
DeCoster, Frank 137
Dee, James 57, 58
DeHart, Jimmy 7, 18–21, 247
Delich, George 177, 179, 182, 205, 221, 223, 224, 238, 245, 248
DeLuca, Al 93

DeMarino, Dan 245
Demoise, Frank 16
Dennison, Harry 27
Detzel, Art 150, 159, 207
Dickerson, John 223
Dickinson System 113, 143, 145, 146, 174, 183, 206, 250, 252
Dickson, Paul 113
DiDonato, Joe 63
Diedrich, Yutz 40
DiMeolo, Albert 39, 50, 51, 143
Dittberner, Art 157
Dixon, Jamie 193
Dodd, Ed 243
Dolly, Edward 57, 58
Dolly, Richard 224
Doloway, Cliff 173
Donato, Sammy 197
Donchess, Joe 15, 19, 31, 34, 39–42, 48, 50, 51, 114, 263
Donohue, John 93
Dorsett, Tony 8, 40, 56, 178, 179, 181
Dotson, Leo 60
Douds, Jap 33, 34
Douglas (Carnegie Tech) 174
Douglas, Bud 212
Doyle, John 60
Doyle, Ted 243
Dream Backfield 222, 254
Dreshar, Henry 72
Dresher, John 36
Druze, John 194, 231–233
Ducanis, Alex 72
Duff, Joseph 3, 13
Duffield, Marshall 49
Dugger (Carnegie Tech) 107
Dulkie, Joe 196
Dye, George 46, 50
Dye, Tippy 184
Dyer, Braven 213

Earl Jenssen Ratings 207, 208, 252
Economos, Jack 245
Edelson, Harry 46, 48–50
Edwards, Charley 16, 17, 19, 22, 25, 28, 39
Eisenhower, Dwight 76
Ellwood, WT 245
Elser, Don 133
Ely, Lawrence 81
Enders, Paul 245
English, Lowell 243
USS *Enterprise* 170
Erskine, Robert 120
Esso Gas Ratings 9, 11, 206, 208
Eugle, Roy 102
Ewing, Buck 72

Fazio, Foge 221
Ferrall, Junius 98
Fesler, Wesley 29, 31
Fields, Ken 76, 95–97
1st-N-goal 86, 87, 208, 252
Flanagan, Christy 187
Fletcher, Don 72
The Football Thesaurus 206, 208, 250, 252
Forbes, John 137
Forsman, Carl 72
Fort Duquesne 137
Fortunato, Angelo 232
Four Horsemen of Notre Dame 254
Francis, Sam 167, 200–202
Franco, Ed 194, 231
French, Cooper 39, 40
French & Indian War 137
Fry, Robert 65

Gales, Charlie 184
Galloway, Clark 46, 50
Garbo, Greta 157
Garvey, Vin 234
Gauthier, George 108, 180, 222
Gelini, Frank 93
George Trevor Ratings 252
Getto, Mike 11, 16
Giannantionio, AJ 245
Gilbane, Bill 162
Gilbane, Tom 162
Glassford, Bill 179, 190, 192, 197, 200, 203, 205, 208, 218
Glenn, Marshall "Little Sleepy" 22, 224, 227
Goldberg, Marshall 13, 52, 177–182, 184, 188, 189, 191–195, 197–200, 202, 204, 205, 214, 217, 218, 221, 223, 225, 228–233, 235, 236, 238, 240, 241, 243–250, 252, 254, 256, 259, 261, 263
Goodell, Roger 75
Goodwin, Charlie 154
Grabenhorst, Coburn 212
Grabinski, Ted 230
Graham, Jim 57
Grant, Ulysses S. 76
Graveno (Carnegie Tech) 74
Greene, Arnie 162, 174, 177, 182, 188, 201, 202, 204, 211
Greeney, Norm 66
Griffith, Homer 115, 117, 118, 120
Griffith, John 257
Gussie, Mike 224
Gwosden, Milo 261

Hackney, Elmore 248, 249
Hagan, Jimmy 8, 152, 209, 220, 236, 250, 251, 253

Index

Hagan Plan 220, 235, 237, 251, 253, 256
Haines, Byron 212, 215
Hall, William 50
Halloran, WT 233
Hamilton, Thomas J. "Tom" 170, 172
Hanley, Vincent 170
Hannum, Max 9, 22, 25, 36
Harding, Ann 157
Harman, Harvey 101, 102, 108
Harper, Hueston 157
Harpers Weekly 147
Harpster, Howard 22, 108, 143–145, 172, 204, 237
Harrison, Don 6, 139, 205, 206, 217, 219
Harrison, Harry 198
Harry Frye Ratings 252
Hartwig, Charley 90, 120, 122, 150, 159, 173–175
Hasson, Bill 70, 73
Hayes, Jim 194
Heath, George 155
Hefferle, Ernie 187, 227
Heinlen, John 180
Heinz Chapel 1
Heinzer, Clyde 72
Heisman Trophy 210, 246, 252, 254
Heller, Eric 55
Heller, Warren 53, 55, 56, 58, 59, 61, 67, 68, 73, 74, 77–79, 82–84, 90–92, 94, 96–99, 102, 103, 105, 107–111, 116–118, 120, 123, 169, 261
Helms Foundation 44
Hendrick, Olan 224, 226
Henrion, Nestor 173, 203
Hensley, Don 178, 179, 182, 188, 198, 212, 215, 218, 221, 224, 228, 235, 245, 248
Herb, Ed 76
Hess, Al 30
Hickman, Randall 57–59
Higgins, Bob 69, 196, 197, 244, 245, 247
Hill, Jesse 46
Hinchman, Lew 97–99
Hirshberg, Ed 53, 76, 78, 81, 82
Hoel, Robert 90, 98, 122, 131, 134, 150, 173, 261
Hoffman, Fabian 182, 188, 190, 192, 197, 218, 221, 225, 232, 240, 241, 248
Hoffman, Nordy 66
Hogan, Bob 53, 58, 60, 66, 78, 79, 81, 83, 84, 90, 91, 94, 96, 100, 102, 106, 109, 117, 119, 120, 122, 124, 126, 129, 136, 142, 144, 145, 149
Holcomb, Stuart 29
Holland, Don 123, 150
Hood, Franklin 15, 17, 18, 261
Hoover, Herbert 19

Horn, Bob 29
Houlgate System 208, 252
Howard, Bill 158
Howarth (Carnegie Tech) 238
Howell, John 201, 243
Hubka, Elmer 141
Hudson, Earl 203
Hulsbeck, Harold 180
Hurley, PJ 76
Hyatt, Don 18

Ickes, Lloyd 245
Immaculate Reception 8
Ingwersen, Bert 56–59

Jacunski, Harry 194, 231
James Howell Ratings 252
James Whalen Ratings 252
Jaskwhich, Chuck 66, 68, 100
Jenkins, Dan 41, 147–149, 196
Jessup, Walter 56
Jim Koger Ratings 208, 252
Johnson, Dick 212, 218
Johnson, Paul 76
Jones, Howard 44, 46, 47, 49, 56, 57, 115, 117–119, 156, 157
Jones, Lawrence 242, 244
Jones, Tad 15
Jones, the Rev. Thomas 228, 229
Jorgenson, Elwood 157

Kakasic, George 137
Kalzo, Steve 232
Karcis, Johnny 36, 37
Karrs, Johnny 188, 228, 230
Kavel, George 72–74, 106, 107
Keady, Tom 62–64
Kebe, Tony 72
Keefe, Tom 99
Kellar (Carnegie Tech) 205
Kellett, Don 103
Kelley, Fred 173
Kern, Bill 4, 11, 237, 238, 261
Kerr, Andy 108, 109, 110
Kilday, Tom 76, 78, 95, 96
King, Bill 150
King, Richard 77
King, Tom 170, 171
Kirksey, George 33, 57
Kirlin, Bob 86, 87, 146, 207, 208, 252
Kish, Ben 261
Kistler, Harry 18
Kliskey, Nick 125, 126, 128, 133, 136
Kochel, Mike 194, 231
Koken, Mike 66, 67
Kopcsak, Coleman 203, 238

Kopsak, Pete 77
Kostka, Stanley 161
Kovalcik, George 193
Krause, Ed 66
Kreizinger, Everett 81
Kristufek, Frank 261
Kubale, Eddie 135
Kuharich, Joe 240
Kuhn, Gil 157
Kurth, Joe 66
Kutz, Frank 125, 237

LaBorde, Henri 108
Lambert Trophy 205, 209, 211, 219, 250, 256, 263
Laraway, Jack 162
Larsen, Frank 161
Larson, Butch 159
Larue, Bobby 150, 151, 158, 161, 166, 168, 171, 173, 179, 180, 182, 184, 188–190, 192, 193, 195–197, 200, 204, 205, 211–215, 218, 221
Larue, "Bus" 22
Lasich, George 69
Layden, Elmer 92, 93, 95, 108, 138–141, 164–166, 176, 187, 190, 191, 193, 234, 240, 241
Lee, Jack 203, 204
Lee, Robert E. 76
Lee, Whitey 238
Lehman, Freddy 172, 203
Lemieux, Mario 223
Lemons, Sam 18
LeVoir, Vernal 132
Lewis, John L. 257
Lewis, Lib 72, 144
Lewis (W&J) 33, 34
Lezouski, Albin 190, 197, 221, 224, 246, 248, 249
Litkenhous System 250, 252
Lock, John 196
Loehr, Bill 19, 25
Lombardi, Vince 13, 194
Loren Maxwell Ratings 252
Lorenz, Harold 181
Love, John 63
Luch, Jimmy 53, 60, 61, 63, 64, 66–68, 73, 76, 77, 108, 132
Lukats, Nick 100, 134
Lund, Francis 131, 132

MacMurdo, Jim 16, 50, 52, 54, 58, 59, 67, 74, 78, 82, 85, 261
MacWilliams, Joe 95
Magnussen, Marcus 57
Malarkey, Leo 180, 182, 183, 189, 199
Malcolm (W&J) 150
Malesevich, Bronko 234

Marker, Harry 60
Markov, Vic 218
Marks (Centre) 135
Marks, Jim 176
Massey Ratings 252
Masterson, Bernie 81, 105, 141
Matelan, Jerry 204, 205
Matesic, Richard 55, 71, 91, 94, 122–124, 132–134, 137, 139, 140, 261
Matisi, Tony 179, 183, 193, 194, 201, 215, 218, 21, 222, 224, 240, 245, 248, 252, 262
Matronic, Carl 212
Matsik, George 188, 189, 228–230
Matthews, Leon 18
Mazziotti, Tom 133, 134
McBurney (W&J) 151
McCarthy, Bill 193
McCarthy, John 240, 241
McCarty, Pat 240
McClure, Bobby 162
McConnell, Arden 29, 31
McCracken, Herb 5, 108
McCurdy, (Carnegie Tech) 37
McDonald, Jim 184
McDonald, Lester 167
McDonald, Romeo 126
McGinnis, Ken 200
McGuff, Al 101
McKeeta, Vince 228
McMillen, Bill 71
Mehring, Bob 200, 243
Meier, Franklin 141, 167
Melinkovich, George 66–68, 100, 165
Merideth, John 52, 54, 63
Merkovsky, Elmer 202, 221, 262
Merten, James 57
Michelosen, John 1, 179, 182, 188, 201, 203, 218, 221, 223, 225, 228, 239, 240, 245, 258
Mihm, Joe 172, 173
Miller, Don 165, 234
Miller, Edgar "Rip" 127, 129, 170
Miller, Jack 141
Miller, Wayne 133
Milligan, Mike 53, 82
Milligan, Walter 28
Montgomery, Ray 15, 39–42, 44, 50, 51, 114
Moonves, Phil 69, 70
Moran, Kelly 181, 182, 224, 226
Morgan, Cliff 26
Moroz, Pete 238
Morris, Bob 63
Morris, Hart 15, 53, 63, 69, 72, 73, 76, 77, 82, 90
Mortensen, Jesse 49
Moses, Don 46
Munger, George 102

Munjas, Miller 100, 106, 107, 122, 131, 132, 136, 142, 150, 158, 160, 161, 173, 174
Murphy, Emmett 66
Murphy, Leo 19, 29
Murray, Hugh 128
Murray, Jack 235
Murray, John W. 141
Musick, James 46
Myers (W&J) 153

Napoleon 71
Napotnik, Leo 204, 238
National Championship Foundation 252
Neale, Earl "Greasy" 59, 60, 91, 92, 125–127, 153, 154
Nerlin, Roy 234
Nesser, Bill 29
Newspaper Editors Association 174
Newton, Charles 218
Niccolai, Armand 139
Nicksick, Mike 90, 94, 121–123, 125, 128, 137, 142, 150, 155, 158, 160, 163, 166, 168, 169, 171, 173, 262
Noel, Ted 86
Noll, Chuck 197, 258
North American Newspaper Alliance 174
Nowogroski, Ed 212, 215, 218

O'Brien, Gail 81, 141
O'Dell, Howdy 122, 124, 125, 126, 128, 129, 131, 132, 134, 136, 139, 140, 142, 144, 145
O'Donnell, Hugh 65
O'Hara, Frank 197
Olejniczak, Stanley 160, 262
Onder, Angelo 154
Onder, Geno 228
Onder, Tarciscio "Tar" 63, 70, 73, 77, 90, 106, 120, 122, 125, 126, 136, 144, 154
O'Reilly, Chuck 193
Ormiston, Ken 90, 122, 150, 162, 169, 173, 174
Ostrosky, Tony 72, 74
O'Toole, Jerry 72

Palmer, Ford 117, 118, 120
Paquin, Leo 194
Paret, J. Parmly 147
Parkinson, Thomas 15, 17, 20, 23, 25, 26, 30, 31, 33, 34, 36, 39–42, 46, 48–51, 262
Parriot, Bill 60
Parsheghian, Ara 148
Parsons, Bud 141
Passarelli, Luigi 39
Patrick, Frank 180–182, 186, 189, 194, 195, 197–201, 208, 211, 214, 215, 218, 221, 223, 225, 228, 232, 233, 238, 239, 241, 242, 244, 245, 247, 249, 252
Patrick, Johnny 197, 198
Patrick Premo Ratings 259
Patton, George 76
Paul, Marvin 81
Pawlina, Ben 93
Peace, Lawrence 230, 236, 262
Peden, Don 108
Peel, Joe 245
Penn State Alumni Club 41
Perry, Lawrence 40
Pershing, John 76
Peters, Frank 218
Peters, Marty 166
Petersen Events Center 14
Petro, Steve 178, 214, 218, 221, 223, 232, 248, 262
Pflum, Walt 141
Phelan, Jimmy 206, 212–214
Pierce, Nat 194
Pilney, Andy 165, 166
Pinckert, Emy 46, 48–50
Pitser, Charlie 54
The Pitt News 225
Pittsburgh Post Gazette 61, 70, 71, 84, 250
Pittsburgh Press 4, 5, 9, 15, 19, 22, 25, 36, 38, 41, 44, 55, 69, 70, 128, 130, 149, 220
Pohl, Neil 234
Poling System 252
Pouncey, Bert 72
Powell, Johnny 103
Powers, Francis 211
Pratt, Rich 170
Presnell, Glenn 7
Price, Clarence 43
Price, Johnny 76
Principe, Dom 232, 256

Quatse, Jesse 52–54, 68, 82, 83, 85, 87, 114, 262

Randour, Herb 124
Rankin, Bolton 129
Rapaswick, Tony 224
Raskowski, Walter 190, 200, 221, 223, 224
Reid, William 110
Reider, Paul 53, 55, 56, 58, 59, 61, 69, 73, 74, 78, 79, 82–84, 90–94, 96, 98, 100, 102, 104, 106, 108, 113, 115, 117
Rennebohm, Dale 161
Rhea, Hugh 81, 82
Rickey, Branch 222
Rissman, Jack 113
Rittersbaugh (W&J) 124
Roby, John 141

Index

Rockne, Knute 15, 25, 33, 35, 44, 51, 56, 57, 64, 65, 112, 113, 132, 133, 143, 164, 165, 187, 191, 194, 234
Rodgers, Alex 57, 58
Rodgers, Ira "Rat" 59, 125, 153
Rollins, Steve 245
Rooker, Harvey 90, 107, 122, 125, 127, 132, 142, 150, 155, 160, 173
Rooney, Art 105, 151
Rooney, Jimmy 18, 21, 22, 26, 28–32, 34
Rosenberg, Aaron 120
Rosso (W&J) 150, 153
Ruetz, Joe 240
Rush, Maury 33

Sagarin Ratings 252
St. John, Lynn 222
Salata, Andy 262
Salvaterra, Joe 98
Sample, Hooks 72
Samuelson, Loe 57
Sansen, Oliver 57
Sasse, Ralph 77–79, 95
Sauer, George 81, 84, 141
Saunders, Russell 46, 48–50
Scarfpin, James 170
Schiralli, Rocco 134
Schmidt, Frances A. 183, 211
Schmitt, Ted 262
Schmitz, Bill 234
Schultz, Ed 21
Schwartz, Marchy 66–68
Scott, Harry G. 79
Scott, Jimmy 154
Sebastian, Mike 55, 61, 63, 64, 68–70, 79, 82–84, 90, 92–94, 96–104, 106, 108, 109, 116–118, 120–126, 128, 129, 131, 133–135, 137, 141, 142, 144, 145, 149, 262
Seidel, Glen 161
Seifert, Karl 160, 170, 173
Seigel, Fran 63, 70, 106, 108
Sekay, Art 108
Sell, Jack 61
Seven Blocks of Granite 194–196, 231, 233
Seven Mules of Notre Dame 127
Shakespeare, Bill 166
Shaver, Gus 46, 50
Shaw, Bill 184, 190
Shaw, Paul 230, 238, 240
Shedlosky, Leon 129, 142, 143, 150, 151, 153, 155, 162, 163, 166, 168, 172, 174
Sheeketski, Joe 66, 67
Shelogg, Alex 240
Sheridan, Richard 75, 76, 95
Sherrill, Jackie 221
Shindehuette, George 108

Shirey, Fred 243
Shotwell, George 92, 100, 122, 125, 128, 133, 136, 141, 150, 159, 173–175
Sieg, Dr Lee Paul 206
Silvano, Tom 197
Sim, Bill 109
Simms, Jimmy 63, 64, 70, 91
Sims, Bob 8
Sinko, Steve 93
Sites, Vincent 162, 165, 170, 262
Skemp, Dick 245
Skladany, Joe 63, 90, 84, 96, 97, 110, 111, 115, 118, 120, 122, 124, 136, 139, 140, 142, 145, 146, 237, 262, 263
Skoglund, Leonard 240
Slaminko, Joe 203
Slate, Patsy 92
Slivinski, Steve 218
Sloan, Clair 24, 26
Slusser, Tom 69
Smith, Chester 128, 130, 157
Smith, Dick 159
Smith, Ed 210
Smith, Ernest 120
Smith, Harry 28
Smith, John "Clipper" 187–189, 227, 228–230
Smith, Sammy 16
Snyder, Bob 69
Sokolis, Stan 102
Soren Sorenson Ratings 10
Sorenson, Soren 7
Sortet, Will 92
Souchak, Bill 178, 179, 184, 185, 190, 202, 221, 222, 224, 229, 230, 232, 239, 240, 244, 245, 248–249, 252, 262
The Spalding Guide 41, 87, 175
Sparling, Raymond 118, 120
Spears, Clarence "Fats" 47
Spisak, Bill 105, 144, 145, 172, 173
Spotovich, Ed 239, 249
Stahley, Skip 40
Staples, Bill 162
Stapulis, Bill 178, 179, 182, 186, 188, 192, 200, 201, 211, 221, 223, 225, 226, 228, 235, 239, 243–245, 249
Starcevich, Max 218
Stebbins, Harold 180, 182, 186, 192, 197–199, 202, 212, 214, 221, 223, 225, 226, 228–230, 232, 233, 235, 236, 238, 241, 243, 244, 248, 254, 256
Steffen, Walter 35, 36, 41, 72, 74, 105–108, 143
Steven Foster Memorial 1
Stevens, Lawrence 120
Stevens, Mal 88
Stewart, Colen 72

Index

Stiles, Maxwell 212
Stilley, Ken 133
Stone, Doug 60
Stoughton, Gene 170
Stuhldreher, Harry 165
Stumpp, Eddie 22–24
Stydahar, Joe 125
Sullivan, Larry 92, 93
Sweeney, Chuck 240
Sweeney, Ray 162

Tallman, Charles "Trusty" 127, 154, 181–183, 224
Tappaan, Francis 46, 50
Tatsch, Herbert 157
Tenner, Bob 131, 159, 161
Tenner, Robert 131, 159, 161
Terebus, Steve 144, 174
Thompson, Russ 141
301st Tank Battalion 95
Thurbon, Bob 262
Timmons, Robert 123, 125, 142, 144
Tipton, Eric 248
Tiptop25 148
Toman, Ray 169
Tompkins, Nelson 57
Tormey, Joe 53, 63, 90, 92, 97, 100, 108, 114, 120
Trbovich, Steve 144, 173, 174
Tully, Charles 34, 48, 50

Uansa, Toby 12, 15, 17–21, 23, 24, 26, 30–35, 37, 39–42, 46, 48–51, 114, 180
Ulrich, Lyron 63
United Press 33, 39, 57, 85
Urban, John 196, 198, 199, 201, 214, 221, 226, 230, 233, 239, 243, 245
U.S. Open 185

Vairo, Beto 187–189
Valenti, John 170
Varano, Nick 28
Veterans Athletes Body Ratings 9, 11
Vidol, Felix 97
Volkin, Dave 181, 224

Waddell, Bob 35, 36, 72, 74, 105, 107, 108
Wade, Wallace 248
Waggoner, "Speed" 22
Wagner, Bucky 15
Waitkoski (Fordham) 196
Walinchus, Whitey 17, 18, 21, 23, 25, 28–30, 35, 37, 40, 48–50
Wallace Wade Stadium 19
Walton, Frank "Tiger" 98, 120, 122, 126, 144, 145, 238, 262

Wanger, Bucky 19
Warburton, Irvine 113, 158
Warner, Glenn 1, 3–5, 8, 9, 12, 13, 15, 16, 21, 43, 60, 88, 89, 106, 107–109, 116, 125, 145, 152, 235
Waskowitz, Frank 212, 214
Wear, Wendell "Windy" 198, 247
Weinberg, Harry 137
Weinstock, Izzy 90–93, 96–100, 102, 107, 109, 114, 117, 118, 120, 124, 125, 128, 129, 131, 132, 134, 136, 139, 140, 142, 144, 145, 150, 151, 153, 155, 158–160, 162, 163, 166, 168, 169, 171, 173–175, 238, 262
Weisenbaugh, Heine 90, 91, 93, 103, 118, 121, 122, 124, 127, 129, 131, 134, 136, 142, 14, 150, 151, 158, 160, 166, 168, 172–174, 262
Weiss, Howard 234
Welch, Gibby 4, 7, 8, 11, 114, 181, 262
West, Mae 157
What's What Ratings 252
White, "Dutch" 24
White, Homer 60
Whitney, Casper 147
Wiatrak, John 213, 218
Widseth, Ed 159
Wilcox, Ralph 49
Wilkie, Bob 190
Willaman, Sam 29, 98
Willer, James 57
Williams, Josh 17, 18, 20, 23, 25, 26, 30, 31, 33–35, 37, 46–49
Williamson System 250, 252
Wilson, Stew 33, 123
Wilson, Walter K. 75
Wilton, Frankie 8, 9
Windwood, Ervin 234
Wissinger, Henry 262
Woitkoski (Fordham) 233
Wojchihovski, Vic 190
Wojciechowicz, Alex 194
Wood, John 180, 182, 193, 196, 199, 201, 214
Woodruff, Jim 262
Woolridge, CL 47
Wotkyns, Haskell 157

Yarr, Tommy 66
Yeknich, Wayne 203
Yonel USC 120
Yost, Fielding H. 222

Zaninelli, Silvio 93, 139
Zawacki, Manuel 204
Zoppetti, Frank 187, 189
Zuppke, Bob 54

www.ingramcontent.com/pod-product-compliance
Ingram Content Group UK Ltd.
Pitfield, Milton Keynes, MK11 3LW, UK
UKHW041930140426
5217IPUK00014B/397